Shuckin' and Jivin'

Daryl Cumber Dance

Shuckin' and Jivin'

Folklore from Contemporary Black Americans

INDIANA UNIVERSITY PRESS • BLOOMINGTON AND LONDON

Manufactured in the United States of America

Library of Congress Cataloging in Publication Data
Dance, Daryl Cumber.
Shuckin' and jivin'.
Includes bibliographical references.
1. Afro-American folk-lore--Virginia.   2. Afro-
American tales--Virginia.   I. Title
GR103.D3   1978   398.2'09755   77-23635
ISBN 0-253-35220-7   2 3 4 5 82 81 80 79

To my mother,
Veronica B. Cumber,
and to the memory of my father,
Allen W. Cumber

Contents

4. Somebody Clapped for Edith Las' Night: Conjure Tales / 37

5. I Hears de Call: Tales about Religion / 41

6. A Nigger Ain't Shit: Self-Degrading Tales / 77

7. Oh, Lord, Will I Ever? The White Woman and the Black Man / 101

8. I Could Eat Her Up: Tales about Women / 110

9. Be True to Me: Tales about Marital Infidelity / 143

10. Goldstein, Pat, Mike, and the Like: Ethnic Jokes / 151

11. The White Man Is the Devil: Tales about the Cruelty of Whites / 165

12. The Bottom Rail Comes to Be the Top Riser: Outsmarting Whitey / 179

13. I'm A Bad Motherfucker: Tales of the Bad Nigger / 224

14. Down in the Jungle, Out on the Farm: Miscellaneous Animal Tales / 247

15. Are You Ready for This? Miscellaneous Risqué Tales / 262

16. A Potpourri: Miscellaneous Black Folklore / 306

Acknowledgments

The fieldwork for this book was begun while I was working on my doctoral dissertation under a grant from the Ford Foundation in 1970 and 1971. Most of the materials included herein were collected and assembled during the 1974–75 school year with the support of a grant from the National Endowment for the Humanities. The final work on the book was completed during the summer of 1976 with the support of a grant from the National Endowment for the Humanities. I am grateful to both these agencies.

I am indebted to the many informants who graciously received me and generously shared their folk materials with me. They include Elton Askew, Esther K. Blount, Charles Bowman, Gary Bowman, Richard Bowman, Viola Bradley, Byron Brown, Julius Brown, Beatrice Buck, Cynthia Buckra, Ethel Burrell, Louise Butler, Charles E. Calender, Charles Cheatham, Martha Cheatham, Clarence Craddock, Veronica B. Cumber, Robert T. Dance, Sr., Mabel Dandridge, Marion Davis, Lela Diggs, Leslie Dixon, Esther Douglas, Lemuel Vaughan Eggleston, Edward Ellis, John M. Ellison, Erselle Epps, Ada Foster Fisher, James Franklin, Mr. and Mrs. Richard Foster, James Giles, S. P. Granderson, Arnold Harris, Phillip M. Harris, Jr., Jack Harvey, Blanche Haskins, Charles E. Hayes, Thelma Hedgepeth, Lillian J. Hinsley, A. O. Hope, Calvin Hudson, Marie Hunter, Richard Jackson, Mae C. Johnson, Phoebe Johnson, Julia Jones, William M. Jones, Joan Kersey, Velma L. Kitching, Mary E. Lewis, Robert Libron, Hopson Lipscomb, W. H. Mackey, Eugertha Mason, Walter Mickens, Jr., Estelle Minton, Louise Mitchell, Quallie Moon, Sr., Eugene Mundle, Mary Oliver, Bernard L. Peterson, Delores Robinson, Thomas Robinson, W. E. Robinson, William Jackson Straughn, Louise Taylor, Ellen C. Thompson, Alte C. Thornton, Lewis W. Tyler, L. D. Wilder, Edith C. Williams, Mollie Williams, Virginia Wyatt, and Preston Yancey.

I am grateful also to the numerous friends and acquaintances who gave me valuable leads to informants and aided me in arranging interviews. For such assistance I wish to thank Richard Bowman, Doris Britton, Veronica B. Cumber, Rozeal Diamond, Walter Gay, Pat Glass, Berbenia McDougald, Margaret Mead, Quallie Moon, Sr., Gerald Poindexter, Frances Roane, LaVerne Spurlock, and C. E. Thompson.

I appreciate the kind reception of administrators of various institutions, who made it possible for me to arrange interviews at their respective establishments. I especially wish to thank Velma L. Kitching of the First Street Senior Citizens' Center; Linda McGowan, Activities Counselor of the Church Hill Senior Citizens' Center; Notis Taylor, Director of the West End Senior Citizens' Center; and C. E. Thompson, Program Coordinator of the Virginia State Penitentiary. I wish to thank also all those workers who offered me assistance but whose names I failed to record.

I am indebted to Joseph Jenkins, who assisted me in collecting folklore from students at Virginia State College in Petersburg, Virginia, and to some of my students at Virginia Commonwealth University, who contributed material which they collected. They include Linwood Lewis, Gregory Pleasants, Dennis Folly, Leonard Lambert, Thomas Beatty, and Marilyn Gordon.

I am grateful to my friends and colleagues who offered me encouragement and assistance. I would especially like to thank Jacob D. Levenson of the University of Virginia for his encouragement; Charles Purdue of the University of Virginia for his many helpful suggestions; Michael Linn of Virginia Commonwealth University for his assistance in transcribing some of the difficult tapes and for his critical reading of my manuscript; and Richard Priebe of Virginia Commonwealth University for reading my manuscript and offering many suggestions for improvement.

I wish to thank my husband, Warren Dance, and my children, Warren, Jr., Allen, and Daryl Lynn, for giving me understanding and encouragement but never allowing this endeavor to become an obsession by constantly reminding me that my major responsibility was to them.

My greatest debt is to my mother, Veronica B. Cumber, who inspired my love of Black folklore, contributed numerous tales herself, gave me several leads, arranged frequent sessions in her home for me, and whenever necessary took over my home and family responsibilities to free me to work on this book.

Introduction

THE PROHIBITIONS against education for Blacks during the time of slavery and during the period of segregation following emancipation have resulted perhaps in at least one advantage for Black Americans. Forced into a closed society, often largely lacking in literacy, Black Americans developed and maintained an oral tradition probably unmatched, and certainly not surpassed, by that of any other group in America. Their folklore reveals the history of Black people in this country and their psychological reactions to their experience. The similarities of themes appearing throughout their tales, from the slave anecdotes to the contemporary stories, suggest that for Black Americans basically very little has changed. The Black principals in the tales may face Old Massa in the slave narratives, they may confront Big Boss in the Reconstruction tales, they may encounter Mr. Charlie in the accounts of the period of segregation, or they may contend with a "Honkie" or a "Pig" in the contemporary anecdotes; but the sense of injustice and oppression and the need to vent their anger, to relieve their frustrations, and to fulfill their fantasies in a created world are much the same. As William H. Grier and Price M. Cobbs have expressed it, "For white America to understand the life of the black man, it must recognize that so much time has passed and so little has changed."[1]

Undoubtedly Black folktales are a form of amusement. They have served as a diversion for the storytellers and their audiences through the years, and one may anticipate many hours of entertaining reading in this book and in other collections of Black folklore. But through my comments I hope to call attention also to the political, psychological, and sociological meanings that lie beneath the humor in most of the selections presented here. Frantz Fanon has noted that, "when a story flourishes in the heart of a folklore, it is because in one way or another it expresses an aspect of 'the spirit of the group.'"[2] A careful reading of this work will, I hope, provide insight into the spirit of Black Americans—into their loves and hates, their joys and sorrows, their values and concerns, their hopes and fears. Insight into the true meaning of much of Black folklore is sometimes lacking even in many of the white folklorists who have provided a valuable service in preserving and presenting this folklore, from Joel Chandler Harris, who contended that the teller of the Brer Rabbit tales "has nothing but pleasant memories of the discipline of slavery" and who suggested that Brer Rabbit is moved, not by "malice, but mischievousness," to Bruce Jackson, who insisted that "Shine expresses little hostility toward the whites."[3] Such insight is lacking also at times among the Black storytellers who reveal in their lore frustrations and fears of which they themselves are not fully aware. Such insight is lacking among those Blacks who are ashamed of the tales because of their own fears and psychoses regarding themselves, their race, and their past. To those who would prefer to ignore and to suppress the folklore of their race, as their counterparts of yesteryear preferred to repress the blues and the spirituals, let me address the admonition of Niles Newbell Puckett: "Those who ignore the past never really understand the present; for the past gives shape to the present. . . . Such ultra-modern worshippers of race-pride would do well to visit again the great Kindergarten of Folk-Thought. . . ."[4]

In selecting material for this collection, I have applied Jan Harold Brunvand's definition of folklore: "*those materials in culture that circulate traditionally among members of any group in different versions.*"[5] Included here are traditional prose narratives, anecdotes of local characters, folk songs, folk verses, and accounts of individual experiences which, to borrow a phrase from J. Mason Brewer, "possess a distinctive and unique folk flavor."[6] Many of the accounts of individual experiences turn out to be in effect folktales. There is admittedly little balance among the varied types of folk material presented here. I did not aggressively solicit specific types of materials or specific tales, since I was interested in observing the kinds of tales, anecdotes, and so on, that people like to tell and voluntarily relate. With the exception of maxims which are not ordinarily recounted unless some specific act or incident motivates them, the prominence of certain types of folklore in this collection generally suggests their popularity among the people whom I interviewed.

The material included here comes from all sources. Some of the tales, for example, can be traced back to early European, Asian, and African origins. Others suggest white American and American Indian influences. Some undoubtedly stem from printed sources and from radio and television. But they have all become a part of the oral lore of Black Americans, who have adopted them as their own and who pass them on by word of mouth.

Numerous anthologies of Black folklore which have appeared through the years have contributed significantly to the preservation of Black American folklore. Collections often, however, reflect a certain selectivity that destroys their representativeness as general collections. (Many of them, of course, do not purport to be general collections.) Certain anthologies have limited themselves to specific types of tales—animal tales, religious tales, toasts, and so on. Other collections, which claim to be general, have omitted obscene tales or have published them in expurgated form. Still others have limited themselves to tales told only by selected groups of Black

Americans—for example, Black prison inmates, Black ghetto dwellers, Black rural folk, and illiterate and semiliterate groups. Others have merely taken tales from a variety of printed sources and brought them together in one volume.[7] I have attempted here, however, to present a more general and more fully comprehensive collection than can be found among other publications. This book includes materials collected from both rural and urban areas, from informants of all ages, and from storytellers of all educational and economic levels, from the completely uneducated and illiterate to the most highly educated, from some of Virginia's poorest, most obscure, and most inconspicuous Black citizens to some of Virginia's most affluent and most prominent Blacks. Though the collection is limited to informants who now live or who once lived in Virginia, the tales which appear here are not exclusively Virginia tales, as innumerable texts given to me were first heard in widely scattered areas of the country. The material presented here is not new; a new folktale is a rare phenomenon. Certain tellers add new dimensions and original perspectives to many of the old tales, however. And several of the tales included here, as far as I have been able to determine, are appearing in print for the first time.

Some readers will no doubt be disturbed by the inclusion of certain of the obscene, crudely bitter, sardonic, and "sick" tales in this volume. The fact is that the myth of the "quaint," "delightful," and "darling" folktales is just that—a myth perpetuated by some folklorists (perhaps the more accurate term is *fakelorists*) through their selectivity or through their tampering with the texts they have received. Most folklore is, as Richard M. Dorson has noted, "coarse and obscene,"[8] and this book honestly presents folklore as it exists among Black Virginians and among Black Americans generally.

One will note in reading these tales that the contemporary selections, particularly those from younger correspondents, are frequently more blatantly hostile, sadistic, and obscene than are some of the older tales. Many of those young people, witnessing the continued plight of their Black brothers in America, noting the persistent strength of racism in this country, and feeling discouraged by the slowness and ineffectiveness of integration, have become frustrated and disillusioned by the hypocrisy, the insanities, and the horrors they view daily in American government and society (as well as in world affairs), and their bitter pessimism finds expression in perverse and sardonic tales, which have their bases in some of the veiled attacks in earlier narratives. Frequent obscenities and lewd tales are not, of course, unique to Black folklore but are common to folklore generally. In the Black community they serve the same purpose as in other groups—that of expressing aggressiveness and rebellion against societal repression. A brief apologia for the obscene tales appears in chapter fifteen.[9]

Except for an occasional comment in the Annotations, I do not deal with origins. More important than the origin of an item are the reasons for which Black Americans adopted it as their own and the implications of any variations they may have added to it. The point, it seems to me, is to view the types of folklore that have a wide appeal to people and to discover the functions they serve to the teller and to the listener. My approach is consistent with Alan Dundes' philosophy of the study of folklore: "It is how a people thinks and how individuals perceive themselves in relation to the world they see around them that folklorists ought to be investigating."[10]

I have made every effort to present the actual texts, to transcribe them word for word from the taped version.[11] I have corrected the events in an item when an informant noted an error in the chronological order during the course of the interview. I have incorporated into the text corrections and additions provided later by the informant and have omitted obvious repetitions. Where necessary, I have placed clarifying information in brackets. In those cases in which words or passages were unintelligible and in which clarification could not be obtained (either because the informant could not clarify it or could not be reached), I have inserted the word *unclear* in brackets.

It is important to note that practically all of the tales included here were delivered in dialect. Even the most sophisticated joke tellers usually revert to dialect in closed company. Indeed, the tales lose much of their flavor in standard English. As Chapman J. Milling aptly averred, "a Negro story not told in Negro dialect is about as successful as a honeymoon shared by the mother-in-law."[12] I have thus given careful attention to rendering the dialect faithfully. Of course, speakers are not always consistent in their use of dialect; the same speaker may, for example, pronounce a final g at one time and drop it on another occasion. I have attempted to reproduce the informants' exact pronunciations and not to force any false consistency onto the dialect.

I have struggled diligently to convey to the reader some sense of the oral performances of the tales, which were colored by dramatizations (described in brackets) and frequently characterized by a rhythmical, musical, and rhyming delivery, with a variety of fascinating tonal variations, sometimes difficult, and often impossible, to render in writing. The transcriptions cannot do justice to the facility with which some of the informants mimicked the sounds of animals or captured a fervent religious service with the chants and shouts of the minister and the impassioned responses of the congregation. Indeed, it is unfortunate that some of the tales which, because of the effectiveness of the delivery, elicited the most uproarious responses from audiences appear rather dull in print. Would that I could recapture those performances on paper! I hope those who take up this book will imaginatively reinvest in these tales the energy that charged them in their initial telling.

Annotations for each item, which appear at the back of the book, provide information about the collection of the item and indicate other printed sources. I have keyed references to Stith Thompson's *Motif-Index of Folk-Literature* and to Ernest W. Baughman's *Type and Motif-Index of the Folktales of England and North America* because they are the best known, most commonly used, and most easily accessible indexes. Both of them suffer certain limitations in the areas of African, Afro-American, and erotic materials, however. African materials and erotic materials are better covered in the two following indexes, which, because of their lack of general use and of availability, I have not keyed: Kenneth Clarke, "A Motif-Index of the Folktales of Culture Area V West Africa" and G[ershon] Legman, *Rationale of the Dirty Joke: An Analysis of Sexual Humor*, respectively.[13]

Brief biographies of most of my major informants are included in the book. A few informants preferred to remain anonymous. My greatest frustration is that I am unable to convey adequately either the pleasure of meeting some of these fascinating Virginians or the thrill of their masterful presentations. Whether illiterate or well educated, whether rich or poor, the informants whose texts appear here have much in common: they appreciate their folk heritage and they preserve it; they delight in telling a good tale and they are adept at it; and they are all intelligent. A good storyteller is invariably witty, creative, and eloquent. During my interview with Charles E. Hayes, a ninety-six-year-old informant, someone asked me if I wanted tales and other items from *old* people. Mr. Hayes quipped, "What she needs is people who *know* something!" Attend these people who know something, peep in on them as they are shuckin' and jivin', and perhaps, like me, you will come away knowing more as a result.

NOTES

1. William H. Grier and Price M. Cobbs, *Black Rage* (New York: Bantam Books, 1969), p. 31.

2. Frantz Fanon, *Black Skin, White Masks* (New York: Grove Press, 1967), p. 64.

3. Joel Chandler Harris, *Uncle Remus: His Songs and His Sayings*, rev. ed. (New York: D. Appleton, 1947), pp. xvii, xiv; Bruce Jackson, "*Get Your Ass in the Water and Swim Like Me*": Narrative Poetry from Black Oral Tradition (Cambridge: Harvard University Press, 1974), p. 36.

4. Niles Newbell Puckett, "Race Pride and Folklore," in *Mother Wit from the Laughing Barrel: Readings in the Interpretation of Afro-American Folklore*, ed. Alan Dundes (Englewood Cliffs, N.J.: Prentice-Hall, 1973), p. 4 (reprinted from *Opportunity: A Journal of Negro Life* 4 [1926].

5. Jan Harold Brunvand, *The Study of American Folklore: An Introduction* (New York: W. W. Norton, 1968), p. 5.

6. J. Mason Brewer, *American Negro Folklore* (Chicago: Quadrangle, 1968), p. 227.

7. Some of these anthologies are very poorly annotated or are not annotated at all. A few fail to provide any information about the sources of their tales and are therefore of almost no value to the study of Black folklore.

8. Richard M. Dorson, *American Folklore* (Chicago: University of Chicago Press, 1962), p. 4.

9. For additional discussions of the social and psychological functions of erotic humor, see G[ershon] Legman, *Rationale of the Dirty Joke: An Analysis of Sexual Humor* (New York: Grove Press, 1971); and Sigmund Freud, "Wit and Its Relation to the Unconscious," in *The Basic Writings of Sigmund Freud*, ed. A. A. Brill (New York: Modern Library, 1938).

10. Alan Dundes, ed., *Mother Wit from the Laughing Barrel: Readings in the Interpretation of Afro-American Folklore* (Englewood Cliffs, N.J.: Prentice-Hall, 1973), p. 402.

11. Instances when a joke was not taped but was given to me in manuscript form or when I reproduced it from memory or from notes have been individually noted.

12. Chapman J. Milling, "Foreword," in J. Mason Brewer, *Dog Ghosts and Other Texas Negro Folk Tales* (Austin: University of Texas Press, 1958), p. xii.

13. Kenneth Clarke, "A Motif-Index of the Folktales of Culture Area V West Africa" (Ph.D. diss., Indiana University, 1958).

Shuckin' and Jivin'

1

In the Beginning:
Etiological Tales

They say that, in the beginning of time, God was
getting the races together, and . . . .
"In the Beginning"

A SUBSTANTIAL NUMBER of Black folktales may be designated as
etiological "myths" in that they tend to focus on the world as it
evolved and to offer explanations for why things are as they are.
Several of these tales emphasize the role of God in explaining why
Blacks are, to quote from one tale, "so messed up," why they are
Black, why they have big, ugly feet and hands, why their hair is
kinky, and why they must remain poor laborers in a rich society. The
causes of all of these "inferior" traits appear to be certain alleged
character defects—tardiness, ignorance, disobedience to God, greed,
laziness, and so on.

   At first glance these tales appear to suggest a self-hatred, a rejection and denial of Blackness, which Blacks have been taught by
white Western culture. Looking at these tales Fred. O. Weldon, Jr.,
noted that "the important fact here is that the Negro has accepted his
inferiority so completely that even in jest he must give supernatural
explanations for the condition."[1] John Lomax, viewing similar
themes in the Black folk songs, suggests that it is deeply tragic that

Portions of this chapter appeared as "In the Beginning: A New View of Black American Etiological Tales," *Journal of the Richmond Oral History Association* 1 (Autumn,
1976): 1–11. Reprinted by permission of the publisher.

"over and over, from many angles, the negro expresses his feeling of a race inferiority, and sings of what seems to be to his mind his badge of shame—his color."[2] Certainly, there are those Blacks who see themselves as standing apart from "my people" and laughing at "their" shortcomings in tales such as these.[3] It appears to me highly questionable, however, to accept the general interpretation of these tales as self-debasing narratives which suggest that Black people accept the derogatory stereotypes, that they regard the physical traits of their race as a curse, and that they view their economic plight as a badge of their inferiority. Several factors combine to make such an interpretation suspect.

First, a careful study of the extant accounts of Black people from the time of slavery to the present, including accounts from both the illiterate and the well educated and including many of the folk materials, tends to suggest that, although Blacks could not escape the fact that in white America whiteness was certainly a preeminent convenience, there have always been considerable numbers who never accepted whiteness, in and of itself, as a positive quality—a virtue—and Blackness, in and of itself, as a negative quality—a curse. It is difficult to believe, therefore, that tales would arise and endure with such widespread currency if they were indeed completely self-defeating tales, since popular folklore inevitably reflects something of the culture, values, and innermost desires of the people who create it.

Second, my own observations of the reactions of Black audiences to the tales indicate that they may chuckle lightly at the Black characters who seem to be the butts of the jokes, but they tend to react more to the absurdity of the situations—all of which have a white orientation and arise from white values, white prejudices, white stereotyping, white hypocrisy, white economic institutions, and so on.

Finally, it seems to me that an interpretation of the "myths" that is more consistent with the interpretations of much other Black folklore, such as the animal fables and the spirituals, might tend to reveal the tales more accurately as veiled satires of situations rather than as indications of blind acceptance of them. It would not be the first time Blacks have appropriated whites' stereotypes of Blacks and have used those same stereotypes for a counterattack: the contented and devoted slave, the Uncle Tom, the minstrel buffoon, the sexual superman—all appear in countless Black productions (folk and literary) in the same guise but with very different souls and subversive motives. Moreover, if we consider the tales and their apparent purpose in terms of the usual function of folklore, we cannot help but see them as satirical commentaries. William R. Bascom has noted that folklore helps to validate its "culture, [to justify] its rituals and institutions to those who perform and observe them."[4] In those tales which purport to provide a logical explanation for illogical values, we find that, instead of validating and justifying them, they make those values appear ridiculous. Further, those values appear even more ridiculous if we attempt to explain the tales as myths. Bronislav Malinowski notes that "the function of myth, briefly, is to strengthen tradition and endow it with a greater value and prestige by tracing it back to a higher, better, more supernatural reality of initial events."[5] On the surface, of course, the tales in this chapter appear to be mythological tales, explaining certain traditions in terms of their creation by, or at least in conjunction with, God. But as we look at the paradoxical nature of the full body of the tales, we see that no amount of mythological explanation will rationalize or give prestige to any of the situations. In their very effort supposedly to give some logic to prevalent attitudes toward the Blacks, the creators of the tales make those beliefs appear so ridiculous that one must conclude that the views and attitudes of whites are positively ludicrous. An additional bit of irony may derive from the Black narrator's use of the whites' God to explain most of these situations, especially when one considers the fact that white Americans have used religion to justify some of their most hypocritical and sacrilegious actions toward Blacks.[6] The unavoidable conclusion is that these tales are not myths—they are only parodies of myths. They are indeed jokes, and the butts of the jokes are only ostensibly Blacks—the real targets are often whites or America.

There is no possibility of providing value and prestige to situations in which the principals lose both if they are first and if they are last; both if they work and if they fail to work; or if any choices that they make are the wrong choices. The only constant in the illogical situations under which Blacks function in these tales is that they must lose. They may be told that they are punished for particular shortcomings, but the fact remains that they must suffer because of only one thing—their race. In a tale in Philip Sterling's Laughing on the Outside: The Intelligent White Reader's Guide to Negro Tales and Humor, which is a variant of my tales "Why the Black Man's Hair Is Nappy" and "Why the Black Man Has Big Feet" (both p. 8), the Blacks get the "worst" hair because they were the last to respond to God's call. The next time He called, they came first, and therefore they got the "worst" feet.[7] Whether first or last they lost. In some tales God offers a package; when the Blacks select the big package, as in most versions, they suffer; and when they select the small package, as in my variant, "Why the Whites Have Everything" (p. 9), they still suffer.[8] In other words, to use an expression commonly heard in Black conversations regarding the political, economic, and social systems in this country, "The nigger can't win!" One can certainly more clearly detect that same sentiment echoing throughout the tales than one can perceive the idea that Blacks are inferior. A vivid example is "Upon This Rock" (pp. 9–10), which is an eloquent commentary on the injustices of the American economic system. If, as in version B of this tale, the Black man rushes, cognizant of how often he is punished for being late, he ends up with a biscuit, whereas the Italian and the Jew get several loaves and a bakery, respectively; if he struggles, as the others did to earn the rewards they received, the rules of the game are changed again and he gets nothing. Inevitably when this joke is recounted, the members of the audience do not so much laugh at the industriousness of the Black man as they react to the hypocrisy of the Lord (here the American economic system), because they know that He will inevitably modify the rules so that, whatever that nigger does, he is never going to get more than a biscuit.

A second group of etiological tales explains the origins of the animals. Those included in this section represent only a small number of the animal tales, which make up a substantial portion of Black folklore and which are discussed in some detail in chapter fourteen.

NOTES

1. Fred O. Weldon, Jr., "Negro Folktale Heroes," in *And Horns on the Toads*, ed. Mody C. Boatright, Wilson M. Hudson, and Allen Maxwell (Dallas: Southern Methodist University Press, 1959), p. 183.

2. John Lomax, "Self-Pity in Negro Folk-Songs," *The Nation* 105 (August 9, 1917): 143.

3. The term *my people* is a common one which, when used in a sense such as I employ it here, suggests disgust or scorn on the part of the speaker for the fellow Blacks to whom he or she refers. For a discussion of the derogatory use of the term, see the chapter "My People! My People!" in Zora Neale Hurston, *Dust Tracks on a Road: An Autobiography* (Philadelphia: J. P. Lippincott, 1971), pp. 215–37. The term also has widespread currency with positive connotations, however, as it is used, for example, in Margaret Walker's well-known poem, "For My People" (Margaret Walker, *For My People* [New Haven: Yale University Press, 1942], pp. 13–14). The context in which it is used and the intonation of the speaker would leave little doubt in the listener's mind as to how to interpret the term. It is interesting, that, as

my colleague Richard Priebe pointed out to me, from an African perspective the term can be explained "entirely in terms of a positive recognition of duality in the universe."

4. William R. Bascom, "Four Functions of Folklore," in The Study of Folklore, ed. Alan Dundes (Englewood Cliffs, N.J.: Prentice-Hall, 1965), p. 292.

5. Bronislav Malinowski, Myth in Primitive Psychology (Westport, Conn.: Negro Universities Press, 1972), pp. 91–92.

6. Slave narratives and testimonials offer overwhelming evidence that slaves frequently saw through the white masters' ridiculously hypocritical use of Christianity and made the whites' behavior the subject matter of jokes.

7. Philip Sterling, Laughing on the Outside: The Intelligent White Reader's Guide to Negro Tales and Humor (New York: Grosset and Dunlap, 1965), p. 170.

8. In a tale collected by Zora Neale Hurston, the Black man finds a shovel, a hoe, and a plow in his package whereas the white men gets pen and ink. The Black man, of course, ends up working while the white man sits down "figgerin'" (Mules and Men [Philadelphia: L. P. Lippincott, 1935], p. 102. In "Colored Man, Jew, and White Man," collected by Richard M. Dorson, the Black man's big package contains a mule and a plow whereas the small packages selected by the white man and the Jew contain knowledge and money, respectively (Negro Folktales in Michigan [Cambridge: Harvard University Press, 1956], p. 76; reprinted in American Negro Folktales [Greenwich, Conn.: Fawcett, 1967], pp. 172–73).

1   In the Beginning

They say that, in the beginning of time, God was getting the races together, and He told the people, He say, "Now . . ." (He was telling them what to do, you know—couldn't hear so good). He say, "Yawl git to the right." They got white, you know.

He say, "Yawl stand aroun', stand aroun', git aroun'!" They got brown, you know.

And [He said], "Yawl, git back!" And they got black.

2   Why the Nigger Is So Messed up

When the Creator made man, He was making the white man first, and all of the scrap pieces, the ends of the fingernails and the toes and the backsides, and what have you, He said, "Well, I don't know what I'm gon' do with all of these ends. I'll throw them over here in the corner, and when I get time, I'll decide what to do with them."

And, ALL OF A SUDDEN, something popped out of the corner, say, "Lawd, here me!"

And He turned around and it was a nigger—he made himself. He say, "Since you so smart, now, you stay like that."

And that's why the nigger is so messed up. He couldn't wait until the Lord fixed him right. He had to make himself.

3   Why the Black Man's Hair Is Nappy

A. At the beginning of time, the Lord, you know, decided that He was going to give out hair. And so first He called up a white man and asked him what kind of hair he wanted; he said he wanted straight hair.

And then He called up the Jew, and said, "Now, Mr. Jew, come on, what kind of hair you want?" He said he wanted curly hair. So the Lord gave him curly hair.

And in the meantime, the niggers were back there playing dice. And they weren't about to stop. And the Lord said, "Niggers, what kind o' hair yawl want? Come up here and tell me."

And they hollered out, "Aw, J. C., just ball it up and throw it back here."

And that's the way we got our nappy hair.

B. All right now, we going to our races; we going to find out where the Black people got their hair from, and how they got it. When it was time for the Lord to give hair, He called all three of these men, and this is what he said. Well, first he called the white man to come on and get his hair. All right, the white man he went right on up there and got his hair. So the Lord called the Jew man to get his hair. So the Jew man went up there and got his hair, and said, "Thank you, Lord."

So when it got down to the Black man, the Lord called him. And do you know what the Black man said? Black man said, "Lord, ball it up and throw it to me." And it's been balled up ever since.

4   Why the Black Man Has Big Feet

A long time ago, when they were givin' out hands and feet and heads and all, say we saw the other people gettin' all the small hands and all, you know. So to make sure that we would get the good part, say, we grabbed all the big feet we could get and all the ugly feet and the big hands. Say that's why we have such large, ugly feet and ugly hands, 'cause we wanted to be sure we would get the large portions.

5 Why the Whites Have Everything

God was making the worl' and He called de people, you know, de white people to get a bag and de colored people to get a bag. De colored people went to get the little light bag and the white people get the big, heavy bag; and the heavy bag [there] was money in it, and the light bag ain't have nothin' in it. And they say dat's why us ain't got nothin' today; white people got it all.

6 Upon This Rock

A. When the good Lord was traveling on earth, you know, they had such a bunch of people following him 'round, and they say He had one of us with Him, you know. So they say, "Lord," say, "We're hungry."

He say, "Well, you go up on the mountain and bring me down a stone." So the others (Jewish fellows and all like that, you know) brought down a pretty good size stone, you know.

Colored fellow say, "I ain't gon' carry no great big rock. He say, 'Bring down a stone.'" He picked up something like that [gesturing with fingers to indicate a tiny pebble] and he walked on down there, you know. So He prayed and commanded the stones be turned into bread. And they had enough bread to satisfy 'em. All he [the colored fellow] had was a lil' loaf like that [indicating a tiny piece the size of the pebble].

So the next time they got hungry, they say, "Lord, we're hungry."

He say, "Go up there on that mountain and bring me down a stone."

Say us say, "I'm gon' fix 'im this time." He went up there and got a great big boulder; he could just barely be capable of gettin' it down there. He say, "I'm gon' eat this time."

And say when he got down there, He commanded the other stones be made into bread. When He got to this fellow, He put his foot on it and say, "Upon this rock I'll build my church."

He say, "Oh, naw, NAW you ain't! You gon' make bread out o' that rock. You ain't gon' build no church on it!"

B. On the side of a mountain once, the Lord summoned three people to help Him with a project, one being a Black man, one being an Italian, and the other Jewish. And the Lord said, "I am simply looking for people to follow simple directions." And He said, "I simply want the three of you to go out and bring me back a stone, or as much stone as you'd like." And so the Black man, thinking that it was a timed thing, rushed right back with a pebble. The Italian took a couple of hours, and finally he came back with a wheelbarrow piled with crushed stone. And they waited until midnight. Finally they heard a rumbling. And the Jew was shoving a mountain. So the Lord in His patience blessed the stones and said, "These stones I will now turn into bread." Well, the Black man had a biscuit. The Italian had a wheelbarrow *filled* with loaves of bread. And the Jew had a *bakery*, of course.

So the next day, the Lord said, "Same gentlemen, same assignment. Go out and fetch stones." Well, the Black man was *extremely* happy for a second chance. So sometime later that evening, the Italian was the first one back, with his same wheelbarrow filled with stones. And the Jew took very long to come, but here he is with his mountain. And they waited until midnight. The Black man didn't show ... Two A.M. .... Three A.M. .... Four A.M. .... Well, just about dawn they heard a rumbling sound. And a whole avalanche of mountains and boulders—just everything—was being hurled at the Lord. And finally the Lord said, "Upon *these* rocks I'll build my church."

And the Black man said, "I be *damned* if you will. You gon' make *bread* today!"

7 How Blacks Got to America

I hear that the colored people one time was all on *one* side of the river. And the white people was all on *this* side. And they had a red flag, red handkerchief or sumpin'. They took that and kept on waving it, wavin' it and *wavin'* it, and that caused them to get those slaves—by that red flag. That's how they managed to come over here. They waved and got 'em over here—through that red flag. Yeah! So that's the way the colored people mostly got here—got here through that red handkerchief—that red flag. They [whites] was on one side of the river—and they [Blacks] was on the other, and they [whites] waved, kep' on waving and they got over there where the white folks at and when they got over here, see, they kep' 'em.

8 Why the Bear Ain't Got No Tail

This boy, this little boy, he'd been fishing in the winter time. He had a sled. And he went down there to the river, cut a hole in the ice and caught a good swing of fish. He had gone on home, and the Fox saw 'im, and he wanted some of 'em. So he *ran* around in front of 'im and laid down, stretched out like he was dead. And the boy saw 'im. He say, "Well, this is fox pelt; I kin make me a cap." So he throwed him on top of where the fish were, and when the Fox got a chance, he shoved the fish off and he rolled on off. The boy never felt it.

He [Fox] went on down the road; he met the Bear. He say, "Hey, Bro Fox!" He say, "Where you get such a fine swing of fish?"

He say, "You go down there where you find that hole cut in the ice; you sit down and stick your tail in there; when the fish bites, snatch it out."

So he went on down there, you know, sit down and stuck his tail in the ice. They was so long bitin'. In the meantime the water froze over, and he didn't know it. So he say, "Well-l, I might as well go home, cause they ain't bitin' today. When he went to get up, sumpin' had 'im. He say, "Oh-h-h, this a terrible big one; if I get this one . . ." And he pulled so hard, he broke his tail off; left his tail stuck in the ice. And that's why the Bear ain't got no tail today.

9 How the Gopher Got His Name

When they were giving out names, the Gopher was somewhere messin' around, goofing off, somewhere, so when the guy came back, the Gopher says, "Well, what is my name?"

The guy say, "We've run out o' names."

He say, "Well, what—I—you know—what I gon' do?"

He say, "Just go!"

"Go? . . . Go what?"

"Go fer anything you wanna go fer!"

That's why they started callin' 'im Gopher.

10 Why Dogs Smell Each Other

They say the Dogs had a masquerade party and they had to check their tails when they enter; and a fire broke out and they grabbed each other's tails; and the reason they smell each other now is to try to get their own tails.

11 How Black Birds Got Black

It seems like this airplane was carrying some dynamite, and at a certain point this airplane released the dynamite, and *all* the beautiful birds that were in that vicinity were blackened. That's why all the birds of different colors are now black. The beautiful Egrets—they were one of the few that were saved because the dynamite was released and they began to get out the way in time—and their plumage remained all *snowy white*.

2

I Raised Hell
While I Was There:
Tales of Heaven and Hell

So some of 'em had told 'im, you know, to stop because if he didn't he was gon' turn the table over. So
finally he kep' on and kep' on until the table went
over, and when the table went over, then they put
him out of heaven.
                    "I Raised Hell While I Was There"

SEVERAL TALES IN the Black repertoire deal with a person's going to
heaven or to hell, or to both, after death or in a dream. Most of these
tales are impious accounts of Black people's conflicts with Saint
Peter, God, or the Devil, who frequently is just another Big White
Boss such as they suffered under in America. And heaven is all too
often a duplication of the America that they have left behind. At
times it even reproduces the same system of segregation found in
America, as suggested in one prevalent old tale in which a person
visits heaven and returns to earth to relate the wonders to be found
there; when he is asked about the Blacks, he replies that he didn't see
any because he didn't go into the kitchen. Almost always heaven is
too repressive for the Black characters who disturb the nature of
things there and who are frequently thrown out or who occasionally
decide that they would rather be in hell. Often the Black characters
actually prefer hell because of the good times to be had there—the
hell-raising. In the few tales where heaven is heavenly and highly

12

attractive to the characters, it is usually appealing for some impious reason, such as the free availability of beautiful women.

In many of these tales, the Black characters in one way or another revolt. They may lose in the end, but, as in a large number of the other types of Black folktales, they take pleasure in the rebellion itself. They may be put out of heaven, but at least they turned the table over. And after all, hell originated from a rebellion against God, who in these tales is frequently the chief authority figure, the ultimate representative of the repressive Big White Boss.[1] Of course, rebellion also occurs frequently in hell, as in the jokes that deal with putting the Devil's fire out, having sexual relations with the Devil's wife, or, particularly in some of the toasts, having sexual relations with the Devil himself.

Tales which deal with the minister in hell and the Bad Nigger in hell are included in chapters five and twelve.

NOTE

1. That the tellers of these tales relate to the Devil in his rebellion against God may be seen in version B of "Flying Good Time" (p. 14), where the Devil is cast in the role frequently assigned to the Black man in this same tale.

12   I Raised Hell While I Was There

This guy died and went to heaven, and when he got up there, say, all the angels were 'round at the table, you know, and he wanted to show off. So he ran around. He did the left-wing dive and the right-wing dive—all kinds o' stunts. So some of 'em had told 'im, you know, to stop because if he didn't he was gon' turn the table over. So finally he kep' on and kep' on until the table went over, and when the table went over, then they put him out of heaven. So after they put him out of heaven, they say he said, "Well, they put me out," he says, "but, HEY! HEY! I raised hell while I was there."

13   Flying Good Time

A. This Black man died and he went to heaven. And he was so glad to get to heaven. Saint Peter was giving out the wings, and he was so happy 'cause he had made it, he decided he would get his wings himself; so he picked up two wings—didn't care which two—whether they were right or wrong. But it was two left wings. And he put 'em on. He was flying all one-sided, *all* 'round the walls, knocking down things. Saint Peter say, "HEY!" Say, "Come here." He say, "*Who* gave you those wings?"

He say, "I put 'em on myself."

He say, "Now look, you niggers done tore up earth. You not coming up here and tear up heaven. Just gimme those wings!"

He say, "Well, I had a flying good time while I had 'em on though!"

B.   This Ole Devil was up in heaben from the beginnin' of the world. So God told Saint Peter, say, "Saint Peter, everything quiet up here." Say, "Let's git everybody 'round here a pair o' wings."

Saint Peter say, "God, let 'em git their own wings."

So God tol' Saint Peter, say, "Let 'em take what they want." Devil was up there too—having a good time.

Everybody went there and got a left wing and a right wing—'cept the Ole Devil. The Ole Devil, he went up there and got two left wings. He start to flying *all* around heaben, knocking down pretty pictures and *everything*. So God say, "Saint Peter, come here!" Saint Peter went to 'im. He say, "Put 'im out." Saint Peter put 'im out.

So the Devil say, once he got in hell, "One thing 'bout it; I had a heck of a good time while I was up there."

14   Don't Wake 'Em!

Once there was a Preacher, and he had a dear friend; and the friend died. And after the friend died, he wandered about, wandered about. And after a while, he [the Preacher] died. So he went on up to heaven, and he was walkin' around with the angels 'n' the angels was showin' 'im all the beautiful things. After a while he said to the angel, "Where is the colored people? I don't see *one* of 'em."

He say, "HUSH-H! Don't wake 'em up. They down the hill sleep. Don't wake 'em up 'cause they'll tear heaben to pieces!"

15   I Don't Want to Staaay!

This guy went to heaven [and he asked this guy], "What's all that noise down there? All that hell-raising down there?"

And he say, "Well, that's what it is. That's hell down there." He say, "But you kin gone on down there. You kin gone on down there! But at six o'clock these pearly gates close. And if they ever close on you once, they close forever for ya."

So he goes on down there and stay till 'bout 'leben o'clock that night. He comes back [obviously intoxicated], "HE-E-EY, BABY!" BAM! [Knocking.] "Open the gate! BABY!" BAM! "HEY!" You know. "Peter, open the gate!"

He say, "Now I told you that you couldn't come back in here if you stayed and the gates ever closed. Now the gates close at six—"

"Look, man, I don't want to STAAAY! I just want to get my clothes. I'm going back!"

16 Fund Raiser

There was a lady in heaven that was always giving programs—to raise money, you know. So she give programs. So they were gettin' tired of that, so the Lord asked Saint Peter, say, "Can't you get rid of her; is it anywhere you can put her?"

So Saint Peter called down and asked the Devil, say, "Do you have any room down there for her? She's up here—keep raising money. We don't wan' no more money now."

So the Devil say, "Well, sen' her down here then."

So she went down there and she started working on the programs. It was so hot down there, she told 'em, say, "Listen here, let us have a program and raise some money and get us a air-conditioner." So she got a air-conditioner put down there.

Say the Devil call Saint Peter, say, "Listen here, you got any room up there for 'er?"

He say, "Yeah, but what's the matter? I thought yawl was havin' a good time down there."

He say, "Yeah, but she raised so much money down here—down here buying air-conditioners. We can't do nothin' with the air-conditioners down here."

17 The Niggers Done Put the Fire Out!

The Devil makes a long distance telephone call to the Lord, and he says, "J. C., you—you—you just got to help me. Since integration, I have been bogged down with niggers! I'm overswamped with niggers. Long time ago, I could keep 'em all in a room, but now that you've integrated I—I—I—"

The Lord said, "I *cannot* help you."

He said, "You've gotta help me with these niggers, Lord. They've *taken* over down here. I can't turn for them, an—an—and they're into everything. PLEASE help me. You've been *known* to help."

The Lord said, "I *cannot* help you."

He said, "Well, Lord, well just listen to me a little longer! Just wait a minute, Lord! Somebody's at the door—just hold it a minute—somethin's happening out in the hall."

And he rushes out into the hall, and he comes back. He say, "Lord, just forget it. The niggers done put the fire out! Just forget it."

18   Three Surprises

If you die and go to heaven, you can count on three surprises: the first surprise is the fact that the persons you thought would be there would not be there; the second one is that the ones you thought wouldn't be there are there; and the third surprise is that you'd be there.

The third great surprise is how *you* got there.

19   No Men in Heaven

Man died one time. His brother goin' 'round here cryin', "My brother's dead and gone to heaben!" So someone told him to go up there and see Saint Peter and ask Saint Peter 'bout 'em. So he went there. Saint Peter told him ain't nah man died and gone to heaben for *twenty-five* years.

20   Teacher Shortage

Two good teacher friends agreed that, when they died, if one went to heaven and one to hell, they would meet about halfway between and talk about how each was faring at his new destination. So they died and later met at the designated place. The one from heaven said, "I'm teaching and the classes are so large."

The one from hell replied, "I'm teaching too, but our classes are very small. I wonder why yours are so large in heaven."

Then they came to the conclusion that there were so many more teachers in hell.

21 I Know I'm in Hell Now

This guy died and went to hell. When he got down there he was all disturbed and everything. "Why did I have to live a life like this and be sent to hell?" But when he got down there he was surprised—it was a very beautiful place, very beautiful place. So, he ran into the Devil; he say, "Mister Devil, is this really hell?"

He said, "Yes, sir, this is hell." He say, "I'm the boss here."

He say, "Well, it certainly is a pretty place."

He say, "Yes, it's pretty; that's why a lot of people are disappointed. If those people up in heaven knew how nice it was here, a whole lot of 'em would want to be down here."

He said, "Well, what do I have to do?"

He say, "You don't have to do nothin'—just have fun. Do anything you wanta do. Eat any time. Drink any time. Socialize any time."

He say, "Man, I can't believe—"

"But don't tell me you can't believe it you're in hell, I'm tellin' ya."

So he looked all around; everything was so beautiful, you know. Finally he ran into the Devil again. He say, "Mister Devil, I hate to bother you, but anyplace 'round here I can get something to drink?" Say, "I drank a little liquor. Long as I'm down here I might as well continue to dissipate."

So he say, "Yeah." Say, "See up there where it says 'bar.'" Says, "Go on up there; you can get all the liquor you want, any kind."

He say, "What's it cost?"

Say, "It's not gon' cost you nothin'. I told you that. It's no cost. Help yourself."

So the guy went up there and got himself a big bottle of whiskey and put it in his hip pocket.

He walked all around and he saw all these beautiful women—all in the nude, you know. So he ran into the Devil again. He say, "Mister Devil, I know you a busy man," he says, "but it certainly is some pretty women." Say, "Can I have social relations with 'em?"

He said, "Sure, any of 'em; it's all yours. Just yours for the asking."

So he went up and tapped on one very beautiful doll. He say, "Baby, can you and I have a little sport?"

She says, "Why sure."

So they went on up in this fine boudoir room. She took off her clothes and he took off his clothes. She had all this beautiful bust, figure and everything that creates a real sexy atmosphere. So he was gettin' ready to make his approach for his landing and wouldn't nothin' go in. So he says, "What's the matter, Baby?"

She say, "It's no hole."

He say, "I know I'm in hell now!"

22   Don't Make a Wave

This man went to hell, and the Devil told him, say, "There are three doors, and you can hear what's going on *outside* the door, and then you decide where you want to spend the rest of eternity."

So the man went to the first door, and, boy, he heard all of the *dancing* and music, you know, and they were just having a ball. He say, "I don't want to spend the rest of my life dancing and jumping 'round." And he went to the next door, and he heard nice soft music and tinkling of glasses. He say, "I don't want to spend the rest of my life drinking liquor, either." He went to the *third* door, and he heard, [softly and cautiously] "Don't make a wa-a-a-ve, don't make a wa-a-a-ve." All these voices, "Don't make a wa-a-a-ve."

"Lord have mercy, what are they doing?"

"Don't make a wa-a-a-ve."

So he told the Devil, he said, "*That's* the door. I'm caught. I—I don't know what they're doing, but that's where I want to go."

The Devil say, "You're sure now, 'cause that's *eternity.*"

"Don't make a wa-a-a-ve."

And so the Devil opened the door, and it was just *loaded* with folks standing up in shit right below their mouths, and they were hollering, "Don't make a wa-a-a-ve."

23   Hard Luck Sam

This is about Sam. Sam was born and bred in Mississippi, and he'd been a good man all his life. His family had died; his wife had cancer. All his kids had died. And he was going to church *every* Sunday, trying to be as *good* a man as possible. And all of a sudden Sam was accused of having raped a white woman. He was totally innocent. So this was really a tragic thing.

So when he got to hell—he ended up *straight* in hell—the Devil say, "You know, of all the people I've seen, you *really* have had your problems." Say, "You the first person I'm gon' give another chance to, 'cause I really think that you should just have a second chance. What I'm gon' do is carry you and let you peek into several rooms, and all you have to do is look at me and *smile* and you can have anything that's in that room." So the Devil proceeds to carry old sad Sam. Sam will have a chance.

First door. Pulled the door open. Inside the room, there was all the food that you would want. 'Cause Black people love to eat. Looked at Sam? Sam didn't smile. So he proceeded down a lil' further. He opened the second door. And there was nothing but *money!* He looked at Sam. Sam didn't smile. He must not want the money. The Devil say, "I got 'im now." He goes down to the third door. Devil say, "I got 'im." And there were *all* the women—just ready for business—no clothes on. Looked at Sam—he didn't smile. Devil say, "Goddamn! What I gon' do now? I only got one more door. Let me try this." So he opened up this fourth door, and he opened the door and Sam burst out laughing. And Sam was just cast right in there. And what was in there? A big room full o' shit.

24   Sam Goes to Heaven

A.   Sam was out drinking and he had quite a bit. He went home, tipped in, pulled off his clothes, and got in the bed. The whiskey began to take effect upon him and threw him into a deep slumber. Then he began to dream. Contrary to his usual dreams, this was most peculiar. He dreamed that he was going up some golden stairs. When he got to the top, someone hollered, "Sam!"

He looked up, he say, "How you know my name?"

He say, "Well, I'm Saint Peter, and this is heaven. Welcome! Come in!"

So he went in. It was the most beautiful place he had ever seen! The grass was greener than any grass that he had ever seen and soft like cotton. He was walkin' with Saint Peter. He said, "Saint Peter, this is a very pretty place."

He said, "Yeah, you'll like it here."

As he walked he saw on a green knoll surrounded with flowers a woman—brown, wavy hair, very shapely, lying there basking in the sun in the nude. He say, "Saint Peter, what is that?"

He said [very nonchalantly], "Oh, that's one of the pretty women we have in heaven here."

He said, "Who is she for?"

"For you, if you want her."

[Incredulously.] "Oh, NAW, Saint Peter?"

"Yes."

He say, "Well, I like heaven. Now can I touch her!"

He said, "Sure, go on touch her." He touched her and she just rolled over and looked at him, smiling. So he said, "Look, Saint Peter, I know this is out of order—or is it?—can I have a sexual relationship with her?"

He said, "SU-U-URE, go right ahead. You're in heaven!"

So he got it, enjoyed it to the utmost. He say, "Saint Peter, this is al-l-l-l right! I really like this. I-I-I don't want to leave."

He say, "Well, naw, you not gonna leave."

So they were walkin' on 'round heaven. In another garden they saw another woman, more beautiful than the first. He say, "Look, Saint Peter, how about that one?"

"YOURS! Anything you see here is yours!"

"Can I get it?"

"Go get it!"

So he jumped on there. Say, "Buddy, this is all right! Saint Peter, you're my man!"

So they walked on. They came to this beautiful palace—diamond wallpaper, golden lights, plush carpets so thick that you could go up to your knees almost. He say, "Look, Saint Peter," say, "uh, where is the toilet around here?"

He say, "Oh, we don't have any toilets in heaven here."

"What?"

"Naw, we don't have no toilets up here."

He say, "Look, I'm coming out and tell you what I got to do. I got to shit."

Saint Peter: "All right, put it on the carpet there."

"Oh, no."

"Yes, right there, that's all right."

[Incredulously] "All right, this is your heaven." So he pulled down his pants, bent over, cut loose. "You got any toilet paper?"

Saint Peter say, "Naw, no toilet paper."

He say, "Well, what am I gon' wipe myself with?"

He say, "Take a handful of that brustle off the carpet there and wipe yourself." So he *reached* down there and grabbed that handful and *pulled* it.

'Bout that time, something hit him on his head, woke him up. His wife say, "Look here! Let me tell *you* one thing! I don't mind you screwing me twice a night. And it's bad that you got to *shit* in the bed. But you did have it on your side. But when you want to pull the hair from around my vagina, that's it!"

B. Say John came in from work happy and everything, thinkin' 'bout his wife, say, "Honey, don't wash dishes tonight. Come on get in the bed."

She say, "All right, John, I be there in a few minutes."

And John drift on to sleep while he was waitin' for her. And say he dreamt he was in heaven, and Saint Peter met him at the gate and tol' 'im, say, "John, anything up here you want," say, "you kin have it while you up here." Say, "Look all around." Say, "Anything!"

And John seen these pretty girls over there. He say, "Lawd have mercy!" Say, "How 'bout them?"

He say, "It's all right." Say, "If you want them, gone on."

So he got them, took 'em behind a cloud. Say John went on behind the cloud, you know, and screwed the three girls, and he came on back and he told Saint Peter, "Now I feel like I got to go to the toilet."

Saint Peter told him, say, "John, anything you want to do or see you want," say, "help yourself. All you got to do is go on, pull the cloud back, and go on back there and do what you want to do." So John went back there ('course this was in a dream), went back there and did his business. Then when he got through, he tore off a piece of the cloud for to wipe his hindparts.

That time his wife hit 'im, WOP! Say, "Wake up, wake up! you bastard you!" Say, "You done fucked me three times, now you tearing the sheet to wipe your ass!"

3

Dese Bones Gon' Rise Again: Ghost Tales

And say after while the man rose up out the casket,
and say EVERYBODY took out and ran.
"Dese Bones Gon' Rise Again"

My RESEARCH in Virginia suggests that no other group of tales enjoyed greater popularity in the past and yet today is disappearing faster among Black Virginians than the ghost tales. Many people with whom I talked vividly remembered hearing numerous ghost tales as children and being "scared to death" by them, but very few were able to tell more than one or two to me. The former popularity of the ghost tales may be attributed to a belief among many in the supernatural and in ghosts. Suggestions that a belief in ghosts contributed to the effectiveness of the Ku Klux Klan in terrorizing Black people have been discredited, however, by H. Grady McWhiney and Francis B. Simkins. They found ample testimony from the Black victims of the Klan to suggest that the victims feared the terrorists in white sheets, not because they believed they were supernatural beings, but because they knew of the violent acts perpetrated by their white neighbors clothed in the ghostly garb.[1] Only one of the tales which I collected, "Look Over Yonder" (p. 36), may show some vague connection between the activity of the Klan and a belief in ghosts. However, many of the tales, several of them accounts of the informants' (or one of their acquaintances') own encounter with spirits, do suggest a belief in ghosts. Hopson Lipscomb, the source of many of my ghost tales, affirmed, "There *are* such things as ghosts. Some people can see 'em.... My foster mother, she

21

would see ghosts; she actually could see 'em."[2] Although he did not claim ever to have seen an apparition himself and although several of hs tales turn on the explanation of what the butt of the jokes thought was a ghost, Mr. Lipscomb, as did other informants, insisted on the authenticity of the spirits' appearances in many instances.[3]

NOTES

1. See H. Grady McWhiney and Francis B. Simkins, "The Ghostly Legend of the Ku-Klux-Klan," *The Negro History Bulletin* 14 (February, 1951): 109–12.
2. Conversation with Hopson Lipscomb, January 31, 1975.
3. For numerous ghost tales from the white and the Black communities, see Harry Middleton Hyatt, *Hoodoo-Conjuration-Witchcraft-Rootwork: Memoirs of the Alma Egan Hyatt Foundation* (Washington, D.C.: American University Bookstore, 1970), pp. 19–164.

25 Dese Bones Gon' Rise Again

A long time ago they used to set up with the dead, you know, and sing and pray all night long. And they were down at this particular place doing this, and, uh, a man was singing this song 'bout "Dese bones gon' rise again!" And they were just singing it, singing it! Say one man there had a cork leg. And say after while the man rose up out the casket, and say EVERYBODY took out and ran. Say the man with the cork leg went through the window and took the whole sill. Say he was two blocks ahead of them— and folks scattered every where!

26 Papa Beat the Dogs

This man had some boys and the boys loved to go hunt, and so one evening, come running, the boys say, "Less go down in the woods and try to hunt and catch a ole 'possum or sumpin' and carry old Papa down in the woods." And old Papa ain't never walked for so many years, and they set old Papa right under the tree, and sompin' come to dat tree and went up dat tree, and the boys ain't know what it was, and they thought old Papa was settin' under that tree yet. Those boys run to the house and set down. Dey say, "Lord, uhn, less go back and get old Papa."

Papa say, "Papa WHO? I come here head o' de dog!"

27 Oh, Me

A girl died in this house, and this man rode his horse up there in the rain and tied his horse outside, and made 'im a fire there in the fireplace. Say a lil' girl came down the steps, [very weakly] "Oh, me, ohme, ohme."

He say, "What's the matter, baby?" Say, "I ain't gon' hurt."

She turn 'round and went on back upstairs hollerin' like somebody was killin' her. She come on down there again. She say, "Oh, me, ohme, ohme."

Suddenly he got scared. He jumped on his horse, and say he could look right 'tween the horse's head. Every time the lightning struck, that little girl sittin' up there, "Oh, me, ohme, ohme."

Scared him to death!

28 When Midnight Struck

A man had gotten killed years ago, you know, in one of those one-room cabins that sell whiskey and everything. One fellow had taken an ax and split the other one right through here [indicating from the middle of the head through the chest], all that blood and everything ... And, uh, they'd always say when you go 'long by there at twelve o'clock at night you could see this man. He'd come out there with his shirt open like that [opening shirt to reveal split chest], you know. So this guy say, [unbelievingly] "Ah, ain't nothing to that."

He say, "I'll bet you a gold watch and ten dollars. You go by there at midnight and don't see it, you'll get it. You got to walk back and forth, back and forth, six times."

And that's 'bout time that midnight struck, and say, when he got to the door (this was the seventh time he walked back and forth), this man come out like that [pulling his shirt open], and he ran and dropped dead at the door.

29 Ole Man Straws

An ole man died up there, name of Ole Man Straws, but he was kind of a funny lookin' ole fellow, you know. And they was out there 'possum huntin' one night, and say the dogs ran all 'round that place until they finally treed somethin', and the dogs was trying their best—them dogs was tryin' to climb that tree for all they worth. So one of the fellows come up there and looked up the tree, and—he say, "Come on, let's go way from here."

So when they got away, they say, "What did you *see*?"

He say, "Ole Man Straws—" Say, "He was sittin' up on that limb hunched over just like a monkey, like that [indicating the way a monkey sits hunched up in a tree]. 'Twas *him* all right."

30   Uncle Butler

Way back there in the days gone by 'twas an old vacant cabin; say the people had died out years ago; and they had made a path right by it going back and forth. And when they come by there at night, a little black and white dog would come out there and run right along beside them, and look up in their face, pant and all like that [dramatizing], and most people wouldn't go by there. They went on by; they wouldn't bother the dog, see. This here ole man named Arthur Butler, he and this white man he call Judas, they come 'long on by there, been over to the village. And just before they got to this ole house he began to get 'im an armful o' rocks. "If that dog come out from there, I gon' *pin* him to the face of the earth."

Judas say, "Uncle Butler, don't you bother that dog."

"If he come out here now, I gon' *pin* 'im to the face of the earth!"

So Judas, he took a lil' *trot* and he got on by there. So Ole Man Butler (that ole dog came out there), he hauled back and he threw a rock at 'im like that [dramatizing]. It never touched 'im. He threw his rocks and it didn't do any good, and he jumped up on the fence (ole rail fence) and grabbed a rail like that and hit at him, and the rail broke. He took the other part and he punched down [trying to stab the dog], and it just went on through to the ground. And it scared him so—that old dog turned, he say, into everything imaginable— from a cow, to a horse, anything imaginable. Then he turned back to his natural shape. The only way he got off that fence, he fell off. He fell off the fence.

This man [Judas] he had gone on down. He'd taken a lil' cut. He [Butler] yelled, "O, Lord, Judas! Wait, Judas! Wait, Judas, WAIT, WAIT, WAIT, JUDAS, WAIT, MAN!" Say he took a step a lil' further like that, and that man hollerin' wait. And he come on by his house, and somethin' say, "Ole Man Butler out there messing wid them dogs. I'd advise you not to open the door for 'im tonight."

By that time, he [Butler] come on home, say, "Oh, Lord, Judy, open the door! OPEN the door, Judy," and 'round the house he'd go, 'round and 'round till she finally got the door open. He ran in the house, ran back against the wall and dropped! It didn't kill 'im, but he fell out just like that [prostrate]. That lil' dog had done run him to death—almost.

31 Loping Black Dog

Use to be years ago when they had horse and buggy. Up there [was] some church where the graveyard was up on the cliff. And say you come on by there at night, and you see a big dog, a great big black dog, just loping on—just loping on—like that [dramatizing]. They say you pass the church, that dog—[dramatizing dog loping along]. He would lope on right between the wheels of the buggy till they get to the graveyard and then—BAM [loud clap of hands and then swoop of hands] disappear!

So a lot o' people said, "Naw-w-w, I ain't goin' by there, with a horse and buggy or nothin', I ain't goin' by there."

32 Spirit Dog

My foster mother, she would see ghosts. She *actually* could see 'em. It didn't scare her. She say one night she was working for a set of people named Morrison. They had a big colonial-type house, back porch sitting up high like that. And say they sittin' out on the porch, and moon shinin' just like day, 'n' say a great big dog, a great big black dog come on by the porch, just like that, head down, and tail down, wasn't lookin' nowhere, like that [dramatizing]. And say people was buried over there by the garden spot. With his tail like that, say he went over there where that grave was, and went right on through the fence through the graveyard and disappeared. And the people say, "Just some o' them people where died, just some o' them people where died."

33 You Gon' See Peace

Well, anyway, these people hunted all the time—Sunday night—all times. And so one night they were out there, and the dog was runnin' somethin' all 'round the field there. And they couldn't see nothin'—it was running all 'round by their feet like that [dramatizing alarm of people who are being frightened by something running by their feet], and one man say, "That ain't right 'round here now!"

Say presney [presently] somethin' run on by there and they say, "Saturday night—Sunday night—Monday night—Tuesday night—Wednesday night,

ThursdaynightFridaynightSaturdaynightSunday—poor 'possum can't see no peace!"

[Dramatizing men dashing away.] "Naw, but you gon' see peace from now on!"

34   You Gon' Pick Me Up?

These fellows was out there coon hunting one day—they was out there 'round the graveyard. And say the dogs jumped sompin' up there in the bottom, and they come *tearing* to 'em like that [gesturing to indicate speed], runnin' all 'round in a circle there; they couldn't see nothin'. Say finally sompin' (they never could see nothin') come runnin' 'round in circle like that [indicating something unseen running all around their legs], say, "Boys, when you gon' pick me up?"

They say, "NAW—[slapping hands to indicate hurried departure]. Naw, I ain't pickin' nuthin' up but my feet!"

35   Take Your Apple!

Another place over there the people had died, and they had a big orchard. So this man had been down there sellin' tobacco and had a wagon. And he stopped over there in that orchard (won't nobody livin' there) and got him a wagon load o' apples. The sun was going down, and say as he was going along, sumpin' say, "Apple!—APPLE!"

Say he started to whip the horse over his head.

"APPLE! APPLE!"

And the horse started . . . And he [voice] say, "I say appleappleappleappleapple!"

He [man] say, "Damn it, take your apple!"

36   When a Man Gets Scared

This actually happened. There was a old man named Samuel Miles and he was a deacon in the church. And they was talkin'—at a church affair—they was talkin' 'bout when a person gets scared—when a man gets scared, he can do most anything. He say, "Well, brother, I'm gon' tell ya the truth, I agree with you for that. When I was a younger man we would call ourselves logging the mill, you know, and we cut down enough logs and load 'em on the cart. So they carry 'em out there where they could get 'em, and we back there, we cuttin' logs till they come back. So that day we had just loaded a cart and he drove off with it, and I was cuttin' down trees till they come back. And one tree, instead of falling the way I wanted it, it fell backwards and fell across me, and caught me under it. It didn't hurt me, but it had me in such a way, I couldn't get from under it. I scrambled and scrambled, and scrambled, and I made up my mind, 'Well,' I say, 'I know I can't get from under here, but when they come back with the cart, they can put what we call a pry-stick under it like a jack and lif' it up high enough for me to get from under it.'"

He done made up his mind. He laying there all satisfied. And 'twas a graveyard up on top of the hill. And say somethin' made a kind o' peculiar noise up on the graveyard, and say when he know anything he was up from under that tree, standin' on top of it, lookin' up at the graveyard.

37 Death in the Graveyard

There was a murderer. So they buried him up in this graveyard. And people wouldn't go anywhere near there, 'cause he'd come out there at night. And this fellow, he said, "Ah, I don't believe it."

They made a bet, and they say, "Now what you got to do (it was a rainy day), you gotta take this stake and this hammer, and you go down to that grave, and drive that stake down, and then we'll know you've been there."

So he goes on and climbs over in the graveyard; so he had on his overcoat, and he squat down and took his stake and drove it down there by the grave, like this, you see, and when he went to get up, sompin' had 'im by his coattail holdin' him. And the harder he pulled, the harder he [whatever was holding him] pulled. So he had a heart attack and he died.

And they went back there to see what was wrong wit' 'im. He done taken that stake and drove it through the tail o' his coat there; that's what pinned him down to the ground.

38 Ain't But Two of Us in Here, Is It?

A. This man went to this house to stay all night, and he was sittin' in this house all night, reading his Bible. And he was reading the Bible, reading the Bible, and something come in and say, "How do you do?"

He [the man] say, "Howde do."

He walked around and looked, and then he says, "It ain't but two of us in here, is it?"

He say, "No, and it ain't gon' be but one of us in here in a few minutes."

So he got out and started to run, and he run and run till he got out of breath almost. And so he stopped to rest; and when he stopped to rest, this thing walked up there beside him and say, "Great day! Didn't we have a good race?"

He say, "Yeah, but 'tain't gon' be no sech a one as we gon' have now!"

B. There was a haunted cabin, 'cause all the people had died years ago, but the cabin still stood. And *everybody* avoided it, you know. So this Preacher was drivin' 'long in this horse and buggy and it was raining so hard, he stopped in there and put the horse in the lean-to, and he went in the cabin. The old fireplace was still good, and he got some old scrap wood, and sit down there and build a fire—drying off you know. He was sitting up there—say a great big black cat walked in the door, come right up to him and sit down, and looked up in his face. He [the cat] say, "Unnh, ain't nobody here but you and I tonight, is it?"

Say the Preacher say, "You damn right, but in a minute ain't nobody gon' be here but you!"

He ran so fast, he jumped a deer; and you know he and that deer run nose to nose for a solid mile. And he looked back at that old big buck, he say, "Look, brother, you better take that chair off your head if you gon' run with me, 'cause you gon' run from now on!"

39 Pass the Collection Plate

A. This house was haunted. Couldn't nobody live in it. And say everybody tried to live in it, couldn't anybody stay in it overnight. So a Preacher came to town, and Preacher didn't have anywhere to stay. All the places were all filled up and he couldn't stay there, so the Preacher didn't have anywhere to stay. So they told him there was one house there that was vacant, but it was haunted, and couldn't anybody stay in that. Say the Preacher say, "*I* can stay in there." Say the Preacher took his Bible and he went on in, went on upstairs, and got ready to go to bed. And say he took out his Bible, and he read the Bible. Say then he sang a hymn; he preached a little short sermon, and say, the noise was just *rumblin'* all over the house and everything, but he say, "I'm gon' stay here *tonight*." Say he just kept on preachin' and prayin' and the noise just kept on. Say he took his hat and started passing it around. Say the noise was goin' on and he passed it around to collect offering, say he just went 'round the whole room, passing the hat around, and say he didn't hear *no more* noise—everybody left!

B. This man was supposed to be a Christian man, see, and he woke up one night, woke up one night in the middle of the night, and there was a ghost at the foot of the bed. He didn't know what to do—just didn't know *what* to do. And he started to *singing* . . .

Ths ghost started to *singing*.
He started to *singing* . . .
The ghost started to *singing*.
Started to *praying* . . .
Ghost started to *praying*.

He just didn't know what to do. So then he reached down here under the bed and picked up a collection plate (he was a deacon, see), picked up a collection plate and started to pass it around. The ghost left! You know, like some people, he didn't want to put nothing in the collection.

40 Up from the Cooling Board

It was one haunted house up there in the country—that's what they say—and a man *died*, my Daddy say, and they had 'im on this board called cooling board. And say he was lying out on the cooling board there and people all sittin' around—horses and things tied up outdoors in the moonshine. And after while they looked, this man was sittin' up on the cooling board. Say EVERYBODY *ran* out but him [Daddy]. He stayed there 'cause it was a friend of his—a cousin of his or something. And he say, "Ben! What am I doing on this?"

He [Daddy] say, "Jim, what you doin' *sittin'* up?" Say, "You s'posed to be *dead!*"

And say the man got up—they took 'im off the cooling board—and he got up and put his clothes on and lived five or six more years.

41 In the Name of the Lord

This little girl (this actually happened), she was living with these people. They was makin' a Cinderella out of her, see, and at night when they get through supper, they use to make her go out on the back porch and wash dishes. And say, every time that she would go out there, something would scare her, and she'd run back in the house. And they'd make her run right back out there. Then she run back—keep on till she get through. So they told the Preacher about it, you know, and he said, "It could be possible the child see something. I'll come over sometime and sit."

And say after they got through with supper, they sent her out on the porch in the dark to wash the dishes, and all at once she screamed and run back in the house, say she saw somethin'. He say, "Now look, daughter, don't get scared now, but whatever it is, when this thing come to you again, say you ask it, 'In the name of the Lord, what do you want?' Say, 'Either speak or leave me alone.'"

Say she went back and the thing appeared again. She say, "What in the name of the Lord do you want with me?"

He say, "Take—take a pick and shovel and follow me."

So she got a shovel and pick and followed him. Say he went on-n-n down—led her down in this little valley like, and say, he say, "Now you dig right here by this tree, and you gonna find a big earthen jar—full of money." He say, "Lil' o' that that runs out, I'm gonna tell you who I want you to give it to, but what stays in there will be yours. And she dug and found it. And they poured it out till it stop runnin' and they left enough in there for her and everybody else. And never did pay her no more visits.

See somebody had buried it and died and they wanted somebody to have it.

42   Where Money Is, Evil Is

That was kinda like true. Down in Orangeburg, South Carolina, wasn't too far from us, and the governor started buying these land and sharing 'em off. It was a house up dere and nobody couldn't stay in it. So a Preacher went dere and so he read his Bible and do everything, and it get so bad, the Preacher had to get out and go. And after the governor buy that land, he sell it to different people, you know. He clean it off, he farm, and one man in Orangeburg buy that land, and he send a man out there to plow de land up and he found a pillow of money there. Where money is, evil there. That was so.

43   Didn't Die Right

A. Yeah, I heard somethin' like that where go like dis here. Say it was a Preacher and say he was tired, and he had his little dog wid 'im. He came to this place, and the owner, you know, was out in the yard. He asked him, say, "Brother," say, "I'm tired. Could I sleep in your barn or somethin' tonight?" Say, "Anything. Could I chop a little wood for a little food?"

Say the man told him, "We just build a *brand* new house down the road there." Say, "But whoever lived there didn't die right." Say, "But you welcome to stay there if you kin tonight."

And the man told him, say, "I be able to stay dere."

So the man say, "Well, my wife got cush [a type of food made from meal] up in de house." Say, "You gone on and make you some fire, and I'll bring the pot of cush to you. As I told you before, whoever stayed there didn't die right, and if you kin stay there, you welcome to it."

So the old Preacher made the fire and hung his pot o' cush up over the fire. [He took out his Bible and started reading. After a while two arms fell down the chimney. Say, "I didn't die right, I didn't die right." The Preacher took one look and kept on reading his Bible. Then a head fell down, say,] "I didn't die right, I didn't die right!" The old Preacher took one look and continued on readin' his Bible. And say, a little while after that, say a whole body fell down out the ceiling, and the head got on it and kept on going 'round the chair, "I didn't die right, I didn't die right." So the lil' dog done got so scared he done curled up underneath the chair, 'cause you know dogs really don't bother ghosts.

And in a few minutes when the pot started to boiling real fast, you know, the legs fell down and joined the body and start to dancin' 'round the chair, "I didn't die right, I didn't die right," right 'round the Preacher, "I didn't die right." So the old skeleton made a misstep, and hit the pot, you know, and knocked two of the great big dumplings out the pot, and the old Preacher was hongry.

The Preacher got up and put the Bible down. Say, "Listen here, who and whatever you are. If you knock another one of them damn [unclear] out dat pot, you gon' die right."

B. One time three dudes was in the graveyard cookin' steaks. So the white man told the Jew, you know, he said, "Gimme some pepper, man, gimme some pepper!"

Two got to talkin' and put pepper on the steak, and so after a while the white man look around. He say, "Did you hear something?"

Jew say, "Naw, I ain't hear nothin'."

Then somethin' say, "I D-I-I-I-E-D wrong!"

White man say, "Hey, Jew, did you hear somethin'?"

Jew say, "Naw, naw, I ain't hear anything."

"I D-I-I-I-E-D wrong!"

White man got up and hauled ass.

Jew didn't go and the nigger didn't go. This nigger say, "Hey! Turn the steak over, man, turn the steak over."

So Jew turned the steak over and put the salt and pepper on the other side.

Somethin' say, "I D-I-I-I-E-D wrong."

Jew looked all around. He say, "Did you hear that?"

Colored man say, "Naw, Jack, I ain't hear nothin'—Cook the steak, man, cook de steak!"

"I D-I-I-I-E-D wrong!"

Jew turned around and got up and hauled ass!

That left the nigger there, you know, with the steak, and the steak was almost done, you know. Nigger started cooking steak, you know, stirring it up, puttin' some onions on it, you know.

So somethin' say, "I D-I-I-I-E-D wrong!"

He looked around. He say, "Yeah, motherfucker, if you fuck with this steak, you gon' die right!"

44   A Visit

This lady I know, she was an elderly woman. And she say she actually saw a ghost of her own boyfriend. Say she was workin' in service out in New Jersey and say the boy friend was in the hospital, deathly sick. That evening, just about, just about dusk dark, she was back in the kitchen, and the other people was in the house, you know, and say the doorbell rang. And when she went to the door, say there was Frank standin' out there with that same suit of clothes on. She say, "Frank, I thought you was in the hospital. Where—?"

He didn't say a word, just stood and looked at her—like that [ghostly, void expression]. Say, "Frank, don't act like that; you scare me." So she turned 'round to run, and she slammed the door. He right along wit' her. And she ran all the way back where the other people was.

They say, "Liza, what's wrong with you?"

She say, "Frank! Something happened to Frank! I saw Frank standin' at the door in that same suit of clothes and he won't say a word, and he act funny."

And pretty soon after that, they got a message from the hospital, said he died at *that particular* time. And that was her boyfriend, and she saw 'im. And she said she'd tell that on her dying day because she didn't know he was dead, but what worried her was he standin' out there at the door and wouldn't say nothin' 'n' lookin' at her so funny like that and it scared her.

So there are such things as ghosts. Very few people can see them.

45   Makin' *Feet* Help the *Body*

After my husband died, I was lying right in the bed where he stayed at and he was sittin' up in the chair there by the bed. I-I-I-I-I-I l-l-looked around like that [fearful turning of the head]. (I have a night table there and 'twas a chair where I had the bedside table.) And I looked around there; he was sittin' on that chair. I could see 'im *plain*, just as plain as I'm lookin' at yawl, but don't ask me did I say anything to 'im. I was makin' *feet* help the *body*! Yes, Lawd, I was gettin' out the way!

46 Hitchhiking Spirit

He said one night he was riding. He was coming along a lonesome road.
And he said he got to a place, where he kind of slowed down and stopped.
And he said a man stepped in the car and sat down beside him. And rode for
about a mile, and then stepped out. The man who stepped in was so heavy
that the buggy could hardly pull it.

My mother said, "Well, why didn't you get out?"

He say, "I was scared to death."

47 Counting Souls

They say that these two little boys, they stole some walnuts. (You know
what walnuts are?) It was gettin' kind of—about dusk. They was comin' on
by the graveyard and decided to go in there and divide 'em up. And just as
they started in the gate they dropped two, but they didn't stop then; they just
went on back in there. So they were down in there pickin' 'em: "This mine,
that's yours; this mine; that's yours; this mine . . . that's yours.

And a Deacon come on by there, about dark, and he heard their voice. He
heard their voice, you know . . . He listened . . .

"This mine . . . that's yours . . . You take this one; that's mine . . . that's
yours."

He went up there; he say, "Reverend, don't you know something. Judgment Day comin' *fast*, 'cause the Lord and the Devil down there in the
graveyard dividing out souls."

Reverend say, "Brother, you know you wrong."

"Come on go down there."

So they went on down there; these kids were still countin' 'em: "This
mine . . . that's yours. This mine . . . that's yours." He [one of the boys] say,
"Now, but it's two at the gate; let's go get them."

They [Minister and Deacon] say, "Ah, naw you don't!" [Makes a gesture to
indicate a hasty departure.]

48 Bob Blount Is Dead

This man met three cats. They had a dead cat, carryin' him on down
there, and say, he stopped and looked: "What, what, what is this?"

Say one of the cats say, "You, man (they had a cat named Nan Can), you,
man, when you go home, you tell Nan Can that Bob Blount is dead."

So he went on [incredulous tone indicating disbelief of man] and when he got home, and he happened to be mentioning about what he saw. The cat was laying down there sleep . . . He say, "When I came home—over the hill, by the place, I met these three cats had another dead cat they was going to bury him." Say, "They tol' me, 'You, man, when you go home, you tell Nan Can that Bob Blount is dead.'"

The cat jumped up, say, "Well, I'll be damned!" And out the door he went!

49   Big Fraid and Lil' Fraid

This lil' boy had a way of coming through the woods at night, you know, all by himself, all by himself. So a fellow said to him, "Boy, ain't you afraid to walk about at night like that?"

He say [very innocently] "What is a Fraid? What it look like? I ain't never seen a Fraid."

He say, "Well, you keep on comin' through the woods at night, you gon' see a Fraid and he gon' scare you, too."

So a night or two later (this man had a monkey), he goes and gets him a sheet, gon' get down in the woods there and gon' jump at the boy. Well, the monkey watched him to see what he did. He didn't know the monkey was watchin' him. The monkey went and got a pillow case and followed him, see. He didn't know the monkey was behind him. So the lil' boy come on through there. He jumps out behind the lil' boy trying to scare him. The monkey jumped right on top of him [the man]. He lit out [gesture indicating speed] and the lil' boy hollered, "Run, Big Fraid, Lil' Fraid'll catch ya! Run, Big Fraid! Lil' Fred'll catch ya!"

50   Hardheaded

This guy's son died. He was away and he couldn't get back, you know. (And getting back to our funerals means a great deal.) And it just shook him up—he couldn't see his son. And he'd go out in the cemetery every night and pray: "Lord, I want to see my son one more time."

The people got tired of this, you know. After two or three months—him out there every night, wailing and moaning, talking 'bout "Lord, I want to see my son one more time."

So one night a fellow dressed up in a white sheet and came out: "Here me, Poppa!"

He say, "Okay, boy, I done seen ya."

"Here me, Poppa, here me."

He say, [impatiently] "Okay, boy, I done *seen* ya."
And he kept coming, "Here me, Poppa, here me!"
He say, "Dammit, boy, I told ya I done seen ya. You dead now 'cause you so damn hardheaded! I told ya I done seen ya!"
No more difficulty with him at all!

51 Haunted House

This fellow who was an ex-slave used to stay in the house with the madam 'cause her husband was a doctor and his practice was here in Richmond, and she didn't want to stay in the house by herself. We was all staying on the lot. And he said that those things [haunts] used to bother him so he couldn't stay there. He got his wife to let me come there and sleep with 'im once on the old couch, and he say it didn't have a bit of effect 'cause I was just snoring with my mouth wide open. Say they was comin' on by me. He had a fire in the fireplace and he could feel 'em when they walk between 'em like that [dramatizing]. And they used to wear satin. He say you could hear that old satin stuff rattlin' and he'd be fussing, fussing, "I wish you'd go 'way from here and let me sleep," and everything like that. And he say now, "He [the informant] won't a bit o' good to me 'cause he layin' there [dramatizing someone snoring] and they walkin' around worrying me to death." He say he could talk to 'em and see 'em.

And they claim the house was haunted, which it probably was. They had a bell on the outside of the window with a cord that reached inside and a spring, so if they want to call the servants, they pull this bell. And I know one day, they say the bell kep' ringing. They say, "Them old folks walkin' 'round here." They say, "I know, each year it's like that."

And I happened to be 'round there one day when that bell started to ringing, and I looked out and saw what it was. The bell was outside the window, and the wind was blowing, and the blinds was loose, and every time the blinds would hit that bell, it would ring. And that was the ghost they saw.

52 If It's Gon' Ketch Me

Fellow say he was walkin' along one night. Now he was scared. And he started to run, and runnin' 'cross that field ('twas pine shrubs like that, you know) and he looked *back*; and this thing was *moving* and he thought it was runnin' after 'im. He let out and started to runnin'. Next time he looked back, it done got much closer—waving like that, you know [indicating manner in which a tree branch would wave after being hit]. He run and run, and each time it was gettin' that much closer to 'im. So he say, "Well, if it's gon' ketch me, it's gon' ketch me." So he stopped and went back there. It won't nothin' but those pine shrubs. Every time he'd run by one it looked like it got that much closer to 'im—waving like that [dramatizing]—and he thought that thing was gaining on 'im all the time.

53 Look Over Yonder

Grandma said that they [whites] used to go outside and stob the horses and put sheets over them, and that's where the people started talking about it's ghosts outside. And it frightened 'em so *bad* it made them afraid to go *outside* at night. Put sheets over 'em and tie 'em to trees at several places and you look down—there's that song. "Look over yonder, what I see—"
"See!" [Audience.]
"—white horses comin' after me."
"Comin' after me!" [Audience.]
Said really was horses—
"Yeah-h-h!" [Audience.]
—with sheets over 'em. I wonder 'bout that, but Grandma said it was true.
"Um-hunh!" [Audience.]
I wonder 'bout that. You ever heard about that?
"Yeah. I heard about that. That's where the song came from." [A member of the audience.]
Yeah!

4

Somebody Clapped
for Edith Las' Night:
Conjure Tales

So the next morning Jacob came over. [They] say,
"Uncle Jacob, how is Aunt Edith this morning?"

"Ah-h-h, Brother, I tell ya, she's faring mighty
poorly, *mighty poorly*."

Say, "What's the matter? She was might spry last
night."

"Somebody done put a hant on her," he say.

"What you talkin' 'bout?"

"Yep, somebody clapped for Edith las' night—the
worse lookin' conjure you ever saw!"

    "Worse Lookin' Conjure I Ever Saw"

I WAS SURPRISED that in my research I found only three conjure tales,
and all of these from one informant, Hopson Lipscomb. Moreover,
my informants made very few allusions to such tales. It appears that
conjure tales are not now very popular in Virginia, particularly not
in the Richmond area, where I conducted the majority of my interviews. However, I include this small collection of conjure tales since
any study of Black folklore must take into account the folk beliefs
and tales stemming from the rather prevalent early belief in conjuration among Black Americans, a belief that obviously has African
origins.[1] It is significant also that much early Black literature, including several of the slave narratives as well as a substantial portion
of the works of Paul Laurence Dunbar and of Charles W. Chesnutt, is

based on or influenced by conjure tales. Charles W. Chesnutt also wrote one of the early studies of conjuration.[2]

The three tales in this chapter are all rather derogatory and humorous accounts of conjuring, though they do give some indications of certain beliefs and practices. Several beliefs and superstitions related to conjuring are included in chapter sixteen.

NOTES

1. Many beliefs alluded to in numerous tales throughout this book have their roots (pun intended) in conjuration; see particularly "Superstitions" (I–IV, pp. 307–310), "Conjuring Your Lover" (p. 310), and "Folk Remedies" (p. 312). Many of the ghost tales, such as "In the Name of the Lord" (p. 29) and "Didn't Die Right" (p. 30), incorporate similar beliefs. The significance of the snake and the cat is also relevant, as in "Controlling the Slave" (p. 167). The title "Put the Snake on Her" (p. 296) may be a play on the expression "to put the snake on [a person]," which means to put a curse on a person.

2. Anyone interested in learning more about conjuration should see Charles W. Chesnutt, "Superstitions and Folklore of the South," *Modern Culture* 13 (1901): 231–35; Leonora Herron and Alice M. Bacon, "Conjuring and Conjure-Doctors," *Southern Workman* 24 (1895): 117–18, 193–94, 209–11; Zora Neale Hurston, "Hoodoo in America," *Journal of American Folklore* 40 (October–December, 1931): 317–417 (reprinted in *Mules and Men*, pp. 229–304); Newbell Niles Puckett, *Folk Beliefs of the Southern Negro*, pp. 167–310; and Harry Middleton Hyatt, *Hoodoo-Conjuration-Witchcraft-Rootwork: Memoirs of the Alma Egan Hyatt Foundation* (Washington, D.C.: American University Bookstore, 1970). Other interesting studies of conjuration are included in Alan Dundes, ed., *Mother Wit from the Laughing Barrel: Readings in the Interpretation of Afro-American Folklore* (Englewood Cliffs, N.J.: Prentice-Hall, 1973).

54   Worse Lookin' Conjure I Ever Saw

William [the son of the lady who raised the informant] was quite a devil. So this couple lived over on the next farm named Aunt Edith Clarke and Uncle Jacob Clarke. Uncle Jacob Clarke was supposed to of been a conjure doctor. And so they [Aunt Edith and Uncle Jacob] come over there and talk a whole lot o' that stuff, and this boy [William], just like the Devil, he went out there and (you used to get quinine in lil' blue bottles like that) he got one o' them lil' bottles and went out there and got 'im three, four of them white pebbles or somethin' else and mixed it up in there, put the stopper in it, and he went, slipped out that night when the folks was in the house sleep, you know. He slipped out of there at night while the folks were in there sleep. It was a peach tree at the back door. He took some horse hair and hung that thing right over the door, like that [illustrating] and he went on 'bout his business.

So the next morning Jacob came over. [They] say, "Uncle Jacob, how is Aunt Edith this morning?"

"Ah-h-h, Brother, I tell ya, she's faring mighty poorly, *mighty* poorly."

Say, "What's the matter? She was mighty spry last night."

"Somebody done put a hant on her," he say.

"What you talkin' 'bout?"

"Yep, somebody clapped for [put a spell on, conjured] Edith las' night—the worse lookin' conjure you ever saw!" He say, "Edith, this morning, she come out the house; she didn't look at the peach tree; she went down to get some water. She come back and looked up there, and that thing was hanging over the door. She went and got right straight in the bed. I believe I'm gon' lose Edith."

So when he went out this guy [William], he started to sniggling back there. She [William's mother] say, "Come here, you lil' devil. What you done to Edith? What you done?"

"I ain't done nothin'."

"Don't you tell me no lie; I'll skin ya. You done done something to those old folks."

So he tol' her what he'd done.

She say, "You go there and pull that mess off that tree and bring it away from there and throw it in the fire. That ole woman gon' die and you responsible."

We went there and took it down and she got all right. And Ole Jacob, now he s'posed to be a conjure doctor, and he say, "Ah-h-h, it's the worse lookin' conjure I ever did see!"

55   This Will Carry 'Im or Bring 'Im

This was a ex-slave, too, and they had what you called the medical doctor who used to treat people around there. This man had got deathly sick. Well, now, the white doctor, he would come there treatin' 'im, and the root doctor would treat 'im. So one night, the root doctor had just come in, and they looked out and saw this white doctor comin' down the path. They took him and put 'im in the closet because, you know, he ain't supposed to be practicing no medicine. And after the white doctor came on and prescribed and went on 'bout his business, they got this ole fellow out there for him to work his roots. So the first thing he tol' 'em, he wanted three spoonsful of red clay out of somebody's fresh graveyard, and he wanted three tuffs of hair off a black cat's tail (black cat with one white foot); three pinches of ashes out o' somebody else's fireplace, and he wanted a weasel toe, you know (you know, a weasel is somethin' like a rat). He had some herb. He took that stuff and put it in there, put some mess in there, stirred it up just like you stir a soup. (The wife's name was Lucy.) He say, "Lucy, you give 'im this. This will carry 'im or bring 'im one!"

Somebody say, "Great God, you never see a man die so fas' in all my life!" Say he just took it, "Gulp, gulp" [dramatizing quick swallowing] and went [swooshing sound with hands to indicate speed]. Say he say it was gon' bring him or carry him one; it sure carried him!

56   The Devil Took Her and Went Airship

Old folks used to say if you get a black cat bone, you could become invisible any time you wanted to. So I wanted that black cat bone. They say, "What you do, you catch a jet-black cat with one white foot, and you go to a old vacant house; you get you a pot o' water and put it on the fire; take that cat and throw him in there alive and boil him till he come all to pieces. Then you take that mess and you go to a runnin' stream o' water, and when you dump him in there, all that's going down except one bone that's gon' detach itself and going upstream; that's the black cat bone." So I'm working after this black cat bone, you see, but they say, "Another thing you got to do; you got to cuss God on the throne." I say, "Naw, I ain't comin' on that one. I ain't comin' on that one!"

One of 'em tol' this tale: they say this man, he got this black cat bone; and say one day somebody rang his door bell, and he was sittin' at the supper table. And say he got up, went to the door, took his bone, and disappeared. Say some of his friends say, "The devil took him and went airship."

5

I Hears de Call:
Tales about Religion

Big holes is the onlies'
  Things in my pocket,
So bein' a bishop
  Is next on de docket

Lawd, Lawd, yas Lawd,
  I hears de call....
         Sterling A. Brown, "Slim Hears the Call"

CONSIDERING THE historical importance of religion in the life of the Black American and the revered role of the minister as a unique and important leader in the Black community,[1] it is something of a paradox that the target of abuse or of ridicule in a considerable number of the tales in the Black repertoire is the Black church leader, usually the Minister but also often the Deacon or the Old Sister. The Minister has been the butt of jokes from the time of slavery until the present, not only as an egotistical, vain leader, but also as an ignorant lover of big words, a hypocrite who chases women and loves booze, an avaricious materialist who covets Cadillacs and fine clothes, and a glutton who causes concern in the barnyard whenever he comes to dinner. Following the Minister as the popular butt of jokes is the self-righteous Deacon, who frequently is pictured as envious of the Minister's power, material possessions, or female conquests and who often is seen in competition with the good Minister. Other humorous Christians who are quick to see and to repri-

41

mand bitterly the mote in another's eye but quicker still to rationalize their own faults include gossipy Old Sisters, who stand out in this third group of church people who are the butts of many of these jokes.

The sacrilegious tone of many of these tales should not mislead the reader into assuming that the tellers are either irreligious or antireligious. Several of the harshest anecdotes that I collected were related by sincerely devout Christians, many of whom were deacons, and by others who were unquestionably conscientious and dedicated church workers (including even an occasional minister or minister's wife). They, as did their counterparts in other times and as have groups from antiquity through the Middle Ages to modern times, simply derive and inspire laughter by lampooning their religious leaders, particularly by revealing the moral defects of those who set themselves up as exemplars.

Some of the humor in the following tales stems also from the frequent liveliness of some Black sermons and church services in contrast with the staid and solemn religious worship of other groups, as suggested in the following folk verse:

> White folks go to chu'ch,
> He nevuh crack a smile.
> Nigguh go to chu'ch
> You heah 'im laff a mile.[2]

In some of the tales, the informants' accurate reproductions of the catchy rhythms of the old-fashioned church service—the shouts of the minister and the enthusiastic replies of the audience—furnish additional interest and entertainment.

NOTES

1. Something of the importance of the role of the Black minister as a model for youths was suggested during my interview with John M. Ellison, retired president of Virginia Union University, who observed, "When I grew up, the first person I knew of a professional nature was my minister." Such testimonials are commonplace. My own observations and reading suggest that the minister has been instrumental in inspiring, encouraging, and assisting in the development of many young Blacks. Further, the minister's role as a leader in civil-rights movements from the time of slavery through the present is unassailable.

2. From J. Mason Brewer, *The Word on the Brazos: Negro Preacher Tales from the Brazos Bottoms of Texas* (Austin: University of Texas Press, 1953), p. 12.

57 Half and Half

A Minister came in, and he, you know, like a lot of them take these different texts and see what they can do with the audience to get people out. And he said he could make half of his audience be *laughing* at one time and the other half *crying*. And *nobody* believed him. So he had one of them split-tails on. And he was *preaching* away to this one side, and they were crying; they were *filled*, you know. And then he would hold that tail up in the air, you know [pantomiming], just take the tails—that split-tail—and hold it up to the people on the other side. And they were laughing.

58 What Did Paul Say?

A. This Minister was preaching a sermon, and he took the text of "What Did Paul Say?" He kept hollerin', "What did *Paul* say?" Little boy was down there, and he had sent this boy to get some meat from a storekeeper named Paul. And he kept hollering, "What did *PAUL* say?" Still he didn't say nothin'. The old Preacher hollered again, "What did PAUL say?"

Boy say, "Paul say you can't get any more meat till you pay for that you done got!"

B. It was one Sunday morning this Minister took his text on "What Did John Say?" And he had been going to this man's house that was named John, drinking whiskey.

So he was up in the pulpit, and he was just *preaching*, "What did John *say*?"

So a little boy, John's son, came in church, and he say, "Wonder why is he up there in the pulpit asking what did Daddy say?"

So the little boy sat down, and the Minister kept on preaching, "I say, *what* did *John* say?"

So the child say, "If he ask *one* more time, I'm gon' tell 'im what Daddy say."

He say, "*What* did *John* say?"

The little boy jumped up and say, "Daddy say he gon' beat your ass if you don't pay him for that whiskey that you owe him for."

C. Here's a Minister who lives in the country, and he needs his cow to be breeded by the bull. And he owes the man who has breeded the cow before some money for past breeding. So he says, "Now, Jacob, you go over there and tell John that *I* said to breed it and I'll pay him for *both* of 'em at the end o' the month. Now I'm goin' on to church and preach the *gospel,* and you come on to church and you let me know what he said." So he goes down there to carry the cow. The Preacher goes on to the church to preach. When the boy gets back to the church, he's preaching on John. So he's there crying, "What did (BAM!) [banging lectern with his fist] JOHN say? What did (BAM!) JOHN say?"

The boy say, "I wonder if he really want me to tell 'im what John said?"

He say, "I SAY (BAM!) SOME-E-E-BO-O-O-DY tell me, what did JOHN say!"

He looked up and say, "John say, 'If you want that cow fucked, you gon' fuck 'im your *damn* self!'"

59 Move Your Finger

This Preacher was a guest speaker that morning at church. So the Minister of the church introduced him to the congregation. So he reached in his pocket for his glasses, and he didn't have his glasses. So he turned to another Minister in the pulpit and told him that he had left his glasses at home, and would he tell him what to say (from the sermon he had already written out)? So then the Minister said he would help him.

So he stood up in front of the congregation and started to preaching. The Minister started telling him what to say. He say, [whispering] "In the beginning..."

And the Minister says, [very loud and authoritative] "In the beginning..."

So the other one said softly, "God created Heaven and Earth..."

And he says, [still loud and authoritative] "God created Heaven and Earth."

Then the Minister who was helping him say, [whispering] "Move your finger."

So *real loud* he repeats, "Move your finger."

The man say, "I say, move your little finger."

He say, [loud] "Move your little finger!"

Then he say, [still whispering, but impatient and loud] "I say move your damn finger."

And the Minister yells, "I say move your damn finger!"

Then he realized what he had said.

60 Put It in My Head

This old Preacher had to go to the doctor, and the doctor say, "I'm sorry, Preacher, I got to give you a needle."

And he said, "A needle! I'm afraid of needles, Doctor."

He said, "Well, that's the only thing will cure you, a needle." And say, "Now where you want this needle?"

Say he said, "Well, you can't put it back here [indicating his hips] because I got to sit down."

And the doctor said, "Well, tell me quickly, so I'll know exactly where to put this needle."

So he said, "Well, you can't put it in my arms because I've got to move my arms, you know, when I'm preaching."

So the Doctor said, "Well, I got to give you the needle." He said, "Well, what about your leg?"

He said, "Naw, you can't put it in my leg because I got to prance around." He said, "Well, Doctor, since I got to have the needle, I want to put it somewhere I don't use."

He say, "Okay," you know.

He say, "Put it in my head!"

61   It's Like This

A Minister had a flat tire, somewhere in the area of the Williamsburg Asylum, and he didn't have a jack. He was trying to find some way to raise his car. So a man was looking out the window, and he told him how to raise the car—how to get some blocks of wood and put under it, and he raised it that way. So the man [the Minister] thanked him. He said, "Thank you; you were very helpful." So he said, "You know, with all of your good sense, I don't see why you'd be where you are."

He said, "Well, Minister, it's like this. A whole lot of them that's out there ought to be in here, and a whole lot of us in here ought to be out there."

62   Pre Hoc, Ergo Non Propter Hoc

In old times the Preacher was preachin' 'bout the Red Sea: "The Lord commanded Moses to lead the children 'cross the Red Sea over to the Promised Land." He said, "Moses led the children to the Red Sea," and said, "the children of Israel did not get drowned," he said, "because of God froze the Red Sea over and the children glided 'cross."

And the other fellow (he had been going to college), he said, "You're wrong there, because my geography tells me that the Red Sea do not freeze. The Red Sea is in the tropics."

The Preacher paused a few moments, and he said, "Well, my dear brother, there were no geographies in those days and therefore there was no tropics."

63   Can't Get to the Fire for the Preachers

This lil' boy's mother had company, and he was out playing. So when he went in the house to warm, everybody was sittin' around the fire. He say, "Whooooo! It's cold as hell outdoors!"

So one of the Preachers say, "Well, Johnny, how you know? You ever been down there?"

He say, "Yeah!"

He say, "How was it?"

"Just like it is here; you can't get to the fire for the Preachers."

64   He Might Be Down There

This old Preacher was preaching. He say, "I'm ready to die right now and go to heaven. When I get up in heaven I want to see all yawl there."

So a lil' later the Preacher died, and this Deacon, he died too. So he [the Deacon] went to heaven and tried to find this Preacher—thought he was gonna be in heaven. Couldn't find him nowhere! Gabriel looked for 'im—he couldn't find 'im. Went to the Cherubim, and they couldn't find him. So one of the Archangels say, "Step down—two steps down—in hell; he might be down there."

He walked down and there the Preacher was down there—loadin' all the other Preachers on [the train]—sendin' 'em to hell.

65   No Minister

This fellow and girl was engaged to be married, and they got kilt in an automobile crash. And they both went to heaven. When they got up there, they asked Saint Peter was it a Minister up there to marry 'em. Saint Peter said, "Not yet."

So every day they'd ask the same thing. So finally Saint Peter told them, "As soon as a Minister comes up here, he'll marry you."

66   Notice the Mistletoe

Christmas for the Rev. Leroy was a rather sad occasion. He was called before the church committee because his behavior over the past year had been simply outrageous. He had slept with every Sister in the church, stolen from the collection plate, and even preached while under the influence of alcohol. Finally, the members of the church could stand it no longer, and, a few days before Christmas, they informed him of his dismissal.

Rev. Leroy was silent while they accused him. He looked around the gaily decorated church, at the tree, the Christmas stockings, and the like. He finally stood up, stuck out his ample chest, and began to stride up and down in front of the pulpit.

"Yes," he said loudly, "I did everything you accuse me of, and more. Sure, I've slept with your wives, mothers, and daughters, stolen the little chump change from the collection plate, and had more than a few drinks. Well, you've won. I'm leaving. But one favor before I do leave. As I walk past you down this middle aisle, kindly notice the mistletoe I've got pinned beneath my coattail."

67 Depression

There was this Preacher, and he got so bad they kicked 'im out o' church, and he couldn't get no churches, you know. He bought a little old piece o' land and decided he's gon' farm it. And so he bought a load of manure, and he opened the gate for the boy [delivering the order], you know. He [the Preacher] say it looked like nothing but a load of straw. And so the boy say, "Yeah, Reverend, the Depression has knocked the shit out of everything."

68 See Me Now

There were two buddies who used to go around together every day. One would take one route and one would take another. And they would flimflam—that was their game, flimflamming people out of money. Each night they would meet and split the spoils. And so one particular day, one of them made more money than the other one made. He made a good lump. So instead of meeting his partner like he should, he skipped town and went in the country.

So his buddy heard where he was and he went over there that Sunday and heard he was gon' preach. (You know those kind of folks can do some of everything.) So he walked in church and his buddy was up in the pulpit, and he saw 'im when he entered. And he said, "Oh, members of the congregation, I think I'll change my text. I'll take as my text, 'See me now, and I will see thee *later*!'"

69 Identification

Here's a guy who got *killed* right there on the spot in an accident. And somebody say, "Somebody find a Priest to say the last rites for the man!"
"How *you* know this man is a [Catholic]?"
"I found a' bingo card in his pocket."

70   I Don't Like That Thing

This Minister was baptizing out in this river, like, you know, they did in old days. They didn't have any pools in the church to baptize. So he started to baptize this lady; he say, "I baptize you in the name of the Father and the Son..."
She say, [chanting] "I—don't—like—that—thing—be-hind me-e-e."
He say, "I baptize you in the name of the Father and the Son..."
And every time he would try to dip her down, she'd start singing a little louder, [chanting] "I—don't—like—that—thing—be-hind me-e-e."
He turned around, trying to see, and he saw this *great big* snake. He say, [chanting also in the same tune] "I—don't—like—that—damn—thing—either-r-r."

71   Damn Good Sermon

After a particularly moving sermon one Sunday morning, a man walked up and said, "Reverend, you sure preached a *damn* good sermon this morning!"
The Minister was very upset; he said, "Young man, you mustn't talk like that, especially not in the house of the Lord. You must watch your language."
The man say, "I still say that was a *damn* good sermon! It was so *damn* good I put *fifty* dollars in the collection!"
The Minister say, "Like *hell* you did!"

72   Ain't But One Door

This guy died with arthritis. He doubled up and they tried to strap 'im down so he would stay down in the coffin. And they had the funeral that day. It was a old fellow 'round there in the country [unclear]. Church, small church, AND—just as the man started services, the strap broke loose, and this guy rose up in the casket. Everybody started running! The Preacher hollered and said, "What's wrong with these sonovabitches! Ain't got but one door in this place!" (Everybody trying to get out that one door.)

73 Blow Yo' Horn, Gabrul

One time there was a lil' boy. He like to practice his horn, you know. His mother gave 'im a trumpet for his birthday. So he wants to be a trumpet player like Louis Armstrong. *Everywhere* he go, he carry the trumpet. He carry the trumpet to school, carry it to bed. When he wake up in the morning, that's the first thing he grab, the trumpet.

So then, come Sunday, lil' boy tol' his mama, say, "Well, I've got to go to church." So he put his trumpet under his arm, carried it to church. Lil' boy started to playin' the trumpet in the back. People tol lil' boy, say, "You better go out o' here with that trumpet." So the lil' boy went downstairs, you know, and started blowin' the trumpet.

This same day the Preacher's sermon was on Gabrul. Preacher was preachin' 'bout *Gabrul.* Tol' *ev-e-rybody,* he say, "If any *sinners* in the house, when Gabrul blow his horn, you have to *leave* here." He say, "When Gabrul blow his horn, *ev-e-rybody* is going to hell who have sinned." Preacher looked up, say, "GA-BRUL, *blow yo' ho-orn,* Gabrul!" Nobody heard nothing. "Gabrul, *please,* blow yo' *ho-o-rn,* Gabrul! Gabrul, blow yo' HO-O-O-ORN, Gabrul!"

About that time the lil' boy hit a high note, "D-O-O-O-T!"

Everybody lookin' at each other. Couple o' 'em jumped up and run out the door. Preacher say, "The message . . . comin', the message . . . comin'. *Gabrul,* blow your *ho-o-o-orn* one time, *Gabrul.* Blow your horn, Gabrul!"

"TOOT—T-O-O-O-T!"

Everybody *got* up and *run* out o' the church and left the Preacher in there. Preacher, he say, "I don't believe this; I don't believe this." He say, "The Lord ain't answered." Preacher say, "Gabrul, blow your HORN, Gabrul. If anybody else in here is a sinner," say, "you have to leave out o' here." Say, Gabrul, blow yo' H-O-O-ORN, Gabrul!"

Little boy went "DO-O-O D-O-O-O-T!"

Preacher jumped up and ran, and his robe got caught in that do' sill. So the Preacher looked back over his shoulder. He say, "Look out, Gabrul, I don't play that shit!"

74 It's Your Choice

Here's a very conscientious man. He could preach and preach; and he asked sinners to come up, see. And the old man got up there, and he was talking so much, and he was sweating so much. He said, "Well, I done asked yawl several times to come on up here, come on up here. If you don't wanna come, just go to hell!"

75 Don't Call My Name

They were taking a collection and the Minister hadn't been getting much collection during the revival. So they had this visiting Minister, and he said, "Well, Reverend, let me up there. I'll show you how to get you some collection."

So he walked up to the pulpit, and he said, "Now, look," he say, "there's a man out in that audience going with another man's wife." Said, "If I don't get a five-dollar bill in the collection plate from that man, I'll call his name out in church." He said, "Okay, Brothers, let's take up collection."

So they say when they took up collection they had ten five-dollar bills in the plate, and they had one two-dollar bill with a note on it. It said, "Please, Reverend, don't call my name. If you don't call my name today, I'll bring you the other three tomorrow."

76 The Rest Is Mine

In this small town there was a Catholic Priest, a Methodist Minister, and a Black Baptist [Minister]. All of them had small parishes. They got together and got to talking about how the church paid them, and, you know, what little money they were getting. And they asked the Catholic Priest, say, "How do they pay you?"

He said, "Well, they pass the plates to take up a collection. Then they take it back in the anteroom. There's a table back there that has a undercover, and they put all the plates in there. And I'm allowed to back up to that table and pull a plate out. I cannot see it, but whatever is in it is mine."

The Methodist said, "Well, we have pretty much the same situation, but I am at least given the opportunity to look at the plate that I want and I can take that."

The Black Preacher said, "Now, we don't do ours like that. We take up the collection and dump it all in one plate. And then I throw it up in the air, and all the Lord don't get while it's in the air belong to me!"

77 Preacher Comin' Today

Another time the barnyard fellows was up there, you know. Done got down there, and they look 'cross the field, and there was a *Preacher* walkin' 'cross the path. So they know what that meant: the Preacher come, somebody got to go. So the old Rooster, he jump up on the fence, say [imitating sound of Rooster] "PREACHERCOMINTODAYYYYY!" Everything scattered! Ducks, they run off underneath the house. The guineas flew up the tree; the geese, they ran back and got down under the bushes there.

So after a while, everything got quiet. One ole Guinea up the tree say, "ISHEGONEYET? ISHEGONEYETTTTT? ISHEGONEYETTTTT?"

'Nother one say, "NOTYETTTTTT—NOTYETTTT—NOTYETTTTT."

The Rooster [unclear] like that, "PREACHERHERETOSTAYYYYY."

Preacher grabbed him [dramatizing Preacher grabbing Rooster by throat], "Git you and put you in the fire!"

You know what the old Gander say? "TEARIMUP! TEARIMUP! TEARIMUPPPP!"

78 God Bless the Cow

The church people were having a party at which they served some punch, but the punch was so weak that, every time they got a chance, some of the men would sneak in a bottle and pour some whiskey into the punch. The Preacher enjoyed it so much he just kept nipping. Later, when he was called to pray, he said, "God, bless the cow that gave this milk."

79 I Thank You for Some Corn

A. This Minister went to the big meetings in the country when they have what they call their homecoming. He was a city Preacher, but he would visit these people because he knew them very well. And they had a great big dinner at the home of these people, and the Preacher was busy eating, and they were having a wonderful time. And the Preacher was so busy he had his face down in the plate just eatin' and eatin'.

So the lady said, "Well, Reverend, won't you have some corn?"

He said, "Yes, I thank you," and he passed his glass over.

B. They [the Ministers] had a conference someplace, and they were just about to serve dinner, and say the lady said to him, "What would you like? Would you like some corn?"

He said, "Yes, I would," he said. "But wait a minute, let me get my glass over there."

80   The Minister's Fresh Air

A. One Sunday this Minister was up in the pulpit and he was preaching, and all of a sudden he said, "Sing a lil' song and say a lil' prayer while the Preacher go out and get some fresh air." So he came on back in and he preached a little more. Again he said, "Sing a lil' song and say a lil' prayer while the Preacher go out and get some fresh air."

So the Deacons began to look at one another, and so they say, "If he goes back out, when he comes back in, we gon' go out there and see what this fresh air is all about."

So he came on back in. He say, "Sing a lil' song and say a lil' prayer while the Preacher go get some more fresh air."

When he returned that time, the Deacons went out, and they found he had been drinking whiskey and he had it hidden in the bushes. So they drank *all* his whiskey, and went on back in church.

So the Minister again repeated, "Sing a lil' song and say a lil' prayer while the Minister go and get some fresh air." He came back; he said, "Don't yawl sing another *damn* song and don't yawl say another *damn* prayer until somebody tell me who stole my damn fresh air."

B. This Minister nipped a little bit, and he had hid his corn liquor, you know, out somewhere. So, he'd preach a while, you know. Then he says, "All right, sing another song and pray another prayer while your Minister go out and get some fresh air." He'd go out and he would get this bottle. Say one of them Sisters figured out what he was doing. She went out and she moved his bottle. Say he come back in; he say, "Don't sing another song; don't pray another prayer! Somebody done gone out and stole the Minister's fresh air."

81   Hurried Departure

These ole Preachers were discussing their Old Sisters, the Sisters of the church. And so this Minister was telling the other one, say, "Don't you know Brother John had to leave Sis Mary's house las' week when her husband come home," and said, "He had to leave his coat and hat."

This old Minister say, "What!"

Say, "*Yes*, man."

He said, "Didn't he have better sense than to take off his coat and *hat*? When I go to see the Sisters I don't even pull my hat off."

82   He Remembered

This Minister could not find his hat, and he finally decided that one of the members of his church must have stolen it. He was very disturbed, and he decided to talk to his Deacon about what he should do. The Deacon suggested, "Why don't you preach on the Ten Commandments next Sunday, and then when you come to 'Thou shalt not steal' really lay it on, so that the guilty person will repent and return your hat." The Minister said, "That's a good idea. I'll try it."

So the next Sunday he got up in the pulpit and he was really laying it on strong on those Ten Commandments. He preached on "Honor thy father and thy mother"; then he preached on "Thou shalt not commit adultery." Then—he cut his sermon short.

After the service the Deacon said to him, "Reverend, you were doing so well, but you never did get to the main part of your sermon. What happened?"

He say, "Deacon Jones, I didn't need to use that part 'cause when I got to 'Thou shalt not commit adultery,' I remembered where I left my hat."

83   Playing in a Large Cathedral

This Minister was a very prominent Preacher in a semirural community. He had a big church, but it was a rural community. He would always go around and visit his people, because he wanted to see how they were getting on. So this young woman, she was singing in his choir—very attractive woman—and he decided he would go by one day to see this couple. He had a feeling that the husband wasn't there, but he went there anyway.

And the lady came to the door. She didn't have on anything but just her gown; she didn't even have time to put on a robe. And so she say, "Well, R-R-Reverend, you'll have to wait till I go get my robe."

He says, "No, that's all right. After all, we're Christian people; we know how to act."

She say, "All right." So he came in and she just keppa sitting down there talking with him, and Reverend couldn't *stand* it any longer. So he finally grabbed her and kissed her. She responded by kissing him. So they lied 'cross the sofa, and they started to having a lil' friendly social intercourse. And he was doing all right; so he asked her, "My Sister, are you satisfied? Are you happy with this lil' intercourse that we're having?"

She said, "Yes, Reverend, but you seem to have such a small organ."

The Reverend said, "No, it's not that I have such a small organ, but my organ is playing in such a large cathedral!"

84   Lil' Red Riding Hood and the Wolf

This young Minister had accepted a charge to pastor a church in a rural area. He was very energetic and dynamic. He had just finished theological school, and he wanted to make good, so he accepted this as a challenge because he knew if he could make good in this community, he could get a better charge at a later time.

But there was a little girl—young woman, rather—that would come to the church every Sunday. And he would preach, and she would just sit right in front of him with her legs crossed and a miniskirt, and she just *disturbed* him because she was pretty and everything—she was attractive—and he was a man. So he tol' her, say, "Why don't you take a seat in the other part of the church because you disturb me."

She say, "That's what I want to do—disturb you. If you can't preach with my sitting up here—you just have to take it, that's all."

He say, "Well, since you talk like that, I'm going to get you."

She say, "You just try."

So one day, Lil' Red Riding Hood decided to take some pancakes and some cake down to her grandmother, and so this Preacher saw her going through the woods; so he followed her. And he just stalked behind her and just stayed behind trees and everything. And she was just walking through the woods, shaking herself and carrying on. When she got inside the house her grandmother was out in the back yard, working in the garden. So she laid the basket on the table and she got in the bed, opened her legs up and started reading a book. And the Preacher came in . . . and he looked at her. He looked right down between her legs, and he got excited. He say, "AH-H-H-H, girl!"

She say, "What's wrong with you, Preacher?"

He say, "I'm a wolf! I'm a wolf!"

She say, "If you a wolf, go on out there and chase some foxes."

He say, "I'm chasing you now. I'm a wolf! I'm going to *rape* you! I'm going to *rape* you!"

She say, "Naw you not! You stick to the script. You s'posed to *eat* me."

85   De Preacher Want Chicken

A.   Say John came in and his wife hadn't cooked or nothin'. And say all at once, she jumped up. She spied a chicken out in the yard. Say she jumped up and started runnin' after the chicken. Her husband say, "What in de worl' you runnin' dem chickens like dat for?" Say, "You ain't even cooked no supper or nuttin'."
She say, "De Preacher want chicken."
He say, "Fuck de Preacher!"
She say, "I done did dat, but the Preacher *still* want chicken."

B.   When the old man come in that day from work, 'twas peoples runnin' all 'round. And he say, "What's the matter? What's all this here work-up? What's this goin' on all about here?"
So the ole lady hollered out, say, "The Preacher's here!"
He say, "Oh, *fuck* the Preacher!"
She say, "Well, I've done done *that*—but now he wants some tiddy."

86   The Test

The boy was gettin' ready to marry this girl, and the Priest told 'im, say, "I'll have to sleep with her one night before you can marry her." So the boy agreed, see. So that night when they got in the bed, the girl got in the middle, and the Priest got in the front, and he got in the back. So they went on through the night.
So, the next morning, the Priest called 'im aside and told him, say, "Now, look here. If I was you, I wouldn't marry that girl."
He say, "What's wrong? What's the matter?"
He say, "*Time* I got in the bed las' night, she *grabbed* me right by the dick and held it all night."
He say, "No, partner, you wrong there. That was my hand on your dick."

87   My Legs

This Pastor was sitting up between two Sisters, and after a while he said he was sick and would have to go to the doctor. One Old Sister asked him what was the matter. He said, "I've lost all feeling in my leg. I've pinched it, rubbed it, smacked it, and I can't feel a thing."

The Old Sister said, "Don't worry, you haven't lost any feeling in your leg. That was my leg you were rubbing, pinching, and slapping."

88   Accuser Accused

The Preacher was in the pulpit *just* preachin'! And so the old man—drunk—sittin' back in the back *drunk*. Say the old Preacher got down out de pulpit an' come to de man and tol' 'im, say, [gesturing with an accusing finger] "Yeah, brother, I smell *whiskey* on your breath," and he point his finger in the man's face jus' like dat [still shaking finger]. And the man say, "Yeah, Reverend, and I smell pussy on your finger."

89   The Trap

Here's a man who thinks the Minister is going with his wife. He say, "I'm gon' fix that guy; I'm gon' fix 'im! I think he's going with my wife."

So he lef' his wife by herself, and the Minister came. (He invited him and he came.) So they talked some trash and the Minister went on and got in the bed with his wife. About five minutes later he came in there:

"I gotcha! I gotcha! I know I'd catch ya. I gotcha! I caught you with my wife."

He say, "Well, look, Deacon Jones, any time that you set a trap for me and bait it with pussy, you bound to catch me!"

90   Boo!

Here's a lady who has invited the Pastor of her church to come and have dinner, and then she finds out that her sister in town has taken ill. She's got a daughter about seventeen years old, so she tells her daughter, she said, "Now, what I want you to do is to act as if I was here. And you feed the Pastor and tell 'im what happened and everything."

So when the Pastor came she explained it to him and everything. And of course, she cooked just as good as her mother and everything. She had a nice, lovely meal. And after the Pastor had ate, he sat there by the stove in the big chair, and *kept* looking at that young thing switching around. He laid back in that chair, and he watched her. He said, "Mary Lou!"

She say, "Yes, Reverend."

"Have you ever been scared before?"

She say, "No, Reverend, I haven't."

He say, "You gone on upstairs and take off your clothes. I'm gon' come up there and scare you in a minute."

The Reverend went up there. WHAM! [Slap of the hand to suggest immediate success.] Man, he helped himself. Rev. come down *laughing.* "Oh-ho, my soul! Young! Tender!"

About five minutes later, he heard a lil' tap on the bannister, say, "Reverend!"

"Yes."

"I'd like for you to come on up here and scare me again."

Reverend went up there and stayed about a hour. He come back down. [Dramatizing a return that is much less energetic and enthusiastic than the last one.] He's beat now! He don't want no more. He sat down with the paper.

Five minutes later he heard another lil' tap on the bannister: "Reverend."

"Yes." [Exhaustedly.]

"I want you to come up and scare me again."

He *crawled* up the steps, CRAWLING! He gets up there. He stays up there a hour and a half or two hours. He comes back down [nearly dead and collapses in the chair]. He got the paper upside down.

About ten minutes later he heard a tap on the bannister: "Reverend!"

He reached up there, [hardly a whisper] "Yes."

She say, "I want you to come up here and scare me again."

He say, "Well, BOO, goddamn it!"

91 No Good Sonovabitch

This girl was walking down the street. She was saying, "That *no* good motherfucker! That no good sonovabitch!"

So the *Preacher* walked by. He say, "Excuse me, Lady, don't you have some respect for me? I'm a *Preacher.*"

She say, "Well, I'm sorry, Reverend, but he's *still* a no good sonovabitch."

The Reverend say, "Well, will you tell me what he did to make you use such a name like that?"

The lady say, "Well, I was standing on the street just like this, and he walked up to me, and he *grabbed* me."

So the Preacher, you know, he grabbed her, and he say, "Like this?"

She say, "Yeah, just like that."

So the Preacher say, "Well, that's no reason for you to call him what you called 'im."

She say, "Well, Preacher, that's not all. Then he throwed me in his car."

The Preacher throwed her in the car. He say, "Like this?"

She say, "Yassuh, Preacher, just like that."

He say, "Well, that's *still* no reason for you to call 'im what you called 'im."

She say, "But, Preacher, that's not all. Then he carried me to the motel."

The Preacher say, "Like this?"

She say, "Yeah, just like this."

The Preacher say, "Well, that's no reason for you to call 'im what you called 'im."

"Well, Preacher, then he throwed me 'cross the bed and commenced to have an intercourse with me."

Preacher throwed her 'cross the bed and jumped up and down on 'er two or three times. He say, "Like this?"

She say, "Yeah."

He say, "Well, that's *still* no reason for you to call 'im what you called 'im."

She say, "But, Preacher, that's not all—he gave me the clap!"

Preacher say [jumping up hurriedly], "A *no* good sonovabitch!"

92 Gabriel's Bugle

There was this old Preacher, and he had this old Nun that was working with him about *twenty* years (you understand). But he was getting sick o' her 'cause she was definitely *too* old (you understand). So he went up to the Nun's School and got one o' them young Nuns, you know. So the young Nun came in that day, you know, and like, un-er, he was using her more like his aide, you know, keeping his office clean and getting him—and things like this here. So that evening the Nun came in his room, and he told the Nun to put on some hot water (you understand). So the Nun got him some water together, and so he sat there by the bathtub. He called the Nun over. He grabbed the Nun (you understand), took his hand and ran it up the Nun's dress. She said, "What is that?"

He say, "You know what this is?"

She say, "Naw."

He say, "Well, this is the kingdom" (you understand). So he grabbed his dick (you understand). He say, "You know what this is?" He say, "Well, *this* is the key to the kingdom." Say, "I'm gon' take the key and stick it in the kingdom and let out the evil spirits." (Dig it?)

So they went on and went through they little change and done their old

thing. But in the process of this the *old* Nun peeping through the keyhole.
(You dig it?) So the young Nun come through the do' (you understand). She
walked out. The old Nun *grabbed* her, right quick, WHOOSH! Snatched her
(you understand). She say, "Dig it, what did he tell you?" (you understand).
She say, "Well, he told me that he had the key and he showed me something
on me that was the kingdom, so he stuck the key in the kingdom and let out
the evil spirits."

The old Nun looked at her, say, "Why that *dirty bastard*, he told me that
was Gabriel's bugle and I been blowing it for *twenty* years!"

93 Jump on Mama's Lap

Someone came to the door, and the little boy went to the door. His father
asked him who was at the door, and he told him the Methodist Minister. So
the father said, "Go hide all the liquor."

Then again, there was a knock on the door, and he asked him who was
there. And he told him it was the Episcopalian Minister; so the father told
him to go hide the food.

The next one came up was a Baptist, and he [the father] told him, say, "Go
jump in Mama's lap."

94 Let Her Lay There

Here was a woman jumpin' up in front of the Preacher when Preacher
was preachin' in church: "Yes, the Lord taught me, the LORD taught me!
JESUS!" [Dramatizes lady falling back.] Her dress falls up. She ain't got no
underpants on. So the Deacon ran over to pull her dress down.

The Minister say, "Deacon! DON'T ya touch 'er! Don't *touch* 'er. Let her
lay there like the *Lord* flung 'er!"

95 Let the Glory Shine

The Preacher was preachin', and the lady was sittin' all so wide and all.
[Indicating that legs are stretched open.] And every time the Preacher would
look down, he'd say, "AMAN!" Say, "Let the GLORY *shine!*"

96   A Lie

They told a tale on Brother Isaac Jacobs. He always sermonized after the Preacher. You know they had a way then of when they get up taking the offering, they'd sermonize: "Eenk [in a nasal tone], the Reverend done preach the gospel today." Then he'd go 'round and repreach it all.

So he went down to Mt. Zion Church. They used to have their meeting every first Sunday [of the month]. He went down there and Reverend J. J. E. Horne was pastor there then. And Horne preached that day and Eenk got up and he sermonized on his sermon. And Horne announced his topic for the next Sunday.

And when the next first Sunday rolled around, Bro Isaac right there. And say when he got up then to sermonize, he got up, say, [nasal tone] "Eenk, yes, Brethren, the same mouth that tell the truth will tell a lie."

They say the people couldn't figure out what in the world he was driving at. Say, [nasal tone] "I was here last first Sunday, and Reverend Horne announced that he would preach this topic. And I come back here today specially to hear 'im, and he didn't preach it. And that's why I say the same mouth that tell the truth will tell a lie."

97   Send Down an Angel

A. This Minister had told his son to carry four white pigeons and get up in the tree, and he was going to preach to the congregation and ask the Lord to send down angels. So he went on that Sunday; he got up in church, and the little boy was up in the tree with the pigeons. So he started preaching. He said, "Oh, Lord, please send down an angel this morning for Jesus' sake." The boy let a pigeon go, and the people began to get all excited.

And he said, "Lo-o-o-ord, please send me down another angel," and he sent down another white pigeon.

So he kept on until he got the fourth one. He forgot because he was all excited because the people were all happy and everything with all these "angels" coming down, so he asked the Lord to send him down the fifth angel. The little boy looked at him. He said, "Daddy, you didn't tell us to bring but four pigeons, but if you want us to go home and get another pigeon, we'll go home and get you another pigeon."

B. This Preacher—he was one of them what we called "Jack-leg" Preachers, you know. And he used to start up a scheme where he would get the congregation real excited. So he was workin' wit' the Sexton of the church, see. He say, "Now, I'm gon' take a text next Sunday in the form of a white dove, and I'm gon' bring you a white dove, and if you get up in the belfry, when I get to preaching, you drop the dove down. He'll be flying around. That'll get everything working fine."

So the Sexton was up there with the dove, waiting for the time. And in the meantime (he won't be looking 'round), a old pet ate the dove up, you know.

So when he say, "L-O-O-O-RD, send the do-o-o-ve," he sent this cat down there on the string: "Meow, me-e-ow!"

He say, "Where is the dove, Lord."

"Inside the cat!"

98 Bunkim

A. This Minister and this Deacon were bragging about the different women that they had had relationships with in the church. So they made a bet. The Minister bet the Deacon, "I can point out more women than you can."

And the Deacon say, "Well, I can point out just as many as you can."

He say, "Well, all right, next Sunday morning before I start my sermon, and every time a woman come in, and if I've had something to do with her, I'll say, 'Bunkim,' and if you've had something to do with 'em, you say, 'Bunkim.'"

And so every time a woman would come in the church that Sunday morning, the Preacher would look over at the Deacon and say, "Bunkim." The Deacon would look at the woman and say, "Bunkim." So they kept on; that kept up: "Bunkim!"

"Bunkim."

So finally, the Deacon's wife came in the church, and the Preacher looked at the Deacon's wife, and he said, "Bunkim!" And the Deacon looked at the Preacher and say, "OH, naw you don't. You gon' unbunk that one!"

B. The Minister and the Deacon, they had somewhat gotten bored of the regular Sunday service every Sunday, and they decided they were going to play a little game. And the Minister reached over and whispered in the Deacon's ear, and said, "Look, let's have a lil' fun this morning. Every Sister who come in that door that you've had some contact with, I'd like for you to clear your throat and say, 'Uh-uhm.' And every Sister that comes in the door that I've had some contact with, I'm gon' clear my throat and say, 'Uh-uhm.'" The Deacon looked at him [nodding head to indicate approval].

So he got up and started preaching, "Gabriel blew his tru-u-umpet-t-t!" and started, you know, really going through his thing, you know. And after a while a Sister comes through the door. He say, "Uh-uhm." Looked down at Brother Deacon. Brother Deacon looks up at him and nods his head. So it goes on for about ten or fifteen minutes. Another Sister comes into the door. Brother Deacon: "Uhm-umn." Looks up at Brother Pastor. Brother Pastor says [gesture indicating smiling approval]. So this goes on for quite awhile. After awhile it gets back to the Deacon's turn again, and the Deacon say, "Uh-umn." So the Pastor's preaching stopped. He looked at the door—he reached over there, say, "Brother Deacon, are you sure?"

Brother Deacon say, "Uhm-m-humnn."

The Pastor couldn't preach any further. He say, "Brother Deacon, are you sure?"

Deacon say, "Um-m-humn-uh-humn!"

So he say, "Well, you know, man, that's my wife."

Deacon say, "I don't give a damn, I still uh-uhm-uhm-uhm!"

99   Deacon Brown Is Dead!

This Negro Deacon who had the largest sex organ in town had a habit of making all of the *Sisters* happy in the church. And at church time, they would all go up and press his hand. The Minister had become sort of *jealous* of it. He didn't do anything.

So he [the Deacon] died. And they couldn't do anything at all to get his sex organ in the casket with him. He died seemingly with a hard-on and they just couldn't get the thing to do *down*. So they had to cut it off. And place it beside him—open, of course. His last will said let his remains remain open.

All the women were *just* coming by there, just hollering and crying, "Oh, LORD, Deacon *Brown* is *dead*! Whatever WILL we do, oh-h-h-h-h, Lord! What SHALL we do?" So the Preacher got a little jealous of it. He was tapping these girls *himself*.

So everything was all over and they carried the body on down to the grave—and buried the body. But they forgot that they had left his penis in this little case they had for it. So the Minister said, "Well, I won't be that rotten. I'll take it on home and tomorrow I'll take it on to the cemetery and tell the man to put it on in there."

So he [took it home and] put it down there, and his wife came downstairs to fix him some broth and hot tea. And she turned and looked and she saw the case. And she broke down. She said, "Oh, oh, LO-O-R-RD! Deacon Brown is *dea-ea-d*!"

100   Here Go One Eye

A woman had gotten happy. She *screamin'* in front o' the pulpit. And fell out. Fell right out! And her dress flew up—no underpants on. And the

Preacher say, "Thou who cast their eyes upon this naked woman shall go blind!"

The Deacon looked around and say, "Well [covering one eye with his hand, but looking with the other], here go one eye!"

101 Deacon Jones Gon' Lead

This boy [Deacon Dick Jones] was playing cards all the time. Couldn't nobody tell 'im, couldn't nobody catch 'im, couldn't nobody tell 'im—nothing like that—about to stop playing cards. So they went to the Pastor and told the Pastor, say, "That Deacon been playing cards right often." Say, "He sit up all night and then come in church and sleep, just like that [dramatizing]." Say "Look at him now, fast asleep and you preaching [unclear]."

Pastor say, "Well, next Sunday, we gon' get 'im next Sunday."

So next Sunday they concocted this wherein the Pastor said, "We're going to sing Hymn 496" . . . and Dick slept on. And the Pastor said, "We're gonna sing Hymn 496," right loud . . . "and Deacon Jones gon' lead" . . . and Deacon Jones slept on.

And the Preacher got a little hot there and he said, *"We're gonna sing Hymn 496 and Deacon Jones is gonna lead!"*

And Jones woke up right there, said, " 'Twon't my deal; I dealt the cards last!"

102 If You Want to Go to Heaven

This Minister was conducting a revival in this big church. And this particular day, the church was *full*. The people had told the Minister in advance that there were a lot of sinners in the church, so the Minister preached a very stirring sermon. And after the sermon, he opened the doors of the church [asked for converts], and no sinners came up. And he was rather indignant because he knew that sinners were in his congregation. So he asked the sinners again to come up—to stand where they were. And no one would stand. So then he said, "Everyone in the church who wants to go to heaven, come over on my right side. Come over here."

So everybody went over there and stood—including the sinners—but one Deacon sat over there and he didn't move.

And so when the Preacher saw this Deacon sitting over there, he say, "Well, Brother Deacon, didn't you hear what I said?"

He say, "Yes."

He say, "Well, uh, I said, 'Everybody who wants to go to heaven, come on this side.' Why didn't you come over?"

He say, "Well, I tell ya, Reverend, I heard what you said. But I thought you were gitting up a trip to go *now*."

103 Shall We Gather at the River

One Sunday the Preacher got up in the pulpit and he started to preachin'. He say, "For my part, you can take *all* the whiskey and throw it in the river."

A old Deacon in the front say, "A-A-A-MEN!"

He say, "For my part, you can take all the *wine* and throw it in the river."

The Deacon said, "A-A-MEN!" again.

He said, "For my part, you can take *all* of the alcohol and throw it in the river!"

The Deacon say, "A-A-A-MEN!"

So he ended his sermon.

The Deacon jumped up. He say, "Let us sing page 392, "Shall We Gather at the River."

104 Lord, Fill 'Im

Have you heard the one about the Deacon who *prayed* and *prayed*, you know? And his prayer was for the Lord to fill 'im, you know, fill 'im with the spirit.

Say his wife come there one day, said, "Lord, please, please don't fill 'im, 'cause he got a hole in 'im. It all run out before he get home."

105 Don't Know Nothin' 'Bout *Morehouse*

This Preacher with his B.D. from Morehouse preached this *magnificent* sermon about how he had been trained at *Morehouse* and how he could *exegesis* texts and how he could read in Hebrew and Latin, thanks to *Morehouse*; and he was going to send so much money to *Morehouse* to develop all these preachers to go out and save the world—the Africans, the heathens—all over! And thank God for *Morehouse*!

The old Deacon, after the sermon, prayed, "Lord, I ain't been fer and I don't know much, so I don't know nothin' 'bout Morehouse. But if you'll just do like I want you to do, then you'll let me into your house."

106 The New Rectum

These Old Sisters always came to church before anyone else and sat looking at everyone else as they came in [crosses arms and rolls eyes around, mimicking an Old Sister].

"I hear we got a new pastor," one says to the other.

"Yes, have you seen him?" the other asked.

"No, I sure haven't."

About that time a man walks in with eyeglasses with a chain hanging down from them [mimics the posture of a dignified, pompous man strolling down the aisle].

One hunched the other one: "Rachel, who is that?"

"I don't know," said Rachel, but she hunched her neighbor and asked, "Who is that pregnating looking man urinating down the aisle with gold testicles on?"

"That's the new rectum of the church," was the response.

107 Gone to Meddlin'

A. This Minister decided that there was just too much sinning in his church and he was going to deliver a fire and brimstone sermon. He said, "I'm gettin' personal wit' yawl 'cause you all guilty of somethin'!" He said, "In this church, some in my choir and usher board, I've got some whores!"

And some of the men hollered, "AMEN!"

He said, "Now I want all-l-l you whores to get up an' come over here on the left-hand side of this pulpit."

And with their heads hung, all of the whores got up and went on the left-hand side.

He said, "Now I want all the women chasers, you men that got five and six different women! Come up here and get on the right-hand side!"

And, OH, the people just yelled, "Tell it, Reverend!"

They got up on the right-hand side.

He say, "Now, ALL-L-L you faggots, come on up here by these whores!"

"Amen, Brother!"

And the faggots tipped on up.

And it was *one* old lady sitting there. And he said, "Now, I know you fit some category!"

She say, "Preach, Reverend, PRE-E-E-EACH, PREACH! You got 'em all!"

He say, "No, I want all the bulldaggers to come up here by me."

She say, "You done stop preachin', GODDAMN IT, and gone to meddlin'!"

B. The Preacher was preaching one Sunday, and he was talking about the youngsters. And this Old Sister was sitting up there with a big ball of snuff in her mouth. Say the Minister said, "Yes, these youngsters now days, you can't do anything with 'em. They drink; they smoke; they stay out all late hours of the night."

The Old Sister say, [mouth obviously full of snuff] "Dat's right! [Chewing.] Pweach it, Reverend, you jes' pweach it!"

So, all of a sudden, he say, "Yeah, and some of these Old Sisters walking 'round here with snuff in their mouth and comin' to church and sittin' up here gossipin'."

She say, [mouth still full] "Shee dat," say, "now, he done stop pweachin' and gone to meddlin'."

108   Fifty Adults

One member of the church said, "We have fifty adults going to be baptized."

The person she was talking to went to tell someone else, "Yes, we'll baptize fifty adulteresses."

109   Do You Believe?

This boy was very sinful, and when they got to baptize him, just like that, say, the Preacher baptized him, say, "I think it'll be a good thing to make an example of him, baptize him right good."

So he baptized him once and said, "John, you're very sinful now; I gotta baptize you." Said, "You believe, don't you?"

"Yeah . . ."

He baptized him the second time. He said, "John, do you believe?"

"Yeah . . ."

So the third time he slammed him down good. Splash-ah-ah! He said, "Yeah-h-h, John, do you believe?"

John said, "Dog-gone, I believe you're trying to drown me!"

110   Washing His Sins Away

There was this bad boy, and his mother thought so much of the boy that, after her little boy professed religion, the mother say she was going to carry him to church. They dressed up. There were a lot of biscuits on the table. And this boy, true to his sinful way, he took all the biscuits and stuck the biscuits down in here [indicates down in his shirt].

So, after a while it come time for baptism. The Preacher was baptizing, and he flung down the little boy, and then the old mother—poor child, she didn't know—she said, "La-a-wd! My child, I know, I *know* he's right now. I know he's got religion, 'cause there all his sins just coming out in chunks!"

All them biscuits come out and floating on top o' the water.

111   Duck!

They was baptizing in the river, and this man lived a long ways. So he carried his bag of lunch. And before time to go in the water to be baptized, he hung his lunch up on this tree.

And so the Preacher was trying to baptize 'im; and each time that he would go to put 'im in the water, he'd tell the man, he say, "Duck!"

He'd jerk his head up, you know, still looking, and the Preacher told 'im three times, he say, "I say, DUCK!"

He say, "How in the world I gon' duck when them dogs there tryin' to get my lunch?"

112   Quit Your Foolishness

They were having baptism in the river, and they were baptizing this man. And a lil' twig was there; the Minister didn't know it. So when he carried him down in the water, the twig kinda hung 'round his neck, and he couldn't get 'im up right away. So when he did get 'im up, the man said to 'im, "Here, Mr. Minister, you quit your *damn* foolishness 'fo' you drown somebody!"

113   I'm Not a Member

This Minister was in church, and he said to all the folks, "If you do *not* want to go to *hell* when you die, stand." Everybody in the church stood up but this little boy on the front row. So he repeated it again, "Will all the members. . . ."

So it *worried* him—everybody standing up but the little boy on the front row.

"Will all the members of this church please stand if you want to go to heaven when you die."

The little boy, "Da, da, dum, hhmmm, hhmmm . . . [dramatizing little boy nonchalantly glancing around and humming softly, unconcerned]."

So finally the Minister looked down on the front row. He said, "Boy, why don't you stand up? Don't you want to go to heaven when you die?"

The boy say, "I'm not a member of this church."

114   Cream Color Will Do

The old Negro Preacher was singing, "Wash me and I shall be whiter than snow."

An elderly lady responded, "Just a cream color will do for me."

115   You Hit 'Em Today

Reverend Jones said he had this Deacon that always, when the Minister would get through speaking (you've seen 'em, we've seen 'em) that would get up and almost give you another sermon and preach back to the congregation. And he did this *all* the time.

So it happened this Sunday, it snowed. Didn't nobody get to church but him and the Preacher. And the Preacher went on and preached. Say he still got up; he say, "Reverend," say, "if they had-a been here today, you certainly would of told 'em somethin'. Reverend, you certainly hit 'em today."

116   Look—Look—Look!

Old man Zeke Brandon—back in that time they didn't have no choirs. They used to sing from the floor. The congregation would sing and one would lead off a song. He'd work it out and all the others would sing it. Old man Brandon was slow in pace; he didn't have no fast tempo. He stuttered. And say, he say, "Look—l-look—l-look—l-l-look—" And say he was pointin', standing in front, pointin' out. Everybody turned 'round and looked at the door 'cause they thought the man had saw somethin' on the outside. He say, "Great God-a-mighty gonna cut 'em down."

117 Same Old Crowd

This man had a Parrot that had been raised by a man who ran a night club. The Parrot had learned all kinds of profane language at the night club. But this religious man who had him now was trying to reform him and teach him not to use such vulgar language. After the man thought he had reformed him, he took him to church. And right in the middle of the church service the Parrot yelled out, "Damn!"

The man hunched the Parrot. He said, "Don't talk like that. You're in church. These people don't talk like that! You're not in the night club now!"

The Parrot say, "Same old crowd. This is the same old crowd!"

118 A Prayer

There was a old fellow, you know. He used to stay around the corners with the young fellows at night, you know. He didn't have no particular place. So he went to church one Sunday morning, and this Minister seen this old man in church, you know. He know he was a good old Christian. So he called on him to pray.

The old man got up, say, "Lord, you know I ain't nothin', and these deacons around here, they ain't nothing'" (and the Minister was named Cheesley), and he say, "Reverend Cheesley, he ain't nothin'." Say, "Lord, if you stay 'round here, you ain't gon' be nothin'. AMAN!"

119 Can't Pray

This gentleman, his name was Claiborne Johnson, went to church and they called on Brother Johnson to pray. He got up and he say, "Lord, I can't do that thing, I know I can't. AMAN!"

120 Let the Piano Do It All

A person went to church once, and she started to sing a hymn, started to sing one of those old hymns. Somebody say, "Naw! Let the piano play it, let the piano play it."

After they played the piano, and then they called on her to pray. She say, "Now, you called on the piano to sing; now let it pray!"

121   Read It for Yourself

This man got tired every night of gettin' down saying his prayers. So he thought he would find a solution to that—so he wouldn't have to do that. So he wrote his prayer and put it up on the wall. And each night, when he got ready to go to bed, he said, "Lord, there's my prayer up there on the wall. Read it for yourself."

122   Who Is Going to Play the Chandelier?

This church had saved some money, you know, to get something to beautify the church, something for the church, and say that, uh, they had this meeting, and they had the old brother there, the church clerk to take the minutes down, and say the old brother was writin' and then they got up and voted. He wrote everything until they got ready to vote to get a chandelier for the church. He put his pencil down and stopped writing. So they all was lookin' at 'im, and he didn't take no more minutes. So when they reached the [unclear], say they asked him why did he stop taking the minutes.

He said, "Well, number one, I didn't know how to spell it. And number two, if you gon' do anything for the church, you ought to do something worthwhile. And number three, if you get that chandelier or whatever you gon' to call it, who gon' play it?"

123   Pot's Boiling Over

The woman had a little boy, and the church was close by the lady's house, and she go and put on a pot of sheep head and put the dumplin's on top the pot, and tell him when those dumplin's about to boil, you know, "Come and let me know."

And the little boy was *dirty* and *nasty* looking, and the 'oman was watching for the little boy, you know, so when he comin' to the do' 'cause she didn't want nobody to see the little boy. The little boy was runnin' and shout, "Hey, hey! You jump and shout like you got religion, but the sheep head bubblin' all the dumplin's out the pot."

The dumplin's was comin' out the pot. When she got there, the dumplin's all over the floor.

124 The Lord Sent It

There was an old lady. She believed in prayer, and she say she felt that anything she wanted, the Lord would give it to her. And so one day she wanted some bread. She was down on her knees, praying, asking the Lord to send her some bread. She was praying—and she just *prayed* and *prayed* and *prayed*. So some boys was passing, and they heard Aunt Mary praying. They say, "Let's have some fun."

And they went to the store and bought a loaf of bread. And Aunt Mary was still praying. So they dropped the bread down through the chimney, and when the bread hit the floor, Aunt Mary started hollering, "Thank God! Thank God! You sent me some bread!"

So the boys, they came 'round to the door laughing, knocked on the door, and she went to the door. They said, "Aunt Mary, you were praying for the bread, and *we* dropped the bread down through the chimney. That was us; it wasn't the *Lord* that *gave* you the bread. It was *us!*"

She say, "Well, the Lord *sent* it if the Devil did *bring* it!"

125 I Ain't Ready to Go Yet

This is an old lady who loved to pray. And she was found praying any time during the day and any time during the night. Some of the farmhands came around. They heard her praying and got tired of listening to this prayer. And her prayer was, "Oh, Lord, I'm tired down here. Come down here and git me." So she prayed and prayed and prayed, and they finally got together and decided that they were going to play a trick on her.

So one day, after some length of time, they came and went up in the old barn. You know, in the country they have these barns where they store feed for the cattle and all. They went up in the barn and tied a rope up there and just put a loop on the end of that rope and dropped it down. While she was on her knees praying, this loop came down and fell around her neck and began to draw her up. And then she hollered, "Oh, dear Lord, no! NO! I ain't ready to go yet."

126 Don't Help That Bear

A. A preacher went a-hunting
       On one Sunday morn.

He laid aside his religion
And took his gun along.

He was telling tales
About killing whales
. . . .
And he spied a [grizzly] bear.

He said, "Lord, you delivered Daniel from the lion's den,
Jonah from the belly of the whale,
And the Hebrew children from the fiery furnace,
The Good Book do declare.

"Lord, Lord, Lord, if you don't help me,
Don't help that [grizzly] bear."

B.   This man had been to visit this friend in the country. And so he had to go through the swamp to get back home, and it begin to get dark. So when he was coming on through the swamp he met the bear, and the bear commenced to coming towards him. And so he started to running, and he found out that the bear could outrun him. So he say, "Lord—if you don't help me, PLEASE don't help *that bear!*"

127   Prayer Is All Right in a Prayer Meeting

This man was going down the country road, and he met this bear come runnin' to him, and he got so excited, he started runnin'. He say, "A prayer is all right in a prayer meetin', but it's nothin' in a bear meetin'."

128   Saying Grace

This fellow wanted to learn how to hunt, see. He heard about the hunting out in the country. He wanted to learn how to hunt, and he wanted to learn how to hunt *bears.* And they gave him a book, see, and he went to every class, and he learned how to handle the gun, and how to do everything else—how to hunt bears. And he finished the twelve lessons that he was supposed to have, and then he went on out bear hunting.

And he went on out in the woods and—he had his gun, you know, and everything, and after a while, he walked and walked and walked. And after a while he ran up on this big . . . black . . . grizzly bear. So he did what the instructions said. He thought back in his mind just what he had learned in school. The instructions say, "When you see a bear, get down on your knees"—you know!—"and put your arms on your shoulder, and raise the gun up like this [illustrating the manner of putting the gun in position to take aim and to shoot] and take aim, and then shoot." So he got down on his knees and put the elbow on his knee, and put the gun up there and pulled the trigger . . . and the gun just *clicked*. Didn't nothing happen. The gun just clicked. So he pulled the trigger again, and the gun just clicked. He had forgot to put the bullets in the gun. So the bear came on up closer—the bear got right up to him. And he didn't have nothing else in the book to go by, so he just, in his own mind, he decided to get down on his knees and pray.

And he prayed. He said, "Oh, Lord. There's the old bear. I know he must be a Christian bear. Lord, take care o' me. I *know* this must be a Christian bear. Brother Christian bear, I know you just wouldn't eat me." His eyes closed, down there on his knees praying. He got up and looked up, and the *bear* was on his knees praying. And he looked. And after a while, when the Bear got up off his knees, he looked at him. He say, "Brother Bear, what you doing?"

The bear say, "What you doing?"

He say, "I was praying."

The bear say, "You mighta been praying, but I was just saying my grace."

129 Children Will Play

My friend say she had a neighbor, and the neighbor was sick. She said, "I want you to—"

"Yeah?"

"—tell God I'm sick! And tell God don't send his son. Come *hisself* to see 'bout me *right* now 'cause children will play by the wayside."

130 Who Made You?

This Minister was going from school to school. He was asking questions from the Bible. And this particular teacher had gotten the questions, and she was trying to line the kids up. And she would tell them, you know, what to say when the Minister come in. The first question was "Who made you?" and the second one was "Who was the first man that God made?" So this particular day the teacher was so sure that this Minister was going to get to her class that she had lined them up and told them, say, "When the Minister comes in and I tell you to line up, you must get around the wall like I'm showing you now."

So when lunch time came, the Minister hadn't gotten there. So this little boy who was number one went home for lunch. The bell sounded for them to return back to class, and the little boy hadn't gotten back. So time they got in class, the Minister came. And the teacher told them, say, "You all get up and line up around the wall," and they went on and got up and stood up around the wall. She told them that this was the Minister and he was going to ask them questions from the Bible.

So the Minister said, "Now, look, I know all of you-all go to Sunday school, and I know you're going to know the answers to these questions." So he said to the little boy, he said, "Who made you?"

He said, "Adam."

He said, "No, son, I know you don't mean that. Now you think *real* hard. Who made you."

He said, "Adam."

He said, "No, son, Adam didn't make you. God made you."

He said, "No, sir, the little boy that God made went home for lunch and he hasn't gotten back yet, but Adam made me."

131   There Goes God's Nickel

This boy's mother gave him two nickels. She tol' him, "Now you put one in church; one is for God and one is for you."

So, on his way to church one nickel dropped and rolled in the gutter. He say, "Oh, there goes God's nickel."

132   I Wasn't Talking to You

A young man sitting at the dinner table was about to eat; then he was interrupted by his father.

Father: "Son, did you say your grace?"

Son: "Yes."

Father: "I didn't hear you."

Son: "I wasn't talking to you."

133   Let's Eat!

This actually happened. It was Christmas time. A neighbor who grew up with me—we were all around the table. So my old man, on Sunday mornings and on special events, he had to have these *lo-o-ong*, drawn-out prayers. And he went through all of this "Bless my boys; bless my neighbors; thank you for having us all here to have dinner...." And, you know, we were getting hungry!

So then after he finished, my friend said, "Here the bread and there the meat; come on *yawl*, let's *eat!*"

134 Your Good and Faithful Servant, Joe

Nigger Joe had lost his wife, his children, and all of his friends, and he lived all alone on his farm except for his dog. And after all these bad things happened to him, every morning he would get up, and he would pray to the Lord. He would say, "Lord, I'm your good, faithful servant, Joe. What have I done to deserve such bad things?" And he got no answer. And finally his dog died, and again he prayed, "Lord, this is your good and faithful servant, Joe; what have I done to have such bad things happen to me?" Still no answer. So finally one day he was out in the field plowing, and the plow fell on top of him, and there with his last few breaths he said, "Lord, this is your good, faithful servant, Joe. What have I done to have so many things happen to me?"

And then there was this thunder in the background, and the Lord answered and said, "Nigger Joe, you know, there's just something about you that turns me off."

135 Don't Give Me No Shit!

Once upon a time a young man was having trouble keeping his girlfriend. So he went down into the woods and held out his hands, asking the Lord for help. And suddenly something splashed in his hand. The boy looked over and said, "Lord, don't give me no shit!"

136 I Ain't Doe Tuss No Mo'

This man who lived in a house made out of nothing but glass was trying to refrain from being a sinner. He wanted to be good. He got on his knees, and he said (he lisped), "Oh, Tord, I ain't doe tuss no mo! Oh, Tord, I ain't doe tuss no mo!"

So two of his friends came by, and they said to him, "John, come on, let's shoot some crap."

He was still praying, "Tord, I not doe tuss no mo."

So they went on around the street and left him. And then they came back again, and they said to him, "John, they fighting around the street."

He was still on his knees, saying, "Oh, Tord, I ain't doe tuss no mo!"

So they said, "John, they threw a brick."

He's still praying, "Tord, I ain't doe tuss no mo."

Then they said, "John, the brick hit your house."

Then he *jumped* up off his knees, and he say, "Who in de Doddamn tru dat Doddamn brick at my Doddamn house!"

(He had forgot he was praying.)

137 Glory and Honor

Glory and honor, praise Jesus,
Glory and honor, praise the Lamb.

I must go; time I was gone,
That old sow is in my low-ground corn.
Track I see; I pursue,
And them little pigs was in there too.

I got the glory and honor, praise Jesus,
Glory and honor, praise the Lamb.

6

A Nigger Ain't Shit:
Self-Degrading Tales

If you're white, you're right;
If you're yellow, you're mellow;
If you're brown, stick around;
If you're black, step back.

Folk Verse

IN "RAPPIN' WITH MYSELF" Black novelist John Oliver Killens relates that, when his daughter went to Fisk University, she was upset to find that "the password [among the girls in her dormitory was] 'a nigger ain't shit!' "[1] Killens goes on to note that "the same password was prevalent in my college days."[2] Self-deprecation among Black people has been frequently observed and commented upon. In the chapter "My People! My People!" of her book *Dust Tracks on a Road*, Zora Neale Hurston, exploring the contrast between Black racial pride and the self-degrading attitudes frequently found among many Blacks, points to self-abasing jokes in the Black folk repertoire.[3]

Indeed, a large number of popular Black folktales seem to fall into the category of self-abasement. In *Black Manhattan* James Weldon Johnson asserts that "a Negro audience seems never to laugh heartier than when laughing at itself—provided it is a *strictly* Negro audience.[4] Many jokes are intended solely for Black ears and contain severe criticism of alleged character defects in Blacks. Other tales ridicule the Black person's color and hair, apparently indicating an acceptance of them as badges of inferiority, or deal with the Black person's preference for things white. Self-abasing humor has been so widespread among Negroes that a study published in 1959 reported that more anti-Black jokes were found among Black college students than among white.[5] The ensuing years, however, have witnessed a revolution in the Blacks' view of themselves. The more recent, prevalent rejection of white values and the reaffirmation of Blackness as a positive virtue have undoubtedly caused a decline (though certainly not a demise) in the popularity of this type of humor.

One cannot overlook the fact that even during their popularity, the self-derogatory tales were grim indeed—tales about situations and events that were not really funny to the Black person, who in everyday life had to face the harsh realities of stereotyped expectations from whites (many of whom believed and acted consistently in the belief that all Blacks steal, smell bad, are lazy, are ignorant, and so on) and the generally accepted idea that to be white is to be the summum bonum in America—both white and Black America. Undoubtedly some of the Blacks who relish these tales see themselves as standing outside of and apart from the group being ridiculed. Whether that view represents a healthy detachment from the pain and anxiety of being Black in America or a sick effort at escape from self and culture is an issue of some import which unfortunately cannot be resolved here.

Like the Black etiological myths, several of the tales generally assumed to be self-derogatory contain subtle elements which raise the question of whether the tales are ridiculing Blacks or are satirizing others. I have included the more obviously satirical tales in other chapters, but some items in this chapter contain elements of both self-criticism and social commentary, as do, for example, "Glad It Ain't Twelve O'Clock" (p. 81), "Pi-R-Square" (p. 88), and "Apt Lil' Boy" (p. 90). Finally, it should be noted that self-derogatory tales are popular also in other ethnic groups (Jewish, Irish, Puerto Rican, and so forth) in America. Several of the items in this chapter have a currency within other groups, the principals in the tales being changed to reflect the stereotypes of those groups. Indeed, many of the fools in these selections have appeared in different guises in innumerable countries for hundreds of years.

NOTES

1. John Oliver Killens, "Rappin' With Myself," in *Amistad 2*, ed. John A. Williams and Charles F. Hann (New York: Random House, 1971), p. 117.
2. Ibid., p. 118.

3. Zora Neale Hurston, *Dust Tracks on a Road: An Autobiography* (Philadelphia: J. P. Lippincott, 1971), pp. 215–37.

4. James Weldon Johnson, *Black Manhattan*, 2d ed. (New York: Alfred A. Knopf, 1940), p. 173.

5. See Russell Middleton and John Moland, "Humor in Negro and White Subculture: A Study of Jokes among University Students," *American Sociological Review* 24 (February, 1959): 66.

138   If This Tail Hole Break

Sam and Mose, they was off that day from work and walkin' 'round through the woods, and they saw a big hole and the fish bucket; and they think a bear was livin' in there. So they could see the young cub. So he [Sam] say, "I tell you what you do, Mose; you go down there tipsy-toe, and I'll stand up here and watch. If I see Ole Bear coming, we'll get away."

So Mose went on down in there; and Sam Boy, he was so busy lookin' 'round, he won't paying attention. The ole bear come up there and squez righ' by 'im; got everything by but his hine quarters, and he [Sam] rare back, grabbed that tail 'n' rared back, RARED BACK (to keep from letting him in). Mose say, Mose say, "What for you makin' that hole so dark up there, Sam?"

He say, "BOY, if this tail hol' break, you'll find out pretty quick what make it so dark up there."

139   Dumbest M.F.

One time there was a cop in New York, you know. See. He don't allow nobody on his beat. So here this dude, he's standin' on the corner, raring back; he's *slick*, you know. So the pohleese come up there and say, "Hey, nigger, what you doing on this corner? You know I don't allow nobody on the corner on my beat?"

The dude looked at the pohleese, say, "Sucker, you don't know who I am." Say, "I ain't thinkin' 'bout that shit!"

Pohleese say, "Well, all right, I tell you what. You be here when I get back." Say, "It take me a half an hour to roam my beat. If you be here when I get back, we gon' fin' out what you thinkin' about."

Dude, he *standin'* up on the corner, layin' up side the pole, you know. Pohleese came back. He *still* hadn't gone nowhere. Then he tol' 'im, he say, "Nigger, didn't I tell you that I don't 'low nobody on my beat?"

He say, "Sucker," say, "I tol' you that you don't know *who* I am." Say, "I stan' anywhere I *want* to stand."

Pohleese say, "You may stand *somewhere*, but you not gon' stand on the

corner on my beat." Say, "I don't 'low nobody on the corner." He pulled out
his *blackjack*, swung at that nigger, say, "Don't (BAM!) you know (BAM!)
that I'm (BAM!) the HEAD (BAM!) BEATINGNESS (BAM!) cop (BAM!) in
(BAM!) *town*?"

That nigger say, "Don't—you—know—that—I'm—the—dumbest—mother
—fucker—in—the—world?"

140 Big Bimbo

One time there was a dude in New York, you know. He was standin' on
the corner. So then the pohleese come up there to the corner and tol' 'im,
say, "Look-a-here," say, "you know I don't allow nobody on my corner." Say,
"What's yo' name?"

He say [in a tough voice], "Big Bimbo Bottom, motherfucker, Big Bimbo
Bottom!"

He say, "What's yo' wife name?"

He say, "Miz Bimbo Bottom, Miz Bimbo Bottom!"

He say, "Yeah?" Say, "What kind o' car you got?"

He say, "Cadillac, motherfucker, Cadillac!"

He say, "What you smokin' there, buddy?"

He say, "The best o' cigars, motherfucker, the best o' cigars."

He say, "Where you work?"

He say, "Nowhere, NOWHERE!"

So he say, "Well, I'm gon' take your ass down for vag [vagrancy]."

So he carried him on down the pohleese station, you know. When he got
down pohleese station, Judge asked him, he say, "What's yo' name?"

He say, "Big Bimbo Bottom, motherfucker, Big Bimbo Bottom!"

He say, "Yeah, what's yo' wife's name?"

"Miz Bimbo Bottom."

Judge tol' 'im say, "Well, I'm gon' ask you again, what's yo' name?"

He say, "Big Bimbo Bottom, motherfucker, Big Bimbo Bottom."

Then here come this ole big, *greasy* Black cop. He come in there, say, "Yo'
honor," say, "lemme have that nigger in the back room for a couple minutes." He say, "I'll fin' out all the information you *want*."

So Yo' Honor say, "Yeah, take 'im away!"

He carried 'im back in the back room, pull out that blackjack, tol' that
nigger, say, "Now, what's you name?"

He say, [with slightly less gusto] "Big Bimbo Bottom, motherfucker, Big
Bimbo Bottom."

He drawed that blackjack and hit that nigger up side his head: BIP!

Say, "What's yo' name?"

[With even less gusto.] "Big Bimbo Bottom, you fuckin' motherfucker, Big
Bimbo Bottom."

He drawed back and hit that nigger, and let that blackjack stayed on his head and hit him 'bout twenty times: BIP! BRRRRRD! "Nigger, what's yo' name?"

[Whimpering.] "Big Bimbo Bottom, motherfucker, Big Bimbo B-B-Bottom."

BIP! BIP! BIP! BIP! "What's yo' name?"

[Crying.] "Hhuh, hhuh, Big Bimbo Bottom, motherfucker, Big Bimbo Bottom."

BIP! BIP! "What's yo' name?"

[Sobbing loudly.] "Thomas Lee."

BIP! "What's yo' wife's name?"

"Hhuh, Lu*cille*."

BIP! "What kinda car you got?"

"Oldsmo*bile*."

BIP! "What you smoking?"

"Oooh-wahhh, Chester*fields*."

BIP! "What changed yo' mind?"

"The blue *steel*."

BIP! "If I turn you loose, will you go home?"

[Completely humbled.] "I showly *weel-l-l*."

141   Glad It Ain't Twelve O'Clock

This takes place in Mississippi. This Black fellow had been to New York about twenty years. So he's coming back home. And he's all dressed up in his pimp suit. And he's on the bus. And gets off the bus, and the first person he sees is a policeman. He say, "HE-E-EY, Mr. Policeman, what time is it?"

That policeman, seeing this Black like this, say, "Come here, *nigger!*" Grabbed him by the collar, took his billy club, say, BIP! BIP! BIP! BIP! [Dramatizing policeman hitting Negro four times.] "It's four o'clock."

So the Black guy say, "GO-O-ODDAMN! I glad it ain't twelve o'clock!" He jumped back on the bus and went back to New York.

142   Listen to the Wheelbarrow

He decided to go in some friend's watermelon patch and steal some watermelons. And it was kinda moonshiny down there like that. And he had one of these old wooden wheelbarrows with the—it was all wood except it was a steel bar goin' through it, like that, and the old thing was rusty, and as it go turn over, it would say, "I'syouIwouldn'tgo, I'syouIwouldn'tgo!"

But he went on down there anyway. He got out in the middle of the patch and reached out and picked up a great big watermelon like that and put on the—

A man say VHOMP! [Dramatizing man hitting thief.] He grabbed the wheelbarrow! The ole wheelbarrow say, "ITOLYASO, ITOLYASO!"

143   Watermelon

This man had a watermelon patch, and the people used to steal watermelons. So one day he was sittin' up down there watchin' 'em. This fellow came in there and got the biggest watermelon in there and bust it like that [illustrating] and just took the heart out and ate it. He crept up on 'im. He say, "Yeah, you did it. It's yours, eat it EVERY BIT!" He made 'im eat all the watermelon, chew up the rinds. Then he said, "Next time you want a watermelon, ask me."

And if you want to fight that man [the thief], you just holler, "Watermelon!"

144   I Ain't Scared o' You

My mother said back in their days, you know, they used to call each other Aunt [pronounced ahnt] and everything. They didn't say Mrs. Julia Jennings, or Mrs. So and So. They used to call 'em Aunt Julia. So they say, Aunt Julia was awfully scared of thunder storms, and say every time she see a black cloud comin' she would always try to make her way to somebody's house. She say, but that day every house she went to, everybody was gone. Say, she kep' runnin', kep' runnin', kep' runnin', and say she started to the next house, went over there. The lady named Cindy. She say, "Well, I think I'll go over there to Aunt Cindy's house." Say, when she got almost there, the cloud had al-l-l-most caught her. Say, it looked like the cloud was just driving down on her. Say, she looked back there. She say, "GOD! You know I ain't running from you, but I'm just running trying to git whar somebody at. But I ain't scare o' you, 'cause I know you can reach me anywhere I go, but I ain't runnin' from you. I'm just running tryin' to get where somebody live."

145   Noisy Oil Can

The father sent this fellow down to the place to get some oil, you know, and it was dark. And he had a oil can didn't have no top on it. And he was kinda halfway scarish, and he started runnin' and sumpin' would say, "Whompf, whompf, whompf-whompfwhompf!" And he LAID out. He ran till he finally got down to a place where he had to stop—and it won't a thing in the world but the oil can top. He was runnin' and the wind was blowin' 'cross the top, and he didn't know it.

146   Running

A.   This fellow say he went out to the battlefield when he was a younger man. Say he was scarry, you know. So when they got out to the battlefield, say the battle had started up, and said a fellow shot at 'im. He heard the bullet pass 'im, and he turned 'round and caught up and passed the bullet.

B.   And another fellow say they shot at him out in battle like that, and say one o' those high-powered bullets, say, he felt it slap right back here, SWIP! like that [striking the back of his neck] and say he carried it for 'bout a mile [dramatizing a man running too fast for the bullet to penetrate], and he stumped his toe and fell. The bullet passed on 'cross and kill a mule standing up on the hill.

147   Striking Twelve

A buddy of mine went over in the next county to see a girl, a little girl over there. But you know the boys had a way o' runnin' you back over your side. And say one night when he left the girl's house, say good-bye at the gate, say the village clock was striking the hour of twelve: BONG, BONG, BONG! And said he lived a mile away, and when he run in his gate, the clock was still striking twelve.

148   Contest

Two masters were debating on what their niggers could do. One said his nigger could do anything a bear could do. So they put the nigger on one end of a stage and a bear on the other end, facing each other.
The bear came toward the man and shook his head.
The man came toward the bear and shook his head.
The bear came nearer and pawed.

The man came nearer and pawed.
The bear dumped a big load.
The man said, "Umph, I did that when I first seen that bear."

149   He Is Lazy

This man had some slaves, and he was saying that he had the laziest slave in the world. And said he was so damn lazy he wouldn't do anything for himself. And the [other] man say, "Naw-w-w, you don't have a slave this lazy."
He said, "Yes I do."
He said, "Naw you don't either. I bet you don't."
So he say, "I got a slave, named John. He is so lazy he won't even fuck."
Man says, "Oh, now, wait a minute now. Them slaves, now, fucking, that's their thing."
He say, "I was sittin' outside the barn, and all I could hear there was, 'Git up, mule—Whoa!—E-e-e-easy now!' I couldn't figure it out to save my life."
He say, "What was he doing?"
He say, "I don't know what he was doing. But all I could hear was John saying, 'Git-up, mule—Whoa!—E-e-e-easy now!' I cracked the damn door and here the nigger was standin' up on two feet of barrel head with the damn mule in front of him, and he had his thing in his hand, tryin' to make the mule move ahead. He say, 'Git-up, mule.' The mule would move on; he'd say, 'Back up—Whoa!—E-e-e-easy-y-y now.' When you find a nigger too lazy to fuck, he is lazy!"

150   Tongue and Teeth

Mr. Charlie, he was the boss man. He had a lot of slaves. He had one of 'em, he told everything he knew. One day he was coming through the woods; he walked up on a skeleton, and he saw the skeleton layin' down. He kicked 'im. He say, "Skeleton, what are you doing here?"
The skeleton tol' him, "Tongue and teeth brought me here and gon' bring you here."
So he goes home and he tells his master 'bout this skeleton down in the woods talking. And the master said, "I tol' ya 'bout lying to me!"
But he swore that he was right.
His master said, "I'm going down there with you, and if that skeleton don't talk I'm gon' kill ya."
He picked up his shotgun and the two went on back in the woods and ask

the skeleton what he was doin' there. He asked 'im three times, kicked 'im, but the skeleton wouldn't say a thing. Master drawed out the shotgun and shot 'im [the slave].

The skeleton say, "I tol' ya tongue and teeth brought me here, bring you here too!"

151 Accidents

This is supposedly a true story. I heard it from another party. There was a driver who works for the [name deleted] Bus Company, and he'd been in a couple of accidents—about two in a six-month period—and so the supervisors and some of the big people there called him in to see what they could do about him having all these crashes with their buses. So the guy came in, and they decided they were going to put him on probation, and they were going to send him through a specialized drivers' training course. Now he was upset about having to take this drivers' training course because he considered himself a good driver. And so he finally blasted out, "I never woulda had these damn accidents if I hadn't been drunk!"

And so they fired him.

152 Same Ole Goddamned Cat

One time there was a white man, a Chinese, and a Black man. So they come down here and stopped at this house. So they [the man at the house] tol' 'em, say, "I need some help."

So all three of 'em volunteered and worked. So that evening they went in there and ate. And the man say, "Yawl kin stay on here," say, "but yawl got to sleep outdoors. I can't have nobody sleepin' in here with my young daughter in the same house. My daughter ain't nothin' but sixteen, and if anybody come in here, I got a old tomcat here. He'll let me know."

So everybody say, "Awright." They went on out there. 'Bout 'leben or twelve o'clock, they thought that the ole man was sleep. Lil' girl had tol' 'em, say, "When Daddy go to sleep you try to sneak in the house."

So the white man, he the first one. He go on in there. He was going upstairs and here a step squeak. When the step squeak, the ole man say, "Who dat? WHO DAT?" and grabbed the shotgun. The ole white man froze, and then he thought about the cat. White man say, "Me-ow, me-ow." Ole man say, "Oh, it ain't nothin' but that old cat." He [white man] went on up there, grabbed the girl up and turned around; he come on back.

Then the Chinese and the Black man asked him, "Well, how you go?"

He say, "It's a step in there; you gotta watch the step, but if anybody holler, just pretend you a cat."

So the Chinese went on in there. The step squeaked and the ole man say, "Who dat? WHO DAT?" Chinese say, [assuming Chinese accent] "Me-oh, me-oh." Man say, "Oh, shit! It ain't nobody but that old cat." So the Chinese went in there. He screwed her and he come on back.

Black man say, "How'd it go?"

He say, "Oh, it went all right, but you gon' hit a screechy step, and he gon' ask you who is that, and you got to tell 'im it's the same old cat."

The Black man went on in there and the step squeaked. Ole man say, "Who dat? WHO DAT?" Black man say, "Ain't nothin' but this same ole goddamned cat!"

153   Shove It Up You

One time they had a white man, a Chinese, and a Black man. They were working on this man's farm, you know. Man tol' 'em, "Now yawl kin work here. I'll give yawl somethin' to eat and everything; but I'm gon' tell you. If I catch any *yawl* messin' 'round wid my daughter—" Say, "Yawl out there pickin' them fruit." Say, "I'm gon' take some o' them fruits and ram it up your ass."

They say, "Awright."

So then that night they turned around and all o' 'em got on her; they just rode on the daughter. Next morning ole man found out. Ole man say, "Well, I told yawl what I was gon' do to you. Now go out there and git somethin' out the garden, 'cause I'm gon' *shove* it up you."

White man went out there and he got a *tomato* and he [the father] took hol' of it and tried to push the tomato up him.

Chinese went out there. Chinese got a little string bean, and he [the father] pushed it up there.

All of a sudden the Chinese and the white man bust out laughing. Farmer turned around, say, "What yawl laughin' at?"

They say, "Look at that *goddamned* nigger over there tryin' to pick up a goddamned watermelon!"

154   Does Polly Want a Cracker?

There was this Black and he wanted to have a real unusual pet. So one day he went to the pet store that specialized in unusual pets. So he asked the owner if he had a pet that was real unusual that no one else would have. So the owner goes out and brings back an owl, and the Black says, "Owls are not that unusual."

So the owner goes out and brings back a boa constrictor, and the Black man says, "I don't want a boa constrictor. I know a lot of people who have boa constrictors."

So the Black man continued to look around in the store, and he came across this really unusual Parrot. The Parrot was in a cage smoking a pipe, reading a newspaper, and crossing his legs. So the Black man says, "Polly wants a cracker," and the Parrot says nothing and politely turns a page of his newspaper. So the Black man says it again, "Polly wants a cracker," and the Parrot says nothing and turns another page of his newspaper. So the Black man gets angry and says, "Goddammit, does Polly want a cracker?"

So the Parrot takes his pipe out of his mouth, puts down his newspaper, and uncrosses his legs and says very calmly, "Does nigger want a watermelon?"

155 Confused Undertaker

This fellow, he was an undertaker, and he was kind of backward, not knowing how to carry on his business or anything. He always, when he got ready to bury a body, go up and ask somebody. So one time he got so *confused* he went on with the people to the graveyard. And he was so excited, say, he buried the hearse and kept the body.

156 Buzzard Oil

I heard the old folks say that you could get buzzard oil; you could put it on your joints, and you'd be like those acrobats, get all limber like that, see, you know. Well, I wanted some buzzard, oil. I say, "Where you get it?"

They say, "You kill a buzzard, you boil 'im, and you get the grease."

So I shot a buzzard. Buzzard ain't got nothin' but his framework, and I went down there and I just boiled him to pieces. Didn't nothin' come out there.

So they say, "What you do, when you shoot a buzzard, you take 'im and bury in the ground nine days, and then the earth will fatten 'im."

I shot another one and put him in there. Ain't nothin' come out o' that one. So they say, "You was dumb, won't you?"

157   Back to the Cotton Fields

This Negro out the cotton fields went to Morehouse. They checked him out at Morehouse, and they told him, say, "Son, you better go on back down in the cotton fields. You can't make it here at Morehouse—On the second thought, you just go on over to Morris Brown; you *might* make it over there."

The sonovagun went on over to Morris Brown, fooled 'round there and he finished with an A.B. degree, cum laude. So he decided he'd further his education. Went on over to Atlanta U. Sonovagun got his masters, magna cum laude. He say, "Well, I keep doing all right." Just about the time the computers came in, the sonovabitch came on up to Washington, to Howard, got his Ph.D., this time *summa* cum laude. That Negro was feeling *real proud* of himself. He went down to one of the big Federal Buildings to get him a job. He dropped his credentials down; he say, "Daddy, read 'em and give me somethin'!" He say, "I'm *here!* You know it's equal employment now."

The guy looked at him, he say, "Well, mister, with your qualifications we can put you over here in this office. You'll have three hundred and fifty people under you, three secretaries, a supervisor . . ."

He say, "Shit, that's the trouble with you white folks, you want to make a [unclear] outta me. Look, I don't want that bullshit. Put *my* stuff in that computer; let the computer tell me what I'm gon' have."

Guy say, "Well, what's your education?"

He say, "Well, I have Morris Brown, cum laude, Atlanta U., magna cum laude, Howard, summa."

He say, "Well, look fellow, you have to—for a computer—you gotta go all the way back to grammar school, get everything from grammar school all the way up."

"All right, I'll be back Monday with everything."

Monday he came back and the guy put that stuff in the computer for him. BA-BA-DA-DA! [Sounds of the computer.] All of a sudden it came out and the guy looked at it. He say, "Well, Mister, say, I tell you what, say you better read this *yourself.*"

He looked at it . . . It say, "Nigger, you better take your raggedy ass back to that cotton field in Georgia."

158   Pi-R-Square

They say during the time, you know, they were trying to get all these job opportunities and everything for Blacks and get 'em spotted in these places, they had an office up there in Washington and they had to fill it. They ran out of qualified Blacks, so they just picked up this Black and put him in

there. They told 'im, says, "All you got to do is interview people coming in."
So he's settin' up in this big office, you know, like he's buyin' it, so the first
guy come in. He says, "What did you major in college?"

The fellow told him, said, "Uh, I majored in French."

He said, "Speak a little French."

He says, "Parlez-vous français?"

The guy said, "Okay, we'll keep your application, and I'll call you, you
know, when I make a selection."

That guy left and another guy walked in. He says, "What did you major in
college?"

He says, "I majored in German."

He say, "Well, speak a little German."

He says, "Guten morgen."

He says, "Okay, we'll take your name down, and, uh, you know, if we hear
anything, we'll call you."

Another guy came in. He says, "What did you major in in college?"

He said, "Mathematics,"

He said, "Speak a little mathematics."

He said, "Pi-r-square."

He say, "Look," say, "Hold it a minute, don't—don't leave," say, "Set
down." He said, "I know I shouldn't have this job"; he say, "They put me
here, and I'm trying to do the best I can; I know I'm not qualified, but let me
tell you one thing: Don't you ever go anywhere and tell nobody pie are
square; pie are round! Cornbread are square."

159 You Count to Two

This concerns a Black student aviator, who wanted to be a pilot. And he
had failed every possible exam, and finally the commissioned officer in
charge said, "Why don't you try parachute jumping?"

And he agreed to this, and they put him in the parachute outfit, on his
back, and they put 'im in the plane and the C.O. said, "Now, wait a minute. I
don't think we've schooled him properly."

He said, "Oh, yes you have. You-you-you've sc-sc-sc-schooled me properly."

So the man said, "Well, it's a very simple process. You simply count to ten
and pull the rip cord." And this is all the instructions that were given to the
man.

As they climbed higher in altitude, he went, "I don't b-b-b-believe I uh-
uh-uh-under-st-st-st-stood-d-stood you. How-how-how-how much d-d-d-did
you say to c-c-c-count?

And the commissioned officer said, "You count to two."

160　Wait Till I Learn

Here's a guy sticking mail [dramatizing someone throwing mail in several slots, under one leg, over his head, and so on, with unbelievable speed], BAM! BAM! BAM! BOOM! BANG! He just sticking—all up under his legs! He just stickin' it!

A guy say, "Great-t-t day! That's what I call a *clerk!* That guy kin stick some mail!"

He say [without any interruption in the speedy slinging of mail—under his arms, over his back, under his legs], "Yeah! You wait till I learn where this stuff *really* go! I'm gon' show ya sumpin."

161　I'll Gratify Your Wishes

One day a maid overheard her mistress and her boyfriend talking. As he was leaving she heard the young lady say to her fiance, "The next time you come I'll gratify your wishes."

When the maid went out on the next date with her boyfriend, she was satisfied that she knew exactly what to say when he left her. So when he said good night, she replied, "The next time you come I'll grab it out your britches."

162　Apt Lil' Boy

My daddy wasn't a slave, but he was a—I think his mother was a slave. And he was a little boy and his mother cooked—for those slave-time people—and he had to take the food from the kitchen to the dining room. They had a group of men sittin' around the table, he said, "plottin' on what to do with us and things like that." And he said he was carrying (his mother made hoe-cakes) and he had to pass 'em 'round to everybody. And he was standin' there with this plate and gave it to one man—one man took the *whole* cake. And he was standin' there waitin' for 'im to break it and put some back, and he say, "Go on, *boy!* If I want any more I'll let you know."

Then the man said, "That's a *apt* lil' boy."

And he cried—he went in the kitchen and cried—told his mother, he said, [sobbing] "The man say I was a apt lil' boy, and I thought he meant I was *apt* to steal a biscuit."

163 Potatoes in de Jackets

The white peoples was goin' out on a visit, and she told huh cook to bake some potatoes in de jackets. And she [the cook] didn't know what "the jacket" mean, and she couldn't think. So she went in there and got all the white lady's cloth where she was gon' make clothes out of and cut it and baste it 'round the 'taters—making jackets to bake the 'taters in. Put the 'taters in the stove and then made the jackets out the white lady's sewing cloth. When they come in for dinner, and there she had all the cloth around the 'taters on the table.

164 Ain't No Sense in Killing Two Horses

Two Blacks walked into the bar, and the bartender said, "What are you going to have, fellows?"
He say, [drunkenly] "I don't know. The same thing I been drinkin' all the time."
He say, "What was that?"
He said, "Oh, horse's neck."
He said to the other one, "What you gon' have?"
He say, [even more drunkenly["Well, ain't no sense in killin' two horses."

165 Jesse's Cut

This lady was riding on a train, and she had a son named Jesse. Every stop that they would get to, the conductor would holler, you know, what stop it was. So they were riding along, and so they got to this stop called Jesse's Cut. So the conductor say, "All aboard for Jesse's Cut! All aboard for Jesse's Cut!"
She *jumped* up! "MY GOD! Who cut Jesse?"

166 Those Ritis Brothers

This lady was sick, and she met a friend one day that she hadn't seen for a good while. And he said to her, "Well, I haven't see you for *months!*"

She said, "No, I've been laid up with arthritis."
He said, "Oh, I know those Ritis brothers. The one they call Arthur is a dog!"

167   We Shave and Shampoo

This lady's husband was named Bob Cock. So she went to this barber shop and hollered in the door at the barber, "Do yawl Bob Cock?"
And the barber said, "No, we shave and shampoo."

168   Pass Your Plate

This lady was going into the big city of New York, and, you know, it's a true saying, "You can get the girl out the country, but you can't get the country out the girl." And this girl went to New York to live with her rich cousins.
And say, they took her out to all these fancy homes, and feedin' her, and so, she was so elated over what was happening. She finally said—no, somebody said, "Lucy, pass your plate!"
Say, she say, "Which one? The upper or the lower?"

169   Who Wrote That Thing?

The teacher had this boy in school. And he wrote a note to a little girl, telling her how much he loved her and all. And when she [the teacher] asked a question, said, "Who wrote the Declaration of Independence?" (He was smart, this little boy.) But, he got up and he couldn't answer it. She was positive this little boy knew the answer (but he really didn't) and so she got angry with him. She said, "I know you know it." So she said, "I'm going to write a note to your Daddy that you just playing in class today and wouldn't answer questions that you know."
So she wrote this note and the daddy came to school the next day. And she told him, "I asked him who wrote the Declaration of Independence."
And the old man [imitating father looking suspiciously] said, "And he know it?"
"Yes."

He said, [angry that the boy is tryin' to protect some culprit] "Boy, if you don't tell that woman who wrote that thing, I'm gon' beat the devil out of you!"

170   Lesson Completed

When my mother was teaching she had this child who was always saying "I have went." And, say, she tried her best to make her say "I have gone." And so she said one day, "You stay right in here (she excused the other children) and you write 'I have gone' one hundred times."

So the child sat down and wrote, "I have gone, I have gone" one hundred times. Then she wrote on the bottom of the paper, "I have written 'I have gone' one hundred times; now *I have went home.*"

171   Learn Her

Another time Mama was teaching, and she smacked this girl, and she went home and told her mama. Say the mother wrote her a note, say, "I'm sending Sue to school for you to learn her. Don't slap her, and don't hit her. Just learn her."

172   All Those Pencils

This lady lived in the country, and she brought her daughter in town to church. So when they was playing the organ, she was sittin' there, and, after a while, she said to her mother, say, "Mother, look at all those pencils." Say, "You know it took a long time to trim all them pencils!"

173   Jesus Died to Save You

This ole fellow was sittin' in church one *Sunday* morning, and this new preacher was just preaching! And he [the old fellow] didn't attend church too much, but he was sittin' up there in front. This man was preaching away, and he said, "Brothers and Sisters, didn't you know Jesus died to save you?"

This ole Brother looked at him, said, "I didn't know Jesus was even sick. If they'd tol' me I woulda gone to see 'im."

174   Doctor, You Treat Her

A. This fellow took his wife to the doctor and say, "Doc, my wife— sumpin' wrong wit' huh! I don't know what's wrong wit' huh. She jest sick all de time 'n' she didn't wanna come, an' I jest made huh come to you today." Say, "I want you to examine huh."

The doctor said, "All right, I'll see what I can find out."

He said, "Well, I'm gon' wait out chere."

The doctor said, "Well, that's my procedure, Sir."

So he examined her and called him in. He said, "I've examined your wife. She's perfectly healthy, but the problem here is your wife needs constant intercourses."

He say, "Uh, hun, all right, Doctor, anything you say. Well, now, Doc, I wan' you jest give it to huh. Give it—"

He said, "Naw, I think you can—"

He say, "I don't know nothing 'bout no constance instacourses or whatever that you say. I'm payin' you. I wancha—'cause I'm tired o' huh being sick."

He say, "But this is somethin' you kin do."

He say, "You do it, Doctor, and if you do it, I know 'twill git done right."

So she, not knowing what an intercourse was (not knowing what the word was), said, "All right, Sir."

So finally he took her in. He said, "This is the strangest request I've ever had." He said, "You've got to take your clothes off again." So he put her on the table (and she proceeded to look at him strangely), and he took off his clothes (and she looked at him strangely), and he got on top of her, and she said, [very meekly] "Well, I guess this is all right." Well, the doctor just tore her up, and she just MOANED AND GROANED.

So the husband heard the moaning and groaning, so he peeped in there. He say, [upset voice] "Doc, what's goin' on?"

He said, [very professional tone] "I'm giving her the intercourse that she needs."

He say, [obvious relief in his voice] "Oh, that's all right—'cause for a minute there I thought you was fuckin' huh!"

B. This is an individual who had been married to a young lady for about two or three years, and he had not made any personal contact with her—at least not often enough. And she began to be rather upset. So he decided to take her to the doctor. And he took her to the doctor and waited out in the waiting room. He waited quite a while. The doctor had her in there, talking to her and everything like that, trying to prescribe some type of medicine for her. And after a while the doctor sent his wife out and stuck his head in the waiting room and asked the husband to come in; he wanted to have a little conference with him. So he decided to tell him, "What your wife needs is intercourse."

So he say, "Well... thank... you, doctor."

So he carried his wife home. And after he carried his wife home, he decided to go down to the drugstore, and he asked for a dollar's worth of intercourse. And the pharmacist, he sort of sniggled a little bit, you know. Went back in the back and told one of his other assistants, "Somebody out here asking for a dollar's worth of intercourse." He say, "What shall I say?"

Guy say, "I tell, ha, ha, you what to do. Send him to the next drugstore."

So the pharmacist went out there. He say, "Well, look, we fresh sold out; we don't have any more; we sold out. Why don't you try the drugstore down the street?"

So he went and asked for another dollar's worth of intercourse. And they went through the same routine. And he just went all 'round the loop, everywhere in the neighborhood. And he went back to the doctor, he say, "Doctor, you know you told me my wife needed intercourse. I went everywhere, all the drugstores, in my area, trying to buy a dollar's worth of intercourse, and they all say they've sold out."

So the doctor looked at 'im, kind of turned his head a lil' bit and laughed. He say, "I tell you what to do. Bring your wife in to the office and let me talk to her again."

He say, "Okay, doctor." So he went and got his wife; arranged an appointment, carried his wife back to the office. And his wife went into the examination room. After he had been seated there for quite a while, and all the other patients had left—even the secretary had left; the receptionist had left—and he was there by himself for two or three hours. He kept looking at the keyhole. He say, "I should peep and see what's going on in there. She's been in there so long!" He say, "Naw-w-w-w! I guess I'll read another magazine." After a while, he say, "Well, I'll take a little peep."

So he went and peeped through the hole there and saw his wife up on the examination table with her clothes off, the doctor on top of his wife. He opened the door up quick! He say, "Doctor! Doctor! What are you doing?"

He say, "I'm only giving her a lil' intercourse."

He say, "Oh-h-h, that's all right. For a moment I thought you were..." (I wouldn't say it).

C. The doctor told him, "In the meantime you go home and practice. In the meantime you come hold my balls up and see what I'm doing."

Okay, so the man went home and he got ready to have his intercourse, but he ain't have no operating table. So he got the ironing board. And then he thought, "I ain't got nothin' to hol' my balls up."

So...

Okay, the wife had to call the doctor. This joker's back was broke and all that kinda stuff. So he tol' the doctor, say, "You know, everything was going fine, except to get somebody to hold my balls up." So he tied 'em up to the damn light fixture, and . . . the damn ironing board broke.

175   That's Right!

This man drank real heavy, you know, and he was so used to stayin' out at night that his wife thought he was gon' stay out that night. She had her boyfriend there and they had gone to bed.

He came in there and looked in the bed there. He know 'twas somethin' wrong. He got ready to get in the bed. He turned the cover back and count the feet. He say, "One—two—three—four." He say, "That ain't right!" He count 'em again. He say, "One—two—three—four." He say, "That's right. Ain't s'posed to be but four feet in there."

He forgot his feet was on the floor.

176   How Are You So Smart?

There were three prisoners in jail—a white man, Jew man, and a Black man. The warden said, "The smart man will be released, if you tell me the various parts of the body." The warden asked the white man to step forward. The warden pointed to the man's kneecap. The white man said, "This is my leg." The warden pointed to the man's elbow. The white man said, "This is my arm." The warden pointed to the man's toe. The white man said, "This is my foot." The warden said, "Shut up! You too stupid to leave. Step back in line."

The warden asked the Jew to step forward. The warden pointed at the same things. The prisoner said, "It is my leg; it's my arm, it's my foot." The warden said, "Step back, you're stupider than the other."

The Black man stepped forward, and said, "This is my leg [kneecap], my elbow, and my toe."

The warden said, "You're right. How are you so smart?"

The Black man pointed to his head and said, "I got it from my ass!"

177   Damn If I Remember

It was a drunk going down the street. And he was standing there drunk and hanging on the post. And he had to heave up everything. And this old dog came up and start to eating it.

The drunk [looked down] said, "I remember eating them *beans*; I remember eating that *ham*; but I be damn if I remember eating that *dog*."

178   The Wrong Man

Once was two men going to association, and before they get there, they had to lay down and went to sleep. And both of them had on a long coat. Somebody slipped there and cut one of the men coat off short. So when the man get up to wash his face to go on, he look 'round. He say, "Oomp!" Say, "You must be wake up the wrong man 'cause when I lay down just now, I had on a long coat. Now I got on a short coat. They shore wake up the wrong man!"

179   Missin' 'Possum

There was a ex-slave, you know. Had a lil' cabin all to himself. He had been out and caught himself a 'possum—picked 'im, baked it all like he wanted, you know. Sittin' there at the table anticipating how good it was gon' taste, he dropped off to sleep. His son came in, saw him sittin' there with it. So he took and slipped the 'possum out from there and ate it. Then he took the bones, put the plate—and the ole man was sleepin' so sound he even greased his hands and his fingers with it. He got behind the curtain to see what was gon' happen when he woke up.

The ole man woke up: "Well, now I gon' eat my 'possum." And he looked at the plate—the 'possum was gone—a whole lot o' bones around there. He was trying to figure this thing out among himself: "Now I know the 'possum was there when I went to sleep. I don't see how I coulda ate it, but I kin say *one* thing: If I did eat that 'possum, it done me less good and give me less satisfaction than any one I ever et in *my* life before."

180   New Bathroom

They said that out in Powhatan County there was an old colored couple, and they raise tobacco mostly up there. And they had a bad year. So the boy's sister had left and gone to New York to get work. So the boy decided later on that he wouldn't farm any more. He was going to New York where his sister was. So that year they had a *bumper* crop.

So the old lady thought she'd sit down and write to the boy and tell 'im about it. So she said:

"Dear John: I'm writing you dis letter to tell you how we been gittin' along. We's doing jest *fine*. We done made a big crap o' tobacco, and we took it to Richmond and we *sold* it. And den we went to dat Sears and Roebuck, and dey were awful nice to us. I bought yo pappy a new suit; and dey done sol' us one o' dem *bathroom* suits. And dey put it in. And *dat thing* is a *humdinger!* You got *three* white bowls: one you kin wash yo' hands and face; and the big one, you kin get in it and take a bath *all* over; and that one in the other corner, with the top on it, you kin put one foot in there and wash it; den you kin flush the water and get clean water and wash the other foot. Now it had two tops to it. But we ain't find out what dem tops is for. But we makin' de biscuit dough on *one*, and de tother one, we done framed your grandpappy's picture in it and hung it on de wall. Den dey was so nice, dey give us a roll o' writin' paper to go wid it."

181   In Hell, Just Like I Thought

This fellow lived in the country, and they had put the rumor out that the world was coming to an end. So he didn't know what to do. He climbed up there on the wagon, which was full of hay, and put 'im a chair up there. And he sat up there waiting for the world to come to an end. So while he was waiting he lighted his pipe, and he dropped off to sleep smoking, and a spark flew in the hay. And it put the hay on fire, and when he woke up, the hay was in a flame. He say, "Oh, Lord, just like I thought. In hell, just like I thought!"

182   Dumb Negroes, Dumb Bosses

There were two old farmers (they were white), and they had two Negroes working for 'em. They were sittin' out in the yard, and one sez to the other, sez, "You see that guy there. He's the *dumbest* that I've ever seen!"

And he sez, "Oh, no, you haven't seen a *dumb* Negro." Sez, "You ought to see mine. I'll prove it to you." He said, "Come here, Bill." He said, "Take this *quarter* and run downtown to the Cadillac place and buy me a Cadillac."

"Yassir!" He went on down.

The other one called his. He said, "Come here, Job. You run down to my house and see if I'm *there*."

So he runs on down to his house, and he met Bill coming back, out of breath, and said, "Where you going, man?"

Bill said, "Do you know what that fool dumbbell that I work for said?" He said, "That *dumbbell* tol' me to go down to the Cadillac place and buy a Cadillac—and *how* I gon' buy dis Cadillac if he don't tell me what color or what kind?"

The other one said, "Well, this *fool* tol' me to run down to his house and see if he was there—and the fool sittin' right by the phone. Why didn't he call up down there and see whether he was home?"

183　Had to Get Away

Segregation was rampant even between the mulattoes and other slaves. One mulatto ran away from his master " 'cause he could not live in that town no longer. Nothing there but sea ticks and chiggers; po' white folks and black niggers."

184　Where? Where? Where?

Riding through the white areas of Georgia, a Black man slipped unnoticed on the bus. He sat beside a white woman, unnoticed also. She finally turned around, and said, "Nigger!"

And he shouted, "Where? Where? Where?"

185　What Makes Me Hot

Say three girls (a white girl and a Chinese and a colored girl) was talking together. And the white girl say, "Lawd, a man feel my legs, it makes me so *hot!*"

And the Chinese girl [said], "A man feel my tiddies, it makes me hot."

The old colored girl sittin' over in the corner say, "Humph, man feel my legs don't make me hot; feel my tiddies don't make me hot neither. Fuck me and don't pay me, that's what make me hot."

186　*I* Can't Stand It

There was this big show in town. And on the gate there was a sign which said "One hundred dollars for the person who stays in the tent with this skunk for five minutes only." Three young men from in and around the little town came by the show. They read the sign and decided that they would give it a try. All three of them went home, took baths, and put on cologne. They came back to town and one by one went into the show. The first man went in, stayed only two minutes, and came yelling, "Whew! I can't stand it!"

The second man went into the show, stayed for about two minutes, too, and also ran out, yelling, "Whew! I can't stand it!"

The third man wouldn't give in. He went into the show, stayed about three minutes, then ran out: "Whew! I can't stand it!"

The events went on all day, with no one being able to collect the $100.00.

Late that evening an old farmer who had been working in the field all day came to town. The farmer read the reward sign and decided to give it a try. He went into the tent, found a seat, and got comfortable. Finally, he decided to take his shoes off to relax even more. Three minutes later the skunk ran out shaking his head, yelling, "Whew! I can't stand it!"

7

Oh, Lord,
Will I Ever?
The White Woman
and the Black Man

Black Man: Oh, Lord, will I ever?
White Man: No, nigger, never!
Black Man: As long as there's life, there's hope.
White Man: And as long as there's trees, there's
rope.

Folk Verse

A POPULAR folk motif is the Black man's preference for the forbidden white woman, a motif which at times also includes the white woman's attraction to the tabooed Black man.[1] Expressions so commonly heard in the conversations of Black males that they have become part of the Black folk idiom include "The only thing black I want is a Cadillac," "The only thing a Black woman can do for me is to lead me to a white woman," and "I don't haul no coal." The Black man's predilection for the white woman (Sterling Plumpp claims that "black men are addicted to white women") may be accepted generally as fact, as Black psychiatrists such as the renowned Frantz Fanon, William H. Grier, and Price M. Cobbs have recognized.[2] It can be confirmed through observing the choice of mates of successful and prominent Black American males.[3] It finds frequent substantiation in many confidential conversations among Black men and in frank accounts such as those recorded in Eldridge Cleaver's *Soul on Ice*. It can be seen in efforts such as those of Wilt Chamberlain to explain his frequent choice of white dates.[4] Ironically, just recently one of my close friends, a prominent citizen of Richmond, laughingly boasted that he had told a Negro woman that he would much prefer a French woman to her. His audience (all of us were Black women—there were no other men present) smiled politely, but none of us seemed to appreciate the little anecdote as enthusiastically as he. (I might note that we could at least smile politely because, though we are Black women, we aren't *black* women, and the fact that we aren't is undoubtedly why we have made "successful" middle-class marriages and are a part of this clique.)

The many complex issues in the Black man's experience in white American and European society that motivate his preference for the white woman and his rejection (and often hatred) of the Black woman cannot possibly be treated here, but I would like to mention a few. Probably the most prominent is that in American society whiteness is synonymous with beauty and status. In addition, the white woman is the one object that has been most forcefully forbidden the Black man, who might be subjected to all manner of violent punishment ranging from beatings to ritualistic castration for any familiarity with her.[5] Thus she, of necessity, becomes the one object he most desires—the ultimate symbol of success and of victory. Grier and Cobbs have noted:

> For the black man, the white woman represents the *socially identified* female ideal and thus an intensely exciting object for his sexual possession. She has been identified as precisely the individual to whom access is barred by every social institution.... He feels a sense of power at having acquired this highly valuable woman and a sense of power that she finds him desirable and indeed that she finds him more desirable than a white lover.[6]

And one perceptive inmate in jail with Eldridge Cleaver asserted:

> I know that the white man made the black woman the symbol of slavery and the white woman the symbol of freedom. Every time I embrace a black woman I'm embracing slavery, and when I put my arms around a white woman, well, I'm hugging freedom. The white man forbade me to have the white woman on pain of death. Literally, if I touched a white woman it would cost me my life. Men die for freedom, but black men die for white women, who are the symbol of freedom.[7]

Another reason for the Black man's desire for the white woman is obviously the sense that in subduing her he is in effect overcoming the society that has attempted to repress him. René Maran has commented on the element of revenge inherent in the Black man's conquest of the white woman: "The majority of them [Blacks in Europe] . . . tend to marry in Europe not so much out of love as for the satisfaction of being the master of a European woman; and a certain tang of proud revenge enters into this."[8] Further, Grier and Cobbs have pointed out that "the sexual act itself carries aggressive overtones. . . . In possessing the white woman he sees himself as degrading her (a function of his own feelings of degradation). . . ."[9] Finally, as Grier and Cobbs have suggested, the Black man sees the winning of the white woman as a direct victory for him in that eternal combat with the white man. They observe that "finally, and perhaps most importantly, he sees himself as having vanquished the white man in the field of love and of having rendered him impotent and castrated, for the white woman, in fantasy at least, has embraced a white lover and then chosen a black one."[10] Numerous jokes in Black folklore picture the Black man in a sexual contest with the white man, and, in this contest at least, the Black man is always victorious. (Those jokes involving white women which deal directly with that contest are included in chapter twelve.)

The idea that the sexual conquest and ultimately the destruction of the white woman are necessary for the achievement of a sense of manhood and freedom in the Black male is also a theme in much of Black American literature, most notably in Richard Wright's *Native Son*, Amiri Baraka's "Madheart," Eldridge Cleaver's "On Becoming" in *Soul on Ice*, Hal Bennett's *Lord of Dark Places*, and Ed Bullins' "A Minor Scene" in *The Theme Is Blackness*.[11] In "A Minor Scene" this theme is combined with that of the white woman's eagerness to give herself sexually to the Black man as an act of expiation for the guilt she feels for white racism. During the course of this short, absurd drama, the significantly named Peter Black heaps vile and violent abuses upon the appropriately named Miss Ann, who simpers and begs forgiveness for the sins of the white race. While he scurrilously assails her, he also longingly fondles her; and despite his hatred and her guilt (with all their equivocal implications), one thing is manifest—their uncontrollable lust for each other.

NOTES

1. While there are obviously Black women who are attracted to and who

prefer white men, this preference is not a subject of folklore (at least not as far as my research shows; I did not collect any tales of this nature) and therefore is not included in this discussion.

2. Sterling Plumpp, *Black Rituals* (Chicago: Third World Press, 1972), p. 93. See also Frantz Fanon, *Black Skin, White Masks* (New York: Grove Press, 1967), pp. 69, 72; and William H. Grier and Price M. Cobbs, *Black Rage* (New York: Bantam Books, 1969), p. 76.

I attempt here to suggest merely the historical prevalence of the situation and not to imply that every individual Black man prefers a white woman. While the term *white woman* is used in this discussion to indicate a woman of the white race, the general preference frequently accorded lighter Black women (and those whose hair and features closely approximate the Caucasoid's) is also relevant here.

3. See also Alex Bontemps, "Startling New Attitudes on Interracial Marriage," *Ebony* 30 (September, 1975): 144–51. Bontemps discusses intermarriages and reports the findings of a recent poll which show that Black men are more receptive to interracial marriages than are white men, white women, or Black women. He also points to the 1970 census, which shows a marked increase in the number of Black men married to white women.

4. See *Wilt* (New York: Macmillan, 1973), pp. 259–62.

5. A passing comment from one of my informants, "My luck was so bad I musta slapped a white woman," suggests that this is the sin for which one might expect the most severe punishment. The fact that racism in America (as well as in Africa and in Europe) is and always has been closely allied to the white man's belief in and fear of the Black man's sexual superiority is discussed further in chapter thirteen. The very nature of the lynch mob's punishment of Blacks—the sexual mutilation of the victim—suggests the white man's efforts to wrest from the Black man that symbol of manhood (that testiment of superiority) which he so fears.

6. Grier and Cobbs, pp. 76–77.

7. Eldridge Cleaver, *Soul on Ice* (New York: Dell, 1972), p. 149.

8. René Maran, *Un homme pareil aux autres* (Paris: Editions Arc-en-Ciel, 1947), p. 18, cited in Fanon, p. 69.

9. Grier and Cobbs, p. 77.

10. Ibid.

11. Leroi Jones, *Four Black Revolutionary Plays* (Indianapolis: Bobbs-Merrill, 1969), pp. 65–87; Cleaver, pp. 17–29; Ed Bullins, *The Theme Is Blackness* (New York: William Morrow, 1973), pp. 78–83.

187   She Forgot

My oldest brother, Willie. My grandmother took Willie over to the Christians where she worked, and this woman (the mistress of house) was *so* elated with Willie that she forgot Willie was a Negro and kissed him!

188   Swing Miss Susie Jane

A Negro slave used to call numbers for the whites' square dances. He'd be calling numbers, walking through the crowd, yelling, "Swing Miss Susie Jane and send her on back to me." In the meantime he would sometimes attempt to pat or touch a particular white girl whom he liked. The whites caught up with him. They took him and tied him to a tree. One got on either side of him with a whip and beat him back and forth, saying, "Hit that nigger on his ass and send him on back to me."

189   I Run My Hand Up Missis' Dress

During slavery days there were house hands and field hands. Well, this man was a house hand, but he had a friend who was in the fields; and every time he got a chance he would go out and talk with him. Well, the field hands very rarely got an occasion to come in the house, but every time he would talk to his friend that worked in the field, he would tell him how wonderful he was living in the house. He say, "OH, man, Ah tell ya, Ah have a good time up in that house." Say, "It's *wonderful* up there. They treat me *good*. Give me all kinds of good food and just let me have the *whole* use of the house. I just have a good time." Say, "I tell ya, every time I go upstairs," say, "you know what I do? I run my hand up Missis' dress."

He say, "Man, do you do that?"

He say, "I certainly do."

[Dramatizes the field hand pondering this at length.] "If I could get in that house *one* time. Don't they ever need extra help?"

He say, "Well, I tell ya what I'm gon' do." He say, "Next time it's time to do a lot of cleanin' I'm gon' tell 'em I need some help, and I'm gonna ask them to let you come up there to do some of the heavy lifting and," say, "then you can see."

OH, he went back to work so happy! Every time he'd see him, he'd say, "Hey, man, when they gon' start the cleanin'?" Say, "I'm *ready!*"

He say, "It won't be long now."

Finally, it was almost time for spring cleaning, so he suggested to the mistress, he said, "I have a friend who is real strong and he kin do a lotta work 'round here. Kin he come up here and help me when you start moving things around?"

She says, "Oh, I would be happy to have him. That's all right. Just tell him to come on and help."

So next day he went down there and said, "Man, the chance is here. We're gon' start today, and she said you could come."

He came on in and helped around, you know, and finally he say, "I'm going upstairs now to do some work," and there the mistress was in the room, and ALL of a sudden, such a SCREAMING, "HELP!"

He ran up the stairs; he say, "What's the matter, what's the matter?" And there she was, screaming. OH, she was just out! Everybody was around, and they was holdin' him. He said, "What happened? What happened?"

So he saw 'em carry him out. He didn't even know—and he heard all this hollering, "Kill 'im, kill 'im, kill 'im!"

So he say, "What happened, what happened? He just said he was gonna help me." So he got near him and whispered, "Man, what happened? What happened? What happened up there?"

He say, "I ran my hand up Ole Missis' dress."

He say, "Man, didn't you have better sense 'n that? You fool!"

He say, "Well, you said you ran your hand up her dress."

He say, "Yeah, man, but those dresses were hanging behind the door!"

190   Pretty Like a Peacock

White mistresses wanted some of these big black dicks, but they were afraid to death of their husbands, and could never let on that they felt so—even though they knew that their husbands slept with any nigger wench any time they felt like it. Had a special room and bed for it.

This particular Mistress would flirt with John whenever she got a chance. She would squeeze his dick and always say, "I want to be pretty like a peacock. Lord, make me pretty like a peacock. John, you are a wise nigger. Can't you make me pretty like a peacock?"

One day John got bold and told her to go down into the barn and get down on her hands and knees. John went down to the barn and thrust his rod up her. He went to town. She was panting and gasping, "Pretty like a peacock."

John bust his nuts a couple of times and then he started feeling and fondling her head and her hair.

She said, "Pretty like a peacock. John, don't bother about them head feathers. Just keep sticking them tail feathers in!"

191   I'd Make Your Ass Sparkle

A.   One old slave man used to watch his old Mistress and say to himself, "If I could get you one night, I'd make your ass sparkle."

One time he forgot and said it out loud, and she heard him. So she said,

"All right, I'll meet you one night, and if you don't make it sparkle like you said you could do, I'll tell Marsta."

So she set the night and the place. The old slave was worried because he didn't really know how he could make the sparkles. Finally he decided to catch him a jar of lightning bugs. When they started screwing he let one lightning bug go every now and then. When they reached the climax, he turned the whole jar of lightning bugs out.

Old Mistress never did tell old Marsta.

B. The one that had to do with the forbidden fruit of the white woman we used to tell all the time—especially when we were working on farms with white people. They used to get very upset about it.

This guy was out chopping wood: [chanting, with the sounds of chopping interspersed] "If I could just get a hold of Miss Ann's pussy (CHOP!), I'd make that pussy (CHOP!) strike fire! (CHOP!)."

And she heard him; she heard him. She say, "Un, hun, I heard ya. You better! You better make it strike fire. If you *don't* make it strike fire, I'm gon' tell on ya and they gon' hang ya."

So he say, "Okay, okay, I'll be down here 'bout nine o'clock."

She had the lil' boy down there watching. He started working out, and he had this bottle of lightning bugs, fireflies. He let one out, and the boy say, "There one spark." He let another one out: "There two sparks . . . there three sparks." Dropped the whole jar and they all flew out. He say, "You jest well get up 'cause he's settin' yo ass on fi-i-ire!"

192 Not Even for a White Woman

Master's daughter was oversexed and she just demanded from her daddy to get her any man with a sixteen-inch dick. Master couldn't find such a man. She demanded again. White man or nigger—but sixteen inches.

Master got his slave with the longest dick and told him the story: He said, "I don't want no black screwing my daughter, but she wants sixteen inches."

John said, "Naw suh, boss. Not even for a white woman. I wouldn't cut two inches off my dick for nobody!"

193 I'm Gon' Get Me a White Woman

This Black guy say, [excitedly] "I'm gon' get me a *white* woman, a *white* Cadillac, and a *white* suit, and ride down the roads o' *Georgia* in dat car!"

The guy say, "Well, you go right ahead—you know what I'm gon' do. I'm gon' get a *black* woman, a *black* Cadillac, a *black* suit, and ride down them *same* roads o' Georgia—and see your black ass hanging."

194   Please Give Me a White Woman

There was a nigger who wasn't a Christian, and they tried to convert him; said they were gon' make a Christian of him. Well, he said, "Well, I don't kn-o-ow; yawl haven't never proven to me that Christianity works or is worth anything atall. How do I know that you mean it?"

They say, "We gon' baptize you."

He say, "That doesn't mean anything to me. Make it *mean* something to me, and I'll go along with it."

They say, "All right. We gon' give you some wishes."

He say, "Give me *three*."

They say, "All right, we gon' give you three wishes. After that, can we *baptize* you?"

He say, "Yeah, you kin baptize me AFTER the three wishes."

So they carried him on; they say, "Well, we got to make it symbolic—we wancha to know what you're doing." So they carried him on over to the place where the monuments were. And they had a [statue] of the crucifix, arms adrape, and nails driven through the feet, thorns upon his head as a crown, and they said, "You must supplicate!"

He say, "What do you mean by that?"

They say, "Get on your knee-e-es and pray, and ask for something, but ask it in the name of the cross: 'Oh, Lord, I want...' and go on from there. You got it?"

He say, "I think I got it. Oh, Lord, I'd like to have a house for my mother; the poor woman hasn't had anything in her life. She wants something. Give it to her."

The man tapped him on the shoulder and say, "Rise, nigger, here's a deed to a brand new house for your mother."

He say, "Well, it worked."

Say, "Okay, we gon' baptize ya."

He said, "Nope! You said *three*. Don't start that. You said three."

"All right."

He said, "Well, I don't want to be selfish; you might have given that to her because she's my mother, but I'm gon' really test you. Give *me*, give ME a house. I want a house for myself."

So they gave him a house. He tapped him on the shoulder and said, "Here's the deed to a brand new house for *you*." So he got it. After that, the man standing by the side said, "How much longer we got to wait for this thing? We're wasting a lot of time."

He say, "You don't have much longer to wait." He said, "Well, I guess you know what the rest of it is. I've GOT to have me a Cadillac car. I've got to have it."

They said, "Well, we figured that and we got it ready for you. Look around, look around."

Say there it was—a brand new nineteen-seventy Cadillac car. He said, "Okay, come on, get the water ready. We gon' baptize. . . ."

"NOPE! Don't start that. Wait a minute. Don't do it like that. Yawl haven't been tested. Cars don't mean nothing to you, and these two houses—you got plenty of them. I never told yawl what I really wanted, and what I just got to have."

"Well, you just said that about the house for your mother and yourself and then this car."

He said, "I've got to have and want yawl to give me what I'm gon' ask for. Let me ask for it in my way." He got back down on his knees: "Oh, Lord, please give me —a *white woman!*"

The [statue] of the crucifix came alive and start shaking and trembling, and Christ said, "*Nigger*, if my *feet* weren't nailed to this *goddamn* cross, I'd kick your *ass!*"

195   Wag Your Tail

A Brother standing on the corner yells, "Yo, Mama!" to a white chick passing by. She does not turn her head. So he yells, "Damn, bitch, if you can't speak, wag your tail!"

8

I Could Eat Her Up:
Tales about Women

> He say, "Well, Reverend, it's like this: the first sev-
> eral months I was married to that woman, I felt like I
> could *eat her up!* And every since then I been mad
> with myself for not eatin' her up when I felt like it."
> "I Could Eat Her Up"

THE TALES THAT Blacks tell about women run the gamut from those
in which the man desires the woman so much that he could "eat her
up" (love her ardently) to those in which the man regards her with
such hostility that he could "EAT HER UP" (destroy her). Oddly
enough, there often is little distinction between the two attitudes, for
frequently the sexual desire for the woman is in itself a longing to
violate, to humiliate, to injure, and even to kill the woman.[1] Most of
these tales, obviously created by men, are blatantly antifemale. (A
few exceptions will be noted.)

In many of these tales, the man's one goal is to seduce the woman,
usually not because he wishes emotional involvement, love, or re-
ciprocal gratification, but merely for the pleasure of the conquest. If
he causes her pain, so much the better; and if he "fucks her to
death," the joke is even funnier. If on some occasions he meets a
woman (almost always a Black whore) who is too much for him and
instead dies himself, then he becomes a martyr whose great exploits
(that is, sexual prowess) are inscribed on his tombstone. See, for
example, "Peter Revere" (p. 239), in which the "awful whore" and
"dirty bitch" kills the sexually prodigious Pete instead of dying as a

nice lady would. Pete's epitaph reads, "Here lies a fucked-up fucking machine."

In those tales in which the woman is unwilling to submit or in which she makes certain stipulations such as the requirement of tenderness, affection, children, or marriage, the joke revolves around the man's overcoming or tricking her. In others the joke turns on the woman's great willingness and sexual insatiability, both of which immediately suggest her vulgarity or even her bestiality. These eager nymphomaniacs are usually either white women who have never had Black men, and therefore have never been satisfied, or Black women who can be satisfied only by animals or by men with phenomenally large or enlarged penises. (The common assertion in Black folklore that the Black male is sexually superior to the white male is discussed in detail in the introduction to chapter thirteen.) In the tales about rape, we find the common male belief that the woman really wanted it.[2] Then, of course, there are the jokes about prostitutes, the women who solicit sex for a price.

Much of the humor in the tales about women revolves around those physical and physiological aspects that distinguish the female from the male (her breasts, her vagina, her menstrual period), and most of the jokes are bitter. Extremely large or small breasts are the subject of many of these tales. The jokes about the genitals frequently turn on the inordinately large vagina. Gershon Legman suggests that the male fear that the penis is too small causes him to project his guilt onto the woman by suggesting that the problem is rather that her vagina is too big.[3] A perfect illustration is "Playing in a Large Cathedral" (p. 53), in which the minister insists that the problem is, not "that I have such a small organ, but my organ is playing in such a large cathedral." Several of the jokes also deal with the general repulsiveness of the malodorous genital area; it is no surprise that one of the most bitterly derided male victims in these jokes is the one who performs cunnilingus. An interesting exception is the popular group of tales about the dying man who decides to perform cunnilingus before his death, and this act, performed on a menstruating woman, restores his health, as in "The Transfusion" (p. 128). Menstruation is usually treated as a hindrance to the sexual gratification of the man. Several jokes deal with the loathsomeness of dirty sanitary pads, and others depict the menstrual period as some sort of injury. At times a male is the butt of some of these jokes, but even then the humor often revolves around the repulsiveness of the menstrual period.

One group of jokes about women deals with a boy's having sex with his mother or with his grandmother. Although some of the tales falling into this group may certainly be interpreted as expressive of an Oedipal complex (the boy's jealousy of the father and his positive libidinal feelings towards his mother), almost always the view of the mother or grandmother as completely complacent is derogatory. Other female butts of jokes include the nagging wife; the old, unattractive woman; the obnoxious, intrusive mother-in-law (invariably the wife's mother); and the lesbian.

I have placed those tales which emphasize racial stereotypes in chapters six and ten even when the subject is a female. The instrumental factor in placement of a tale in this chapter was the subject's sex rather than her race. My task was difficult because, in many instances, both race and sex are pertinent to the tale. Sexual jokes revealing hostile attitudes towards women are also included in chapters twelve, thirteen, and fifteen. In addition to those placed here, jokes about prostitutes occur also in various other chapters.

Certainly not all the folktales involving women are degrading. Occasionally the woman is triumphant over the male, who is the butt of the humor. Additionally, there are a few paeans to the female, which were found among Black Virginians during the course of this study.

NOTES

1. William H. Grier and Price M. Cobbs observe that "the sexual act itself carries aggressive overtones, and in the fantasy of all men there is a likening of male aggression in the sexual act to murderous aggression and a likening of the female partner to the victim of murder" (Black Rage [New York: Bantam Books, 1969], p. 77). In his perceptive analysis of the sadism and hatred inherent in the sex jokes, G[ershon] Legman asserts that fantasies of sexual murder "are more popular than is suspected" (Rationale of the Dirty Joke: An Analysis of Sexual Humor [New York: Grove Press, 1972], p. 276).
2. See Frederic Storaska's discussion of male attitudes toward rape in his How to Say No to a Rapist and Survive (New York: Random House, 1975), particularly chapters one ("What Do You Mean—Rape?" pp. 3–16) and fourteen ("And If It Happens Anyway," pp. 217–31).
3. Legman, p. 377.

196 I Could Eat Her Up

See this man, he had gotten married, naturally, and about several months after, when all the glamour wore off, he went back to the Preacher

and asked him could he unmarry 'em. Preacher said, "No-o-o, can't do that."
He says, "What God has put together, no man puts asunder. Don't you love
the woman no more?"

He say, "Well, Reverend, it's like this: the first several months I was
married to that woman, I felt like I could *eat her up!* And every since then I
been mad with myself for not eatin' her up when I felt like it."

197 Just in Case

This man was playin' with the girl. She says, "I can't. I can't do anything like that. I'm on my period. I just can't do it."

So he went on 'round to the back, you know. She says, "No! Don't touch
me back there. I got hemorrhoids," you know.

"Ah-ha-a-a!"

So he gets out of his car, goes back in the trunk of his car. She's wondering
what he's doing. Here he comes back—with a *crowbar*. She says, "What the
crowbar for?"

He say, "Well, just in case, damn it, you got lockjaw too!"

198 The Guy in the Fur Coat

A. Now this gal was a travelin' salesman, you know. And she was out
there on the road, and she got stranded. And she stopped by my man's place.
And she made a deal with him, you know.

He said, "Well, I'll tell you what. I don't have too much room in the inn.
But, I'll let you come on in. Now, you can stay over in *my* place." Say, "Now,
I got quite a few *men* here, and if you, uh, want to, uh, turn a trick or two,
you go ahead and do it. Split with me fifty-fifty."

She say, you know, "Well, what the hell! Fifty-fifty is all right."

And say, this innkeeper had a pet bear . . . And the pet bear was outside in
the garage, had 'im in the garage. He was a pet. No harm, you know what I
mean. All right.

So this chick went all through the whole motel, took care of *all* the business up there, you know.

So the next morning, she told the farmer, say, "I made a thousand dollars
last night. Your part is five hundred."

So he figured that was pretty good. He say, "Did you have any problems?"

She said, "Naw, everything was *fine*. Everybody paid up . . . Who is that
cheap sonovabitch you got out in the garage with a damn fur coat on?"

B. There was this traveling salesman, and when he go from town to town, he used to carry a big bear with 'im, say he used to carry a big bear with 'im; and, uh, he claimed he was tired, so he came to this lil' inn, and the man told him, "Yeah," say, "I'll be glad to rent *you* a room, but I ain't got no place for your bear."

He say, "*Anywhere*, 'cause I am tired and I can't go no further." Say, "Anywhere, any place you got where the bear can stay," say, " 'cause he ain't gon' bother nobody? Anywhere you got will be *all right*."

So the man tol' 'im, "Well, I tell you, today is Thursday, and today is the maid' day off. She stay in the basement . . . You can put the bear down in the basement."

And they put the bear in the basement and shut the do'. They ain't know the maid was still there.

So the next morning, the maid came upstairs *singing* and *doing*. And the boss said, "Wonder what the matter with Mary this morning she so happy?"

And she say, "GOOD MORNING, Boss!"

And he say, "Hi, Mary? What's the matter wid chu?"

She say, "I *thank* you for what you did last night."

He say, "What I did?" He trying to think o' what he had did.

She say, "Boss, you know 'bout that man you sent downstairs there."

He say, "What man?"

She say, "That man you sent downstairs." Say, "He screwed me five times and ain't never pull his fur coat off."

199   That Las' Dude

This *very* huge Black woman was washing outside of her old shack with a washboard, very scantily clothed. And these three salesmen passing by wanted to know the directions to the town, the quickest way to town. And they had car trouble and some farmer had loaned them a mule. And all three of them were on this mule, and they were so tired. And she said, "Jest keep on going down the road, and you'll come to it."

And one of them *meddled* with her and said, "I wonder if we can get a lil' action here."

She said, "You kin get all the action you want if you just don't stop me from washing."

So the first guy jumped on her back and he proceeded to backskuttle, so to speak, and he finished, and she kept right on washing . . . and the second one . . . and the third one . . . and so finally, they shoved the mule up to her, and he worked out.

And finally they said, "You're a strange woman. You didn't say anything!" Say, "Kin we give you anything? Do we owe you anything?"

And she said, "Yeah, the name and address o' that las' *dude!*"

200   They Don't Come Too Long and Hard for Me

So one day everybody sittin' in class, had a nice meetin' goin', and the Teacher said, "Today, children, for our lesson, we gon' spell *Peter*." So she told one girl to stand up. She say, "Darlene, I want you to spell *Peter*."

She say, "Uh-uh, Teacher, I can't spell no long, *hard* words like *Peter*, but I try." She say, "P-P-P—"

Teacher say, "Sit down, girl!"

So one girl jumped up. Her name was Sally. She say, "Teacher, Teacher, Teacher, I can spell it: P-E-T-E-R, Peter! Peter! They don't come too long and hard for me, baby!"

201   You Got to Do Better Than This

Everybody thinks in terms of—most Negro gals, rather, say the size of a man's penis is the thing that determines his sexibility, you know what I mean, and a whole lot of people believe this thing, you know, that if he got this great big joint, he s'posed to be powerful, you know.

So my man was doing all right. Hell, he was 'bout—nine inches, you know. Shit! But this chick, man, I don't know what her problem was, but she tol' him, say, "Man, you got to do better than this."

This was on his wedding night, you know, and the cat wanted to please his old lady.

So she say, "Well, what you think?" She say, "Look, I'll give you one year, and you got to make it larger. Otherwise, we'll just have to get a divorce."

So my man say, "Well, what you want?"

She say, "I don't give a damn what you do. You gon' do better than *this*."

So my man thought about it. He loved his ole lady. So he thought about it and he decided he would go to Africa. So he went over in Africa, and he was using his damn dick, you know, to plow, and he was plowing up the soil, and turnin' over the shit, you know, cuttin' down trees, you know, and fuckin' gorillas and giraffes and all that shit. He was *determined*, man. That cat say he got to make it. And all of a sudden it was gettin' larger, you know what I mean. So the cat was cracking coconuts. He thought—he say, "Well, it's time for me to go back," you know. Three hundred and sixty-five days had just about passed, and my man caught the boat and he was on his way back.

So as he walked up his walkway, you know what I mean, he knocked on the door, and his ole lady came. She looked at him, and my man had his dick wrapped all 'round his neck, *all* 'round his neck, and it was dragging on the *damn ground*, man! She looked at him. She say, "GOOD GOD, I didn't mean for you —I didn't mean for you—What in the world you got in—"

He say, "You ain't seen nothin' yet, baby. My nuts are comin' by first."

202   In Your Good Sense Now!

Right down at Williamsburg at this crazy house there was a woman walkin' 'round in there, shouting, "Send me a man with a ten-inch prick! Send me a man with a ten-inch prick!"

And a *old* lady what leaned up on the fence said, "Hummph!" Say, "Old lady, you mought o' been crazy when they sent you there, but you sho' talkin' in your good senses now!"

203   Shoot the Habit

Papa Rabbit, you know, he got kinda tired. He won't for no stuff, you know. And so Papa Rabbit told Mama Rabbit, he say, "Look here, honey, screwing ain't nothin' but a *habit!*"

She say, [very sexy, seductive tone] "Well, shoot the *habit* to me, *Rabbit!*"

204   I'm Hiding

A male mouse asked a female mouse, "Where are you?"
The female mouse answered, "I'm hiding!"
The male mouse said, "Where are you?"
Female mouse said, "I'm hiding!"
Male mouse said, "When I find you I'm gonna screw you!"
Female mouse said, "I'm hiding in the bread box!"

205   Signs

Once there was three prostitutes in this city, you know. They was lookin' for three men. So they put this sign on the back of their car: "THREE YOUNG MEN WANTED!" The cop came along, noticed the sign, and stopped the three women. "Don't y'all know it's illegal to have a sign like that on your car?" the cop asked.

"What's wrong with the sign?" asked the ladies.

"It's immoral," said the cop.

While the cop was talking to the prostitutes, a preacher came by. On the back of his car was a sign saying, "JESUS SAVES."

Seeing that sign the ladies asked why the preacher could legally have a sign like that on his car and they couldn't.

"That sign is moral," said the cop.

The ladies didn't say anything. But the next day the cop sees the same three ladies. This time they had another sign on the rear of their car: "THREE ANGELS LOOKING FOR SAINT PETER."

206   Forget the Small Change

This girl was getting ready to get married, but she didn't know anything about sex. So she went to an advisor who had her come in for five sessions to learn what to do. During the first session he hung a penny down by her left side so that it came to the level of her hips, and had her sway her hips, rhythmically hitting it and chanting, "Hit the penny, hit the penny, hit the penny." [This and all actions in this joke are dramatized by the teller.] During the next session, he hung a nickel on her right side and had her go through the same routine of swaying her hips to hit it, chanting, "Hit the nickel, hit the nickel," et cetera.

At the third session, he hung a dime behind her and had her sway her hips back and then in place, chanting, "Hit the dime," et cetera. During the fourth session he hung a quarter in front of her and had her swing forward to hit it, chanting, "Hit the quarter," et cetera. At the final session, he had her coordinate all of the moves she had learned, "Hit the penny, hit the nickel, hit the dime, hit the quarter," et cetera. When she had mastered this, he said, "Now you are ready for sex. Just picture this penny, nickel, dime, and quarter, and say to yourself, 'Hit the penny,' et cetera."

On her wedding night she remembered everything she had been taught, and she was just working out, saying softly to herself [while oscillating her hips left, right, backwards, forward], "Hit the penny, hit the nickel, hit the dime, hit the quarter; hit the penny, hit the nickel, hit the dime, hit the quarter, OH-H-H-H! [Obviously carried away by passion.] Forget that damn small change! Hit the quarter, hit the quarter, hit the quarter" [frantic forward thrusts of the hips].

207   This One Knows

We had a tragedy this afternoon on the campus [Virginia Union University]. Two freshman girls who apparently had never been off the campus decided that they would, on this cold night, walk downtown via Leigh Street. And when they got to Harrison and Leigh, two young men grabbed them and pulled them up in the alley.

In questioning them, I asked them, "What happened *then?*"

And one girl said, "Well, you know, the usual thing that happens. But what struck me was as soon as they started, the other girl said, 'Father forgive them for they know not what they do,' and I told her to *shut* her mouth up: 'This one does!'"

208   Encore

This man was going around raping people. He'd drag 'em in the alley. So he dragged this one woman in the alley and raped her. And say, she didn't report 'im. She went back the next night looking for 'im.

209   Pass the Pussy, Please

This woman was getting so disgusted with her husband about the way he made love to her. He was a truck driver, and he would come in after being out on the road for days, all dirty and smelly! And without taking a bath and without one caress or romantic statement, he would just jump in the bed on her. So finally she told him she just wasn't going to put up with that any longer. She said, "You're just going to have to have a little tact and finesse about the way you approach me. Why, you aren't even courteous! Clean yourself up and make yourself appealing and be more romantic. Don't just come in here jumping on me all dirty and smelly and expect me to respond."

So when he came home next time, he took a bath, shampooed his hair, shaved, put on some sweet-smelling aftershave lotion, slipped into some silk pajamas, and got in the bed. He caressed her gently and whispered sweet words in her ear. He said, "How am I doing? Is this tactful enough for you?"

She said, "Oh, yes, this is lovely."

"Am I being tactful enough?"

"Oh, yes!"

"Am I using enough finesse? Am I being courteous enough?"

"Oh, yes!"

"Well, would you pass the pussy, please!"

210   Houdini

Here's a woman enticing a sailor to go home with her, and she tol' 'im, say, "Listen, I want to have intercourse with you because I want to have a baby. I don't have nothin' to call my own, NOTHIN'—no husband, no children, no nothin'!"

He say, "Lady, I don't want no—I can't take care no—"

She say, "I don't wancha to take care of 'im."

And so she finally persuaded him to go ahead and have intercourse with her. Well, he went on and had his intercourse, and when it was over, she *laid* back. She say, "I *know* I'm gonna have something." She say, "If it come out a boy, I'll name 'im *John*. And if it come out a girl, I'll name 'er *Mary*."

He held up this rubber, and he say, "And if it come outta this rubber, I'll name 'im *Houdini!*"

211   You Still My Baby

She wanted to get pregnant, you know, but she never could. So she went to the doctor, and he sewed up a monkey in her, you know. And he left a little piece of string, and he told her to take a lot of walks, exercise, and if she felt a terrible pain to pull that string.

She was out in the park, you know, and the pain *hit* her. She was sitting on the bench and she *snapped* that string, and the monkey jumped out 'tween her legs. And she said, "Come back here, you black sonovabitch. You still my baby!"

212   Mary Had That Little Lamb

Something I used to get by with a long time ago, was, ah, Mary. When people named a girl Mary, I told them I had three Marys in my life.

I took one out a long time ago, and we had a dinner. And at that time I was kind of a dude. Didn't have but a dollar, so I thought I'd take Mary out and have a good time and everything like that; so I gon' let her have fifty cents, and I use a quarter, and I was gonna give a quarter to the waiter, just like that. So I had that thing all prepared. But after a while, here comes the waiter. He came in and brought the menu to me. Put it right in front of Mary there, and she looked on that menu and saw lamb on there.

And she said, "Um-hun, lamb!" Said, "I believe I'll take a little lamb."

Well, I thought I was all up then 'cause I didn't have but so much and so much money. I didn't know what she was gonna do:

Since Mary had that little lamb,
She also had some candied yams;
Some mock turtle and some consommé,
Caviar from Russia way.

She had some roe, and she had some shad;
And there were some other things that Mary had.
Before the lamb came in I was stuck
Two dollars for some kind of duck.
You may think that I'm a joke,
But I also ate some artichoke.
And just before the lamb came in
She had à la Newburg terrapin,
Alligator, peas, and some imported caviar, apple sauce and spinach greens,
All stuffed with peppers in between.
She had juice from three grapefruits in a glass;
Two cups of coffee and a demitasse.
Salted peanuts by the peck;
I know because I got the check.
She used to be my heart's delight,
But, Heaven! What an appetite!
I'm living now on bread and jam,
Since Mary had that little lamb.

213　Expensive Fruit

There was a lil' boy sittin' on the corner with a big apple, and the apple
was that big [gesturing to indicate a very large apple], I mean shin-n-n-ny,
and it was, you know, it was a *beautiful* apple.
So the man said, "Listen, you wanta sell that apple?"
Guy say, "Oh, what'll you give me for it?"
He say, "Well . . . I'll give ya a nickel for the apple."
"A nickel! For *this* apple! Is you crazy?"
So he say, "Well, I'll give you a *quarter* for it since you think so much of
the apple."
"A *quarter!*"
So the man started to gettin' interested in the lil' boy holding on—for a big
quarter wouldn't give the apple up. So he say, "I'll tell ya what, I'll give ya a
dollar for the apple."
He say, "Man, I ain't gon' sell this apple for no dollar."
He say, "Well, what would you take for that apple?"
He say, "You see that pink Cadillac down there? My sister got that Cadil-
lac for a *cherry.* I should get a *Greyhound bus* for this apple."

214　Here's to the Little Girl

Here's to the little girl that wears the red shoes;

She'll drink your whiskey and she'll drink your booze.
She doesn't have a cherry, but that's no sin,
'Cause she has the fine drink that the cherry came in.

215   It Runs in the Family

This fellow was courting a girl, and the mother was doing most of the courtin'. So she was telling him that no man had never been with her, you know, and nothin' like that.

So he married her, but 'fo' he went up that night, he hid him a pint underneath the bed, you know. So he went up there and went in the room. And the mama crept on to the door. And so he reached in and got his liquor, and somebody had drank some of it. And he told the girl, he say, "Somebody's been hittin' this thing!"

Say the old lady say, "Naw, it ain't!" Say, "It's just that big pussies run in this family."

216   The Problems of the Wives of Servicemen

These three wives of Air Force men got together at a bridge party one day and they got to talking. And one of them said, "You know, I don't know what to do about my husband. He's a pilot in the Air Corps, and he goes out on these missions every day, and he works hard, and he comes home, and he falls right out in the bed and he's sound asleep. All of a sudden that thing will come up and he'll grab it and holler, 'Right 'round! Left 'round!' Now that disturbs me!"

The other one said, "Well, I'm glad you said that because my husband is a radio man in the Air Corps, and he goes out on these missions. And when he comes home he does the same thing. He falls out in the bed and goes sound asleep. And way in the night, he'll reach over and grab one breast and holler, 'Roger!' He'll grab the other one and holler, 'Bacon!' That's very abnormal behavior. I just don't understand it."

The third one said, "Well, girls, I had an appointment with the psychiatrist this morning about my husband. He's a bombardier in the Air Corps, and when he comes home he falls out in the bed and goes sound asleep. And he throws his hands over right between my legs and then hollers, 'Good God! Who opened the bomb bay door?'"

217 I Used My Head

Man tol' his daughter, he say, "Daughter, when you get eighteen, I'll gi' you *anything* you want. On your birthday, you kin ask for *anything*."

Lil' girl say, "All right, Papa."

Lil' girl was sixteen years old, hoping and praying she hurry up and git eighteen. See her parents were real strick on her, wouldn't even let her have dates. She got to stay at home and all that. Go to movies—big brother or big sister got to go with her. Couldn't do nuttin'. Turned around, and her eighteenth birthday rolled around.

Then she tol' her daddy, say, "Daddy, Daddy," say, "remember you tol' me say when I get eighteen you say you give me *anything* I want for my birthday?"

Daddy say, "Yeah, Gloria, I tol' you *that*." Said, "I mean it. Now what you *want* for your eighteenth birthday?"

She say, "Well, Daddy, I'm eighteen years old, and I ain't never had nah man. I want a good man. I want you to give *anybody* a thousand dollars that can make me holler."

So her daddy say, "Well, if that's your wish," say, "that's what I'll do." So her daddy sent out the note that he got a eighteen-year-old daughter. Anybody that could ride her and make her holler he give 'im a thousand dollars.

Everybody from all around come. So this dude, he came to the house and he went in there; he fucked her for 'bout half an hour. She just laughed. She ain't paid no attention to 'im. Next dude come in there. He had a nine-inch dick. He fucked her. She still ain't do nothin' but *laugh*. Dude with a twelve-inch dick, he rolled her. She ain't paid it no mind.

Daddy say, "Damn!" Say, "I done got 'em from [six] inches to *twelve* inches, and they still ain't doing nothin'."

A dude come in there with *eighteen* inches and rolled 'er, and she still ain't do nothin', you understand.

Then this lil' colored boy 'bout *nine* years old, he come in there. His dick won't no more than three inches long.

Daddy say, "Look, what you want to do?"

He say, "I want to try to git that reward, that thousand-dollars reward you givin' out."

Her daddy looked at him, say, "Son, I don't think you'll stan' a chance." Say, "I had 'em come in here from six to eighteen inches ridin' my daughter."

Boy say, "Mister, *please* gimme a chance."

Man say, "Naw, son, come on, let's git out."

Lil' girl came to the door when her daddy was kickin' the little boy out. She say, "Naw, Daddy, don't put 'im out." Say, "Reward go for *anybody*, *anybody!*"

So then the man say, "All right, go 'head on in there."

The lil' boy went on in there. Lil' boy start throwin' somethin' in there.

Then after 'while, the girl started hollering, "Ooh, ooooh, ooooooh, stop 'im! Stop 'im! Daddy, Daddy, HELP! STOP! HELP! HELP!"

Lil' boy come on out.

Man say, "Men been coming in here with six to eighteen inches. They couldn't make her holler." Say, "Tell me, son, how did you, how did you do it?"

Lil' boy say, "Ain't nothin' to it." He say, "Ain't nothin' to it." Lil' boy say, [swinging his head around] "I used my head man, I used my head!"

218   Put It Up Possible

This lady and her husband . . . The part of the country they were living in, it was a lot of robberies going around. So they was in a horse and wagon, and she had valuable jewels. So he said to her, "Well, listen, let's separate, and they won't get *everything*. They'll get the horse and wagon or either they'll get the jewels, but they won't get 'em all."

So sho' nuff they met him, and they took the horse and wagon. And when they got to her, they couldn't find the jewelry.

When they got home, he said, "Well, they got me, and they got the horse and wagon."

She said, "Well, I met 'em too, but they didn't get my *jewelry!*"

He say, "What did you do with it?"

She said, "I put it up possible" [her vagina].

He said, "Well, we should have stayed together. We could've saved the horse and wagon too."

219   It Smelled Like Roses

This nigger hadn't had sex relations with his wife in quite a while. And every night she'd try it, but it wouldn't work. And she suggested many things for him, but of no accord.

So he came home that evening, and he said, "Hi, Sugar." She fixed a fine meal for him, and she had everything she thought he wanted. And he went on to bed, turned himself from her.

She say, "I don't know *what* to do."

So she went to a doctor, and he—asked her, say, "What does he love? What does he really *love?*"

She say, "You know what he's got a weakness for? Flowers! He loves roses."

And he said, "You do everything to surround yourself with the fragrance—the smell of roses. Make it be a part of you."

So she say, "All right."

So she picked the roses and put 'em in the living room and the bedroom and kitchen, in the dining room, and as an extra precaution she took the roses and rubbed them all between her legs and just smothered her body with the smell of roses, you see. She took these roses and put 'em back in the vase in the hallway.

So sure as hell the nigger came home that day. He's still distressed and upset. He opened the damn door, went in the dining room. It smelled like roses. He went in the kitchen; it smelled like roses. And he went to the bedroom; it smelled like roses. *Everywhere* was smelling like roses. And he was as *happy* as he could *be!* "Oh this is just—I can't describe it!" So he went to hang his hat and coat up, to put them in the closet.

In the meantime he saw the vase of roses standing there, the first time he'd seen [those roses in the hallway] . . . He grabbed them and put his nose right down in them. Snuuuuuuuuuuuuuum! [Smelling.] "Oh-oh, God! Call Ripley. Call Ripley! I've smelled a many a goddamn pussy that smell like a rose, but this is the first time in life I've ever smelled roses that smell like pussy!"

220   Mighty High in the Bed

This boy was fifteen years old, and every night before he went to bed he had to suck on his mama's breast. So the mama was getting tired of that mess. So one day she was telling one of her neighbors. She say, "You know Steve acts just like a little baby. Every night before going to bed he comes to get some tiddy."

So the neighbor said, "Well, next time, why don't you put some sardine juice on your tiddies and let's see what happens."

So that night, when the boy was ready to be to bed, he tipped up to his mama, and asked, "Oh, Mama, I'm ready for my tiddy."

She took 'em out, and he started sucking on 'em. And quickly he jumped up and said, "Mama, ain't you mighty high in the bed?"

221   Couldn't Stand More

There were two young boys seeing these men going to this house and paying this woman at the door. It was a house of ill repute. And these boys kept watching, wondering why they kept giving this woman a dollar— dollar, or whatever money they were giving her. They wanted to go up there and find out, but you gotta give that lady at the door something.

So he say, "Well, how much money you got?"

He say, "I got a penny."

And he say, "Well, I got a penny."

He say, "Well, less go up there and give 'er a penny, pay 'er a penny, and see if we kin go in."

So they went to the door. The lady, the Madam, looked at 'em [disgustedly].

They say, "We come to pay you like the grown men paid you—give you a penny to come in."

She say, "Well, you lil' *bastards* you!" She grabbed both of 'em, one at a time, ran their hand under her dress, pushed their hand in there, and pushed 'em out of the door.

So both of 'em walkin' down the street [dramatizing smelling their hands and frowning]. One of 'em say, "GODDOG-G-G-G! I glad I didn't have but a penny. I couldn't stand a dollar's worth o' *this stuff!*"

222 Mose Pushes the Wrong Button

This is about Mose. You know Mose hit the numbers, see. Never had anything before in his life. So he decided to take a trip abroad on one of the luxury airliners. So he was there looking around, enjoying drinks from the bar and the likes of that. So, he had to go to the lavatory—hurry call! And he went to the gents' room and it was occupied. He said, "Oh, no! I can't hold it. I've got to go somewhere." So the hostess in the meantime was passing. He said, "Listen, I've got to go to the toilet. The men's room is occupied. Where can I go?"

She said, "Well, I'll find out whether or not the ladies' room is occupied. If so, I'll let you go in there while I stand guard."

So she looked and found out it was empty. So he went in. He said, "GOL-LEEE! This ladies' room is a *palace* compared to the gents' room. This is a beautiful thing here!" So he went and sat on the stool. He said, "Damn, look at all these buttons here." While he was observing the buttons he was going through his actions and everything. Then when he finished he decided to look for some paper. He couldn't find no paper. So he said, "Well, let me see here now. That damn button here says W.A." So he pushed that—warm air! "This one says P.P." He pushed that. Powder puff! "God durn," he say, "this is REALLY-Y-Y out of this world! Ha, ha! What in the hell is this one, say A.T.R. What in the hell is it? I'm gon' *push* it!" Say he pushed it . . . and passed out.

When he awakened he was in the hospital in England. He said, "Where in the hell am I?"

The doctor say, "You in the hospital in England."

He said, "I thought I was on the *airplane.*"

He say, "You were, but they had to bring you to the hospital here in pretty bad shape."

He say, "Well, the *last* thing I remember I was in the *damn* ladies' room on that airplane."

He say, "Yeah, you touched the *wrong* button. You touched the A.T.R."

He say, "What the hell was that?"

He say, "That was the automatic *Tampax* remover."

223   Plenty of Excitement

One day this teacher told her class to go to the board and write a word that suggests excitement. One boy went to the board and wrote *fire*. "Very good," said the teacher.

The next little boy wrote *war*, and the teacher praised him.

Finally, it was Sam's turn, and he went to the board and put a dot on the board.

The teacher said, "How can a dot cause excitement, Sam?"

Sam said, "That's not a dot. That's a period. And my sister just missed one. And it has caused a plenty excitement around my house."

224   A Minor Cut

One time this lady, she had a Parrakeet, and every time some guests come to the house—old Polly Parrot had picked up a whole lot of foul language. The lady told all the guests that the Parrakeet had learned how to talk. So one lady, she went over there and spoke to the Parrakeet. She say, "How you doin', Parrakeet?"

Parrakeet tol' her, say, "Kiss my ass; kiss my ass!"

The lady was shocked. The lady jumped back.

So then, another one o' her guests went over there, say, "Good evening, Parrakeet." Say, "Say somethin' for me, say somethin' for me, you little, sweet devil."

Parrakeet say, "Kiss my ass, bitch; kiss my ass."

The lady heard it; so after all the guests left, the lady say, "I don't know why you embarrass me like that!" She say, "I gon' kill you!" She reached up there and grabbed the Parrakeet, cut the Parrakeet's throat; and then turned around and th'owed the Parrakeet down the toilet and flushed the toilet. She walked out. She hadn't noticed that the Parrakeet hadn't went down.

So 'bout a couple o' weeks later, you know, the lady went in the bathroom. She sat down on the toilet. Then after awhile she heard the Parrakeet holler, "Aaah! Aaah! Aaah!"

The woman *jumped* up, say, "I thought I had killed you! I thought I had cut *your throat."*

The Parrakeet looked at the woman, say, "Aaah, aaach, if you can live wid that big gash in your ass, I know I can live wid this little one in my throat!"

225 You Gon' Cutcha-Self

This man had a old Parrakeet, old *nosy* Parrakeet. He was sitting in the bathroom. Every time the man go in there to shave, the Parrakeet holler, "AACH, you gon' cutcha thoat, you gon' cutcha thoat!"

He say, "I gon' kill your ass [if] you keep saying that shit!"

So the man went in there three days later, start shaving. The Parrakeet holler, AAAH, you gon' cutcha thoat, you gon' cutcha thoat!"

Man say, "I'm tired o' this goddamn shit!" So he took the Parrakeet out the cage, you know, thowed the motherfucker in the toilet stool and *flushed* it.

So 'bout a month later, his wife came on her period. So she went in the bathroom and sit on the toilet stool—and she start bleedin'. And the Parrakeet say, "AAAH, you done cutcha-self. I tol' you you gon' cutcha-self!"

226 Out for Blood!

A representative from the Campbell's Bean Company was talking with a local radio station about placing an advertisement on the air for his company, but he was very much disturbed about the amount of money the station wanted to charge him. When he complained about this, they told him that all the companies were paying large fees for advertisement. "Even Kotex pays a substantial fee for their ads," they told him.

He retorted, "Well, I can understand that. They're out for blood. We're just farting around!"

227 Peepin' Tom

Once in the country long ago when they used to have parties, and the girls used to have to dress wherever they gon' have the party. You know, they'd go and dress at their house. And there was this old boy used to blow the harp, and he know the girls gon' dress where the party gon' be, and come, and they used to call 'im Peepin' Tom. And he blowed a harp. That's the way you could tell he was comin'.

One night the girls looked out the window. She say, "Old Peepin' Tom be 'long 'cause I heard his harp blowin'."

The other girl say, "Yeah." Say, "If he comes to that window tonight," say, "I'm gon' fix 'im."

And she, you know, she was—unwell [menstruating]. Say, sho' nuff, old Peep came up to the window and stuck his head in there, and the girl pulled that thing off and hit 'im right 'cross his face with it.

He wiped his eyes and run 'round to the door, say, "I didn't come here for no fight. I ain't come here for no trouble. But, if I knowed who hit me with that damned piece of liver, I'd shoot 'em!"

228   The Transfusion

In this house it was a Doctor Jones had as his favorite patient, Moses. Moses became very ill. The doctor found that Moses was sinking very fast. And he hated so badly to tell Moses that he really was on his way out. But he felt that he owed it to him. So he went into Moses' room and closed the door and told Moses about his plight and that he was on his way out. So Moses asked how long did he have.

He say, "Moses, you will not be able to make it until morning."

He say, "Well, that's tough." He say, "Doctor, I tell you. You know, I've been hearing about this all my life, 'bout men using their mouths on women, and since I'm going to die, I'd like to do that."

He say, "Well, damn, Mo, you know, this is in the hospital. I don't know who in the hell I'm gon' get to do that."

He say, "Well, Doc, you promised to do something for me."

He say, "Wait a minute, Mose, let me see what I can do." So the doctor went out in the hall, and there was Mary, the maid. Mary was a pretty good timer. She liked fun and pleasure and everything. So he asked Mary, he say, "Mary, now, listen. I want to ask you a question. I have a dear friend who's going to die. I wonder if you'd let him use his mouth on you, 'cause that is his last request. I'll give you twenty-five dollars."

She say, "Doctor, let me tell you something. I need that twenty-five dollars, and I'd do it for that twenty-five dollars, but I'm menstruating."

He say, "Oh, hell. He wouldn't know the difference. He's dying anyway. Go 'head, let 'im go ahead."

So she say, "All right, it's his funeral."

So she went in, performed the operation.

So the next morning, the doctor making his rounds, and he passed Moses' room. He say, "Poor Moses . . . Look like somebody . . . Look like another patient's in there. Lemme take a look."

Mo was sitting on the side of the bed, shaking his head and smiling, his

feet going up and down! He say, [very animated voice] "Doc! You know *one*
thing! I believe I'd make it if I could get another transfusion like I got last
night."

229 The Only Two I Can Trust

An old lady was asked why she carried her money in her bosom.
"Well," replied the Negro woman, "them's the only two suckers I can trust!"

230 All That Meat

This little boy sitting with his mother watched a lady across the aisle
nursing her baby. Afterwards, he asked his mother what she was doing, and
his mother said, "Oh, she was giving her baby his dinner."

"What?" said the little boy. "All that meat and no potatoes!"

231 *Fried* Egg

This dude was going shopping, you know, so his wife had tol' 'im to get
her a bra, you know. So this ole man, he went on down town, you know,
went in the store and start shoppin'. So then when he started payin' for the
clothes and everything and the ticketress [saleslady] asked him, say, was
that all, you know, he say, "God, naw, I was s'posed to git somethin' for my
wife, somethin' for her to wear . . ." and finally they figured out it was a bra.

So the woman asked him, say, "Well, what *size*?"

He say, "Well, uh, uh . . ."

She say, "Well, how big is her tiddies?"

He say, "Uh . . . uh . . . uh . . ."

She say, "They like a watermelon?"

He say, "Naw, naw, that's too big, too big."

She say, "What about a grapefruit?"

"Naw, naw, naw, that's too big."

She say, "What about a apple?"

He say, "Naw, naw, naw, naw."

She say, "What about a egg?"

He say, "*Yeah!* Fried!"

232   I'm Gon' Get in the Drawer

A.   This newly married couple were ready to retire on the first night, and the husband was already in bed. So the lady removed her contact lenses. She put those in the drawer. Then she removed her teeth and put those in the drawer. She removed her falsies, and she even had on false hips. She put all that in the drawer. And then her husband got up. She said, "Now, where are *you* going?"
He said, "I'm gon' get in the drawer."

B.   Here's a guy who just got married. He's known this girl for several months, but he had never had anything to do with her sexually. He gets in the bed there, and she start to taking off false hair [mimicking lady removing her wig and laying it on the table], false teeth [mimicking lady removing her false teeth and laying them on the table], false eye [mimicking]. So she had all this stuff laying all up on top o' the table. He kept on looking back over at her and looking back over at the table.
She say, "What you looking at?"
He say, "I'm trying to decide whether to get in the bed with you or to get up here on that table. It's as much of you on the table as in the bed."

233   What Size?

This old woman went to the store to get a pair of shoes. So she walked in the store and she said, "I want to see a pair of shoes."
The man said, uh, "What size?"
She say, "Well, I usually *wear sixes;* but I can wear *sevens* nicely. Once I got a pair of *eights* 'n' they was even better. These I've got on now are number *nines* and they hurt like the dickens!"

234   We Return *Anything*

This girl applied at this motel, say, "I sees, suh, you wants a maid."
He said, "Yes, do you know how to clean up rooms?"
Say, "Yas, suh."
He said, "Now if there's a 'No Disturb' sign on the door, you don't bother it." He said, "But I have one strict policy here—What's your name?"
She say, "Ma-ary."

He say, "Well, I'm gon' have to call you Mary. I want you to come to me with *any* article after people have checked out, that they leave. I don't care *what* it is, and give it to me, and I'll put the room number on it, because so often people will come back and say, 'Did you fin' somethin'?' and we have a strict policy here. We like to keep our customers, so we will return anything that's lost."

She said, "Anything?"

He said, "ANYTHING!" He said, "And whether I'm busy or not, you give it to me and be SURE you have the right number on it. That's one of my strictest things I want you to pay attention to. That's our *biggest* policy."

And he *kept* telling her this. So this was the uppermost thing in her mind. So as she would clean, she would *look* for things. So one day, he was at the desk and she went running to him, and say, "Mr. Charlie, I found dis in Room 221."

And it was a whisk broom. He labeled it. He say, "That's *fine*."

And so the next day she ran to him. She say, "Mr. Charlie, look, somebody left some earrings. This was in 225."

He say, "That's *fine*. You're doing very well."

Well, the third day he was registering some guests, and she was standing there with somethin' behin' her, just standin' [mimicking girl nervously shifting from one foot to the other]. He said, "I'll be with you in a minute."

She said, "Yas, suh, but hurry up!" [Still more nervous agitation.]

He said, "Do you—have to go to the bathroom?"

She say, "Nawsuh, just hurry!"

He say, "Well, just a minute."

So she waited, and waited, and finally he said, "What is it?"

She said, "LOOK!" [Dramatizing girl bringing something forward that she is loath to hold in her hands.]

And he said, "Well, Mary, you just throw that in the commode or in the trashcans."

She say, "NAWSUH, this is uh-uh-uh-uh—he might *miss* it. He's sick or sumpin's wrong."

He said, [exaggerated patience] "Mary, haven't you ever been to bed wit' a man before?"

She say, "Yaas, suh, but when he got through, he ain't pull the *skin* off it!"

235   Too Old for That

This old lady came into the colored bank to apply for a loan. The bank officer, whom she knew, said, "Now, let's see now. I can let you have this money, but you'll have to give me some *collateral*."

The lady said, "Oh, go on, Mr. Jenkins [name changed], you know we too old for that!"

236   I Expect I Had Plenty

A.   A woman was keepin' sto' and a man come by and asked for some syrup. She tol' 'im, "I'm sorry, we don't have any."

He say, "Yes you do. There it is right up there."

She took it down and say, "You know, we always call that molasses, but they changes names now so fas', you never know what you got. Man come by here the other day and asked for some poontang, and I tol' 'im I didn't have none. And I expect I have *plenty!*"

B.   This here drummer was in this place, and so a man come in and asked the old lady, said did she have any syrup.

So she told him, "Naw," she didn't have none.

So he looked up on the shelf, say, "Yeah," say, "there's some syrup up there." Say, "There's some Karo."

She say, "Lawd, have mercy!" Say, "Things have changed so." Say, "We used to always call that molasses." Say, "A man come in here the other day and asked me for some poontang, and I told 'im I didn't have nah bit. I bet I had a plenty of it right here."

237   You First

There was this grandmother who became very ill, but you know how older people are: they don't want to go to the doctor and be examined. So she [her granddaughter] told her grandmother, "You've *got* to go to the doctor and take off all your clothes and let him examine you."

So she finally got her grandmother to go to the doctor. When they got to the office, the doctor took her on in his room and he said to her, "Now, Mrs. Brown, pull off your clothes—*all* of your clothes—and get up there on that table."

She turned around and looked at him and said, [coyly] "You pull yours off first."

238   I Want My Money Back

This old lady went to the racetracks. Somebody told her to bet on a certain *horse*. And she went to this window and placed her money on this horse to bet. Then, the horses came out and they started *trotting* and trying to get together. And this one she bet on jumped out there and his—whatever he got—fell, you know. And the woman saw 'im. She made up her mind, say, she ran up to the desk. She say, "I want my money back! I want my money back!"

Say, "Why you want your money back?"

"That horse don't have his mind on racin' today. I want my money back!"

239 Who Wouldn't Be Mad!

'Twas a old lady in the country, and she used to smile *all* the time. Don't care whatcha do, you couldn't make her mad, you know. So three boys say, "Well, when Miss Sarah go to town today," say, "we gon' fix her. I mean she gon' be mad when she come home."

They went up there and took all the water out the well; they caught the cat and cut all the hair off the cat; and took the donkey and paint the donkey red.

So Miss Sarah came home, and she grabbed the bucket and went to the well, and won't no water in the well. She look around and see the cat with all the hair cut off and see the donkey painted red. So the boys came up, say, "How you feel, Miss Sarah?"

Miss Sarah ain't said nothing.

They say, "You act like you mad, Miss Sarah."

She say, "Who in the hell wouldn't be mad!" Say, "You done drawed my water, done cut all the hair off my pussy, and done paint my ass red."

240 The Precious Little Thing

A. It was a lady, and she went to a funeral. And this funeral was of her husband. And it was a little baby, and since the baby died, they put the baby in the casket with the man. So when she went up to look at her husband, she broke down and she got to crying. And she say, "Oh, the precious little thing between his legs! Oh, the precious little thing between his legs!"

Everybody [remainder of joke is inaudible because of laughter].

B. A baby had died and they went to the undertaker place to get the man to try to give 'em a way to bury the baby 'cause she wasn't able to bury the baby. And the man tell her, the undertaker man say, "Well, I got a man to bury today. I'll tell ya what I'll do. I'll git your baby and put him right between his legs." And say, "Today, when I bury 'im, baby'll be all right."

And see the lady know her baby was buried down 'tween the man's legs. And so when it was time to let de man's corpse down in the grave, the 'oman just screamin' and hollerin', carryin' on.

The other lady say, "What you cryin' about that man for? Dat ain't none o' ya husband."

Say, "I ain't cryin' 'bout dat man. I cryin' 'bout dat thing 'tween man's legs."

241   Not a Single Bedbug

'Twas a fellow, he was kind of a travelin' fellow—he traveled around, and so he stopped in this place and went into a rooming house. The woman charged him a dollar and a half a night. So he goes up there and turns the lil' light on in the ceiling and went to bed.

And all at once he ran down the stairs, say, "Landlady! I can't stay in that room. Them bedbugs eatin' me up!"

She say, [sternly] "Listen here, young man, let me tell you sumpin'. I don't have a single bedbug in this house, and if you brought any—"

"Naw, you ain't got a single one. They all married and got big families! Come on up there then. I'll show you what I talkin' 'bout."

So they went there and turned the light on. Say they was out there playing baseball and football all on the sheets. He say, "There they is, lady, there they is!"

She say, "What you call them things?"

"Bedbugs! They're bedbugs!"

"We call them things chinches up here."

But they bite just as hard.

242   Absent-Minded Man

We had a man was so absent-minded who lived about three blocks from my house, from where I live at. He was so absent-minded that he went home one night and kissed the cat and put his wife outdoors.

243   The Cow's Better

This couple was married and the wife caught the husband screwing the cow. So she said, "That's all right, John. I'm going around and tell all the neighbors that you screwing the cow."

So he said, "You be sure to tell 'em that the cow got better cock than you."

244 Some Are Bachelors

This couple had a spat, you know, and so the wife said to the husband, "Let me ask you something. Are *all* the *men* in the world *fools?*"
He say, "Naw, honey, some of 'em are bachelors."

245 Gifts Are to Be Used

This is a true story. This is really true. This lady asked her husband, say, "What are you going to give me for Christmas?"
He said, "You ain't use the one I gave you last year."
She said, "What'd you give me last year?"
He said, "A cemetery plot!"

246 Rest in Peace—Now

There was a lady whose husband died, and he had been so mean to her and all through his life. So she used to go to his grave nearly every day. And so one day she went to his grave, and she was standin' on his grave. She say, "You devil!" Say, "You rest in peace *now*. But you wait till I come, 'cause when *I* come, 'tis gon' be some *hell* raised!"

247 I Can Measure Yours

It was raining, and the window was open, and the wind was blowing. And the man told his wife to close the window. He said, "If I can tell a joke better than you, then you close the window."
So she said, "Well, that's all right."
So he said:

Three and three will make six.
Six and three will make nine.
I can pee in yours,
But you can't pee in mine.

So the lady got mad, but she closed the window. But she couldn't sleep.

She decided that, you know, "I know I can tell a joke better than that." So *finally*, she thought of a better joke. She jumped up and she opened the window. She woke up her husband and said, "*Dear*, get up and close the window."

He said, "We have already finished that bit."

She said, "But, no, I've got a better joke." She said:

Three and three will make six,
And six and three will make nine.
I can measure yours,
But you can't measure mine.

248   How'd You Make Out?

This old man and old lady were eighty years old, and they'd been together so long that they decided they wanted some younger person and have an affair. So they found a couple of twenty-year-olds. The boy was twenty and the girl was twenty. So the old man eighty took the twenty-year-old girl, and the old woman eighty took the twenty-year-old boy. So they went on and spent the night together.

The next morning when they came out, the older couple got together again. The old man said, "How'd you make out last night, honey?"

She said, "Well, you know twenty will go into eighty four times. How'd you make out?"

249   Changing a Wife

This man came in to this place, and he said, "I want to change my wife." And the lady said, "*Why?*"

And the man said, "I just want to change her."

She said, "Well, how old is your wife?"

Say, "My wife is sixty years old."

"Oh, my goodness gracious! That's not old!" Says, "What do you want to exchange her for?"

Say, "I want to exchange her for a forty."

"Well," the lady say, "we all out of forties."

And he say, "Well, give me two twenties."

250   Plenty Fire in the Furnace

This ole lady, she was flirting with a young fellow, you know. She was standin' around there, and of course the young folks could see she was old, you know. Her hair was all gray and everything. So she say, "Oh, don't pay any attention about the snow on the mountain 'cause it's *plenty* fire in the furnace."

251   B-36, C-47

You know, during the time when we had those airplanes, the B-36 and C-47, this man asked this girl (Janet Knight, I think her name was)—Well, after he asked her her age, she said, "I'll be thirty-six my next birthday."

He looked at her [incredulously], say, "You might *be* thirty-six, but you'll never *see* forty-seven."

252   Ole as the Hills

This census taker came by these two ole maids' house there, and he asked their name.

They say, "The Misses Jones."

He say, "Age?"

She say, "You see those Hill girls where you just passed by their house?"

He say, "Yes."

[Peremptorily.] "We just as ole as they are!"

So he wrote down, "The Misses Jones, ole as the Hills."

253   Wrinkled

These two old ladies in a old folks' home, they was so hot and so uncomfortable, they said wonder what could they do. So one of 'em said to the other, "Let us streak! It's so hot, let us streak!"

And they started to streaking, started running all 'round the table, and these two old men was sitting back of them, say, "What is those ladies got on?"

The other one say, "I don't know, but whatever it is, it sure need pressing."

254   They Came to Buy the Mule

The Pastor went to a funeral at a church, and a whole lot of people were there. The Pastor told the [man] say, "Well, I see that such and such a people in your party are dead." Say, "That was your mother-in-law, ain't it?"

Say, "Yeah," say, "my mother-in-law is dead."

So the Preacher said, "Well, what's the matter with her?"

Say, "A mule kick her. Mule kick her and killed her dead."

The Pastor said, "Uh, my goodness." Say, "I see a lot of men up here today." Say, "What is all these men coming up here for?"

Say, "The men came up here to buy the mule."

255   I Come to Buy the Dog

A dog bit a man's mother-in-law right over across the street some time ago, and his wife she got so excited about it. Said, "What are you going to do because they are going to sue us" and everything like that.

He said, "Well, I don't know what to do. I'm scared to death, too."

Right about that time [tapping on the table to suggest a knocking on the door] and her husband opened the door and said, "Come in."

The man outside said, "Are you the man who owns that dog bit my mother-in-law?"

Say, "Yeah, come on see if we can settle it."

He say, "Settle it! I didn't come up to settle it. I come up to buy the dog."

256   Lucky Horseshoe

The man next door came to the man's house. He said, "Henry, whatcha doing up there?"

Says, "I'm puttin' this horseshoe up there."

He said, "Well, I thought that thing fell down the other day."

He said, "Yes." He say, "It fell down the other day." And say, "My wife left me."

"Well, what are you putting it up again for?"

Said, "I'm puttin' it up again so somebody can come back and get my mother-in-law."

257   Luck to the Duck

Luck to the duck that swim the lake,
Screwed his mother by mistake.
When he found out what he was doing,
He tucked his head and kept on screwing.

258   You Had Intercourse with *Mine*

This was an individual who had a real modest father. This little boy had
never had his first piece. And his father was somewhat concerned—he was
close to seventeen years old now. He said, "Son, have you ever—uh—had a
relationship with a girl?"

He said, "No, Dad."

He said, "Now, I'm concerned about this now. You're going on seventeen
years old." He said, "I'll tell you what. (This was quite a few years ago.) Take
this quarter and go to town and see what you can—you know—go on
Seventh and U Street."

So the son lived about eight miles from town, and he was walking all the
way. He started to walk, and he was twirling his quarter up and down
[dramatizing], singing, "I'll get my first piece today; I'll get my first piece
today." After about three miles down that road, he approached his
grandmother's house, and his grandmother, nothing else to do, was out
there leaning across the fence to talk to anyone who comes down the road.
He's still twirling this quarter, "I'll get my first piece today."

During those days, you know, a quarter was a quarter. You could buy a
steak with a quarter then.

She said, [mimicking her gazing with interest at the quarter which the boy
is twirling in the air] "Son, where you going?"

He say, "I'm going to town, Grandmother."

She say, [mimicking her eager eyes still following the quarter] "What you
going there for?"

He said, "Grandmother, I can't tell you that."

She say, [gruffly] "Boy, don't be sassy! What are you going to town for?"

He still told her, "Grandmother, I can't tell you that."

So she pulled his ear, "Boy, don't be sassing me. What are you going to
town for?"

He said, "Well, Grandmother, if you must know. I'm supposed to be going
to town to get my first piece." And he twirled his quarter up.

She said, "With all that money?" She say, "You come on in here."

He said, "But you're my *grandmother*."

She said, "Stop sassing me. Give me that quarter!"

She carried him on in the bedroom, you know, and undressed him and—and sent him on back home.

So he got home a little too quick. His father say, "Son, did you get your first piece today?"

He said, "Yes, sir, Dad, yes, sir."

He say, "But you got back a little faster than I thought you should have gotten back. Where did you go? Did you go in town?"

He say, "Well, Dad, I didn't have to go all the way to town."

"What you mean you didn't have to go all the way to town? The only house between our house and town is Grandmother's house."

He say, "Well, Dad, I was going down the road, minding my own business, twirling my quarter, singing my little song, 'I'm going to get my first piece today—'"

His father was getting a little impatient. He say, "Go on—Go on—"

He say, "—and I approached Grandmother's house while I was twirling my quarter—"

He say, "Go on—Go on!"

He say, "—and Grandmother stopped me—"

He say, [growing more excited] "Go on—Go on!"

He say, "—Grandmother asked me what I was doing with a quarter and everything, you know, where was I going. And I told her I was going to get my first piece—"

He say, [almost frantic now] "Go on—Go on!"

He said, "—Grandmother told me to come on in there; she'd give me a little bit for a quarter!"

[Long silence.]

He say, [incredulously] "Do you mean to say you had intercourse with my mother?"

He say, "You had intercourse with *mine*, didn't you?"

259   Let Me Be Frank

A. Here's a woman, you know, she's a lesbian. She doesn't want to be this way. So she goes to the doctor. The doctor say, "Well, what you need to do . . . Now, you've begun to think about gettin' yourself healed because you've come for *help*. That's the *first* step. But, what I want you to do is walk out into the far woods and see nature at its rawest. Then you'll start gettin' close to nature, knowing where things should be placed in their *proper* perspective, you know."

So she walks on, thinking about what the doctor say, and walked till it got dark. She got lost out there. So she went to the *very* first house. And when she got there the people who lived there was a woman and her daughter. She say, "Oh, my God! This ain't nothin' but the Devil and temptation! Now, I don't want to bother these people. I'm trying to get myself straight. Why couldn't a man be here to keep me straight."

So she was there. They ate. Boy, they were nice to her and everything. She say, "I'm gon' have to tell these people 'cause I don't want no misunderstanding." She say, "Look, lady, I'm gon' lay it down on the line. I'm gon' be frank wit' ya . . ."

The lady say, "No, don't you be Frank. Let me be Frank tonight. You be Frank tomorrow night!"

B.   These two secretaries had their vacation at the same time, and they both wanted to go to the beach for the summer. And to save money, they decided to share the same room. So they got off and went to the hotel. They got ready to go to bed that night. One of them said to the other, "Listen, you know, it's something about me that I . . . didn't . . . tell . . . you. Now I'm going to be frank!"

The other one said, "Oh! NO! Oh, NO! I'll be Frank!"

260   Miss Lucy Neal

I went over the mountain,
Took my horn and blowed,
Poor little Lucy come runnin' home,
Say, "Yonder comes my beau."

Ah, Miss Lucy, Lucy,
Ah, Miss Lucy Neal,
If I had her by my side,
Lord, how good I'd feel!

And I hold Lucy, Lucy,
Then I hop on Lucy's knee.
If I had her by my side,
Lord, how good I'd be!

Ah, Miss Lucy, Lucy,
Ah, Miss Lucy Neal,
If I had her by my side,
Lord, how good I'd feel!

Ah-h-h, custard board and pine log
And cotton in the field
Come floating down the river stream,
Say, "Ah, Miss Lucy Neal."

Ah, Miss Lucy, Lucy,
Ah, Miss Lucy Neal.
If I had her by my side,
Lord, how good I'd feel!

I wouldn't marry a yellow gal,
I'll tell you the reason why:
Her neck [is] so long and stringy now,
I'm 'fraid she'll never die.

Ah, Miss Lucy, Lucy,
Ah, Miss Lucy Neal!
If I had her by my side,
How good I'd feel!

I wouldn't marry a yellow girl [in one version "an old maid"]
I'll tell you the reason why:
'Cause she wouldn't mend my britches
Till the britches fall in stitches
And the stitches wouldn't stitched—
Yellow gal, I want you to mend my britches.

Ah, Miss Lucy, Lucy,
Ah, Miss Lucy Neal!
If I had her by my side,
How good I'd feel!

261   I Comin' Back

Me and my gal, we had a fallin' out,
And she worried me so I thought about going out.
And when I went on out she came to the door.
She said, "You may go, but you're coming back."
I said to her, "I'm goin' away, and I'm going to stay."
I went downstairs; I packed my bag.
She says, "Where are you goin'?"
I say, "I'm going away-y-y."

I ran away; I went to stay,
But I stayed so long, I said, "I'm goin' back."
So I missed my girl and I commenced writin',
And I commenced tellin' her,
I say, "Ba-a-bie-e-e, I'm comin' back to you!"
I say, "Ba-a-bie-e-e, what will I do?
Ba-a-bie-e-e, I comin' back to you.
What will I do?
I comin' back to you."

9

Be True to Me:
Tales about
Marital Infidelity

There was a fellow who was very sick, and just before he died, he called his wife to his bedside, and he
asked her, he say, "Honey, I'm gon' die, but I want
you to make me a promise that you'll be true to me,
even after death, and that you won't have another
man as long as you live. And when you die and you
come to heaven, you'll be with me, and we'll have a
happy life together."

She say, "Yes, honey, I promise you."
"Pinwheel Charlie"

PERHAPS THE MOST universal of the tales found in the Black community are those treating marital infidelity. In these tales, which are
popular in all cultures and times, the issue is never race but rather
the age-old war between the man and his wife which reaches its apex
in the infidelity of one partner. That it is usually the wife who is
unfaithful suggests perhaps that the majority of the tales are male
creations. The attacks on the wife as the inevitably disloyal partner
in some of these tales are often balanced, however, by the suggestion
that it is the husband's ignorance or naiveté which allows him to be
cuckolded. That several of the tales in this chapter were told by
female informants indicates that both males and females find these
tales humorous.

143

262   Pinwheel Charlie

There was a fellow who was very sick, and just before he died, he called his wife to his bedside, and he asked her, he say, "Honey, I'm gon' die, but I want you to make me a promise that you'll be true to me, even after death, and that you won't have another man as long as you live. And when you die and you come to heaven, you'll be with me, and we'll have a happy life together."

She say, "Yes, honey, I promise you."

And he said, "Honey, any time that you have a relationship with a man, I'm going to turn over in my grave."

And she say, "Well, all right. You won't have to worry about that."

He say, "I'm gon' promise you now. I'm gon' turn over in my grave every time that you have relations with a man."

So the fellow died and went on to heaven. And about ten years later the woman died. And when she got to the Pearly Gates, the first thing she asked Saint Peter was where was her husband, and she called her husband by his name.

Saint Peter say, "I don't recognize anybody by that name up here. Describe your husband to me. Tell me some of the things that happened while you were together."

And she told Saint Peter about this promise that she had made her husband, and her husband said that he was going to turn over in his grave every time that she had anything to do with another man.

Saint Peter say, "OH-H-H, I know who you talking 'bout, but we call 'im Pinwheel Charlie, because every since he been up here, all he been doing is just spinning like a wheel."

263   Revolving Jones

This individual had died and gone to hell. Before he died, he said, "If and when I die, if I die before my wife, I *know* she will *not* have another man in her life. If she does, I will just—just turn over in my grave."

So a few years later, he died and went on to hell. Three or four years after that, one of his buddies died and went to hell. He was going up and down the streets of hell, looking for him. He knocked on a few doors down there, say, "Do you know Ed Jones from Richmond, Virginia?"

They say, "I don't believe I know him."

So he kept on inquiring: "Do you know Ed Jones from Richmond, Virginia?"

He say, "Ed Jones? . . . Ed Jones? . . . *OH!* You talking about old *Revolving Jones*!"

264 He Doesn't Know It

A young man was talking to his father, and he told him that he was deeply in love with a girl by the name of Mary Jones, and he wanted to marry her. So the father said, "Well, son, she's a nice girl, but you can't marry her because I'm her father. But don't tell your mother because she doesn't know it."

But the son was so disturbed that that night he went and talked to his mother anyway and told her, "Mother, I was planning to marry Mary Jones. We were very much in love. And Daddy told me not to marry her because he was her father, but you didn't know it."

She said, "Son, go on and marry Mary Jones if you want her because he's not your daddy, but he doesn't know it."

265 The Father Will Die

There was once a woman who was going to have a baby. There was a bad spell placed upon her. The spell was that one minute after the baby is born the mother will die; two minutes later the baby will die; and three minutes later the father will die. Just as the spell was predicted, the mother died one minute after the baby was born, and the baby died two minutes after the mother, but the weary father sat impatiently, knowing that his time was next. But for some strange reason, when three minutes were up the father was still living. So excited, he leaped up and ran out of the house and tripped up over the dead milkman.

266 Mama Had Another Fit

This little boy happened to pass by his father and mother's bedroom, and he noticed they were doing something unusual to him, and it so happened that he didn't say anything. So he waited until the next morning after he had had breakfast, and he had a chance to talk to his father. He say, "Dad, I passed by your room last night, and it looked like you were struggling with mother."

His father say, "Oh, yes, son, your mother was having a fit, and I was holding her down."

He say, "Oh, I didn't know what was happening. She looked like she was struggling."

So the father went to work. A couple of days later he came home. His son ran down the hall. He say, "Daddy! Daddy! Daddy!"

His daddy say, "What's wrong, son? Why are you so excited?"
He say, "You know, Mother had another one o' those fits today, and the milkman held her down."

267 Why Do I Talk Like This?

This little boy went to his mother and asked her, "Mama, why thu I taut dike dis?"
She said, "I don't know. Go ask your father."
So then he asked his father, "Daddy, why thu I taut dike dis?"
The father said, "I don't know. Go play."
So then the next day the milkman came, and he asked the milkman, "Why thu I taut dike dis?"
And the milkman said, "Wath thu doin', boy? Tryin' to det me tilt or somethin'?"

268 $4\frac{1}{2} + 4\frac{1}{2} = 9$

This country boy got married, and so they had been married about four and a half months. And his wife told him that she was ready to have the baby. He went running down the road for the doctor. So the fellow said, "He-y-y, where you going?"
He say, "I'm going to get the doctor for my wife. She's gon' have a baby!"
And this guy said, "And you've only been married for four and a half months? Man, you're crazy. That baby isn't yours!"
So he stopped. He say, "It takes nine months for a baby—but she been married to me four and a half months, and I been married to her four and a half months. Four and a half and four and a half is nine. I'm going to get that doctor!"

269 Talkin' Barrel

Man wanted to butcher a hog, and he didn't have no barrel to scald the hog in. So he went to the friend's house to get a barrel, and he wasn't home. But when he went there, another man been settin' there, and both of 'em wait till the owner come there. And when he come (he had a barrel behind the house in the chimney corner), when he come one man went and jump down in that barrel, and the other man—he run up the loft.

While the wife and the man was sleepin' in the bed, the man in the loft come down on a seesaw board and come right down side that bed in the flo' and wake the man and he wife up. And he say, "I want to butcher a hog, but I ain't got no barrel to butcher it in."

Man in the bed tell the man, "You go behind the house and get that barrel and butcher him in it."

He didn't know that man was in the barrel. He took it and throw it 'cross he back and go on 'cross the field. And the barrel was so heavy he put it down and rest. He said, "This barrel sho' is heavy!"

The man in barrel say, "I sho' make a 'scape tonight!"

The other man say, "Not you, me!"

He went on and tol' the people the barrel talked to him.

270 Be True to Me

An individual and a girl were marooned on an island, and they had been there for about two years. And they didn't have any life on this island. The only food they had was fruit from trees. And some individuals had been to war, been at sea for about five years—they had not had a woman. Five individuals who lasted through the war ended up going back to the states. They looked through the binoculars, and one individual on the ship saw life on that particular island. He saw this lady, and he almost went berserk. He said, "Look! It's a woman on the island, Captain."

The Captain say, "What! Give me your binoculars."

He looked through his binoculars and looked on the island and saw this beautiful lady there on the island—looked something like Daisy Mae in Dogpatch, in "Lil' Abner," one o' those type o' things.

And they headed for the island. So they went to the island. And this individual, the only thing he had left on the island was a little fiddle. So the Captain ran straight to this lady. He say, "I've got to have her!"

He say, "No, no, no! I'm trying to get back to the States. We're marooned on this island. We have plenty of money, and if you get us back, we'll pay you anything. Name your price!"

He say, "What do you have left?"

He say, "My fiddle."

He say, "Is that all?" He say, "Now, I tell you what. Now, we've been at sea for five years. This is the first woman we've seen in five years." He say, "I'll bet you my ship against your fiddle that I'll satisfy your lady."

He say, "No, no. I'm not going for that. No. I'll pay you anything to get me back. We have plenty of money in the United States. I'm from New York." He told him his name (big name, you know). He say, "I can pay you anything! My family can pay you anything! Just get us back!"

He say, "No, I don't want any money. The only thing I'll do, I'll bet you that ship—that great big ship—against that fiddle that I'll satisfy your lady."

He say, "No, no. I'm not going for that."

He say, "Well, that's the only way I can see that you can get off the island. I'm not taking you back under any other conditions."

So the lady say, "Let me talk to you." So she carried him on back, you know. She say, "Look now, you know I'm your woman. He can't satisfy me. No one has ever satisfied me but you. You don't have that to worry about. We can get off this island!" She say, "Go on and make the bet. After all, you'll never miss it. Make the bet! You don't have nothing to worry about. You know I'm for you all the way."

He say, "No, honey, I can't go for that."

She kept on talking to him, and he kept on resisting. So after a while she kissed him on his ear, you know, caressed his back, kissed him again. He say, "Okay, honey, but you be careful." So eventually he gave in.

So the fellow, the Captain of the ship, took this lady back in the bushes there, and they stayed back there a while. So this fellow sat there with his fiddle, and he started playing this lil' song after he looked back and he saw the bushes quivering—quivering. After about fifteen minutes, he sang:

Be true to me, be true to me, for one little ho-our-r-r,
And the ship will be o-o-ours-s-s.

Another ten or fifteen minutes; nobody said anything. He looked. Bushes shaking. He say again:

Be true to me, be true to me for one little ho-our-r-r,
And the ship will be o-o-ours-s-s.

[Long silence.]

Nobody said anything.

After a while, she finally decided to talk. She says [in a breathless, ecstatic voice]:

I—can't—be true to you;
I—can't—be true to you,
Because he hit a spot
That you forgot,
And you lost your goddamn fiddle.

271   That's Why I Poisoned Ya, Honey

A.   This woman was very sick. She was about to die, and she called her husband to her bedside, and she said, "Honey, I'm gon' leave now. You've been a good husband, and I want to thank you for it—for all the nice things you've done for me."

He was crying. He say, "Well, honey, don't talk like that. I did it because I thought 'twas my duty."

She say, "But sumpin' else I want to tell you, honey. I haven't been true to you. I've had other men. Every time you'd go away in the morning, another man would come in, and he'd spend the day with me. And just 'bout time for you to come home, he'd be just leaving. And I just want to tell ya 'bout it."

And the husband said, "Honey, huhn, huhn [mimicking man crying], I know that's, huhn, huhn, true; that's why I poisoned ya!"

B.   This man was dying and his wife was standing there looking sad. She said, "Well, Dear, you wanna make your confession?"

He said, "I made love to lots of your friends. I made love to my secretary. And you know that thousand dollars we couldn't find—I gave that to a lady, also."

The lady looked down in the bed at 'im. She say, "Nigger, why do you think I poisoned you?"

272   Let Him Buy His Own

Two guys were drinking in a bar. One guy say, "Well, I have run out of money."

The other guy say, "I have too."

He say, "Well, come on go to my house. I kin get some money from my wife. I know she got—she keeps money. She earns it daily."

They went home—and there his wife was in the bed—with a *man!*

He say, "Hey, Honey!"

She say, "What is it?"

He say, "You got five dollars?"

She say, "Gon' in the thing there and get five dollars and lea' me 'lone."

He went and got it. This other guy lookin' in—amazed, you know. Here's a man's *wife*—and he, you know, like he don't see nobody. So he went on and took the five dollars and they went on out. So a little later, they in the bar. The guy say, "Look, give him a drink and give me one."

The other man say, "Well, wh-wh-what about that guy in your house, man?"

He say, "Let him buy his own damn drink. I ain't gon' buy him none!"

273   Joe Survives

This cat would always go by this chick's house, you know. He would take care of business, you know. Every Monday! (Her husband, he was out on the road.) And this particular Monday, her husband—something happened. He got his schedule changed and he was coming back, and my man was in there gettin' ready to take care of business. And ALL of a sudden, he looked! He say, "Y-y-y-your husband's here! W-w-w-where's the closet? W-w-where's the closet?" So he ran in the damn closet.

Meantime this gal has had syphilis, you know, and her husband didn't know that, either. And she was takin' her scabs, you know, throwing 'em over there in the damn closet.

One week passed, and that Monday morning she was thinking, she say, "Well, Joe will be over here in a few minutes, and uh—" She say, "Joe, Joe, JOE! OH, MY GOD! Joe is in the closet!" She realized Joe had been in the closet a whole week. She say, "I know he *must* be *dead*. She ran, she opened the door, and my man was standing up kind o' smiling. She say, "I-I-I'm sorry—I know I uh, uh—"

He say, "Baby, if it won't for these damn potato chips, I'd o' died!"

10

Goldstein, Pat, Mike, and the Like: Ethnic Jokes

One time there was this white man, there was this
Jew man, and it was this Black man....
"It'll Go Off by Itself"

BLACKS, THEMSELVES the victims of the persecution and vituperation of white American society as well as the objects of its vicious stereotyping, have in their own folklore embraced that society's comparable stereotypes of other persecuted minority groups, mainly the Jews and the Irish. Comprising the minority ethnic group most frequently lampooned in Black American folklore are the Jews, who have long been, as merchants and landlords, the most visible symbols of the economic exploitation of Blacks in the slums. As James Baldwin noted, it is often the Jew who does the "dirty work" for the Christians.[1] It may be noteworthy, in this respect, that every anti-Jewish joke that I collected came from urban, rather than rural, areas. These jokes usually depict the Jew as a dishonest, unscrupulous, but successful businessman.

Frequently lampooned as the fools in numbskull stories in American folklore in general were the stupid Irish, most often two ignoramuses named Pat and Mike.[2] Tales about these two dumbbells were very much in vogue also in Black American folklore. Although the Pat-and-Mike tales remained popular in Black folklore (as well as

151

among isolated groups of whites such as the Kentucky hill folk)[3] long after they had vanished from the larger American scene, they are not particularly popular today among the Black Virginians whom I interviewed. Not one of my informants who told me a tale of the comic Irishman was under sixty-five years old.

Other ethnic groups occasionally the butts of jokes among Black folktellers are Italians, Chinese, Japanese, Mexicans, American Indians, and Puerto Ricans. Jokes about particular groups tend to be more popular in areas where there are large concentrations of those groups (for example, jokes about the Mexicans in the southwestern sections of this country), but none of these groups is a common object of humor in the tales of the Black Virginians whom I interviewed.

In several of the ethnic jokes the nigger is in competition with the Jew or with the Irishman, the Italian, the Mexican, or the white man. All of the usual stereotypes obtain in these tales. If it is a sexual contest, the nigger is always victorious. (See chapter thirteen for some of these tales.) If, on the other hand, the contest is economic, the prodigal and thievish nigger is no match for the industrious and wily Jew.

NOTES

1. James Baldwin, "Negroes Are Anti-Semitic because They're Anti-White," in *Black Anti-Semitism and Jewish Racism*, ed. Nat Hentoff (New York: R. W. Baron, 1969), p. 10.

2. See Jan Harold Brunvand, *The Study of American Folklore: An Introduction* (New York: W. W. Norton, 1968), p. 110.

3. See Richard M. Dorson, *American Negro Folktales* (Greenwich, Conn.: Fawcett, 1967), p. 373.

274 How Did the Fire Start?

There was a fire in an apartment house, and it was raging—continually. And the fireman come up there and said to a Japanese man, "How did this fire start?"

He said, "It started, I think, by electric light."

Then he asked one of my folks, a colored guy (notice that I didn't say "colored"; I always say "my folks"), "How did this fire start, John?"

"I think it started by candlelight."

So he asked a Irishman, say, "Vinsky, how did this, how, how, how did the fire start?"

"I think it started by lamplight."

Then he got down to the Jew. Said, "Come here," said, "Lavinsky," said, "How did this fire start?"

The Jew told him, say, "I think it was started by the Israelites."

275 See You Sad-dy

A. A white man, a Black man, and a Jew went to heaven. And when they got to the gates, Saint Peter said, "It's fifteen dollars to come in."

The white man gave him fifteen dollars, tipped him five, and went on in.

The Jew talked with him for *two* days and finally got in for fourteen ninety-eight.

Nigger say, "See ya Sad-dy."

B. There was this Italian guy and this Black guy. They were in hell. And the man tol' 'em, say, "Now, I tell ya what ya do. You want to get outta here, yawl give me two hundred dollars apiece, give me two hundred dollars and you kin get outta this place."

Well, the Italian guy kept saying, "Well, I would like to argue with you, but I'm not. I'm gon' give ya the two hundred."

And the Jewish guy say, "I'm gon' give ya a hundred and ninety-nine, that's what I'm gon' give ya."

And the Black guy tol' 'im say, "Kin I pay you Sad-dy?"

C. There was this Italian guy, this Black guy, and this Jew. The three of 'em was in a foxhole, and a hand grenade fell in there and killed 'em—killed all three of 'em. And there they were in [purgatory]. And the guy told 'em, say, "Now, I tell ya what you kin do. If you kin find enough money to get outta here, say, two hundred dollars, I kin get ya outta here."

The Italian guy went on and paid his money, and there he was, back in his foxhole. So the commander say, "Hey! Where are the other two guys, the Black guy and the Jewish guy who were in here with you?"

He say, "I don't know. Don't ask me no questions. I don't know."

He say, "Well, you better know something 'cause if you don't, you going to jail. Now they were here with you and I wanna know—"

He say, "I don't know where they is. The las' time I saw 'em, the Jewish guy was tryin' to jew 'im down to a hundred and ninety-nine dollars, and that damn nigger was 'round there tryin' to find somebody to sign a note for 'im."

D. Three guys over in Vietnam got killed in a foxhole. It was a Catholic, a Jew, and a nigger. When they got up in heaven, Saint Peter opened up the gates and say, "I'm sorry, fellows, we don't have no room." He say, if you got a hundred dollars apiece you can get some extra time on earth."

The Catholic right away paid his hundred dollars and went back down. The lieutenant came by checking out his casualty list, saw that Catholic down there, he say, "Gee, what you doing back here? I thought you were the one that got kilt."

The guy said, "We got up there and Saint Peter didn't have any more room, so he told us for a hundred dollars apiece we could get some more time."

He say, "If that's the case, why are you the only one back here? What happened to the Jew and the nigger?"

He say, "Well, I'll tell you, lieutenant, I paid my hundred dollars. I turned around and the last time I looked the Jew had gotten him down to forty-nine fifty, and that nigger was still looking for a pistol."

276   Give Me That Nigger's Address

God called a white man and a Jew and a nigger to come before him, and He told them he would give each one whatever he most desired.

The white man said he wanted knowledge [or property or money].

Then God asked the nigger what he wanted, and he asked for a big car, a big house, and a million dollars. So God granted him his wish.

Then he asked the Jew what he wanted, and the Jew said, "Don't bother about any big gift to me; just give me that nigger's address and I'll get all I need."

277   He Can Go to Hell

You know the Jews believe in paying their way through Purgatory—what they call Purgatory. And this was his brother, and he had paid once for one step up into Purgatory. And they come for more money, for him to pay some more money. So he paid some more, and this put him a little further. So he lack just about three steps of being into Purgatory. So after he asked for some more money, his brother tol' 'em, "Well . . . if he can't jump them three feet, he can go to hell!"

278   I'll Write a Check

They say a Jewish fellow died; and they had a way of—when they buried 'em—they drop money in the casket, see. This fellow he come up and he drop fifty dollars in there; another fellow, he dropped in twenty-five. So they got around 'bout two or three hundred dollars. This other Jewish fellow come up there 'n' wrote a check. Say, "If he kin spend any money, he can cash a check; it's certified." He put that in there and took the money out: "I'll take the money and give him a certified check for the whole amount."

279   That's the Thief

I used to work for a fellow when I first came here named Goldberg. And he say one time, you know, say, somebody stole a man's horse. And he got in the crowd. He knew somebody was in there, but he didn't know which one. And he say, "Somebody stole my horse, I know who he is. He's right in this crowd. If you don't come up, I'm gon' disqualify him. I'm gon' turn him in, 'cause that was a rotten thing to do. Oh, [quickly] the thief's hat's on fire! The thief's hat's on fire!"

One man [dramatizing man hitting frantically at his hat as if to put out a fire].

He say, "That's the thief!"

280   It's Worth Ten Dollars

They say this Jewish fellow was standing on a corner like he was in deep study 'bout somethin'. And another one of his Jewish friends come up and say, "Iky, I bet you ten dollars that I can tell you what you thinking."

He say, "Well, I'll have to take that bet." So he put up his ten.

The fellow say, "You thinkin' about going up here someplace, findin' a lil' place where you can have a lil' secondhand shop or store; and of gettin' a big stock of what white folks might sell (just ole cheap goods), and after you get set in there, take out all the insurance you can and then set fire to it and burn it up." He say, "Now, don't I win my money?"

He say, "Vell, you don't exactlee vin the money, but the idea is worth ten dollars. You keep it."

281   One Condition

A.   Bernstein had a store on the corner. Bernstein had three daughters. They lived in the back of the store and ate *beans, sacrificed* to give these girls a college education. Sent 'em off to college.

Spring came, and one of the girls came back home and went for a walk in Byrd Park. When she came back, she came running in, all flustered and everything. She said, "Pop-a! Pop-a! I have some verry bad news to tell you!"

He said, "Vat ees it, my dear?"

She says, "Pop-a, I vent out in Byrd Park and I valked around in the park, and enjoying the sight and all of a sudden, somebody gerrabed me and pulled me behind the trees and rape me!"

He said, "VAAT! This happened to my daughter! I make all of these sacrifices to send her to school and this happen! *Who* done it?"

She said, "Pop-a, I don't know."

He said, "What do you mean you don't know? You been to college, and you don't 'ave the common sense to ask a simple question, 'With whom am I having da pleasure?'"

The second one came home, and they got to talking. And she went out. She came back and she says, "Pop-a, I have some verry bad news to tell you." She says, "I ain' going back to school. I don't like it."

He said, "VAT? I make all o' dese sacrifices, your mother and I, eat beans in the back of the store to give you a college education, and den you tell me you AIN'T going back to school! You still use *ain't*? You don't know no better?"

When the third one came home, she said, "Oh, *Pop-a!* I have some verry bad news to tell you."

"Vat is it, my dear?"

She says, "Pop-a, I'm pregnant."

He says, "Oh! My Godt! We make dese sacrifices to give you a college education, and then you pregnant! Who done it!—I don't care who done it!—Who *done* it? I *kill* 'im! I *kill* 'im!"

She says, "Pop-a, it was Sam Scholtz."

He says, "I don't care! I'll go over to his house, and I'll *kill* him!"

Sam Scholtz was an orthodox Jew—*very wealthy*. And he could not marry her. So when he got over to Sam Scholtz' house, he was in a rage. He said, [exasperated tone] "I came over here to *kill* you. You *ruined* me life! You *ruined* me daughter!"

Scholtz said, [cool and calm voice] "Well, sir, yes I did, I admit I did. But you know I'm an orthodox Jew and I *cannot* marry her. But what I'll do: When the baby is born, if it is a girl, I'll give her twenty thousand dollars, and if it's a boy, I'll give her twenty-five thousand dollars."

Bernstein thought about those days he stayed in the back of that store and ate those beans. He says, "Vell, now, vait a minute! You say *twenty* thousand for a girl, and twenty-*five* thousand for a boy. That's not bad! That's not bad at all. I tell you vat I'll do. I'll accept that under *one* condition. Ven the baby is born, if it is a miscarriage, you fuck'er all over again."

B.   This is Mr. Vanderbilt living *high* up on the hill. And it seems as though he had some problems down in the valley. One evening an individual had gotten sort of plastered, somewhat drunk, in a tavern, and some of the people thought he could have been drunker than he was at the time. And they were talking (the lumberjacks and whatnot), saying, [in a whisper] "You know, Mr. Vanderbilt is supposed to be the father of so and so's child (over there, you know)," and they called his name. So he was sitting over there with his head on the table, and he heard his name called. He heard the conversation.

So he ran home, approached his daughter. He say, "Linda! Are you pregnant?"

She say, "Yes, Daddy."

He say, "Mr. *Vanderbilt* is going to be the father of your child?"

She said, "Yes, Daddy."

He reached in the corner and grabbed his gun. He went straight up on top of that hill, knocked on that door with the nozzle of his gun, BANG! BANG! BANG! BANG!

The butler comes to the door, say, "Yah, may I help you?"

He say, "I want to see Mr. Vanderbilt."

"Come in, please."

Then he paged Mr. Vanderbilt, pulled down the cord. Mr. Vanderbilt comes up to the top of the landing with a robe on, big cigar in his mouth: "Yes, may I help you, my dear man?"

The father pointed the gun at him, say, "I'm Linda's father. I understand that you're going to become the father of Linda's baby!"

Mr. Vanderbilt is real cool. He walks downstairs. He say, "Yah, that's right. And if it's a boy, I'll give her fifty thousand dollars. If it's a girl, I'll give her thirty thousand dollars."

He say, "You say *what*?"

And he repeated it.

Then he eased the gun down on the floor. He say, "If it be a miscarriage, will you give her another chance?"

282   *That* Is the Finger!

This old Jew gathered the family around him. He was going to give them a lesson. He said, *"Life* is a ver-ry interesting t'ing. You can equate life to the fingers on the hand. The litel finger [holding it up and gesturing], the etiquette, the charm, to show your culture. This finger [holding it up] is the ring finger. That shows that you done married, engaged. This finger [holding it up] is the indicator to point out, specify. The thumb is the gripper— that holds. *Ah!* But *that* finger [holding up the middle finger]! *That* is the *finger! That* finger has brought more pleasure to *more* people than anything in the world!" [Long pause.]

"That is the finger that rings the cash register!"

283 Pop-a's Last Vords

Jews have a habit—a custom—when the head of the house has *died*, all of them gather around the bed to "hear Pop-a's last vords." This old Jew was dying, and he was there puffing, and *all* of his kids gathered around the bed. He looked up: [in an exhausted voice] "Ja-a-cob, I-saac, Is-a-bell-l . . . Jo-o-hn. . . you're all here to hear Pop-a's last words . . . Who? Who? . . . WHO is vatching the *sto'a*?"

284 Stop, Thief!

A. They say that years ago when they used to have the clothes out on them stands, you know. Say a fellow ran down there and snatched a coat off the rack, and the Jew ran out there hollering, "Stop, theevf! Stop, theevf! Stop, theevf!"

And the cop ran out there with his pistol like he was ready for to shoot.

He say, "Shoot 'im in the pants! Coat belong to me! The coat belong to me!"

B. This Jew had this store, and all his suits were white, and this man went in and asked could he see a *blue* suit. The old Jew said, "Turn on de blue light, Mary." Say, the man tried the suit on and told him he had to go to the bathroom. So he said, "Go vright tru dat door right dere."

In the meantime, while he was waiting for him to come out the restroom [the man had obviously run away with the suit], another man came and wanted to see a green suit. He said, "Turn on de gween light, Mary." She turned the green light on. And this man told him—after he tried the suit on and looked good on him—he said that he had to go to the bathroom. So he said, "Oh, no!" He screamed for the police. The police came there and drew the pistol. He said, "NO! NO! NO! NO! Don't shoot! You shoot a hole through me suit."

285 My Wife Will Clean It Up

Once was a man cousin had died, and he ain't have no money to get no clothes. So he went to de Jew store to get a suit o' clothes. When he get that suit o' clothes he slip out the back door. The Jew lookin' at the back: "Good fit! Good fit!"

The man look 'round. The man slip out the back door and gone.

Then he went out there and tell he friend how he get the clothes. So he friend went in there and tell the Jew he want a suit o' clothes 'cause his cousin died. And the Jew flit 'round like dat [mimicking the Jew], you know. After while he say, "Oooh, my stomach hurt. Where de bafroom? I want to go to de bafroom."

And the Jew tell dat man, say, "You just shit right down dere, 'cause my wife will clean it up."

286 My, How You've Grown

Say this man went to a Jew store on a Saturday afternoon and bought this suit and went home and he just *knew* he was sharp! Going to church the next morning. He got up and put on his suit, went on out, and it started raining. When he got back home the suit had drawn up. Say he said, "Just *look* at this suit! And I just paid *all* my money for this suit and look how it has *drawn* up!"

That Monday morning he went to the Jew store, and he said, "Just *look* at this! Just *look* at this suit!"

"My!" the Jew said, "but you vreally did grow over the veek-end!"

287 Everyting Has Gone Up

This man went into the Jew store, and he wanted some slacks; so the old Jew came out and said, "Vat kin I do por you today?"

He say, "Vell," say, "I would like to look at some slacks."

So he say, "Vell, come on ober thisa vay."

So he went over there. He say, "MY! Six ninety-*eight!* Vy, befo' the var they were no more than four ninety-*eight!*"

He say, "But everyting is going up since the var."

He say, "Well, I no want tose slacks." He say, "I vould like to look at some sport shirts."

So he say, "Vell, come on ober thisa way."

So when he went over to look at the sport shirts, he say, "MY! They are *five* ninety-*eight* now, but befo' the var they vere no more than *three* ninety-*eight!*"

He say, "Just like I told you, my friend, everyting has gone up since the var."

He say, "VELL, I don't want nuttin'." He got to the door; he turned around, he looked at him. He say, "MY!", he say, "I no see dat hump on your back befo' de var!"

He say, "Dat's my ass. I told ya, *everyting* has gone up since de var."

288   She's in da Tutes

These three Jewish women went over to the corner of Second and Broad one day, and each of 'em had a daughter named Maria. And each of the daughters was in service. And one of them says, "Oh, let me tell you about my daughter Ma-rria. She's in the Vaves, you know, and she's been in the Vaves now three months, and already she's sent back *twelve* hundred dollars to be saved. Eesn't that *great!*"

The other one says, "Ooh, that's good, but *my* Ma-rria, she's in the Vax, and already she's been in four months, and she's sent back over five *thousand* dollars to be saved. That is gr-reat money. My Ma-rria is doing so *beautifully!*"

The third one spoke up, said, "Look, what do you think about *my* Ma-rria? She's in da Tutes, and she's only been in there for four months, and already she's sent twelve thousand dollars home for to be saved."

The others said, "Da *Tutes!* Da *Tutes?* What branch of the service is that?"

She said, "Oh, that is the *biggest* branch of the service, da Prostitutes!"

289   They Worried Him to Death

This porter was on a long trip with these people, a bunch of Jews. The custom of those people was when they'd go on a long trip like that, they'd pay a high price, tip 'em good. Some of these people went to New York; they all walked off the train. Nobody gave the porter anything. Porter was standing on the side. Finally, one came back, and gave him a roll of money.

The porter thanked 'im. He said, "You know, folks say that yo' people killed Christ, but they didn't kill im; they worried him to death!"

They liked to worried him [the porter] to death.

290   It'll Go Off by Itself

One time there was this white man, there was this Jew man, and it was this Black man, and *all* three o' 'em was sittin' at a bar one Friday in this hotel, drinking big champale and lookin' fine. So all o' a sudden this big, *fat* lady came in. She say, "*Baby!* One o' yawl mens show me some *bravery,* and I'll take you home with me."

So the white man say, "I'll show you some bravery." So he pulled out his knife and cut his *thumb* off. She say, "Oh, what bravery! What bravery! I must go home wid you!"

So the Jew man say, "Hey! Hey, lady, gi' me a chance." So he pulled out his knife and cut his ear off.

She say, "Oh! My! What bravery! I must go home wid you!"

So the Black man say, "Hey, baby, gi' me a chance." So he pulled out his dick and laid it on the table.

She say, "O-O-OH! You gon' cut it off! You gon' cut it off!"

He say, "Hell, naw, baby. You kiss it. It'll go off by its goddamn self!"

291   Don't Dress It

This lady had an Irish maid, you know, had just come from Ireland over here. So she say she was gon' serve dinner, and it was some kind of a dish she wanted—she didn't want it dressed, you know, she wanted it raw. So she said, "Nora, such and such a dish, I want you to serve it undressed this evening."

So when it come dinner time, Nora come out there with just shimmies and another lil' piece, say, "Missis, I done took off everything but two pieces. I'll quit my job before I'll take anything else off."

292   Pat Goes Hunting

The Irishman was working on a job, and there come a kinda cloudy day. And everybody knocked off. And he had heard 'em talkin' 'bout squirrel hunting, you know. So he decided he'd get a gun and go hunting. He ain't never been nowhere like that. So they 'uz usin' those muzzle loaders. He say, "Pat, I tell you way you load it. You put your cap on, like that [illustrating], and you put three fingers of powder in there and put a wad on it, and you put two fingers of shotgun on top of that, and you pack it down tight, and put the cap on the back end. Then you got it fixed." Pat goes to work and puts three fingers this way [illustrating that, instead of the amount indicated by three fingers held together side by side, he put that indicated by three fingers held end to end]. That's two fingers; he put three fingers in there like that. And he load it up and went up on top of a hill there, and he saw a squirrel. He blasted away! That gun kicked him way back down to the bottom.

So the man hollered, "Hey, Pat! Did you kill 'im?"

He say, "I had the wrong end pointed up there. If he'd been standing here where I'm standin' 'twould a killed 'im."

293   It's 'Leven O'Clock

This Irishman, he come over to America, and he had never seen no ticks; he didn't know what a tick was. So they tol' 'im, "Pat, I tell you now, over in America they got them terrible ticks; they'll *bite* ya man, and they'll really hurt ya!"

So he had a idea that a tick was a great big somethin', you know. So when he started over there, he got him a big stick, and he say, "If I run across any of these ticks, I'm gon' kill 'im."

So it won't too long; a man just walking along in front of 'im; he dropped his watch. Watch laying there, it was going "Tick! Tick! Tick! Tick!" He say, "Yeah-h-h, here one o' them durn ticks right now!" And he took the stick and beat the watch all up, you know.

Pretty soon, the man come on by lookin' for his watch. He said, "Hey, man! You seen a watch laying up there?"

"Watch? Watch? What is a watch?

He say, [incredulously] "A lil' thing 'bout that big around [indicating size] and it make a noise, Tick! Tick! Tick! Tick!"

He say, "I thought it was one of them things yawl call ticks, and I kill it!"

So the man say, "Come on and show me where it is."

He went over there and he done beat the man's watch *all up*, you know.

He say, "Now next time you see somethin' laying in the path like this, pick it up and put it in your pocket. Somebody 'll tell you what it is."

So a little after that he was walkin' on down, and he saw one o' these dry-land terrapins, crossing the road, and when the terrapin saw him, he just drawed all up in the shell, like this [illustrating]. He thought, "It must be a watch." He picked up this thing and stuck it in his pocket, and going on down the road, you know, the old terrapin started to scratching, tryin' to git out there. And somebody come over, say, uh, "Hey, mister! You know what time it is? You got a watch?"

He say, "I b'lieve I got a watch." He stuck it down there [dramatizing man sticking his hand in his pocket]: "Yeah, it's 'leven o'clock and scratching like hell for twelve."

294   Moving Hell

They say these two Irishmen had just come over to America and had never seen a fire engine; and that night they put up in this room. And they had the horsedrawn fire engines in those days and had that big steamy thing—that pump that was pumpin' water. And a fire broke out in the neighborhood, and they heard that thing going, BLANKA, BLANKA, BLUNKEDY, BLUNKEDY, BLUNK! One of 'em run to the window and looked out there, and just as he run to the window, that big thing come with all that smoke and boiling, and that horse runnin' like that. He yelled, "Hey, Mike! Wake up there, Mike. They're moving hell out here; the first load just gone by!"

295   Littin' Is Hell

A crow was on the courthouse, and the crow fly down on the ground, and he light. And there was a Ishman [Irishman] who was dere lookin' at 'im. And the other Ishman say, "Kin you do dat?"

Say, "Yeah, I kin do dat, too."

So he climbed up on the courthouse. See here he flyin' 'round like a crow. And he fly 'round like the crow. He get heself all break up.

The other Ishman say, "How you like flying?"

He say, "I like *flyin'* all right, but littin' is hell!"

296   Pat and Mike

Pat and Mike was goin' down the road, and they hadn't had *none* for some time. So they run across a sheep, and they thought they'd get 'em a piece there. So Mike was holdin' the sheep while Pat was gettin' his. All at once Mike looked down, and the sheep poked her tongue out at 'im. So Mike hollered, "Pull it back, Pat, it's runnin' out her *mouth!*"

297   Me Sell to Niggers

Well, they tell me one time not too many years ago there was a ole Chinaman up there on Main Street running a restaurant. And say these trash men kept gettin' all this cat fur out the trash. And they reported it.

Say he say, "Me don't sell to white folks! Me don't sell to white folks! Me sell to niggers!"

298   No Sabe

Here's one about a Japanese woman entering the country. And, of course, she was going through customs, and the naturalization officer say,

"Well, who's sponsoring you into the country?"
    She say, "No sabe, no sabe."
    He say, "Well, it's somebody who's s'posed to be responsible for you."
    She say, "No sabe. No sabe."
    He say, "You got a brother or somebody? A sister or somebody?"
    She say, "No sabe. No sabe!"
    He say, "You don't have no *kinfolk* here?"
    "O-O-OH! *Kin fuck!* Kin fuck a lettle beet!"

11

The White Man Is the Devil: Tales about the Cruelty of Whites

Say the fellow say, [pleadingly] "Boss Man, Boss
Man, my feet is cold."
He say, "Damn your feet, let the wheelers roll!"
"Let the Wheelers Roll"

IN VIEW OF the fact that people joke about what frightens or disturbs
them, we might well expect many of the jokes in the Black repertoire
to be about the white man, who is frequently pictured as a devil
who makes the Black's life hell. Although recently jokes about the
white liberal have arisen, the white devil in Black folklore remains
the cruel, racist, white Southerner: the harsh slave master, the un-
feeling white boss, the brutal, sadistic white sheriff, the unjust white
judge, and the ordinary, all-American, white Christian who visits all
manner of persecution onto his Black brother.

Many of the tales in this chapter depict vicious beatings, inhuman
slave drivers, cruel injustices, lynchings, and so forth. These could
hardly be considered funny subjects, certainly not by Black people,
many of whom have suffered under circumstances such as those
recounted here. And yet many of these tales are humorous. Those
who created them have transformed unendurable situations which

they witnessed or suffered into jokes, and they are thereby able to laugh at such absurd incidents. That this has undoubtedly been their salvation was strikingly revealed to me when I recorded "Let the Wheelers Roll" (below) in a session attended by a group of Black men in their seventies and eighties. They laughed uproariously at the end of the anecdote, and then they started talking about their own experiences with similar cruel bosses, one informant asserting, "Yeah, that boss man didn't care 'bout nothin' but let them wheelers roll." At the repetition of that key line, they laughed again; but then, almost abruptly, they returned to the painful reminiscences of the similar suffering that they had endured. I detected an almost imperceptible crack in their voices; I watched their brows slowly wrinkle and their eyes dim with painful memories. For one brief moment I saw in their faces the sufferings of my people, and I felt the magnitude of a pain so deep that none of them could ever have verbalized it. Tears began to well in my eyes, but I was snatched from my sentimental mood when one of them repeated, "What that boss man say? Let them wheelers roll!" And we all laughed heartily again. If they noticed the tear that fell, I am sure they assumed that it resulted from my exuberant laughter. I experienced then, more vividly than ever before, the verity of that old blues line, "laughing to keep from crying."

A number of other tales in this book also depict the cruelty of the whites, but they deal with getting revenge on them, humiliating them, and so on. The selections in this chapter treat only their cruelty. Because there is no poetic justice in these tales, they comprise perhaps the grimmest tales in the book. You will note that many of them are individual experiences which have been repeated so often that they have become a part of the folklore of certain families or areas.

299   Let the Wheelers Roll

They had what you call those rooters—had two mules—go up there and tear the ground up and the other fellows up there had what they call a wheeler—it was more of a scoop with two wheels on it. And they hook four mules there and scoop up in order to get that dirt up and then they unhook these mules, 'n' 'course they had laborers down there to lift up the dirt and carry it up the hill where they gon' dump it. One cold day, you know, said they out there loadin' wheelers and like that, and say, and they slowed down, and the boss man say, [nastily] "Hey, what's wrong with them wheelers up there? Let them wheelers roll!"

Say the fellow say, [pleadingly] "Boss Man, Boss Man, my feet is cold."

He say, "Damn your feet, let the wheelers roll!"

300 Controlling the Slave

Another [superstition] was a cat crossing their path. There were times at adjoining plantations that slaves, after a day of hard work (some of them had a little liberty), so they sometimes would sneak off to the next plantation, I guess, to fraternize with slaves on that plantation. As a way of knowing whether or not they would go a long way, they [whites] would say to them [the slaves] if a cat crossed their path to stop and make a mark in the road. (They kept a lot of cats anyway.) And so when they did see a cat, they'd make a mark in the road. And then in the morning he'd [the master would] go down there and see how many marks he'd see and see how many were moving back and forth from one plantation to another. And that was another device they had in trying to control their slave population.

301 A Slave Escape

Another experience I remember that was related to me [by Mr. Bill Jones]. Right here in this community here [Ruthville], there was an elderly fellow who was owned by some of these landowners here in this vicinity. And he said that he didn't know how old he was. But he was a large fellow. He'd been promised a pair of shoes—something he'd never had in his life. And so he said the Marster promised him he was going to take him in to the city and get new shoes. They got up early that morning before day and they traveled and traveled until they ultimately came to the city—the city, I suspect, was Richmond. And so they went to this place and they carried him in and had him to stand up on a large block or something in the center, and all of the whites would come around and they'd look at 'im and they'd examine his legs and all (he thought they was fitting him for shoes, but actually I suspect they were looking for the condition of his muscles). They said it never dawned on him till nightfall came when someone else came and said, "You're going with me." And it dawned on him then that he'd been sold. He realized then that an exchange had been made for him.

The person who got him carried him up into what, I suspect, is now Hanover County—and there to work on a farm. He was very depressed and despondent because he'd been raised up on this farm in Charles City County and he knew people on the farm—knew this area—he was familiar with Charles City. But on this strange place—on this farm where he was on now—there was a river there, also. He'd seen a river in Charles City County. I suspect he believed that was the only river in the world—that one in Charles City—and he had the intelligence to know that a river flowed in certain ways. So he used to go down there during the day to work on the lower fields near this river—he'd go down there and look at the river and watch the water flowing, and it dawned on him that, if he could follow that river, he could go to Charles City. So he worked for that fellow for the space of about three months, and he said it was near the fall time—apples had ripened— and he had planned his escape.

So he got himself a gunny sack and he put these apples in the gunny sack. And he planned his escape. During the time of the full moon he decided he would sneak off at night and he did. And he followed this river. And he said it was about a day and a half of traveling by walking, and this river did bring him back to Charles City County. And when he came within the county—at that time the Union forces had occupied it and they were hiring all run-aways as workers in the army to build fortifications, breastworks, and to drive supply wagons. And having worked on a farm, he got a job driving a supply wagon in the army.

And down the road that runs into Route Five, it's a place where they call the Kinnard [?], and at that time they had some action in that area and they had captured quite a few of the local militia. And when he carried these supplies down to the compound where the men were garrisoned at, he bring these persons they had captured back up to the stockades where they were keeping them. (It must have been up in this area here.) They said in the first load of prisoners, in that number was the man who sold him. And said that he had a great urge to take one of those spears out of that wagon and just bash him on top of the head, but they wouldn't allow it because the soldiers had guard over them. But he had a great urge to do him bodily harm because of the fact he realized what had happened to him.

But he gained his freedom after the war and he lived up into the early part of the century in this community here—somewhere between here and Charles City Court House.

302 You Could Hear the Whip Falling

This man had a lot of slaves, and they had died out. And say you could come on by there at night—'specially if it rainin'—say you can hear them slaves holler—just like the overseer beatin' 'em: "Oh, me, please, Master, OH, MASTER, OH, PLE-E-E-ASE, Master." Say, everybody'd *scatter!* 'Course they were departed spirits. But that's the way they used to treat 'em in those days, see. They say you could hear them people hollerin' and screamin' and you could hear this whip *fallin'* on 'em.

303 Sure to Go to Jail

If you [a Black person] went there before Judge Whitefield [name changed] you were *just as sure* to go to jail as you went down there!

304 Disturbing the Peace

This fellow went before Judge Whitefield for disturbing the peace. And Whitefield asked 'im, say, "Nigger, how have you been disturbing the peace?"

So he said, "*Judge, I've just been singing.*"

He say, "*What you been singing?*"

He say, "I went down the street and I was singing 'I got a long, tall, sealskin brown; she's on the road somewhere.'"

So Whitefield say, "Lemme hear you sing it."

So this fellow sang this song, you know: "I got a long, tall, sealskin girl; she's on the road somewhere."

So Judge Whitefield say, "I kin beat ya singing that." So Whitefield say, "I've got a long, tall shovel and pick; it's on the road somewhere. *Thirty* days in jail!"

305 The Mobile Buck

The time that Whitefield was judge—years ago—they was dancin' what you call the Mobile Buck, and it was kind of a (in those days *anything* that was "out the way" was what they called indecent) . . . So they passed this law that anybody was dancin' the Mobile Buck out in the street, they was gon' arrest 'im and carry 'im on down to jail and fine 'im. So they caught this young man and this girl out there dancing the Mobile Buck, and the police arrested 'em and carried 'em on down there.

So the Judge said, "What you arrest 'em for?"

They say, "Judge, they was dancin' the Mobile Buck."

So the Judge said to 'em, he said, "What is this? You know better than to be dancing the Mobile Buck out there on the *street.*"

He say, "I *won't* dancing the Mobile Buck."

The girl say, "Yes, you were too. We *both* was dancing it."

So the Judge say, [talking to the girl] "Now, I'm gon' tell you; you go on out here." He didn't do anything to her.

"But *you*, you dance me down five dollars for the Mobile and ninety cents for the Buck, or thirty days in jail!"

306   Shortenin' Bread

It used to be against the law to sing "Shortenin' Bread." So they was out there singing "Shortenin' Bread." So they arrested him and carried him in court. The Judge say, "What is the charge?"

They say, "He was out there singing 'Shortenin' Bread' on the street."

So he say, "I don't even know how to sing it."

So Whitefield say, "Put on the skillet and put on the lead, Mama gon' bring me some shortenin' bread."

So the fellow say, "That ain't the way you sing it, Judge." He say, "Pick up a skillet and put on the lead, Mama gon'—"

Judge say, "That's all right 'bout that. Five dollars for the skillet; ninety cents for the lead. Six months in jail for singing 'Shortenin' Bread.'"

307   Talkin' Like a Damn Fool

This fellow—he was a hardworking man and bought his food, so she never cooked it. When he come in there looking for his supper, she over next door, gossiping and carryin' on. This night he got mad, and he beat her.

So they had him arrested, and the Judge said, [in a confidential tone] "All right, Uncle John," said, "tell me, man to man, what went on between you two. I'm married myself and you know these women are always doin' somethin' to get a man off."

He say, "Well, Judge, I'll tell you the way it 'twas." Say, "I work *hard* and I bring that woman my somethin' to eat home and all she got to do is cook it and have it ready for me. Whenever I come there, she ain't got it ready. She over next door or somewhere gossipin' or somethin'. This time when I came in there, she didn't have it ready, I *hauled* back 'n' I smacked her down on the floor. I picked her up and I *smacked* her down again. In fact, then I hauled back and *kicked* 'er. After I kicked 'er, I pulled her up on the bed; then I opened the door and *threw* her out the door and *locked* the door behind her—" Say, [tone of voice indicates that Uncle John is pleased with himself] "How I talkin', Judge?"

"Talkin' fine, you talkin' fine. Talkin' fine. Anything more?"

He say, "Naw, that's 'bout all."

He say, "Well, Uncle John, I'm gon' tell ya somethin' 'bout that. For *smackin'* that woman 'round like that, that's a fifty-dollar fine. And for *kickin'* her, that's twenty-five dollars more. And for throwin' her out the door and lockin' the door behind her, that's thirty days." Say, [copying same pleased voice as Uncle John's] "How I talkin', Uncle John?"

"You talkin' like a damn fool!"

308 Horse Must Pay

This man' lil' girl want to go somewhere and this man didn't have time to kyar [carry] her. So he hitched the horse to the buggy. And he was telling that man, "This horse is kinda wild." Say, "Be particular." Say, "I don't want my child to get hurt."

And as they get out on the street, a wind blowed a paper in front the horse' face and make the horse run away. And he break up the buggy. And they tumble out, and the lady had to went to the hospital and the baby went to the graveyard. And they put the horse on the gang for lifetime and put the buggy in jail.

309 You Have All the World

Way back there, a colored man was in court. I can't recall his name now, but he was in court. And I suppose he was there as a witness, from what I can recall. And the Judge asked him a question. Well, he didn't want to answer it, so he answered like this: He said, "Uh, Judge, Your Honor, you have *all* the *world* to stand on, and I have just *this* little place to stand." Before he got through the Judge ran him out of court.

(What he was trying to say was, now, to make him say something that he didn't want to say, but more than that, the Judge had *all* the power, but to make him commit himself to something he didn't want to say . . .)

310 Neither Here nor Dar

They tell a story on my great grandfather, who lived to be one hundred and nine years old. They used to tell many stories on him, but I'll tell you two of them. One of the stories was something like this. Somebody had stolen something. (He was a great fisherman, you know.) Somebody had been charged with stealing some nets or something, from the boats, the creeks. And they had my great grandfather called to the court as a witness. He was well over a hundred—And of course, they said . . . (His name was Sam, Samuel [name withheld].) They said, "Uncle Sam, will you swear to tell the truth and nothing but the truth so help [you] God?"

And so the only thing he would say, "I was neither here nor dar . . . I was neither here nor dar," and they couldn't *make* him say anything else. He wasn't going to swear anything.

311　Yawl Used to It

A white guy and a Black guy were in court for rape, and the man had sentenced both of 'em to hang. So the morning of the hanging, the white guy [was] crying, "Huhnhuhn, they gon' kill us, huhn, they gon' hang us, you know they gon' hang us."

The Black guy say, "Man, why don't you *shet* that noise up. Man, you raped the woman and beat 'er—we did all these things, and the only thing we're getting is our *just* due."

The white guy turned around and say, "Huhn [still crying], yeah, you kin talk. YAWL used to it!"

312　I Jest Had a Dream

This Black man worked for this white man, and this white man wanted to date this Black man's sister. So this particular day they were in the truck, and the white man said, "Nigger, you know I had a dream las' night 'bout your sister. We were datin' and, you know, I gave you twenty-five dollars."

So the nigger say, "You know what?" Say, "I had a dream too. I was sittin' in this car along with yo' sister, and we were just hugging and kissing."

The white man say, "SHET UP, nigger! I jest had another dream. I dream that you were dead!"

313　It's a White Lady

But let me tell you one now that will knock you over.

In my county, in Reedville, a woman lost her watch—it was stolen. A white woman stole the watch, as a matter of fact. (But in the town of Reedville [sarcastic tone] anything that was stolen, it was always a Negro that stole it.) The Commonwealth's Attorney was named A. B. Coles [name changed] (I'll never forget), A. B. Coles (I knew Coles). Coles stammered terribly. So somebody said, "Mr. Coles, uh, it's an awful thing that happened. Whatcha gon' do 'bout it?"

And he said, "Uh, uhuh, i-i-i-if it w-w-were a d-d-d-damn n-n-n-nigger, I-I-I'd k-k-know j-j-jestwhattodo, b-b-but it's a w-w-w-w-*white* lady."

314   The Suicide

A Negro was pulled from a river in Mississippi. He had five stab wounds and two gunshot wounds in his head and chest. In addition, his feet had been set in concrete and his hands were tied. The sheriff called a Civil Rights leader and told him it was the worst case of suicide he'd ever seen.

315   Yawl's Blue Heaven

A nigger was on the street in Alabama singing:

It's Molly and me,
And baby makes three.
Happy in my blue heaven.

A white man walked up and hit him on the head and knocked him down: "Now get up and sing that song like a Black bastard s'posed to sing it."
When his head cleared, the nigger got up, shook his head, and sang:

It's the mistress and yawl,
No niggers a-tall.
Happy in yawl's
Blue heaven.

316   Where the Niggers Hang Out

And even after the War the Ku Klux Klan made it so hard for Negroes, scared them to death, whipped them, shot them, beat them, hung them. Niggers were more afraid of them than they had ever been afraid of their masters.

This is how afraid they were in Georgia: A white Klansman asked, "Hey, John, where do the niggers hang out around here?"

And John pointed: "Up dar in that old oak tree."

317   Yo Ami

A Klansman say, "Hey, nigger, what town is this?"

John: "Miami, Captain, Miami."

He hit John and knocked him flat: "Now get up and tell me what town this is."

John: "Miami, Boss, Miami."

He knocked him down again. This happened four times. "Now, nigger, what town is this?"

"Yo Ami, Boss, Yo Ami."

318   I'll Go as Far as Memphis

This man had lived in Mississippi, and they were getting along so poorly during that particular time that he went up North, like a lot of people who migrated to the North to get out of the Deep South because they were being treated so badly. So he went up North and he was getting along *fine*. Oh, he got on top. So some of his friends asked him to come back down to Mississippi and help the others; and so then he said, "I'm going to talk to the Lord about it."

So he talked to the Lord about it, and his friend asked him, say, "Well, what did the Lord tell you?"

So he said, "I told the Lord my friends in Mississippi needed my help and asked Him if He would go back South with me, and the Lord told me, "I'll go as far as Memphis.""

319   No Business Praying in White Churches

I went to a church—revival was going on at the church, and so I assumed to go to the revival meeting. I had gone out in the community. I went to this revival meeting. So there was a big fat man at the door named Boots. (I knew him very well; I had worked on his farm.) And he saw me coming; he said, "John! glad to see you; come on in; glad to see you; just walk—no-o-o, just walk up in the gallery."

And so, of course, I went in the gallery. That was the only thing to do. So I went up there and sat. To be evangelical and to be Christian (he [the minister] looked up in the gallery—saw me, and another minister with me), he said, "I see—I see two ministers here today of another race, of another race." Then he said, "You know one of the things that I say of the colored people is to *educate* 'em." Then he said, "Brother, won't you lead us in prayer?"

I knew he was talking to me, so I stood and offered the prayer. [Long pause.] Of course, you know it was just like, you know, something had happened, *Judgment Day*—everything was so quiet.

So there was considerable comment around about this Negro praying in a white church. Up at the little store about a mile from the church, they said, "Did you hear about young Ellison praying in the white church the other day?"

They said, "Yes, I heard about it. He prayed a right good prayer."

So one white woman said (she was the owner of the store), "You know, I think it's all right for colored people to go into white people's church *sometimes*, but I don't think any colored people got no business praying in white peoples' church."

320   The Master Can't Get In

This Negro sexton of the white church wanted to answer the call. The Minister, you know, didn't want to hurt his feelings, but he asked him to go back and consult the Master about it. So, he come back the next Sunday, you know, and the Minister asked him what was the answer.

He told him the Master say He had been trying to get in there for twenty-five years and He hadn't been able to get in there. You know well his chances was mighty slim. If they hadn't welcomed Him in there for all those years, you know well the sexton's chances were very poor.

321   The Last Thing I Remember

This fellow joined this Methodist Church down Williamsburg, and—he died. And he was up, you know, before Saint Peter, and Saint Peter was asking about his life, you know, what did he remember? And the Lord told him, He say, "You know you belonged to an *integrated* church."

He said, "Yeah," say [haltingly] "I joined a Methodist Church of Williamsburg."

So the Lord said, "Well, what else do you remember?"

He says, "Uh," say, [haltingly] "they . . . took . . . me . . . to . . . baptize . . . me—and . . . Say! You know one thing, that's the *last* thing I remember."

322   Ingratitude

This fellow had a Parrot and he was walkin' 'round out on the lawn there, you know, and a Hawk came on by and picked 'im up—thought it was a chicken. So Polly looked down and saw the man out in the field. He say,

"HEYYYY, POLLYRIDIN' POLLYRIDIN'." So the Hawk took his claws and kinda stuck 'im like that [dramatizing]. Ole Polly say, "DAMNITTTTT, TURNMELOOSE! DAMNIT! TURNMELOOSE!" So the Hawk hadn't been used to nothin' talkin' 'n' he turned him loose and *dropped* 'im.

And as he was flyin' on across the river, you know, he fluttered on down in the water. He was too light to sink. So there was two colored fellows sittin' down there, you know, fishing, and Ole Polly say, "TAKEMEOUT, MARS'LLPAYYA, TAKEMEOUT, MARS'LLPAYYA" [Master will pay you].

So one of 'em knew 'bout who he b'long to. He took his hook and line and threw it over there and pulled him to 'em, and when he got through fishing a while, he went on by the house and the man was out there lookin' for the Parrot.

You know what Polly say: "MASSA!—MASSA! MANSTOLEME! MAN-STOLEME! Give 'im a kick in the rear and send 'im on 'bout his bizness."

323 Why

I wake up and there's no smell of bacon frying . . .
Why?
Because that white motherfucker got it in his house!

324 Put 'Im Back

A colored man was sittin' on the bus, and they had chinches in the cars. Say a white man was sittin' there—saw a chinch on the colored man's shoulder—so he walked up there and took 'im off.

He [colored man] say, "Looka here! LOOKA HERE! Yawl white folks don't wan' to see a nigger have nothin'. Put 'im back up there!"

325 Alligator Bait

During Johnson's administration, you know, he went down to see how integration was. He was flying over *Florida,* and he looked down, and he saw this boat down there, and here was a white guy driving the boat and a Black guy on skis—down there in the Everglades—just rowing away. Johnson said, "Get this plane down, land it, *land* it! These people up North talking 'bout—Black folks ain't—gettin' equality down here." Say, "Get this plane down. I want to see these people."

So they got down and the guys, they come up on the shore. So he told the Black guy, he say, "I want to congratulate yawl down here as well as you people are gettin' along and everything." And he says, "Just like you out there skiing; you don't have a problem, do you?"

Say the Black guy told him, say, "You ever been on a alligator hunt?"

326   You Knew I Was Coming

I think the Civil Rights law had just been passed. And a couple of Negroes went in a restaurant on Pennsylvania Avenue in Washington. And they asked this waitress for some chitterlings and pig feet.

She say, "Well, we don't serve that here."

He say, "Whatcha mean, you don't serve it! Don't you read the papers? You shoulda had it. You know I was coming. You knew I was coming!"

327   White Water

Place: South Africa
Person: Radical Black
Restaurant: White

The radical Black, disgusted that they are kept separate from the white man, hollers out, "I guess I'll try some of this white water."

328   Basic Assumption

Everyone in the hospital wears white. And they pick up their laundry from the same place. One day a Black medical student goes to pick up his intern jackets. The white man behind the counter says, "Sir, what size kitchen jacket do you wear?"

329   Sam Is Definitely Left Out

There were these kids in school. And this particular day the teacher decided to give some homework. So she say, "Kids, I want everyone to go home and use the word definitely."

So the next morning came. So the teacher say, "Did everyone do their homework?" So everybody raised their hands. So the teacher called on Sally. And Sally's sentence read, "I am *definitely* going to have a birthday party."

She said, "Oh, very good, very good!"

So the kids raised their hands, and the teacher called on *Susie*. Susie's sentence read, "I am *definitely* going to the birthday party."

So she said, "Very good, very good!"

So a couple of weeks had gone by and she hadn't heard anything from Sam. Sam, he was the little colored boy. So she said, "Sam, do you have your homework?"

So Sam said, "Yes." So Sam's sentence read, "If a turd is a fart, I'm *definitely* going to shit!"

Sam's sentence read this because he was mad because didn't no one invite *him* to the birthday party.

12

The Bottom Rail Comes to Be the Top Riser: Outsmarting Whitey

> And the old slave lady answered, "Missis, my God know how to make the bottom rail come to be the top riser. . . ."
> "The Bottom Rail Comes to Be the Top Riser"

FROM THE TIME of slavery until the present, Black people have constituted the bottom rail in American society. Wherever they look they see themselves in the demoralizing position of powerless victims in hostile territory. It has been mainly in their folktales that they have been able to find some relief from their frustrations and to give some aggressive expression to their hostilities. The tales have allowed the Black slave, the Black freedman, and the contemporary Black militant to act out their hostility without endangering their physical well-being. The tales have allowed them, in a sense, to revolt against their master, boss, or judge in a created world where obstacles are not quite so great as and the conditions of combat are a little more equal than they are in real life. The psychological rewards of this kind of tale is explained by J. L. Fisher, who points out that folktales provide both wish fulfillment and catharsis. He notes that, by expressing those emotions which have been denied expression, the teller of folktales derives some relief. Even though the tales may deal with fear, sadness, and so forth, they serve a "positive

179

psychological affective function" because they relieve anxiety.[1] By belittling and ridiculing whites and by picturing them as foolish victims, Blacks mitigate some of the frustrations of their daily lives and enhance their sense of dignity and pride.

It is no surprise then that the favorite hero in Black American folklore is the Brother who successfully tackles "the Man" (that is, the system). Unlike the favorite heroes in European and white American folklore, he ordinarily does not fit into the categories of feat hero, contest hero (John Henry is the one possible exception, and his exploits may be read figuratively as a sexual contest, which is extremely popular in Black folklore), defender, or deliverer.[2] He rarely sets out to perform any great feat, to accomplish any notable task, to face any challenging ordeal, or to save a lady in distress. His one goal is usually to outsmart the Man, to humiliate him, to outperform him mentally, verbally, physically, or sexually, or to force him to recognize and to respect him. On a few occasions he works to outsmart or to defeat other Blacks. Unlike the standard Western hero, who is usually a defender of the system, he sees the system as his enemy. He may often be a villain; he almost always violates the accepted mores; he fails to follow any rules for combat; he is often inhumanly cruel and sadistic; he is a braggart, a flashy dresser, a lover of showy material things, an untrustworthy, wily trickster, and a potent and virile lady's man. Roger D. Abrahams points out that the Black hero shares many attributes of the Minister.[3] However, though this hero is the object of admiration, the Minister is the target of abuse in folk humor because he hypocritically denies the attributes at the same time he reveals them in his actions. As Leonard Feinberg notes, folly and vice "are likely to be attacked by satirists only when folly poses as good sense and vice as goodness."[4] The Black folk hero not only defies the system and its mores, but he brags about his defiance at the same time.

This Black hero, who takes two forms—that of a trickster or of a Bad Nigger—has his origin in the Brer Rabbit and Slave John figures. The slaves' Brer Rabbit is an obvious descendant of the African Anansi the Spider and Hare. Like them, Brer Rabbit is a powerless creature, without weapons to protect himself against other, stronger animals. Obviously seeing their own situation mirrored in this help-less animal, the slaves adopted him and invested him with a wily cunning and a scheming nature through which he was in most cases, though not always, able to overcome other, stronger animals. Not only did he usually defeat the enemy, but he frequently also obtained certain privileges denied the slaves, such as competing with stronger rivals for the lady of his choice and continually winning the best food. That he might have achieved these ends through underhanded, unsportsmanlike, immoral methods was not important to the slave. That he bucked the system (a system which never had the slave's happiness at stake anyway) and often won gave them immeasurable psychological pleasure. The aggression released in these stories and the revenge which Brer Rabbit exacts reveal a hatred and bloodthirsty aggression suggestive of later-day militancy. As Bernard Wolfe has pointed out, in Joel Chandler Harris' most famous collection, *Uncle Remus: His Songs and His Sayings*, the Fox (the animal who is the most frequent representative of Old Massa) is made a fool of by all the weakest animals—the Buzzard, the Terrypin, the Bull Frog; Brer Rabbit finally kills all three of his powerful enemies, and sometimes his killing is extremely cruel: he scalds the wolf to death, sets a swarm of bees on the Bear, causes the fatal beating of Fox, and, not satisfied with killing Fox, he takes Fox's head to Mrs. Fox in his wish to fool her and her children into eating it in their soup.[5] Not all the Brer Rabbit tales illustrate this extremity, however; many are merely humorous accounts of Brer Rabbit's trickery or of his escape from more powerful animals.

The Slave John (sometimes known as Tom, Sam, Efan, Jack or Rastus) is the human parallel to Brer Rabbit. He is in perpetual conflict with Ole Massa, whom he frequently, but not always, outwits. The tales of actual physical harm to the master are rarer here than in the Brer Rabbit tales, and most of these stories deal with John's efforts to get out of some predicament that his laziness, talkativeness, or thievery have gotten him into. At best they involve his humiliation of Ole Massa.

Brer Rabbit and Slave John are with us today in varied guises. Their most popular contemporary descendant is the Bad Nigger, who has inherited Brer Rabbit's violent side. Rather than rely on wit, cunning, and persuasion, the Bad Nigger relies on force.[6] The Bad Nigger has been enjoying increasing popularity at the expense of the trickster, whose use of indirection and persuasion frequently approaches the despised methods of an Uncle Tom. (Because of the preponderance of tales dealing with the Bad Nigger, those tales will be treated separately in chapter thirteen unless the emphasis is exclusively on a racial contest.)

It is interesting that, in many of the tales recounting contests between whites and Blacks included in this chapter and in chapters seven and thirteen, the Black man asserts his superiority through his sexuality. The sexual prodigiousness of the Black man is a com-

monly accepted idea in Black folklore.[7] This myth probably originated with whites, whose concern with Black sexuality may be seen
in early American and European "scientific" studies and fiction
(especially in the Plantation School novels but also in later European
and American novels) as well as in an account such as John Howard
Griffin's Black Like Me.[8] Frantz Fanon asserts that whites view the
Black man as "a penis symbol" and cites widespread association
tests to substantiate this assertion.[9] This preoccupation of white men
with Black sexuality lies at the basis of much racial violence, which
is frequently motivated by tales of a Black man's having molested a
white woman. Innumerable "crimes" have been intensified by the
additional rumor of sexual molestation, and the punishment has
frequently—almost inevitably—been a bloody ritual in which the
Black man was sexually mutilated. Laws in certain states in this
country reserved the penalty of castration to Blacks (and sometimes
to Indians).[10] All these acts undoubtedly reflect the white man's
obsession with the Black man's genital superiority and the former's
desire to emasculate the latter.

Whatever the basis for the myth of Black sexuality, Blacks have
accepted it and exploited it in their folk humor as a source of pride
and as an indication of superiority over the white man. And if at
times these tales of Black supersex heroes seem exaggerated and
ludicrous, pause for a moment over some of the serious studies and
comments by whites such as those cited here.

NOTES

1. J. L. Fisher, "The Sociopsychological Analysis of Folktales," Current
Anthropology 4 (June, 1963): 257.

2. These are categories of heroes enumerated by Orrin E. Klapp, "The Folk
Hero," Journal of American Folklore 62 (January–March, 1949): 17–25.

3. Roger D. Abrahams, Positively Black (Englewood Cliffs, N.J.: Prentice-
Hall, 1970), p. 105.

4. Leonard Feinberg, Introduction to Satire (Amos, Iowa: Iowa State University Press, 1967), pp. 29–30.

5. Bernard Wolfe, "Uncle Remus and the Malevolent Rabbit," Commentary 8 (July, 1949): 32.

6. Harold Finestone makes a similar classification of young Blacks into
"Cool Cats," who rely on manipulation and who eschew force, and "Gorillas," who resort to force to achieve their aims ("Cats, Kicks, and Color,"
Social Problems 5 [July, 1957]: 3–13). Roger D. Abrahams also makes a
comparable distinction between the trickster and the bad man (Deep Down
in the Jungle: Negro Narrative Folklore from the Streets of Philadelphia, 1st
rev. ed. [Chicago: Aldine, 1970], pp. 61–85).

7. Langston Hughes notes that "in the category of the bawdy joke there are

hundreds illustrating the prevalent folk belief in the amorous prowess of the Negro male" ("Jokes Negroes Tell on Themselves," *Negro Digest* 9 [June, 1951]: 24).

8. Dr. Charles White, described as an "eminent English physician and surgeon," wrote in his *Account of the Regular Gradation in Man* (1799): "That the *Penis* of an African is larger than that of an European, has, I believe, been shown in every anatomical school in London. Preparations of them are preserved in most anatomical museums; and I have one in mine. I have examined several living negroes, and found it invariably to be the case" (quoted in Thomas F. Gossett, *Race: The History of an Idea in America* [New York: Schocken Books, 1965], p. 48). Another example is a passage from Michel Cournot's *Martinique:* "The black man's sword is a sword. When he has thrust it into your wife, she has really felt something. It is a revelation. In the chasm that it has left, your little toy is lost. Pump away until the room is awash with your sweat, you might as well just be singing. This is good-by. . . . Four Negroes with their penises exposed would fill a cathedral. They would be unable to leave the building until their erections had subsided . . ." ([Paris: Collection Metamorphoses, Gallimard, 1948]: pp. 13–14; cited in Frantz Fanon, *Black Skin, White Masks* [New York: Grove Press, 1967], p. 169). See also John Howard Griffin, *Black Like Me* (New York: New American Library, 1963), pp. 85–90.

9. Fanon, pp. 159, 166. Fanon and his white colleagues administered the association tests over a period of three or four years.

10. See Gossett, p. 47.

330   The Bottom Rail Comes to Be the Top Riser

During the days of slavery and the Civil War, a young mistress said to her slave mammy (as they called them): "What will happen, what will happen if the Yankees win?"

And the old slave lady answered, "Missis, my God know how to make the bottom rail come to be the top riser—my God knows how to make the bottom rail come to be the top riser."

331   You Broke Momma's Vase

My grandmother was a girl back in slavery, and she was a nursemaid in this house. And something happened, and she knocked down a vase. She heard the mistress coming. (She knew she was going to get a whipping.) So this [white] child was sitting down on the floor. So she just took the pieces of the vase and put them down near the child and scooted down the back steps. And so she said the woman came in and when she came back up, she said,

"Oh, Virginia has broken my beautiful vase!" She looked at her and said, "Oh, you broke Momma's vase."

My grandmother said it was better for her to fuss with her [white child] than whip her [slave girl].

332   Turn the Pot Upside Down

They used to say that the old Marster would take them where he want to, take 'em and carry 'em, put 'em on the block and sell 'em, sell 'em! And then if you want to *sing* or *pray*, didn't want them to hear you (hear 'em), they'd take a iron pot and turn it [the pot] upside down, and that keep them from hearing 'em when they pray and sing—*Yeah!*

333   God Delivered 'Em

My stepmother told me that when her mother was comin' 'long, all them was comin' up, say, they wasn't allowed to pray, and say they would git in that place where they would stay—in the lil' cabin—they'd turn the iron pot down—turn it down, bottomwards—so the white people couldn't hear 'em in the house, you know. And they would *sing* and they would *pray*. They would *sing* and they would *pray!* And have that pot turned down to hol' the sound in—'cause if they caught 'em prayin' and singin', they would *whip* 'em. And say that they would turn that pot down and get in there and have a meeting, have a meeting.

So one time—they called 'em Marster or something, my aunt say, they called 'em Marster—Marster Charles, Marster this, Marster the other. And say he came to the door and shook the door—of course, they had a bolt on it—and that fly open, and they all was down there *prayin'* to the Lord. And he say, "What yawl *doing* down there? Git up from there and shet that foolishness up!" Say they was *prayin'* to the Lord, you know, for deliverence—

"Yeah!" [From listener.]

And they didn't 'low 'em to do it!

"Thank you!" [From listener.]

"Shut that fuss up! Whacha doin' down there? Git up from there! And go to bed so you kin git up in the mornin' and go to work at daylight!"

Lawd, they was worried to death. She must o' been 'round there some-where, outside. Well, anyway, say after he left, they turned the pot back down—gon' try it again. And say, "Don't yawl pray so loud—Mars Charles gon' come down here again." But say they prayed for dee-li-vrance, because they was under bondage.

"God delivered 'em too!" [From the audience.]

Yeah, prayed for deliverance—say, "God, deliver us!"

"God deliver!" [From the audience.]

Yeah, and God delivered 'em. And say colored people been prayin' 'long down through the years when they was in slavery, you know, God was with 'em and He taught 'em how to pray.

And they say Mars Charles, or whatever he was, took the pot, took the pot, and carried it in the house, carried it somewhere, but say what was in here [indicating heart], couldn't get it out, say they prayed together . . . and they did that until this lady [Harriet Tubman] came down here and got 'em and carried 'em up North under that underpass. She say Mars Charles, he caught some of 'em and carried 'em back, but she said the majority of the slaves . . . this lady got 'em from down there and carried 'em up North.

That was YEARS and YEARS ago! And I sit up there and cried 'cause I didn't have no better sense.

334 John, John, Tonight

When they [slaves] tried to get away, they would sing a song down the cotton patch and they would carry that message all the way to the end of the cotton patch, as I would tell it to her [informant gestures to person seated next to her], [singing] "John, John, tonight, John, John, tonight."

Then she would start singin', "John, John, tonight."

That means John is tryin' to get away tonight, and that's the way they did all the way down the cotton patch. That was how they planned things and how they managed sometimes to get away from the plantation.

335 John in Philimōdel

During the days of slavery Ole Massa owned a very valuable slave named John. John decided, though, that slavery was not for him and he wanted his freedom. So there was a great underground movement, and John was able to get in on it, and through some friends he finally got to Philadelphia. Well, Ole Massa was certainly disturbed because John was one of his most valuable slaves. He was very strong and had so many children among the slaves; and this was very valuable because he was selling the slaves, you know, and he certainly didn't want to lose John.

So he decided that he would go to Philadelphia and go down into some of the areas where he heard that the slaves who had won their freedom lived. Finally, one day after looking around in the areas, he saw John. Well, by this time John had really began to *live*. He had *fine* clothes, and was looking so *good!* Ole Massa looked 'cross the street and saw this man with the broad shoulders and looking *so good!* He said, "That man walks just like John; I believe that's John." So he called, "*John! JOHN!*"

John by that time had even changed his name, you know, and he was wondering who was that calling *him John*. So he looked around and he said, "Who in the HELL is that callin' me John here in this *gret big* Philimōdel?"

336   Uncle Daniel's Caught

Did I tell you 'bout the old ex-slave where they had out there? See, when they get old, they had them old quarters, you know. And they'd just stop and put them in there—freedom—and let them have a little boy to look after 'em. They call that retirin' 'em, see. So they had retired this old man 'cause he done worked his lifetime out. He had this lil' boy that was takin' care of 'im, and he used to be mean to the boy. And what the old man would do, when all the people at the Big House go to sleep (up in the loft, that's where they kept the sweet potatoes—and he had a fire to keep 'em from freezing), he'd go and put a whole lot o' sweet potatoes in the fire, roast 'em and get his bucket and go out there in the pasture and milk all the cows he want and come back; he would sit down, he would drink milk and eat sweet potatoes.

So he was cruel to the lil' boy, and the boy tol' Ole Master 'bout it. He say, "That Uncle Daniel, he ain't ole as you think he is. At night, when yawl go to sleep, he put a whole lot o' sweet potatoes in the fire and roast 'em, then go out there, gon' take a bucket and milk the cows. He gon' come on back and eat all the sweet potatoes and drink all the milk. He ain't gon' give me none."

He [Master] say, "Oh, go 'head boy, goheadgoheadgohead, I don't pay any attention to that foolishness." But that night, he goes down there and stood outside the door. And sure enough, 'round 'bout four o'clock when he thought everybody was asleep in the house, the old man come on out there with his bucket and went on down to the cow pen and milked the cows, come on back, sit down there, eat his sweet potatoes and drink his milk.

So the ole man [Master] didn't say nothin' to 'im. Next morning, he come on down there, he say, "Ah, Uncle Daniel, how you doing? How you gettin' along?"

[Sickly tone.] "Ah-h-h, Master, the ole man's mighty puny, mighty puny. I don't think I'll be around much longer. Mighty puny! Mighty puny!"

He say, "Well, Uncle Daniel, don't you think if I sent a couple of men down here and let them help you walk out to the straw stack out in the field and let you sit out in the sun, it'll do you some good?"

"Naw-w-w-w, Master, I don't think I could make that, I don't think I could make a walk that far."

He say, "Well, I'll tell ya what I'll do; I'll send a couple o' men with a cart and they pick you up and load you in the cart and carry you, and we'll set you by the straw stack 'cause that sun will do you good."

"Well, just as you say. I don't think it'll do me no good."

So they took 'im, carried 'im out there, set 'im over there by that big stack o' straw; he layin' back in the sun there; and they went behind the straw stack and set the whole stack of straw afire. And that old man see that fire and jumped over top the stack and got up and outrun everybody.

So they took him and put him back in the fields.

337   Abe and Dinah

During the days of slavery there was a couple, Abe and Dinah. Dinah was very devoted to the mistress and master; so was Abe, but *Abe* liked a little *fun.* So every so often the master would go to New York, to some of the big cities, to attend to business. And he had a lot of confidence in Abe, and he would say to him, "Now, Abe, I'm going away and I want you to take care of the household; I want you to look after *everything* for me. Look after my *wine* (I've got plenty wine down in the cellar), and I want you to take charge. I'm gon' give you the keys, 'cause I can trust you, Abe, you never bother anything. *All* those things, my clothes upstairs, I want you to have 'em cleaned up 'n' want you to shine up everything. And, *Dinah,* you take care of the household, too; I want all the silver and brass and all the crystal shined up. You watch it because I can trust you two with this household."

And Dinah was so humble. She was so proud of this trust, and she would say, "OH! Massa, I'm gonna look after things while you gone, not a thing will be outta place; I'm gon' take care of everything for ya."

And Abe, he would come up, "Yep, Massa, you kin depend on me. Everything will be in place when you get back. I'm gon' look after all o' your *wine,* all of your *clothes,* and *everything*—the silver in this household—I'm gon' see that everything's in place." And Ole Massa then would get ready, you know, and go off on a big trip, he and his wife and the household...

SOON as he would get out of sight good, Ole Abe would start to kickin' up: "SO GLAD he gone! SO GLAD he gone! I'm gon' have me a big time now!"

And poor Dinah would say to 'im, "Abe *please* don't do like you did last time; you know this thing is going too far. One of these days you gonna get *caught.* Ole Massa is not going to New York; he may come back!"

"Oh, he's not comin' back. He won't come back until his business trip is over, and I'm gon' have some *life,* Dinah. *You* kin sit back in the corner and be faithful, but *I'm* gon' enjoy *myself.*" And soon as Ole Massa—they'd get out of sight and be gone maybe for three or four hours, Ole Abe would start a callin' up *all* his friends, tellin' 'em, "Ole Massa gone! Ole Massa gone! We gon' have a good time!" Ole Abe would go upstairs and put on Ole Massa's coat, *pants*, dress up in his clothes and strut around and look. He say, "Ah! Don't I look good!"

Poor Ole Dinah would sit there and just shake her head. "Abe, you ought not to do that. Abe, please don't do that, don't put on Massa's *pants!* Don't put on his *coat*, please don't do that."

"SHUT UP, Woman, I know what I'm doing." Then he would go way down on the plantation and get 'em to kill up two or three pigs, and get the hands down there to roast 'em, you know, and OH! then he would go down in the wine cellar, get Massa's *best* wine, all of the silver, make Dinah set the table: "Dinah, I say set that table, SET IT up!" And then he would invite *all-l-l-l* of the slaves in. They would come in their rough clod clothes and looking all shabby and bad. He the man o' the house, all dressed up in Marster's long-tail coat, and poor Dinah—head all tied up still—so sad, oh, she was so worried. And then the guys would bring in the banjos and the homemade instruments, you know, and they would set up their own lil' band, you know, and *they* would play, and then they would all get out (he would put a covering on the flo' so they wouldn't tear it up, you know) and then they would get out and do a ole-fashion jig dance, you know. Then he—*he* would do it, and clap his hands and—Ole Dinah wouldn't take no part in it. She'd just sit there—she was so sad.

So on this occasion, this party, there was a man who was one of 'em—Abe would be at the door, "Well, come on in, boys." (He didn't even know their names.) "Come on in, boys!"

In came this man. He was all shabbily dressed . . . Dinah looked at 'im; she say, "I never seen that face 'round here befo'." Say, "That man certainly got broad shoulders and strict lookin'." Say, "He certainly turn like Ole Massa."

Abe came on in, "Yeah, boys, how yawl feel? Sho glad to greet ya, so glad to greet ya. I'm gon' have a good time tonight . . ." Dinah watched, and Dinah thought, " 'Tis somethin' familiar 'bout the turn of that man." Of course, he had soot all over his face, had his hair all matted down to his head, you know, and had on old run-down shoes, ragged pants, old dirty-looking shirt. "You can't fool me. That man don't look right." So they started dancing. Well, *that's* what gave it away to Dinah, because HIS STEPS—were just a lil' bit too polished. They weren't like those other steps. She come, she say, "ABE, come here, come here. [Whispering.] You see that man there. *That man*, I believe, is Ole Massa. He doesn't turn like the other folk."

By that time Ole Abe had plenty of wine in him, you know, he couldn't see. He say, "WOMAN, haven't I tol' ya to stop meddlin' wid me. I know dat ole nigger. He come from 'round dere on dat other plantation. I know 'im. Now don't come here worryin' me. I know exactly who he is."

Dinah went around, she say, "Lawd have mercy, I know sumpin' gon' happen 'round here because I *feel* it, I *feel* it. That's NOT one o' us. That gotta be Ole Massa and I believe it." So she got in the corner and start worrying ... and they were *dancing*. So *finally*, 'bout break o' day, *every-thing* was over, everybody left, and Ole Dinah, Dinah started cleanin' up the house. She say, "I hate to do this." She say, "I just hate to do this, Abe, because I feel like something is gon' happen 'round here."

"SHUT UP, woman, let me git dis stuff straight here! I'm gon' have another one 'fo' Massa get back. I just want to get things back in order."

And *just-t-t* about daybreak good she looked around. Somebody knocked at the door, started coming in. She say, "Lord have mercy, Abe, I believe it's *Ole Massa* coming in; I believe it's *Ole Massa!* OH my goodness!"

And he walked in. There's Abe, had all o' the glasses on the table, had just washed some of 'em. He saw the wine bottles, everything all tore up. He said, "Well, ABE! what's going on here, what's the matter with the house? What's wrong?"

"Uh, uh, uh, uh, M-M-M-M-Massa, I-I-I was just givin' it a jun-jun-juneral cleanin' up. I just cleanin' up good. I just cleanin' up around here."

He say, "Well, what is all my wine bottles and all those empty bottles doin' on the table?"

"Uh, uh, I just went down in the cellar an-an-and was pouring wine from one bottle to the other, uh, uh, that's what I was doin'."

He say, "Well, wait a minute, Abe, come here, let me see your clothes. That's my *pants* you got on and my *coat*. What's been going on in my house?"

"Uh, uh, uh—"

Dinah, say, "Oh, Lord [crying], ABE, I tol' ya what's gon' happen, I tol' ya."

He say, "Dinah, I'm not gon' touch ya. I was here las' night, and I wit-nessed *all* of it. Dinah, you had no part in it, but ABE, take off those things, and let me call the help down from the field there, who is in charge of the field help, and I'm gonna tell him to give you as many lashes as your body can stand. I'm gon' try to *kill* you! My most trusted slave, and you turned on me like this!"

She say, [crying] "OH, please don't kill 'im, Massa, please don't kill 'im, don't kill 'im, DON'T kill 'im!"

He say, "Dinah, if it wasn't for you I'd *kill* 'im, but because you've been so faithful, I'm gon' spare his life."

338 He Cursed Marster Out

A. One day Marster told John to go down to the stable and fix the horses up. John didn't say anything; say, he went on down there. When he got down there to the stable, say he *cursed* Marster out! So he went and told Jim 'bout it.

Jim say, "Next time Marster tell me to do somethin'," say, "I'm gon' *curse* him out."

So Marster told Jim, say, "Jim," say, "Go down to that woodpile and cut me up some wood."

Say Jim cursed Marsta right in front of his face. Say old Marsta hopped on 'im and whipped the devil out o' 'im. Say he went on back to John, say, "John, I thought you say you cursed Marster out when he told you to hitch the horses."

He say, "I *did!* But, *fool,* Ole Marsta was here and I was down at the stable."

B.   Two slave men were behind the barn talking. One said to the other, "I cussed Old Marsta out the other day and told him what I won't gonna do."

The other slave said, "You mean you cussed Old Marsta and told him what you won't gonna do and you got away with it?"

The first man replied, "Yes."

The other one said, "Well, if you did that and got away, I'm gonna do the same thing when Marsta gets after me."

So in the next day or so when Old Marsta got after him he too cussed him out and told him what he wasn't gonna do. Old Marsta tied him up to a tree and beat the daylights out of him. He went back and told his slave friend what had happened and asked him, "Did you really say what you said to Old Marsta and he didn't beat you?"

The other slave replied, "I said it to myself behind the barn."

339   Free as a Old Rabbit

My father say his master was going out to town, and they surrendered while, you know, while his master was gone. And say he heard it before his master came back, and he came in the house where his mistress was. He say, "I'm just free as a old rabbit in the woods this morning!"

Say, she broke at 'im, runned 'im out the house. So after the master came, said that "Yes, General Grant (I think [obvious confusion of names]), he surrendered this morning and they's free."

340   From King to Queen

A brother was standing beside this white dude in the toilet. The white guy looked at him while they were both taking a leak, and said, "I am a king."

And the Black guy replied after looking at his penis, "Yeah, and three more inches shorter, you will be a queen!"

341 Swinging It Around

Okay! The white man, the Jew man, and the colored man! And so all of 'em was havin' trouble at home with their wives. And the problem was that their "things" couldn't fit up their wives. So all three of 'em went to the doctor, and the doctor said, "I'm gon' give *all* three of you all some pills, and I want yawl to take one a day."

So all three of the men say, "All right, we'll take one a day."

So the white man, he went in to get his pills, and the doctor say, "Now, you take one of these pills *every* day."

So he said, "All right." So the white man left.

So the Jew man went in. He told the Jew man, "Take one of these pills *every* day."

So the colored man went in, and he told him the *same* thing.

All right. So *all* three of the mens went home. So when they got home, the white man, he *took* one a day. Now the Jew man wanted to be bad, and he didn't take any of 'em. So the colored man, he took the *whole* bottle. So a couple o' months passed by. All of 'em went back to the hospital. So the doctor called the white man in. The white man came in, and his was all right because he had taken one a day. Well, the Jew man (he called him in), and the Jew man, he wanted to be BA-AD. He didn't believe anything; he didn't take none a day.

So he called the colored man in. The colored man had took the *whole* bottle. And you know how he came in? He came in swinging "it" around, that's how he came in.

342 The Princess Is Dead

The King said, "My kingdom for someone to satisfy this Princess of mine. I have to have a man for her." So they sent the word out, and the couriers [courtiers] came from far and wide. It seemed as if the Princess had an insatiable sexual appetite, commonly referred to as *nymphomania* amongst the more lettered persons. The Latins had been rumored to have been great lovers, and consequently the King said, "Send me the Latin lover." And he came and he wooed the Princess. (Now the understanding was that if you did not satisfy her, you must die, must be beheaded. They could not afford the scandal of having it said that you went to bed with the Princess.) So they carried the Latin lover there and he lasted about ten minutes, and the Princess was still writhing about. So they put him to death.

So the Englishman is supposed to be very suave, genteel, and in many instances, gallant. This didn't do anything for her. She had to have hard sexual manifestations, and he didn't help her. So they killed him.

Well, the Russian is *brutal* and hard and cold. Maybe this would turn her on. They killed him. The German likewise used the same hard approach, animalistic approach, and he died. They called the American, who was supposedly a combination of all of these things (and mind you, the Negroes having been excluded from the gestation of American life, he's not one of these *people* considered Americans). The American was put to death, too. So finally there came the nigger and said, "Give *me* a chance at the Princess."

And usually at these things they would keep a tally: "The Italian has come *ten* times; Princess, not yet. The Frenchman has come fifteen times; the Princess, not yet." And in these instances they put these people to death. So they brought the nigger and explained to him. They said, "You have *very, very* little to gain. *Every* race of man known throughout this commonwealth is dead. It wouldn't be wise for you to attempt it."

The nigger say, "As you say, I have nothing to gain, but I have *nothing* to lose. First chance I've had to have a white woman in my lifetime. Where is she? Let me have 'er!"

So they carried him to her, and he mounted her. So the heralds and the tribunes would come out: "UM-BA-DA-DUM-M-M! UM-BA-DA-DUM-M-M! Princess come three times; the nigger, not any."

After another twenty minutes: "Princess come *thirteen* times; the nigger not any."

[Long pause.]

Another twenty minutes: "Princess come *twenty-three* times; the nigger, not any."

[Long pause.]

Another hour and a hour and a half. So it got on to the point: "Princess come *hundred* and *thirty-three* times; nigger, not any."

So after a *lo-o-ong, lo-o-ong* silence—no one heard anything from the room. The heralds and the tribunes were tired; they couldn't report—they didn't report. The King became impatient, and he knocked upon the door. No one answered.

The heralds staggered forth ... and said, "The Princess ... is dead ... And the nigger is knocking his fist."

343   Can't Kill Him That Way

There were these three men—Black, white, and Jewish. And they'd all committed capital crimes. And they could die whichever way they wanted. So the Jew say, "I wanna *eat* myself to death. I wanna *eat* myself to death." So they brought a million-course meal, and he ate, and he ate, and he ate. He finally died with a bloated belly and a smile on his face.

And the white man say, "I wanna drink *myself* to death." So they brought him a fifth of every kind of possible concoction of alcohol, and he drank and drank. And he died with this smile on his face.

And naturally the brother say, "I wanna *screw* myself to death." So they brought in *fifty* women. And two weeks later they went back, and the fifty women were laying there dead ... And he was sittin' there jacking off.

344 Fornication Contest

It was generally known that a Black nigger could outfuck a white man. But this particular white man did not believe it, and his friends didn't believe it.

So they had a fucking contest: the Master fucking a white wench, and the nigger fucking a nigger wench. And the scorekeepers were keeping score.

The white man fucked her twelve times and fell away—couldn't do no more. The nigger went right on fucking. When they got to twenty-four times, the scorekeepers got confused. One said it was twenty-four; the other said twenty-five. There was an argument.

The nigger said, "No need to argue and fuss. I will start over again."

345 How Much for That Mule?

One time here's a ole man, he has a ole mule, you know. So he offered a *reward*, say he give five hundred dollars to anybody who could fuck that mule the longest. So *everybody* 'round came around. So one man, he tried. He last 'bout a half a hour, couldn't go no more. They had a ole Chinese. Old Chinese last 'bout a hour and a half; he couldn't go no more. Japanese—he last 'bout two hours. Say he couldn't make it no more. Then this ole *white* man, he came there. White man last 'bout *five* hours. Then he say, "I just can't make it no more."

So, uh, this old Black man came up there, say, "Why don't you give *me* a chance." So he turned around, gave the Black man a chance. Black man rode the mule for *fo'* days and he *still* won't tired. Man tol' 'im, say, "Well, Mister, you done *won* that reward." Say, "I got to pay you off. Here your money." Black man say, "Goddamn that money! How much you want for that mule?"

346 If

The white man, the Jew, and the nigger were caught stealing. And so they brought 'em up before the Judge, and the Judge said, "If you can produce twenty inches of penis, I'll let the three of you go." So immediately the nigger [white man] went over to the corner and started shadow boxing.

And then the Judge called the white man [nigger] up and they measured him, and he was twelve inches. And then they called the Jew up and they measured him, and he was seven inches. And, oh! The nigger [white man] was just shadow boxing! So he came up and they measured him, and he wasn't but a half an inch. So now they got nineteen and a half inches. But the Judge said, "Since you came so close, I'll *still* let you go."

So later they were walking down the street and the white man [nigger] say, "You know, if it hadn't been for my twelve inches, you two would be in jail."

And the Jew said, "Well, you know my seven. That wasn't so bad."

And the nigger [white man] said, "You better shet up, 'cause if I hadn't had a hard on . . ."

347   White Fools from Charles City

A.   This old white man was very old and senile and he couldn't tell time. But he wanted a watch. And so his brother brought him a watch, and he was so proud he went along walking down the road with this watch on his arm. And he met someone. And he was looking at his watch. So this person that he met asked him, "What time is it there, Charlie?" [Name changed.]

Say he looked at his watch and said, "It's *seventy-five* minutes to ten!"

B.   This old white man—they raised chickens and hens—and he didn't have a bit of sense, he was real crazy—cracked. So they asked him, say, "Charlie, how many hens you got now?"

Say, "Well, we did have eight, but now we done et 'em down to 'leben."

348   The Early Animal Gets the Water

It came to be a drought in the land and all the animals were all thin. They couldn't get enough water to drink, and they couldn't get enough food to eat. But the Rabbit was always slick and fat, you know. And they say, "Why is the Rabbit always slick and fat and everybody else is so thin and skinny? We just can't find enough water to drink, but looks like Brer Rabbit is always finding enough water to drink."

So they started to *peeping* on him, trying to figure out what he was doing. And they found out, *every* morning, *early* in the morning, the Rabbit was going out and just licking the dew off the grass and off the leaves. That's where he was getting his water. Early in the morning, off the dew and off the grass, before the others could get any. Which brought out the thing that the early bird gets the worm, but in this case it was the early animal gets the water.

349 The Tar Baby

The animals were tryin' to *catch* Brer Rabbit; and Brer Rabbit would go down to the spring to get water. They thought that would be a good way to catch him. And so they made a Tar Baby and set it up at the spring 'cause Brer Rabbit was very inquisitive. And Brer Rabbit went down to drink, and he saw this Tar Baby; and he said, "Uh, who're you?" And he didn't say nothing, so then Brer Rabbit said, "You better tell me who you are!" And so the Tar Baby didn't say anything. So then Brer Rabbit went up there and say, "Well, I'll *slap* ya!" And the Tar Baby didn't say anything, so he slapped the Tar Baby, and his hand stuck, but the Tar Baby still didn't say anything. So then he say, "I'll kick ya!" And he kicked 'im and his foot stuck. So then he said, "Well, I got another foot; I'll kick ya with that!" And he kicked 'im and *that* foot stuck. And then he said, "Well, I got another hand—I'll slap ya." And so he slapped 'im with the other hand, and *that* stuck. He said, "Now you think you smart, but I got a head—I'll butt ya!" So he butt 'im and *that* stuck. So when the animals came to catch him he was all stuck on the Tar Baby, and he say, "Oh-oh, oh! Turn me loose, turn me loose!"

They say, "We gotcha! We gotcha!"

He say, "Well, I tell you what you do. You throw me in the *briar* patch, because I don't like briar patches. You just throw me in the briar patch and you'll have me—then you kin keep me *forever*."

So then they took him and throwed him in the briar patch, and he say, "O-o-oh!" when he got in the briar patch. "O-O-OH! This is where I was *born* and *raised*—right in the briar patch!"

Then he ran on down through the briars.

350 I Fool You That Time

The Rabbit, understand, *every day*, every morning, understand, the Rabbit come out, understand, commence to eatin' up the fruit, cabbage, and different things like that, you know. So the man set the trap; so when he set that trap, understand, they caught the old Rabbit, and the old Rabbit, understand, he just stood up and commence *beggin'*, "*Please* let me loose. I eat no more cabbage."

"Say what?"

"*Please* let me loose, just let me loose this time, I ain't gon' eat no mo' cabbage."

So they took Brer Rabbit and let 'im loose. When they let 'im loose, understand, he went on just like that. He say, "You ole fool, you, I fool you that time."

351   Bobtail Beat the Devil

They had a saying: they say that "You beat Bobtail and *Bobtail* beat the Devil." So the way it come about, say the Devil and the Rabbit (we call him Bobtail, you know) got to talkin'. Say the Rabbit said to the Devil, say, "I tell ya what let's do, Mr. Devil." Say, "Let's go in croppin' together this year. We gon' plant corn." He say, "You have all the bottom; I'll have all the tops."

The Devil say, "All right."

So when it come to gather the crops, the Rabbit had the feed and the corn, and the Devil didn't have nothin' but roots, you know. So the Devil was put out 'bout it. He say, "Aw, that ain't no fair. I-I'll crop you again next year, but I'm gon' have all the tops you had."

He say, "Naw, I'll tell ya whatcha do. Let's raise sweet potatoes next year. I'll have all the bottoms; you have all the tops."

He say, "Awright."

So when they went to gather in all the crops, the Devil had the vines and the Rabbit had all the sweet potatoes. So he beat the Devil each time. That's why they say, "Bobtail beat the Devil."

352   All the Tracks Goin' In

You know the Lion always has been king of the jungle. And the Lion had this den, see. And Brother Fox came by. And he say, "Brother Fox, come on in have a lil' chat."

Fox say, "Well, you know I got better sense than to come into a *Lion's* den."

He say, "Oh, come on in, Brother Fox. Everything will be all right."

Fox say, "Naw, you know I'm not coming into no *Lion's* den."

"Come on in, Brother Fox, you'll be all right." He say, "A lot o' animals been 'round here today, you know. See all dem tracks! A whole lot o' animals been in here today!"

So Brother Fox say, "I see that, but all the tracks goin' *in*. Ain't none coming *out*."

See, that's what he meant. Everybody went in there and got ate up, and didn't none of them come out.

353   The Signifying Monkey

A. It was bright and early one summer day,
Says the Monkey to the Lion, "There's a bad motherfucker living down
   your way."
Say, "You take this fellow to be your friend,"
Say, "but the way he talks about you is a goddamn sin."
Say, "Now something else, I forgot to say;
He talks about your *mother* in a hell of a way.
Say your sister got the syphilis and your grandma got the pox,
And your little baby cousin on the hill fucking the old red Fox."
Say like a ball of fire and a streak of heat,
The old Lion went rolling down the street.
Say the old Lion let out a terrible sneeze,
And knocked the damned Giraffe on his motherfucking knees.
Say now he left the jungle in a *hell* of a rage,
Like a young cocksucker who fouled his gauge.
Say, now, he saw this Elephant sitting under a tree,
And he say, "Now you bring your big black ass to me."
The Elephant looked at him out the corner of his eyes,
And said, "Now, chickenshit, go play with somebody your size."
The old Lion jumped back and cocked his tail like a forty-four and made
   a crooked pass;
The Elephant cross-stepped him, and kicked him *dead* in his ass.
Say now he broke *both* jawbones, pushed his tail through his face,
Knocked his dick in the dirt and knocked his nuts out of place.
Now they fought all night and they fought all day;
And I don't know how in the hell that Lion ever got away.
Say but the Lion was going back through the jungles more deader than
   alive,
And that's when that Monkey started that signifying.
He said, "He-e-ey-y-y, Mr. Lion, you left here the jungle [king];
Now you come back with your ass damn near hung.
You call yourself a king and a ace,
And gon' take ninety-nine yards of sailcloth to patch up your
   motherfucking face."
He say, "In the morning when I'm trying to get a little bit,
You come around with all that ole 'EIO-O-EEEE' shit."
Say, "Get on out from under *my* tree,
Before I decide to shit and pee."
Say, "Don't you dare roar,
I'll come down out of this tree and kick your hairy ass some more."
Say, "Your mama's got thirteen children, and it's a sight to see,
'Cause everyone of them bastards look like me."
Say the damn old Lion was sitting down there crying,
And the Monkey just *kept* signifying.
Say but the old Monkey got frantic and started jumping around,
And his foot slipped and his little ass hit the ground.
Like a ball of fire and a streak of heat,
The old Lion was on him with *all* four feet.

Say the Monkey looked up with tears in his eyes,
And said, "Mr. Lion, I apologize!"
He said, "In this jungle friends are few;
You know I was only bullshitting you."
The old damn Monkey looked at him and saw he wasn't gon' get away,
So he decided to think of a bold-assed play.
He say, "Mr. Lion, you ain't no hell."
Say, "Everybody in the jungle saw me when I fell."
Say, "Now, if you let me up like a good man should,"
Say, "I'll kick your ass all over these woods."
So the old bad Lion looked at him and jumped back for a hell of a fight.
And say in a split second the Monkey was damn near out of sight.
Say now he jumped up into a tree higher than any human eye can see;
Say he looked down at the Lion,
Say, "Hey, Mr. Lion," say, "it's often said and seldom seen,"
Say, "but the shit I put on you make the grass grow green."
Say, "That is bullshit!"

B. Way down in the jungle deep,
The bad-assed Lion stepped on the Signifying Monkey's feet.
The Monkey said, "Look, motherfucker, can't you see
You standing on my goddamned feet?"
The Lion said, "I haven't heard a word you said,
If you say three more, I'll be standing on your motherfucking head."
The Monkey would sit way up in a banana tree,
Bullshitting the Lion every day of the week.
And every day before the sun went down,
The Lion would kick his ass all through the jungle [town].
The Monkey got wise, started using his wit.
He say, "I'm gon' put a stop to this old ass-kicking shit!"
He runned up on the Lion the very next day.
He say, "Oh-h-h, Mr. Lion, there's a big, bad motherfucker coming your
      way,
'Cause he's somebody that you don't know.
He jest broke aloose from Ringling Brothers' Show."
Say, "He talked about yo' people till my hair turned gray.
He say yo' daddy's a freak and yo' mama's a whore,
He say he saw yo' brother going through the jungle selling assholes from
      door to door.
He say when you meet there's going to be a goddamn scene,
And wherever you meet some ass is bound to be [unclear]."
The Lion tore off through the jungle, tearing down trees,
Kicking giraffes to their knees,
Walked up on the Elephant talkin' to the Swine,
He say, "All right, you big bad motherfucker, it's gon' be yo' ass or
      mine!"
The Elephant looked at 'im out the corner of his eye,
He say, "Awright, you funny-bunny motherfucker, go pick on somebody
      yo' own size."
The Lion reached out with a fancy pass;

The Elephant side-stepped 'im, kicked him *dead* in his ass.
He fucked up his jaw, smashed up his face,
Busted up his leg, and knocked his ass outta place.
They fought all that night and all the next day,
Somehow the po' Lion managed to get away.
He drug his ass back to the jungle more dead than alive,
Just to run into that Monkey with some more of his signifying jive.
The Monkey say, "Oh, Mr. Lion," say, "You don't look so swell.
Look to me like you caught a *whole* lotta hell!"
Say, "I tol' my wife before you left
I shoulda kicked yo' ass my motherfucking self."
The Monkey got happy—start jumping up and down,
His feet missed the limb and his ass hit the ground.
Like a lightning bolt and a ball o' white heat,
The Lion was on his ass with all four feet.
The Monkey looked up and said, "Mr. Lion, you ain't raising no hell."
Say, "Everybody saw me when I slipped and fell."
Say, "If you let me get my nuts out the sand,
I'll whip you ass like a *natural* man!"
This made the Lion mad;
It was the boldest challenge he ever had.
He squared off for the fight.
That lil' Monkey jumped *damn* near outta sight.
He landed way up in top of a banana tree and begin to grin.
He say, "All right, you big, bad motherfucker, you been bullshitted
    again."
The Lion let out with a hellava sound;
That lil' Monkey fell *back* down to the ground.
The Monkey looked up with tears in his eyes.
He say, *"Please,* Mr. Lion, don't take my life.
I got three lil' children and a very sickly wife."
That Lion kicked him in his ass and broke his neck,
Left that lil' Monkey in a hellava way.
And now the sun was slowly going down,
Everything was quiet throughout the jungle town.

354 Oink

A. These two men decided to go home—they were going South, and
they started out driving. And on the side of the road, they saw this pig out
there. So he took the pig and set the pig up between the two men and put a
red coat on 'im and a old cap and some dark glasses. And they turned the
radio on; the broadcaster was tellin' about this pig that had gotten lost; they
think some men had swiped him on their way South. And so when they got
way down the road, say they saw this cop, and he stopped 'em. Say the man
walked up and said [to the driver], "What's your name?" And he gave

'im his name. He say, "Who is this in the middle?" The police say, "What's your name?"

He [driver] hunched the pig in the side; the pig say, "Ooink!"

So when he got 'round to the other side, he walked around, he say, "Where you live?"

The other one hunched him; the pig say, "Ooink!"

He say, "Your name is 'Ooink, Ooink'?"

He say, "Ooink, ooink!"

So he got the name of the other man. So when they pulled off, the old policeman say, "That was the damndest, ugliest Ooink Ooink I ever did see!"

B. It was against the law to ride around with three in the front seat of a car.

So these niggers stole a hog, see, and they seen two state troopers had a roadblock down the road, so they throwed a overcoat 'round him and throwed a hat on his head and got him in the middle. So when they get down there, he stops 'em, and he said, "What's your name, fellow?"

Well, time he stopped them and went to the car door, the hog say, "OINK!" This here was Joe and Jim got the hog, but the old hog answered, "OINK!"

So he let 'em go; he say, "You know you ain't suppose to ride three on the front seat." Say, "I'm gon' let you go this time."

When they left, one of the troopers said to the other one, he said, "That's the damndest thing I ever seen."

He say, "What you mean?"

He say, "That damn nigger in the middle, that OINK!" Say, "That's the ugliest sonovabitch I ever seen."

355 Help!

They say that, you know, when—during all this integration period—the South trying to hold up its end, you know. So they went out, and they said, "This T.V. is putting out too much, you know, about Blacks, saying it's so bad down here in Mississippi." So they went out in the back woods as far as they could to get the dumbest Negro they could find. And they told him, say, "Look, we gon' pay you fifty dollars to be on television, and all you got to tell 'em is how well we white folks treat you down here. That's all! Then you can go on back home. FIFTY DOLLARS! And it'll just take you a few minutes."

They carried him up there and set 'im in front the camera; they say, "We'll tell you when we ready." And they say, "You go ahead."

And say he was settin' there, you know, and he say, "Are you ready? Are you ready?"

They say, "Hold it a minute!" They had *all* the cameras and they had *all* the stations across the country opened up for it. They says, "Go ahead!"

He say, "HELP! HELP! HELP!"

356   We Don't Eat 'Em

A.   I was on the road in nineteen fifty-two with a group from Juilliard—out in the West. And outside Detroit was a neighborhood similar to Colonial Heights. And we pulled into this city at five-thirty in the morning, and there was a Joe's Diner. And we *joked* about it. We said we didn't *really* know a Joe's Diner existed. And we went in for breakfast. We had an engagement at the high school at eight o'clock, and we were going to Wayne [State] University that evening, so we decided we'd get all fresh after we got to the University and relax. So we went into this restaurant and ordered breakfast, and the waitress said, [nasty tone] "We don't serve negras in here!"

And I said, [just as caustically] "*Good!* 'Cause we don't *eat* 'em!"

And this was written in *Jet* as a quote, back in fifty-two. Elizabeth Yates sent it in; she said she thought it was choice!

B.   Black man walks into an obviously all-white restaurant. While all the customers look shocked and disgusted, the waiter comes up to the Black gentleman and says, "I'm sorry, sir, but we do not serve colored people."

To this the Black man says, "That's all right; I don't eat colored people!"

357   Give Me My Change Right Now

The white man, the Jew, and the nigger were all hungry, and they didn't have any money, so they stopped at this restaurant, and they stood outside and decided a scheme of at least how to get a cup of coffee.

So the white man went in and ordered a cup of coffee without cream and sugar, and when it was time to pay, the waiter said, "Give me a dime."

He said, "Oh, no! I paid you when I ordered."

So the waiter said, "All right."

So he left and the Jew went in. He ordered a cup of coffee with a little cream and sugar. He also, when it was time to pay, told the man, "Look, I paid you when I ordered."

And now the nigger thought, you know, "Now that mess not gon' work twice." So he went in anyway and ordered his coffee with as much cream and as much sugar as he could get in the coffee.

And so then the waiter said, "You know, you're the third man who's been in here this morning asking about coffee. Those other two jokers—I *know* they didn't pay."

The nigger said to him, "Well, give me my change *right* now!"

358   The Best Dream

Once upon a time, there was a Mongoloid man, a Caucasoid man, and a Negroid man who were the last three people in the world. They were living in an old hotel, eating whatever food they could find, until there was only one item of food left, a piece of bologna. When the men discovered this, the Caucasoid suggested that they hold a conference. In the conference, the conversation went something like this:

Caucasoid: "I suggest that we cut the bologna into three pieces, then go to bed until the next morning. Next morning, we will tell each other about our dreams. If our dreams are equally good, we will each get a piece of bologna; if one person's dream is better than the other, then he shall get all the bologna."

To this the Negroid and Mongoloid said, "That's fair enough!"

So the next morning they all came down and sat around the table. Then they drew straws to see who would be first to tell his dream. The Mongoloid won, and he told his dream like this:

"I know my dream is better than yours 'cause I rode my pony and I'm gonna get the *bologna!*"

Then it was the Caucasoid's chance to tell his dream, and it went like this: "I know my dream is better than yours 'cause I rode a *white* pony, and I'm gonna get the *bologna!*"

Then it was the Negroid's chance, and he told his like this: "I *know* my dream is better than yours 'cause while *you* rode your *pony*, I *eat* the *bologna!*"

359   I Tell Ya, White Folks

Another fellow, you know, he had raised this mule. And the mule would kick the soda outta a biscuit. But he knew 'im, so whenever the mule kicked where he was at, he was outta the way, you know.

So one day the horse traders came through, and that ole man had the mule down there, gon' trade 'im off to the horse traders. So one of the white fellows say, "Uncle Josh, I thought you and that mule was just like brothers. I didn't think you'd ever get rid of *that* mule."

He say, "I tell ya, white folks, it's like this. I'se gittin' ole, and I ain't spry as I once was. And you know somethin'?"

He say, "What?"

"One o' dese days, that mule gon' kick where I'se at and I gon' be dar!"

360 Guess

"Hey, Sam! Where's Broad Street?"

"Say, man. How did you know my name was Sam?"

"I guessed it."

"Well, guess where Broad Street is."

361 How?

It was said that this large plantation owner had many slaves, and for one reason or another the Devil appeared to him one day and said that he was going to take the man's slave whose name was John.

And the plantation owner said, "Why John?"

He said, "Well, it's just John's time."

He said, "Please don't take John."

And the Devil said, "Well, what's so special about John?"

He said, "Well, John is my record keeper." Says, "I don't keep any records. I keep no books whatsoever. John has a memory that's *fantastic*, and he just doesn't forget *anything*. I can ask him about my crops and what I made last year, and all I have to do is tell him and I call him back and ask him what I made and how many bushels of corn and what have you, and John has the answer [snap of the finger] just like that."

So say the Devil said, "That's unbelievable. Are you sure about that?"

He said, "I'm positive."

So the Devil said, "Well, will you call John up here? I want to talk to John—I want to test him out now. If he doesn't prove you're right, I'm going to have to take John."

So the Master called John up, and he said, "Now, Mr. Devil, you can ask him anything you want."

So the Devil said to John, say, "*John,* do you like eggs?"

And John said, "Yes, sir," and immediately the Devil disappeared.

Well, it was two years to the [day] and John was in the corn field plowing the corn, laying beside the corn, and it was a hot day. John had stopped the mule and sat under a tree. He had his old straw hat just fanning himself, you know. The Devil pops out of the ground, and he says one word to John; he says, "How?"

John says, "Scrambled."

362   Caught the Sly Fox

A.   There was an old Negro man who was in slavery, and he had been pretending to the other slaves that he could guess things that were happening or that he was much more wise than they were, and so the news got back to the Master that John was able to tell or to foresee things. And the Master said, "Oh, is that true?" Said, "If he can guess something that I'm going to do, then, I'll see that he gets his freedom." And so he took an old Fox and put it under a very large container. All the slaves gathered together in the room where the box was with the Fox under it. And the Master said, "Well, John, they tell me that you've been foretelling things and that you can guess things, that you're a very wise person. Now, if *you'll* tell *me* what's under the box, then I'll see that you get your freedom."

Say, everybody sat very, very silently around in order to find out if actually John was going to tell his Master what was under that box. And say John *sat* there for a while, and he thought and thought . . . He had no idea as to what he should say. So finally he said, "Well, Master, I must *confess*, you caught the old sly Fox at last!"

B.   This darky could tell about any and every thing. When white men came in from hunting, this darky could always tell what they had caught. They would put the "catch" under a barrel, and he would *always* tell what was under it (with a sign from his colleagues, of course).

On this day his in-between informer was sick and was not around. Master asked, "What's under the barrel, John?"

John replied, "Don' know . . . yet, suh."

Master: "Don' know? Black bastard, you better know. I'm betting my money that you know."

John: "Don't know . . . yet. Don' know."

Master: "What's under that goddamn barrel, John? Or I'll bust yo' ass wide open."

John: "Well, suh (scratching his head), yawl got the ole coon at last."

(John meant himself, but a coon was actually under the barrel.)

363 Mongrels

During the time (nineteen hundred) when they were organizing the Creek tribe [name of tribe changed], there were some whites in opposition of the organization of it because they felt that, you know, they felt this was moving a special class of Negroes into a special situation. So they were kinda getting their, you know, opposition and so forth against the organization of the tribe. So they had Bro Samuel Braxton [name changed], coaxed him, you know, what to say when they had the hearing relative to their heritage, background. Bro Samuel was to stand to say that they were not Indians, but they were Negroes. So they coaxed him, and then they went back to make a last check on him; they said, "Now, Uncle Sam, you all ready to give your testimony at the hearing?"

He said, "I *don't* know, Mr. Jefferson" [name changed]. Say, "You white folks so unsuhtain," say, "a nigger don't know what to do."

So when they asked him what *were* they, were they Indians or what, he said, "Mongrels, sir, mongrels."

364 My Daddy Was a Lollipop Maker

This white man, colored man, and Chinese man, like they were soldiers, you know, and they had a leave. They had to try to drive to the city. On their way going to the city, the car broke down, ran out of gas and all that stuff. So they started to walking, and then it started to raining, thundering, and lightning, and things. So they had to stop at this farmer's house. So they came in and say, "Look, Jack, I got a car broke down, and we need some shelter for the night."

The man say, "Yeah, well, okay, yawl kin stay here for the night, but you BET' not touch my daughter. If you do, I'm gon' do somethin' to you."

That night every last one of 'em *burned* her up. Next morning she came right straight to her daddy and told 'im. Her daddy came out there and said, "I told yawl not to touch my *daughter!* Why'd yawl touch my *daughter?*" He drawed the shotgun on 'em. So he tol' the white man, he say, "Come here! What *your* daddy do for a living?"

White man say, "My daddy was a carpenter."

He say, "Take your dick out. I'm gon' cut your dick off." He cut it off—SWI-I-SH!

The Chinese fellow—he say, "What your daddy do for a living?"

He say, [imitating Chinese accent] "Oh, my da-dye work in a laundry."

He say, "Take your dick out. I'm gon' *iron* your dick off." SW-O-O-SH!

He asked the colored man, he say, "What your daddy do for a living?"

He say, "My daddy was a lollipop maker."

365 If That Ain't Fuckin'

A. One couple was arrested in Jackson Ward for fornication. This Negro was a witness to it. They went to court, and the Judge called him before the stand and asked him to tell the court what he saw. He said, "Well Judge, all I say—I just saw them fuckin'."

And the Judge berated him from the bench: "I know you, and I know your reputation as some kind of a jackleg poet—at least you have some knowledge of the English language. You tell the court what you saw in decent language or I'm going to lock you up."

The Negro dropped his head, and he said:

Well, I saw his shirttail fanning in the breeze:
I say his "you-know-what" in her "you-know-where";
Now if that ain't fucking, I wasn't there!

B. This cat rode in the park with his girl. He get down in the park all the time, you know (they ain't got no crib), and the cop busted him, you know. So after he busted 'im, carried 'em to court, charged 'im with indecent exposure and fucking in the public. Went to court. The Judge say, "Read off the charges, officer."

So the officer tol' the Judge say, "Judge, Your Honor," say, "I caught this man and woman in the public park."

Judge say, "What's wrong about that, catch 'em in the public park?"

Officer say, "But, Your Honor, they was laying behind the bushes fucking."

Judge say, "Hol' it!" Say, "Officer, I charge you ten dollars for using that kind o' language in my court."

So pohleese, he had to pay the fine.

Then 'bout two weeks later another pohleese caught 'em fuckin', carried 'em to court.

Judge say, "Officer, read the charges."

Officer say, "Your Honor, I caught this man and woman in the park."

Judge say, "What's bad about in the park?"

He say, "They was laying behind a bush out there fuckin'."

Your Honor say, "HOL' IT!" Say, "I charge you ten dollars for using dem words in my court."

So then about a week later another pohleese caught 'em. So he went to court.

Judge say, "Officer, read the charges."

He say, "Yo' Honor, I caught this man and woman in the park."

He say, "What's about the park?"

He say, "Well, the man and woman behind the bush fuckin'."

Yo' Honor say, "I charge you ten for using that word in my court."

So then 'bout two days later the same first officer, he caught 'em again. So the Judge say, "Officer, read the charges."

He say, "Yo' Honor," say, "Uh—I caught this man and woman in the park."

He say, "What's so bad about in the park?"

He say, "Hol' it, Yo' Honor, befo' you charge me ten, I'm gon' describe this." He say:

Now I caught the man in the park; now I caught 'im with his pants below his
    knees.
Say his balls was swinging in the breeze.
Say his ass was going out and in.
If you don't call *that* fuckin', you kin fine *me* ten.

366 The Sandy Bottom Shuffle

Once there was a lovers' lane and this couple drove in lovers' lane and the cop was following them, but they didn't know it. And this old nigger, he was laying out there half drunk; so the cop drove up to him and said, "Listen, did you see a couple drive by here in a car?"

He said, "Yes, I saw 'em drive by here."

"Well, what did they do?"

Say, "They went through the bushes and they done the Sandy Bottom Shuffle."

So he said, "What do you mean by the Sandy Bottom Shuffle?" Say, "You come to court next Thursday and tell us what you saw on May the seventh."

So they went to court next Thursday, and they called this Negro up on the stand and said, "Tell this court what you saw on May the seventh."

Said, "I was out there lying on the grass in the park, half high, and this couple drove up, and they went through the bushes and they done the *Sandy Bottom Shuffle!*"

The Judge stamped his foot. He said, "Just what do you mean by the Sandy Bottom Shuffle?" He says, "We've got to make an affidavit of this case."

So the nigger asked him, said, "Well, what is an affidavit, Mr. Judge?"

He said, "That's a technicality in law that you niggers don't know nothing about. You come back here again next Thursday. We're going to have this trial over."

So next Thursday they went back, and he called him up on the stand again: "Tell us what you saw on the seventh, nigger!"

"On May the seventh I saw a couple that drove through the bushes and they done the Sandy Bottom Shuffle."

So the Judge was *really* mad then. He stamped his foot: "Just WHAT do you mean by the Sandy Bottom Shuffle?"

The nigger say, "That's a technicality in screwing that you *white folks* don't know nothing about."

Court was dismissed!

367 Self-Defense

A. They had this fellow arrested for shootin' a man. So the Judge come up the nex' morning; they had the man in court. He say, "Did you shoot this man in self-defense or not?"

He say, "Naw, Judge, what I did: I shot him in the rear as he jumped over the fence."

B. This man had this man arrested, and he went before the Judge. And the Judge asked him how did he plead. Was it self-defense?

He say, "Yeah! I plead self-defense. I kicked him in the ass, and he jumped over the fence."

368 Suppose

A. This Negro was in court. He was down there for beating up a man. Judge asked him what did he beat him up *for*. He said, "'Cause he called me a black sonovabitch! How would *you* like it if he called you a black sonovabitch?"

The Judge said, "Well, I'm not black!"

He said, "I know that, Judge, but how would you like it if he called you the kind of sonovabitch that you is?"

B. Here's a Black man livin' next door to a white man. So the white man got mad with the Black fellow and called 'im a *black* motherfucker. So he said, "Now, all of a sudden, now, I'm suppose to get angry and fight you, but I am *above* that." (That's what this Black man was telling the white one.) He said, "What I'm going to do, I'm going to have you arrested and carry you to court for calling me out of my name."

So they went to court. And the Judge say, "Well, let's come on with it, let's ... tell me ... I'm tired ... tell me what happened and everything."

He say, "Well, Your Honor, I was conversating with Mr. So and So, and I did it in a very gentleman-like way, and ... so and so ..." and he went on and tol' 'im. He say, "And he got angry with me in our conversation and he called me a black motherfucker." He say, "Now, Your Honor, just *suppose* now, just suppose someone got mad wit' you and called *you* a black motherfucker. Now, how would *you* feel?"

The Judge looked at 'im: "Hummph, hummph [laughing], they ain't gon' call *me* no black motherfucker. I ain't got that to worry about 'cause I ain't *black*."

He say, "Yeah, Your Honor, but suppose he called you the motherfucker that you is."

369 Poor Thing

Poor ole colored lady got on the bus. She didn't have any money, laden down with groceries and all. She got on it, stumbled on to the back and finally took a seat. This streetcar conductor had been so used to ordering people about, you know: "Will the last person who got on the bus please come up and pay the fare!"

This old lady, you know, she's sittin' there, didn't say anything, riding along, jogging, just holding her packages.

"Ump, umn, the person in the middle aisle next to the door, come on up and pay the fare!"

The ole lady, riding along. The other people sitting on the bus. They said, "Poor thing, she probably doesn't hear. I'm gon' touch her on the shoulder and tell her what the man is saying." She's riding on and somebody touched her, say, "Lady, we don't want to bother you, but I think the man is saying he wants you to come up there and pay your fare."

She looked at them. She said, "I know it, children. FUCK HIM!"

370 Sealskin Brown

Colored man went to his boss and said, "Boss, I want a raise in salary." He said, "A raise in salary?" Say, "You getting along fine now."

He said, "I know, Boss, but I gotta have some more money."

He say, "John," say, "I don't see why you want money." Say, "You've got a nice wife, nice sealskin brown wife; all your children are sealskin brown."

He say, "Yeah, but I can't keep a sealskin brown on a muskrat salary."

371 If You Could Be Black for One Saturday Night

These guys were working in the sawmill, and they had some whites, and some Blacks, you know, who did all the menial work. And the Black wanted to be off on Saturday. And so the fellow told him, he says, "Now, you know I don't mind you having Saturday, but you want every Saturday." So he took him aside. He said, "What is it, you know, that you darkies want Saturday off every week?"

So the fellow told him, he say, "Look, if you could be Black for one Saturday night, you'd never want to be white no more as long as you live."

372   Johnny, Can You Give Me a Number?

Johnny is a *bad* little boy in elementary school, and they just integrated. Johnny didn't participate or act right. So the teacher decided they'd have a number game. So she said, "What you're supposed to do when I call on you, you give me a number, and then you reverse it."

She called on a little white girl. She jumped up and said, [very prim, prissy, and proper] "Twenty-three—and if you reverse it, that will be thirty-two."

And then she called on a little white boy, and he said, [just as prim and proper] "Twenty-nine, and if you reverse it, that will be ninety-two."

So Johnny wouldn't raise his hand, but the lady knew she had to call on somebody black, so she said, [hypocritical tone] "Johnny, can you give me a number?"

Johnny said, [nonchalantly] "Yeah, take eleven."

373   Description

When integration first started, and they just had one Black student in the class... So this day the teacher was going over the room asking the children, "What are some things that you can describe that you've seen?" (And naturally Sam was sitting in the back.) So she asked lil' Mary Lou with her lil' pony tail, say, "Mary, dear, what can you describe?"

She said, "Oh, Teacher, I'm thinking about something that's red and round, and it grows on a tree."

Teacher say, "*That's* it! That's a apple."

She say, "Yes, Teacher, that's what it is."

So eventually she goes all around the class. She's getting closer to Sam. Sam's back there just *squirming*, wondering what he gon' say. So just before she gets to Sam, she say, "Susan, dear, what can you describe?"

Susan say, "Oh, this is a kind of yellow fruit that grows in tropical regions."

She say, "Ah! I know what it is. That's a good description, Susan; that's a banana."

She say, "Yes, Teacher."

She say, "Sam! What can you describe?"

Sam didn't know what to say, exactly. He say, "Uh, I-I got something, and I got my hand on it in my pocket. It's long and hard—got a head on it—"

She say, "Stop! Stop! Stop!"

He say, "Naw, Teacher, it ain't what you think. It's a nail."

374 I'm Ridin' This Morning

This fellow had a Parrot who watched the laborers, you know, and he had one man who was named Thornton, and Thornton was the one who didn't work, and he'd [the Parrot would] watch 'im and tell his boss on Thornton, that Thornton didn't work. So a Hawk come through, and this Parrot was on a post watching, and the Hawk picked him up, and he went on over in the air, and he [the Parrot] hollered, "Hello, Thornton," says, "I'm ridin' this morning!"

Thornton looked up at 'im and says, "Yes, you'll soon ride on to hell, too, now!"

375 Dinner Is Served

This maid was working for these ritzy people, you know. So she came to the door one night and said, "Dinner is ready."

So the madam said to her, "That's not the way you say it, Susie. Now, you go back, and you come in again, and you say it right."

So she came back in and she said, "Dinner is on the table."

She said, "NO, Susie, that's not the way you say it. You go back, and you say it right, like I taught you.

So after a while Susie went back in there. She came back again. She said, "Dinner is burned, Madam."

376 Hot Biscuits Burn Yo' Ass

A. 'Twas a woman, a cook, you know, and every day, you know, after she cook sumpin' t' eat, you know, and she was take sumpin' out. After she make hot biscuits, you know, she'd put some away for her children, I reckon, and herself. And one day she cooked hot biscuits, and she didn't know the old Parrot seen her, and she wrapped 'em up and put 'em down in her drawers, you know (old folks then wore them drawers).

And say, the old Parrot tol' her, "Hot biscuits burn yo' ass! Hot biscuits burn yo' ass!"

B. This was a maid, and she went to work for these people. So this lady had to go away to do some shopping or something. So this maid had to cook while she was gone. They had a Polly Parrot, and he was hanging up there, and this little girl, she didn't know he would talk. So she had to cook dinner, and so she went on and cooked biscuits and other foods to go along with it.

So then when the lady came in, she had dinner all ready. She wanted the lady to go right on to the table and eat, but the lady, she went somewhere and sit down. The Parrot had seen this maid put these hot biscuits (when she saw her coming, she grabbed some out of the pan and put over there for her[self], you know, under the cushion in the chair). So this here Parrot told his mistress, "Hot biscuit burn [yo' ass]! Hot biscuit burn [yo' ass]!"

377   I Gon' Tell on You

The white people had a Parrot, and that Parrot, understand, could talk just like I'm talkin' now. So the cook, understand, she used to take sugar and take different things, you understand, and she thought the white woman wouldn't know it. So one day, understand, the old cook, understand, she was diggin' 'round in the sugar, and the old Parrot say, "HAW-W-W, HAW-W-W, I see you, I see you! I gon' tell on you! I gon' tell on you!"

So when the white woman come in there, she tol' the white woman, understand, that the woman was takin' her sugar, but still she didn't discharge her; she kep' her.

378   Talk So Much

The maid went in the pantry to steal some meat while the master and missus gone out. Polly say, [imitating Parrot] "TELLMISSIS!"

She say, "I be damn if you gon' tell Missis anything." And she caught Polly and wrung her neck and threw him down the hill there, you know. She thought she'd killed 'im.

Polly came to, and working 'round in there, tryin' to find her way back out, there was a old dead hog laying down in there. So she walked over there 'round the pig, she say, "AWKKK, Piggy, Piggy, what you doing laying down here, Piggy? You been talkin' 'bout that ham, too, ain't you? That's what brought me down here, my mouth, tryin' to talk so much."

379   Beatin' Cap'n Garrett

This same man, he was kinda a lil' bit touched [tapping head to indicate crazy], you know. His name was Andrew. So we used to call the Man, we used to call 'im Cap'n Garrett. (His name was Garrett.) They had 'im out there shuckin' corn in the field, and they saw Garrett when he drove off in his car. They thought he was going over to the mill. So he [Andrew] comes over there to where the other fellow was shuckin' this corn and sit down, you know, talkin': "Shuh, Cap'n gone away now. I ain't thinkin' 'bout workin' myself to death. I'm gon' sit around a while."

The Man came back and he got so close up on 'em this fellow couldn't tell 'im "There Cap'n."

So he sittin' there talkin' and the fellow come up there right where he was; he say, [gruffly] "Hey, Morton, what you call yourself doing? Ya beatin' me now, ain't ya?"

And Andrew looked up and saw the Man and jumped up to run and ran into a shock of corn and knocked it down on top of 'im.

380 But I Ain't

The white boss hired John and set him out in de woods to cut wood. John sittin' down, pattin' his foot, makin' a lil' noise to sound like he cuttin' wood, singin', "You think I'm cuttin', but I ain't."

That evening the bossman shake his money in his pocket when John come up and sing, "You think I'm gon' pay ya, but I ain't."

381 Guarding the Watermelon Patch

This man had a watermelon patch and people would steal in. So he went and built him a lil' house, but it didn't have no top on it. And he got in there, and he's gonna guard his patch. But he went off to sleep, and the fellows came up there and heard 'im snore. So they goes to work and git many watermelons as they want and took some wire and wired the door together on the outside, so he couldn't get it open, and crawled up on top and took this great big watermelon and dropped it on top his head like that, and it squashed. And he jumped up, almost turned the lil' house over. He thought that was his brain runnin' down like that.

382 The Swimming Match

Master had a nigger that could outswim everybody. He would always bet on his swimming nigger, and he would win.

A white swimming champion of the world came to town, and the Master put up a bet that this nigger could outswim him.

They were to meet at the river at nine o'clock A.M.

The white swimmer was there at nine o'clock in swimming trunks all ready to go.

The nigger came about nine fifteen, trunks on. Big and black and muscular. Had a frying pan, bacon, eggs, and bread.

White swimmer: "What you come here with all that stuff for, nigger? We came down here to swim."

Nigger swimmer: "You mean you ain't got nothing? We will be gone for a couple of days."

The white swimmer paid the bet off and left town.

383   Ain't No Way in the World for the Lord to Catch Your Daddy

There was a man who was a slave, and every night before he'd go to bed, he'd go out and pray and say, "Lord, I'm so tired. Why don't you come and get me? Lord, I'm so tired." And he'd moan and groan like this half the night. He'd wake up all the folks in the Big House.

So the white man up there and his wife couldn't sleep, say, "We're just tired of that nigger down there hollering that "Lord, come git me." So the white man say, "I know what I'm gon' do," say, I'm gon' get that nigger good, next time he start hollering."

So the next night the man got out there and started hollering, "Oh, Lord, please come get me. I'm so tired."

So the white man put on a sheet, walked down there, and say, "Nigger, here I am to get you."

And the nigger started running.

And the little children started jumping up and down in the house, "Oh, Mama, the Lord's gon' get Daddy."

Mama say, "Shut up, Daddy ain't got no shoes on. Ain't no way in the world for the Lord to catch 'im."

384   Turn Out the Sack

The Cat was sittin' out there one day and the old Fox come on by and wanted to strike up a conversation. The Cat say, "Mr. Fox, they tell me you're the smartest thing on four feet. Say you got more sense in how to outwit the hunter and the hounds and everything going."

He say, [boastfully] "Oh-h-h, Cat, you talkin' to a genius in animals now."
He say, "I got a whole sack o' tricks that I can turn around."
 The Cat told 'im, "The only trick I know is to run up a tree."
 The Fox say, "Oh, that ain't *nothin'*."
 While they were talkin' a pack o' Hounds came over the hill and grabbed him 'fore he could even get outa the way. The Cat ran up the tree and say, "Turn out the sack, Mr. Fox, turn out the sack! Turn out the sack!"
 Won't nothin' he could do. They soon killed him.
 The Cat say, "Oh, Mr. Fox, of all your sack full of tricks, if you had known one simple and safe as mine, you wouldn't of lost your life."

385 Shine

A. It was 1849 when the great *Titanic* went down;
 Say the fifth of May was a hell of a day,
 When the great *Titanic* sailed away.
 It was hell, hell, it was some fucked-up times
 When that *Titanic* hit that iceberg and began to go down.
 Came up from down below old Shine,
 Came up on the deck and said,
 "Captain, Captain, water is coming in through the boiler room do'."
 Captain said, "Now Shine, oh, Shine, go back and pack your sack,
 'Cause I got forty-nine electric pumps to keep that water back."
 Shine said, "That may be true because you carrying a load."
 Says, "I'm gon' take my chances in jumping overboard."
 Captain say, "Now, Shine, oh, Shine, don't be no fool and don't be no clown."
 Say, "Anybody go overboard is bound to drown."
 Shine say, "You may have them pumps, and they better work fast,"
 Say, "'cause I'm going overboard when that water reach my ass."
 Say now the Captain's daughter came up on the deck.
 She had her hands in her cock and her tits 'round her neck.
 And say she say, "Now, Shine, oh, Shine, save poor me."
 Say, "I'll give you more pussy than one Shine can see."
 Shine say, "Now, you may have good pussy and that might be true,"
 Say, "But women on land got good pussy too."
 So she say, "Now, Shine, oh, Shine, if you don't save poor me,"
 Say, "I'll cut it out and throw it to the sea."
 Shine say, "Before I let that matter pass,
 I'll cut my dick off to the crack of my ass;
 I'll make my dick into an oar
 And paddle that pussy back to shore."
 All the millionaires looked around at Shine, say, "Now, Shine, oh, Shine, save poor me";
 Say, "We'll make you wealthier than one Shine can be."
 Shine say, "You hate my color and you hate my race";

Say, "Jump overboard and give those sharks a chase."
Now women began to scream, and babies began to cry,
And everybody on board realized they *had* to die.
But Shine could swim and Shine could *float*,
And Shine could throw his ass like a motorboat.
Say Shine hit the water with a hell of a splash,
And everybody wondered if that Black sonovabitch could last.
Say the Devil looked up from hell and grinned,
Say, "He's a *black, swimming motherfucker*. I think he's gon' come on
     in."
Say Shine looked over to his side and got a hell of a surprise,
A forty-foot whale was swimming by his side.
Say, but Shine shook his head and wiggled his tail,
And did the deep-sea shuffle and fucked that whale.
Say, now, when Shine hit the nearest seaport town,
The word had gone around that the great *Titanic* had gone down.
Say, but Shine walked up to the nearest bar and *kicked* down a do',
Women lined all up against the wall and punks laying all out on the flo'.
Shine said, "Houseman, Houseman, fix me a toddy";
Say, "I'm gon' get high and fuck *everybody*."
Shine began to drink and he began to drink fast,
And Shine end up not getting nah piece o' ass.
It wasn't women that killed poor Shine, and it wasn't whiskey that took
     his breath;
Say a little green fly flew up Shine's ass and *tickled* Shine to death.

B. Say the twelfth of May was one *hell* of a day,
When the news got around the seaport town
That the great *Titanic* had settled down.
Step the Black man below the ship
They called Shine; hollered
"Captain, Captain, don't you know,
Why there's forty feet o' water on the boiler room flo'!"
The Captain say, "Git back, you dirty Black!
We got twenty-five pumps to keep this water back."
So Shine came on board, *jumped* over, waved his Black ass and begin to
     swim,
With a thousand millionaires lookin' at him.
So the Captain's wife stepped on board,
Say, "Shine, Shine, please save poor me,
I give you all the pussy you can see."
Shine said, "I got pussy on land, I got pussy on sea,
I got *twenty-five* motherfuckers in New York just waitin' on me."
So the Captain's daughter stepped on board,
She say, "Shine, Shine, *please* save poor me;
I'll name this *kid* after thee."
Shine say, "*Bitch*, you went and got knocked up, that's fine,
But you got to hit this water just like old Shine."
So the Captain stepped aboard,

He say, [pompous voice] "Shine, Shine, please save poor me,
I'll make you richer than any Shine could be."
Shine say, "To make me rich would be very fine,
But first I have to save this *black* ass o' mine."
Shine say, "*Sharks*, look out, I know some o' this black ass you'd like to
    taste,
But from here to New York's gon' be one hell o' a race."
So the news got around the seaport town,
That the *Titanic* had sank down.
Shine was in Harlem on Thirty-Fifth Street
Damn near drunk, fucked his twenty-five bitches,
And his dick got sore; went to the doctor.
The doctor say, "Shine, I gon' have to cut your dick off."
Shine say, "If you cut it off, you better cut it down to the *motherfuckin'*
    bone,
'Cause if you leave any kind o' meat, I'm gon' fuck *right* on."
He say, "If I should die, soak my *balls* in alco*hol*;
And lay my dick on my chest,
Then tell *all* them cocksuckin' whores
Old Shine's gone to rest."
Shine died—went to hell.
The Devil said, "All you bitches, you better clamb [climb] the
    motherfuckin' wall,
'Cause Shine gon' come back down
    here and fuck us *all!*"

386 Peeled It, Cored It, and Diced It

The Negro and white man was boasting on their capabilities. The white
man was a pistol shot. He throwed up a dime, you know, and pulled his gun
out and shot a hole through the darn thing.
The Negro throwed up a apple and pulled out his knife, peeled it, cored it,
and diced it before it hit the ground.

387 He Does Need Some More Sugar

There was a nigger cowboy and he walked in this tavern, bar, and say,
"Bartender, give me some coffee."
He [bartender] say, [unbelievingly] "What the hell he mean—coffee?"
He say, "I want *coffee*."
Guy say, "Well, what does he want?"

"I said I want *coffee*."

Well, he thought on it. So he said, "I can't lose any time—" (you know), "I-I'll give the nigger some coffee."

They say, "Give the nigger some coffee." He looked; Jesse James and the Dalton boys were sittin' at the bar. They say, "Give the nigger some coffee."

So he gave him some coffee. Nigger say, "Upp, uhn-un, give me some *cream and sugar*."

He say, "Now ain't this somethin'? [Pause.] Better give 'im what he wants. They said give it to 'im." So they went on and said, "Okay, well, I'll give the nigger some cream and sugar." So he put some cream in it and some sugar in it.

He say, "Nope! Uhn-un, *two* lumps—*two* lumps of sugar."

"Naw, I be damn if I'm gon' give you two lumps. That's just too damn far. I'm not going that far. Call the sheriff."

So they called the sheriff. Called Wyatt Earp. He came over there and told the nigger, say, "Now, wait a minute here, nigger, first of all we don't serve *yawl* in here. Understand that. I don't know how you got your coffee, don't know how you even got the cream or what little sugar you got, but I think your coffee is *sweet enough*, and I'm gon' stir your coffee for you and let you *taste* it. So he reached in there and took his *thirty-eight* and stuck it right down in the bottom of the coffee and stirred it 'round, said, "Now, nigger, I think that's sweet *enough!*"

The nigger reached over and got a left-hand forty-five, and cocked it on the sheriff. He said, "I don't think it's sweet enough."

The sheriff said, "I think the nigger does need two lumps of sugar. Give him some sugar!"

388   You Ever Kiss a Mule?

A.   These white guys, you know, got this Black guy down in Mississippi somewhere, and they just started to shooting around his feet, you know. Say, "Dance, nigger, dance!" And they were just shootin' and he was *jumpin'!* (That guy was scared.)

So when they got through he said, [meekly] "You use *all* your bullets?" They say, "Yeah."

He pulled out that *blade*; he say, "You ever kiss a mule?"

The white guys say, "Naw, but I always had a inklin'."

B.   During the time of Al Capone, these people they'd do just about *anything* to *anybody*, you know. They'd run the government, *anything*. So they ridin' down a little country road outside of Chicago, and a farmer had his mule out there. So they say, "Let's have some fun with 'im." So they say,

"Listen, kin that mule dance?"

The farmer say, "Naw, you know . . ."

They say, "Let's see that mule—" (BAM! BAM! BAM!—they shooting) and the mule just [dramatizing mule jumping around trying to dodge bullets]. "I thought you say that mule couldn't dance. Well, how 'bout you?"

"Man, I can't dance. I'm seventy-some years ole!"

"Let's see if you kin." BAM! BAM! BAM! [Dramatizing them shooting and the man dancing around dodging bullets.] "I thought you say you couldn't dance."

Well, the farmer had counted the shells. When they emptied out, the farmer reached down and got that shotgun, and put it right in their faces. He say, "Hey, Sonny, both o' yawl come over here. You ever kissed a mule?"

The guy say, "No, but I've always *wanted* to."

389 You May Fall in Yourself

It's sad but this is a slavery-time story, too. Seems like after the slave was abolished, his ex-master left 'im a lil' piece o' ground where his lil' cabin used to stay on. Nobody paid it any mind, but it so happened that a railroad company wanted to run a track through there and the land got valuable. And those poor people—they wanted it, wanted to get 'im out of it. They couldn't *take* it away from 'im 'cause it was given to 'im by this owner where died. So they did everything they could to aggravate 'im and worry 'im to make 'im—just make 'im jump up and leave 'cause they wanted the property. So this man—this white fellow—had a son. They both of the same type.

And that day the old man [ex-slave] had just cooked 'im a 'possum, had it in the stove baking while he was sleep. And this poor white fellow came in and looked around to see what he could steal there, to agitate, and he saw the old man sleep. He smelled the 'possum, and he opened the oven door, looked in at it, all browned up. His first idea was to grab it and carry it off and eat it. And he happened to look up on the shelf and saw this rat poisoning. He say, "Oh, I know what I'll do. I'll git him—I'll git his land." So he took that rat poisoning and put it *all* over that 'possum, and left it back in the stove. He say, "Now, if he eat that, I'll get the land."

Well, now he had a son who was just on his type. The son didn't know the daddy had been in there. So, he come around, snooping around to see what he could do to this old fellow. And he smelled this 'possum, looked in the stove, there it was. So he carried it off and ate it . . .

And the next day the daddy had a funeral for his only son. And he put the poison down for the ole slave fellow and his son ate it and killed him.

You dig a ditch for your fellow man, you may fall in yourself.

390   Good Morning

Good morning, Lord.
Good morning, Mama.
Good morning, Daddy.
And,
White America, kiss my ass!

391   Bad Bluebird

So the Bluebird flew to the grocery store,
Pulled down his pants and shit in the flo',
Wiped his ass on a sardine can,
And say, "I ain't thinkin' 'bout a grocery man."
So he flew over there to the barber shop,
Wiped his ass on a razor strap,
And lathered his ass on a lathering can,
And say, "Shave my ass, Mr. Barber man!"

392   Take My Order

A Black brother in a restaurant tells the white waiter, "I want some black coffee, black toast, and some black butter."

The white waiter looks confused at the brother.

The brother tells him, "If you don't like what I asked for, kiss my black ass."

393   I Won't Take Any Shit

Go to work from nine to five,
While the white man is trying to fuck with my mind.

Come home, tired as shit,
But you better believe I won't take any shit!

394   Only Thing Better Than One Is Two

PLACE: Big City

SPEAKER: Black Radical
BLACK RADICAL: "Today, Brothers, is a new day. We have to stop taking whitey's shit. Now in what way can this be stopped today, this minute?"
BROTHER IN THE CROWD: "Well, it ain't but one thing better than one dead whitey—And that's two of them motherfuckers."

395   Peace (Piece?)

Whitey gives the Peace sign to some Brothers.
They reply, "Yeah, we have been waiting for a PIECE of your ass for a long time."

396   Some Are Going, and Some Are Coming

A.   The Rabbit was coming along, and he looked down in this old deep well (you know how the wells used to be), and he looked down in this well, and he saw what he thought was a piece of cheese down there, but it was only a reflection of the moon. And he said, "Well, I'll git down here and git this piece of cheese." It was two buckets, you know, it was two buckets; you know how people used to have one bucket goes down and the other one goes up. So he got in this bucket at the top, and he say, "I'll go down and get it." So he went on down in this bucket. Then when he got down to the bottom and reached for the cheese, it was only a reflection of the moon. And he didn't have any way to get up, and he say, "I'm down here now in this water, nothin' but this moon reflection 'n' . . ."
And after a while the Fox came by. He looked up there and the Fox was at the top of the well. And the Fox say, "Brer Rabbit, what ya doin' down there?"
He say, "I'm down here eatin' cheese. I'm down here eatin' this cheese. Can't ya see this big cheese down here?"
"Yeah, I see it."
"Come on down, Brer Fox, 'n' get a piece, ya know. Come on down. It's nice."
So the Fox got in the other bucket and he was coming on down. And when they got about half—you know, when they got about, you know, even Stephen, you know, when the Fox was going down and the Rabbit was coming up, he say, "Brother Fox, I tell ya, that's the way it is in life. Some are going and some coming." And he got on up, you know. Some going and some coming.

That's the way it is in life—some going and some coming. When you think about it, like in birth and death. It's some going and some coming.

B.   Brer Rabbit went up to the well to get some water. He jumped in the bucket, but the other bucket hadn't sunk, you know. With his weight, he carried the bucket on down. But he was so *light*, it didn't go down in the water; it sat up on top the water. Brer Fox, he came on by. So he decided he'd get some water. He saw the Rabbit down in there. He say, "Hi, Mr. Rabbit, what ya doing down there? Ah," he say, "is it bitin'?"

He say, "Now-w-w-w-w . . ." (He thinkin' all the time, you know.) So he say, "I tell you what, Mr. Fox, why don't you get in the other bucket and come down and try your luck?"

Ole Fox say, "Well, I believe I'll do that." So he jumped in the bucket and he was so much heavier, he carried the Rabbit back up. And he met 'im halfway. He say, "Mr. Rabbit, what kind of funny way you doing now? I thought you was gon' stay down there with me."

He say, "Aw, man, that's the way of the world: some go and some come."

397   I Owns Old Marster

There is a community known as Lottsburg . . . There was a family named Diggs that lived in Lottsburg on a large farm, an old, a very old man. I went to his home and had a long talk with him. I said, "Mr. Diggs, tell me how you came to possess this large farm."

Then he tells me this very interesting story. He said, "You know, I grew up on this farm. I was a child on this farm, and I lived in the old house—*old house*—way back there" (down in the fields—it had been gone; they'd demolished it—and the old house in which he lived was one of those old, sort of colonial houses). And he said to me, he said, "The house in which I live now was my Old Marster's house." (Those were his words.) Then he pointed and said, "You see—you see that gyarden out there." (The old people said *gyarden*.) He said, "My Old Marster is buried there. And," he said, "I owns my Old Marster in his grave."

398   White in White America

Hey, Brother, what is white in white America?
White slaves in the cotton fields.

399 All Yawl Look Alike

A Black security guard was checking a group of white people's I.D.'s as they entered a hotel. The first whitey shows his I.D., and the cop gives it back and tells the rest to go on through.

The whiteys who didn't show their I.D.'s stand amazed. And the guard turns to say, "All yawl whiteys look alike anyway."

400 Cross Burning

A white family who moves into a all-Black neighborhood is welcomed by the neighbors that evening with a burning in the front yard. Instead of the traditional cross of the KKK, they are met with the BBB (Black Bombers Battalion).

401 Get That White Trash Out of Here

This is a old one. There was a traveling salesman, and he went into this Southern nightclub. They were not welcomed, but they could not put them out. So the manager told the maitre d', "Everytime they order a round of drinks, double the price. That'll get them out of here in a hurry."

So they sat there and drank and drank and drank. Finally the maitre d' went to the manager and said, "They've run up to sixty-four dollars a round and it's just the two of them." Say, "What must I do?"

The manager said, "Sixty-four dollars! What must you do! Go back there and get the rest of that white trash out o' here!"

402 If You Are White

Blacks used to say, "When you are white you are right."

Now it has been changed to, "If you are white, it's best to keep your ass out of sight."

13

I'm a Bad Motherfucker:
Tales of the Bad Nigger

I've got a tombstone disposition, graveyard mind.
I know I'm a bad motherfucker, that's why I don't
  mind dying.
                              "Great McDaddy"

As WILLIAM H. GRIER and Price M. Cobbs have pointed out, "One of the constant themes in Black folklore is the 'bad nigger.'"[1] That the term *Bad Nigger* from its beginning has had positive connotations to certain Black people and negative connotations to white people suggests its early meaning as a Black man who fought against the system. Though at least one attempt has been made to trace the term back to African origins, it is most likely, as Alan Dundes suggests, that the phrase as we know it probably originated in antebellum America.[2] Dundes cites the reference in John Little's slave narrative to the slave in irons as a "bad nigger," by which the whites meant dangerous and rebellious; noting the antithetical attitudes of Blacks and whites toward Bad Niggers, Little continues, "The man who was 'a bad nigger' in the South is here [Canada] a respected, independent farmer."[3] The Bad Nigger is and always has been *bad* (that is, villainous) to whites because he violates their laws and he violates their moral codes. He is *ba-ad* (that is, heroic) to the Black people who relish his exploits for exactly the same reasons.

The Bad Nigger of folklore is tough and violent. He kills without blinking an eye. He courts death constantly and doesn't fear dying, probably because he is willing to do battle with the Devil as well as with his human enemies (and he frequently defeats even the Devil). He values fine clothes and flashy cars. He asserts his manhood

224

through his physical destruction of men and through his sexual victimization of women.[4]

The Bad Niggers in folklore are sexual supermen, but their women are enemies to be conquered, humiliated, and controlled rather than partners to be loved. The hostility toward the Black woman expressed in toasts such as those included here undoubtedly has its basis in the inhibitions imposed by white American society on Black men. As I have pointed out elsewhere, it has usually been the Black mother who, because of her fear of the slave master, the lynch mob, and the legal system, had to teach her child to "mask and repress his normal masculinity and aggressiveness lest these put his life in danger. She had in other words to prepare him for his subordinate place in the world."[5] Black boys inevitably resented their mothers' repression and developed hostility toward their mothers. It is commonly accepted that the Bad Nigger's need to humiliate and subdue the woman (the battlefield is always in the bed) stems from his antagonism toward her for what appears to him to be her collusion with white American society to emasculate and repress him.

The exploits of Bad Niggers are frequently recounted in toasts, long narrative poems peculiar to Black Americans and collected most frequently in jails and in ghetto areas. Their popularity has not, however, been limited to those areas, as I collected toasts from a Black college professor reared in the rural South, from a high-ranking administrator in a Federal government program who was born into an upper-middle-class family, from a scientist born and reared in a rural Virginia county, and from other professional Blacks.[6] Of course, the barrier separating successful Black professionals from Black convicts in America is a tenuous one, as was forcefully impressed upon me a few years ago. I was in the car with the administrator to whom I just referred when he was arrested and thrown into jail in a small town in Virginia for, as the arresting officer put it, "pulling out in front of that *white* woman!"[7] Certainly the conditions that motivate the rebellious tales in this chapter are suffered by both Black ghetto dwellers and successful Black professionals, and the bitterness and aggressiveness expressed in them are felt (if not expressed) by all Blacks. As Grier and Cobbs have put it, "because of his experience in this country, every black man harbors a potential bad nigger inside him."[8]

The language in the toasts is shockingly obscene. The toasts are full of slang expressions current in Black communities. The obscenities and the slang are in themselves representative of further rebellion against white society. The psychological function of obscenities (and the sexual assertiveness that also characterizes these tales) as aggressive tools has been explored by Sigmund Freud in his well-known "Wit and Its Relation to the Unconscious."[9] The slang (with its many double entendres) is, of course, a part of the Black person's language, designed to prevent the white person from fully comprehending (a game that has always been played on the white American with the blues). There are certain common phrases and lines that are repeated from toast to toast, but there also is a great deal of the teller's individual ingenuity displayed in each of the toasts, particularly in the use of metaphorical language and hyperbolic imagery.[10]

The strictly masculine point of view, the scatological subject matter, and the shocking language of the toasts and of the Bad Nigger jokes make this group of Black folk materials wholly male in its origin and appeal. Every tale in this chapter was related by males; I have never seen a reference to a female teller of toasts, nor have I ever heard a toast told by a female.[11] The tales in which the major theme is conflict or contest between the Bad Nigger and the white man are included in chapter twelve.

NOTES

1. William H. Grier and Price M. Cobbs, *Black Rage* (New York: Bantam Books, 1969), p. 54.

2. H. C. Brearley's suggestion that the term is possibly of African origin has been discredited by anthropologist Melville J. Herskovits, who attacks Brearley's attempt to argue African origins as indefensible (H. C. Brearley, "Ba-ad Nigger," *The South Atlantic Quarterly* 38 [January, 1939]: 75–81; and "A Letter to the Editors: Some Comments by Professor Herskovits, *The South Atlantic Quarterly* 39 [July, 1940]: 350–51). For his comments on this debate, see Alan Dundes, ed., *Mother Wit from the Laughing Barrel: Readings in the Interpretation of Afro-American Folklore* (Englewood Cliffs, N.J.: Prentice-Hall, 1973), p. 580 (note).

3. Dundes, pp. 580–81 (note), quoting Little from Benjamin Drew, *A North-Side View of Slavery. The Refugee: or the Narratives of Fugitive Slaves in Canada. Related by Themselves, with An Account of the History and Condition of the Colored Population of Upper Canada* (Westport, Conn.: Negro Universities Press, 1968).

4. For fuller discussions of the Bad Nigger, see Brearley, pp. 75–81; Abrahams, *Deep Down . . .*, pp. 61–85 and *Positively Black* (Englewood Cliffs, N.J.: Prentice-Hall, 1970), pp. 69–96; Bruce Jackson, "*Get Your Ass in the Water and Swim Like Me*" (Cambridge: Harvard University Press, 1974), pp. 30–38; and Grier and Cobbs, pp. 53–55.

5. Daryl Dance, "Black Eve or Madonna? A Study of the Antithetical Views of the Mother in Black American Literature," *Perspectives on Afro-American Women*, ed. Willa D. Johnson and Thomas L. Green (Washington,

D.C.: Educational Community Counselors Associates, 1975), p. 107. For some of the observations following in this paragraph, I am indebted to Grier and Cobbs, pp. 49–52.

6. It is unlikely that any of my professional informants would have performed for white collectors or even for strange Black folklorists. The only Black professionals from whom I collected toasts are my friends.

7. Consider also the large number of Black leaders who have been or who are in prison.

8. Grier and Cobbs, p. 55.

9. See Sigmund Freud, "Wit and Its Relation to the Unconscious," *The Basic Writings of Sigmund Freud*, ed. A. A. Brill (New York: Modern Library, 1938).

10. For fuller discussions of the toasts, see Roger D. Abrahams, "The Toast: A Neglected Form of Folk Narrative," in *Folklore in Action*, ed. Horace P. Beck (Philadelphia: American Folklore Society, 1962), pp. 1–11, and *Deep Down . . .*; William Labov et al., "Toasts," in Dundes, pp. 329–47; Dennis Wepman et al., "Toasts: The Black Urban Folk Poetry," *Journal of American Folklore* 137 (July-September, 1974): 208–24; and Jackson.

11. I should note that at the 1976 Festival of American Folklore in Washington, D.C., I spoke with Jason Dodson, a graduate student at Indiana University, who informed me that he had collected the standard toasts from Black females. None of these has at this writing been published, however.

403   John Henry

A. Say when John Henry was a lil' bit o' boy,
No bigger 'n a lil' bit o' *baby*,
No bigger 'n the palm of his hand,
His mother took a look at him and said,
"My baby gon' be a steel-drivin' man. Lawd! Lawd!
My man gon' be a steel-drivin' man."

Say John Henry had a lil' woman;
Her name was Polly Ann.
John Henry took sick and had to go to bed,
And Polly Ann drove steel like a man. Lawd! Lawd!
Polly Ann drove steel like a man.

Say one day the boss man said to John Henry,
He say, [nasty tone] "Look here, boy,
You gotta be on your P's and Q's now because we got a steam drill here,
And it can drive so many holes in a day, and if you ain't careful,
It'll put you out of a job.

Say John Henry looked at his boss man, and he said,
"A man ain't nothin' but a man;
Before I let that thing beat me to the bottom,

I'll die wid dis here hammer in my hand. Lawd! Lawd!
I'll die wid dis here hammer in my hand."

Say they was drivin' up in the Big Bend Tunnel there and inside the
    mountain
'N' the boss say, "Hol' it, John, hol' it, John!"
It sound like the whole front o' that mountain was cavin' in.
John Henry took a look at the boss man and say,
"Ain't nothin' but my hammer suckin' wind,
Ain't nothin' but my hammer suckin' wind. Lawd! Lawd!
Ain't nothin' but my hammer suckin' wind."

Say when John Henry died,
They buried 'im on the hillside in the sand.
And every time a steel drill go by,
The steel drill say, "TOOTtoTOOTTTTT,
Yonder lies a steel-drivin' man. Lawd! Lawd!
Yonder lies a steel-drivin' man."

B. When John Henry was a little baby,
Sitting on his pappy's knee,
He picked a hammer
And a little bitty nail,
Drove it in his pappy's knee,
Oh, Lord, and drove it in his pappy's knee.

404 Stag

Back in thirty-two when times was hard,
Stag had two forty-fives and a marked deck o' cards.
He had a pinstriped suit and a old fucked-up hat,
He had a twenty-nine Ford and owed payments on that.
Stag thought he'd take a walk down on Vampire Street,
There where all them slick and ba-ad dudes meet.
He wade through shit and he wade through mud,
He come to a crib they call the Bucket o' Blood.
He called to the bartender for something to eat.
Bartender gave 'im a muddy glass o' water and a stale piece o' meat.
He say, "Bartender, Bartender, you don't realize who I am!"
Bartender say, "Frankly speaking, Mister, I don't give a good goddamn."
But just then (the bartender hadn't realized what he had said)
Stag had pumped two forty-five slugs in his motherfucking head.
And in walked this ho [whore] and say, "Oh, no! Oh, no! He can't be dead!"
Stag say, "Then you get back there, bitch, and mend them holes in his
    motherfucking head."
Just then Stag grabbed the ho and they went upstairs and begin to tussle;
Stag fucked her nine times before she could move a muscle.

Fucked her on the bed, fucked her on the flo'.
Come downstairs and the joint got quiet as a pin.
In walked that bad motherfucker they call Billy Lyons.
He say, "Oh were, oh where may that bad motherfucker be?"
Stag say, "Excuse me, Mister, but my name is Stagolee."
Ho come up there and say, "Stag, please . . ."
Stag slapped that bitch down to her motherfucking knees.
And then old Slick Willie John, he turned out the lights,
And when the lights came on Billy Lyons was layin' at rest,
With two of Stagolee's forty-five slugs pumped in his chest.
Somebody say, "Stag, Stag, you know that ain't right.
One o' us tell Mrs. Lyons 'bout this old fight."
Stag went to Mrs. Lyons, say, "Miz Lyons, Miz Lyons," say, "you know what
      I've done.
I've went out there and killed your last and only son."
Mrs. Lyons looked at Stag, say, "Stag, Stag, you know that can't be true!
You and Billy been good friends for the last year or two."
He say, "Look, bitch, if you don't believe what I said,
Go down there and count them holes in his motherfucking head."
And in walked the rollers [law officers];
They picked up Stag and carried him to court.
Judge told Stag, say, "Stag, I been wanted you for a long time."
Say, "I'm gon' gi' you twenty years."
Stag looked up at the Judge, say, "Twenty years!" Say, "Twenty years ain't
      no time."
Say, "I got a brother in Sing Sing doing one ninety-nine."
And just then Stag's sister jumped up and begin to scream.
Judge told her, say, "Sit down, Sis, this is only a dream."
Stag's mama jumped up and begin to shout,
Judge say, "Sit down, old bitch, you don't know what it's all about."
And then—just then, in walked this ho.
By the courtroom's surprise that ho pulled two long forty-fives.
Stag grabbed his forty-five and shot his way to the courtroom do',
Tipped his hat to all the ladies once mo'
Down on the corner of Vampire Street there was Stag,
Old dude called Booty Green.
That's the cleanest motherfucker I ever seen,
With a great big, long, white limousine.
Stag got in the limousine;
They drove 'round the block until they came to their hideout.
They was sittin' in there shuffling them broads [cards], sippin' that gin . . .
That's when them goddamn rollers start tippin' back in.

405 Dolemite

Some folks say that Willie Green
Was the baddest motherfucker the world has ever seen.

Now I want you to light up a joint and take a real good shit and screw your
     wig on real tight,
While I tell you 'bout this *bad* motherfucker called Dolemite.
Now Dolemite was born in San Antoine,
A young, ramping, *scamping* young fellow from the day he was born.
For the day he dropped from his Mammy's ass,
He smacked his grandpappy in the face and said,
"From now on, cocksucker, I'm runnin' this place."
At the age of one he was drinking whiskey and gin,
At the age of two he was eating the *bottles* they came in.
Now Dolemite had a uncle they called Sudden Death,
That killed a *dozen* motherfuckers from the smell o' his breath.
So Dolemite's aunt tol' his uncle how he was treatin' his ma and pa.
He say, "Lemme go and check this little bad motherfucker fo' he go too far."
So one *cold*, dark *December* night his uncle came broking in on Dolemite.
He said, "Dolemite, you better straighten up and treat your mother right,
'Cause if you keep on with your dirty mistreatin'
I'm gon' whip your ass till your heart stop beatin'."
Dolemite was sittin' in the living room floor playin',
He say, "Uncle, I see your lips going up and down,
But I don't hear a motherfuckin' sound."
So that made Dolemite' uncle mad,
He swung for the *right* and lighten the place,
But Dolemite tore his right leg off 'cause he was that damn fast.
So all the men in San Antoine gathered around that night,
To see what they could do about this little *bad* motherfucker called
     Dolemite.
So it took one *hundred* of the *baddest*, the *boldest*, the UGLIEST men in
     town,
Finally throwed Dolemite' ass down.
They throwed him in jail; they held 'im without bail.
If you think his Mammy was happy, you should o' see his pappy;
'Cause it been a *long* eight years since Dolemite's been fed,
And the average motherfucker woulda *long* been dead.
So the warden came to Dolemite and said,
He say, "Dolemite, we gon' do you a favor.
We gon' give you a dollar and a half and a damn good meal,
If you promise to leave us *alone*.
And keep your *ba-ad* ass out o' San Ant*oine*."
So Dolemite *took* the dollar and a half and the damn good meal,
But he said, "I'm gonna tell *all* you ancient motherfuckers how ole Dolemite
     feel."
He say, "Yawl kin suck my *dick*, ass, balls, down to the motherfucking
     bone,"
Says, "I ain't never comin' back to San Ant*oine*."
So Dolemite was thirteen; he say, "Let me try my [unclear] on sea."
He got a job in Africa, kicking lions in the asshole to stay in shape.
He got run out of South America for fucking steers.
He fucked a she-elephant till *she* broke down in tears.
So Dolemite worked five years and a day,

Got his pay.
He say, "Well, I believe I'll go back to the jive-ass U.S.A."
The Sonny Liston heavyweight fight was being broadcasted that night,
And a special bulletin saying, "Look out for storms, bombs, and Dolemite!"
So the first thing that Dolemite ran into
Was two big Rocky Mountains. Dolemite say, "Mountains, what yawl gon'
    do?"
The mountains say, "We gon' part, Mr. Dolemite, and let your ba-ad ass
    through."
Hoboed down to Chi [Chicago], who did he ran into but that bad-assed,
    two-gun Peter.
He say, "Move over and let me pass,
'Fo' the doctor have to pull these triple A's out your motherfuckin' ass."
So he went on down Kansas City, kicking asses till both shoes got shitty.
Went on down Forty-Second Street;
Not for no shit, but for some place he could sleep and eat.
So he ran into this shy-ass Mabel.
Of all the whores, she was the most!
She'd suck you, fuck you, and jack you off.
She say, "Dolemite, come on down to my pad;
We gon' fuck and fight till broad daylight!"
Dolemite say, "Bitch, it's best you not fuck with me."
He say, "I got a job in Africa kicking lions in the asshole to stay in shape."
He say, "I got ran out of South America for fuckin' steers."
He say, "I fucked a she-elephant till she broke down in tears."
Mabel said, "I don't care where you going and where you been,
I'm just dying to wrap this hot pussy all around your bad-assed chin."
Dolemite say, "Bitch, let me run you down some o' my pedigree."
He say, "I swimmed across bloody rivers and ain't never got wet.
Mountains have fell on me and I ain't dead yet."
He say, "I fucked an elephant and there too the mother."
He say, "I could look up a bull's ass and tell you the price of butter."
He say, "I fucked the same elephant and down to the coon,
Even fucked the same damn cow who jumped over the motherfucking moon.
And you talking 'bout wrapping your hot juicy pussy all around my
    bad-assed chin.
Bitch, you ought to be blowing out my asshole and trying to be my
    motherfucking friend."
But WOE! Mabel fought him. That's when the fucking started.
Mabel made that pussy do the popcorn, mojo, the turkey, and the grind,
Left Dolemite's ass nine strokes behind.
She throwed pussy up Dolemite's back, run it down his side, out his pocket,
Damn near knocked his asshole out o' socket.
But Dolemite suddenly made a mojo turn,
Had the crabs around that bitch's asshole hollering, "Burn, baby, burn!"
So the next morning they found old Mabel dead.
With her drawers wrapped around her nappy-assed head.
And the crabs were madder 'n' a motherfucker,
'Cause Dolemite had beat 'em out o' their supper.
So Dolemite kept on kicking asses and fucking up in the hall,

Till finally his *roll* was called.
So they took 'im down to the grave,
And Dolemite was dead, but his *dick* was still hard.
And the preacher said, [solemn tone] "Ashes to ashes,
And *dust* to dust, I'm GLAD this BA-AD motherfucker
Called Dolemite is no longer with us."

406   The History of the Dog

Some o' you guys may be surprised
At what I'm 'bout to say;
But show me the lame who think he knows the game,
And where did he learn to play?
Now the rule o' the game is
Never teach a lame the game unless you make 'im pay.
So let me tell just how I fell,
And what tricks fate played on me.
So gather around, while I run it down
And unreel my his-to-rie.
Now it was a Saturday night,
And the jungle was bright,
And all the hustlers began stalking their prey,
Where the cold was crime
That laid on the line,
And the weakest was doomed to pay;
Where blood was shed,
For the sake of bread,
And most drunks are beat for their poke ["scratch, money"].
By the sight of the hands
Are the Murphy man ["a cat who cons men looking for whores"]
And the words the con man spoke:
Where most winos cringe to a can head binge
And make their graves in the snow;
Where girls of vice sell love for a *hell* of a price,
And most laws are corrupt.
As I keep on going down, trying,
I keep crying, I say, "Now, Jack, this is a bitter cup."
At the grand display lit up like a Christmas toy,
I was making my play for this female prey
Ever since I was just a boy.
Now I was young and prancy,
And reefers was my fancy;
And known as a adequate male,
But I curse the day
When I made my play
At this sidewalking, jazzy belle.
Now she was a brownskin moll

Like a Chinese doll,
Walking in the wages of sin,
Up and down with a trod,
And a wink, and a nod
To the nearest ho-house den.
Her *eyes* shown *bright*
In the neon lights
And from her cheeks teardrops fell.
When I asked her *why*,
She started to *cry*
And told me this bitter tale:
All about how some guy
Had blacked her eye
And took all the scratch she could get,
Let her lie in jail
And wouldn't go the bail,
And dared her to call it quits;
So I looked at her. I say,
"Dig this, bitch, dry your eyes
And have no fear,
For the kind lover is here;
For I'm storking my name on a piece of this game,
And I don't want you to have no fear (you understand)."
So she looked at me like a slave set free,
And said, "Like dig, Dog, I'm your girl."
And that *sucker* o' hers didn't even stir
As I split wit' her and we made it all 'round the world.
She caught on fast
As the months rolled past,
And played it to the bitter end.
A better ho I've yet to know,
Like, dig it! I thought Dog was man's best friend.
Now she rank with the *best* in the East and the West,
And when her boosting hand came down [when she had an urge to shoplift],
She stole knots out o' trees, beat Fido for his fleas,
And thieved in a many a towns.
Now she was a good sharp broad, pro and fraud,
And played drags [put on a false front] like a natural vet;
She played stuff like a ace, and never lost a case,
And leave many a marks in debt.
Now this ho had a good *round* eye [anus; the reference is to anal sex], and
    that's no lie,
Just as sure as a shithouse door swings,
'Cause a many a nut's been busted in her butt,
'Cause the rag [sanitary pad or tampon] didn't mean a thing, you
    understand.
She tricked with Sioux, Arabs, and Jews,
And would go to hell if she had to go;
She'd fuck his do'man [doorman]
Even to his woman,
And get sick as a dog if he didn't show.

407   Bullshitting Murphy

This cat, you know, you ever have gone to a convention or something like that—nothing but *ladies*, you know, and everybody talking, talking, talking, you know, and running off at the mouth. The cat couldn't get *nothing* in sideways. He was a little pissed off, and he decided he would come on and introduce *hisself*. So my man knocked the *damn* door down, and walked in the house. He say:

"Now shut up, shut up your motherfucking mouths.
Let me introduce myself to this cocksucking house.
I wasn't invited, but I'm down here.
I decided to drop on down here."
He say, "I'm thirty-six inches across my chest,
Don't bother nobody but the good Lord and death."
Say, "The good Lord [unclear] and death comin' *anyhow*."
He say, "I walked through the graveyard, and leave the world on a wonder."
He said, "In the mornings I eat my lunch in a gravel pit,
And beg for ass, and that's no shit."
Say, "I woke up this morning with a *hard*-on,
And I was mad as hell 'cause I couldn't find nothin' to start on."
He say, "I was pussy struck and I sure want to fuck."
He say, "I lay my head in a hornet's nest
Where the beasts and the lions come to rest.
Now if anybody ask you who propose this toast,
Tell 'em it's the Bullshitting Murphy from coast to coast."

408   At the Whorehouse

Back in forty-two when the poor man had nothing to do,
All the hoes [whores] had made plans
To fuck each other like a natural man.
So I went to this ho house, I knocked on the do',
The bitch that came was damn good and so'.
She say, "Nigger, what you want?"
I say, "I want to *fuck*."
She say, "How much you got?"
I say, "Two bucks."
She say, "Nigger, befo' I fuck for ten or less,
I'll cut my cock from under my dress,
Hang it up on bamboo wire,
Say, 'Stay there, pussy, till cock get higher.'" (You understand, YEAH!)
I say, "Look here, bitch, before I fuck for two or mo',
I'll cut my *dick* off and throw it in the flo',
Kick it around and stomp it in the ground,

And say, "'Stay there, dick, till cock come down.'" (You understand!)
So I thought I had fired something slick;
So the bitch looked at me and say,
"Look here, nigger, befo' I fuck for the likes o' you,
I'll move in the country and eat oyster stew,
Sew my pussy up stitch by stitch,
And piss out my navel, you bad sonovabitch." (Yeah! Dig it!)
So I went on and left this ho house,
'Cause my pockets was *slack*. (You understand!)
But when I showed back, I had a dyno.
I jumped on this ho; I done the two-dollar shuffle and the loop-the-loop,
The three dollar shuffle and the scoop-de-scoop.
Every time she came up I was there to meet 'er,
With a hump in my back and steady feeding my peter.
So the bitch started to moan,
Say, "Like, dig it, Jack, this is enough."
So I felt sorry for the ho,
And let her *nasty* ass up.
She say, "Mr. Dog, youse the best, it has been said;
Next time you show in town, I keep my poor cock hid."

409 Pimpin' Sam

While sittin' in a deep meditation,
Shuckin' and jivin', dope-poppin', lollygaggin', eating chittlin' stew,
Remind me of a girl I once knew.
She wasn't no bathing beauty, she didn't have long black hair,
But she was a stone good [unclear].
So I pimped this little chick and moved down East; my bankroll got low.
She say, "Ooh-whee, pretty Papa, you *can't* jive me no mo',"
She say, "I know more than you'll *ever* know."
She say, "I'm wicked [unclear] the chorus girl hot from Birmingham."
Say, "When you pimp me you thought you could fill me full o' bull,
But you can't look up a mule's asshole and see how big a load she can pull."
So that made Pimping Sam *mad!*
He say, "Shet up, SHET UP, bitch! Don't you say *another* motherfuckin'
    word!
If you do, I'll put my *foot* in your ass."
And he say, "Now you run around here wid yo' nose all snotty,
If you don't know what the game's all about, you better *ask* some*body*."
He say, "I got eight or ten standin' in line."
He say, "Ain't a day pass I don't kick fo' or five o' they motherfuckin' ass."
He say, "I'll pull a bitch out o' bed like you was half-pass fo'
And make you jump in Lake Michigan if it's ninety feet belo'."
And say, "If you shiver when you come to sho',"
He say, "Well, I'll kick your asshole and make you swim some cocksuckin'
    mo'."

He say, "Catch it, catch it quick, if you have to suck his motherfuckin' dick."
She say, "Daddy, I ain't got on no clothes."
He say, "Catch it out the window, *bitch!* You ain't going out the do'."
He say, "So you done all right, lil' girl with all right looks,
But to a pimp like me, I wouldn't even put you in the book."
He said, "You awright girl from down South, but you ain't nothin' squarer
    than a [unclear]."
He said, "The pistol's in the dresser, and the razor's in the drawer,"
He said, "If you think about ah one o' 'em, I'll break your motherfuckin'
    jaw."
He say, "Don't you roll your eyes or gimme no sass,
'Cause I'll make these brand new Stetsons sing a song in yo' ass."
He say, "If you *ever* think about going back home to Chitlin' Switch,
I want you to tell everybody you met Pimpin' Sam, a bad, *bad*, BA-AD
    sonovabitch!"

410   The Monkey and the Coon

Deep in the jungle, down in the sticks,
All the animals had a poolroom, and the Coon was the slick.
But up jumped the Monkey from the coconut grove,
You could tell he was a pool shark by the clothes he wore.
He wore a one-button robe with a square back;
He wore knob-toed shoes and a Stetson hat.
He wore a ring on his finger, and a watch on his wrist;
He wore long silk socks, and *didn't* take no *shit!*
Now Brother Monkey heard that the Coon gang was up tight,
So he hung around the poolroom *all* this Friday night.
So early that morning 'bout ten to ten, that's when all those fucked-up
    hustlers started jumpin' in.
So the Monkey pulled off his hat and pulled out his gun.
He say, "I'm gonna *kill* one o' you motherfuckers—I'm gonna try me one."
Forty dollars was the table stakes.
The Coon flipped a coin and the Monkey won the break.
So the Monkey ran from the one to the three.
And told the houseman to watch the game while he go pee.
Now he pissed out the window and spit in the flo';
He came back and banked the *fo'.*
He ran from the five to the seven and looked around the room;
He saw Bro Coon chalking up too soon.
Now the eight and the nine was a very difficult shot—
Both balls on the rag and the cue on the spot.
So the Monkey shot the cue on all four sides,
And put the eight in the corner and the nine in the side.
Now he said, "Now, if you think this something where you just *seen,*
Show back tomorrow and I'll run all fifteen.
But then again, if in your mind there's any doubt,

I'll take this sixteen-ounce pool stick and wear your *greasy* ass OUT!"
So Bro Monkey said to Bro Coon, he say, "Don't stand there looking like the
    game was bored [boring],
I wants to know what the fuck you kin do with a deck o' cards."
So the Coon say, "Show me a stump that'll fit your rump,
And I'll coon ya until your asshole jump."
That's when they went on down to Beaver's Creek,
And they cooned for two SO-O-LID weeks.
Bro Coon plucked a card, and had three fives;
He brought boiling water to the poor Monkey's eyes.
The Monkey plucked a card and had three queens,
And put a switch on the deck that the Coon never seen.
Now the Monkey plucked a card and looked at the Coon with a frown,
With what he had in his hand and on the table it made eleven, so he put it *all*
    down.
Say, "Hop, Mr. Rabbit, skip, Mr. Bear,
It looks might shitty, but all eleven is there."

411   Honky Tonk Bud

Honky Tonk Bud, the hip cat stud,
Stood diggin' a game of pool.
Though his pockets was saggin,
Bud wasn't braggin,
'Cause he knew he was looking *real* cool.
Now he was choked up tight in his white on white,
And his charcoal vine [suit] was *down*,
And on his head supported a lead
That supposed to been a gold Stetson crown.
It was the first frame of a nine-ball game,
Hip Bud stood digging the play.
With a idle slug, he suddenly dug
A stranger moving his way.
Now he was a medium-built cat
With a funny-styled hat,
It looks to been ten years old.
He wore a second-hand vine
And his shoes need shine,
And he shivered as though he was cold.
Now to all the rest o' the cats except Honky Tonk Bud,
This cat looked to be a ninety-nine flunky.
But with a minute past high [twelve o'clock] and a way-out trained eye
Hip Stud knew he was just a junky.
Now Bud started to grin as the chump moved in,
And sounded for a boy named Joe.
But Joe wasn't around 'cause his habit came down,
And he *also* went to the man to sco' [score].

Now hip Stud started to grin, and he said, "Like, uh, er, dig this, my man,
My name is Stud from 'cross the way,
I may kin do some good for you."
He said, "Well, yeah, Jack, like I wants to cop a few bags,
And if the shit ain't no drag, I may get you to cop me some mo',
For, you know, we are traveling hustlers
On the road, you know." (Like, dig it, see.)
So Bud say, "You wait here until I get back,
Though I won't be gone for long."
So Bud hurried back 'cause he was all so sick,
And they went to his pad to get on.
Now they pulled out their hypes and unrolled their spikes,
And rolled some dollar bill g's.
They cooked a small taste on the kitchen stove,
And they all begin to roll up their sleeves.
One cat say, "This shit is go-o-o-o-d! It's better than it should.
It makes a man feel real *high*."
That's when one of the cats pulled out his badge
And said, "Freeze, I'm the F. B. I.!"

412   Prison Walls

These prison walls are close[d] at last;
I know my future won't be the same as my past.
I learned the life of a wise man,
I learned the life of a crook,
I learned the life of a no good ho,
Like a school boy learn his book.
I learned that when the man goes to jail for doing something he thinks [is]
     slick,
The ho'll come to see 'im, and that's no shit;
Not to do 'im no good, of course, but to see how much time he got.
If he gets thirty days to a year,
The ho will cry in his face, "Dear, oh! Dear!"
But while out in the hall
Telling his best friend, "Come on, Big Daddy, we got a long time to ball!
For my man is old.
Dumb, simple motherfucker ain't got sense enough to make parole."
But if he get thirty days or more,
He get a one-page letter from that no good ho:
"I was coming to see ya, but God know when;
I went to see your lawyer, but he wasn't in;
I bought you a carton o' cigarettes
And put 'em on the shelf;
Times got so tight I smoke 'em my motherfuckin' self.
Times are still kinda tight.
I had a trick wid your best friend to eat last night.
But you must try to understand,

I'll never leave you for another man."
But now that you're home with money to spend and money to lend,
She'll be the first bitch you see asking for a thin dime:
Well, bitch, 'fo' you get a thin from me,
These are the shape you must be:
You must be blind, cripple, crazy, cannot see,
Have the clap so bad [you] cannot pee,
Jump off the Empire State Building widout a fright,
Git up and do a striptease in broad daylight,
Take out your eyeballs and roll 'em 'cross the sand,
Walk on water like you walk on land;
Get shitty drunk off o' thin strawberry wine,
Then you might get a nickel,
But never nah goddamn dime!
Standing on the corner lookin' slick as the law,
When you ought to be shoveling shit
In some farmer's back yard,
You motherfucking dog!
Get to stepping!

413 Peter Revere

Listen my children and you will hear
Of the midnight fuck of Peter Revere.
Now Pete was born rugged and strong;
He had a dick on 'im seven feet long.
'Twas a sad day for poor Pete
When he met an awful whore in the middle o' the street.
She challenged old Pete to a fuckin' duel
Up the hills and around the pools.
And people came from all around
To see old Pete put his fuckin' down.
There was old Big Ass Bess with her beaver hat;
She was wiggling her ass, so we can't miss that.
There was old Fart-box Sam,
Who didn't give a damn;
He just let out a fart
To give the signal, "Start!"
There was old stinking-cock Sally from Tennessee;
She acted as judge and referee.
They fucked all night and when they was still,
They had worn all the grass all over the hill.
She fucked old Pete to death, the dirty bitch,
And then she died with the seven-year itch.
And while they was carryin' old Pete's body to the graveyard,
Ass still wiggling and dick still hard . . .
And on old Pete's tombstone these words could be seen:
"Here lies a fucked-up fucking machine."

414 Rastus Whatcha Thing

There was a situation in which they needed help. There was a Black man who conceived of an idea to bring some help. There was a gorilla that was in heat, a female gorilla, poor thing! She had killed all the male gorillas that tried to get to her. They had tried crossbreeding her with bears and wolves. They couldn't take it—killed 'em, clawed 'em, crushed 'em to death, in ecstasy. So they scoured the country, looking for someone to serve this beast. And they found a white fellow, and he said, "Well, I'm down on my luck, and I'm not proud of what I've had to do. What is it you want?"

They told him there was a gorilla in heat and they had done everything they could, and he said, "Well, what color is this gorilla?"

They said, "Black."

He said, "Well, that lets me out. I can't do that. You got the wrong man. I can't do that."

So they kept on fooling around. So they gave up and went on to this bar. (They was gon' give 'em five hundred dollars.) So they went to this bar and the man said, "Lord, I don't know what I'm gon' do with this thing." Said, "Things are tough with me. I can't do any good. This damn thing here, laying up there dying, and we don't have any gorillas . . . We need somebody to mate with this thing if we gon' save this species, you see."

So a nigger broke in the door at that time, and said, "My name is Rastus Whatcha Thing. I will do it to anything!"

Man say, "Did you hear what he said?"

He say, "I heard 'im, but did he say that? What did he say?"

"He say his name was Rastus Whatcha Thing and he would do it to anything."

Let's see what he'll do." So they called 'im. They say, "We don't want to interfere in your business, but we were standing inside here, and you said something that you would do it to just about anything."

So he said, "I will take care of it."

And the man came on up and said, "Well, we gon' give you one thousand dollars—that's tax deductible. You can do anything you want with it. We'll ask you no questions."

He say, "Well, you know, I've been drinking, and I might have said a little more than I meant to say. I am known to do it to just about anything. What do you have in store for me, you see?"

And the man told him, say, "We have a ape. That's what you know it as—it's a ape, a big ape. The thing is in heat, and it's not gon' be that hard a job for you. You've got to go up there and serve this ape."

"You mean—is that one of them things with them big, hairy arms and all on it?"

Say, "That's right."

"With them great long legs, strong and muscular?"

"That's right."

"With them big sharp teeth in his mouth can just snap a man's head off if [unclear] at him?"

"That's right."

"And that's what you want me to go to serve?"

"That's right."

Nigger say, "Yawl gon' tie him down?"

"Yeah, we gon' tie him down."

"Strap him up?"

"We gon' strap him up."

"You gon' put one o' them iron muzzles on 'im so he won't bite me?"

"We'll put one of them iron muzzles on 'im so he won't bite ya."

"Are you gon' have anybody around to shoot 'im in case he breaks loose and tries to *harm* me?"

"We gon' have somethin' hanging 'round."

"Are you gon' give me some wine to drink while I'm doing my thing?"

"Gon' give you some wine."

"Where is the ape? Take me to him. I want this thing."

So they carried him on up there to the ape. He mounted the ape, he climbed up on top him and started walkin', see. And the ape started hollering, "OHWAH! OH-H-H, OHWAH-H-H, OHWAH-H-H!"

They said, "Stand steady, stand steady. This ape is going to try to break loose and do the same thing to this nigger he's done to all them other things we tried to mate him with. He's gon' crush this nigger."

"OAOWAH, OHWAH-H-H, OOOHWAH-H-H, OOOHWAH-H-H!"

After a while the nigger started grunting, "Umhhh, ummhhh, ummhhh." The more the nigger would grunt, the more the ape would grunt.

All of a sudden, without warning, the ape broke loose the right arm, say, "OOAOAH, OOOHWAH-H-H," and engulfed half the nigger.

They said, "Oh, Lord, it's gon' kill him; it's gon' kill this nigger."

Without further warning, the ape broke loose the left arm and threw it 'round him: "OOHWAH!"

They said, "Oh, Lord!"

All they could see was the nigger's ass bobbing up and down, *weaving* in and out, doing his thing, grunting still, "Umhmhm, hmhmhm." So all of a sudden, the ape broke loose *both* legs and completely hid the nigger. You couldn't see anything. And all of a sudden, the nigger started hollering, "OOAOAH, OOAOAOOAH, OAOAH-H-H-H!"

They said, "Don't worry, Rastus, we're gon' shoot him."

He said, "NO-O-O! Take the muzzle off the sweet motherfucker. I'm gon' kiss him."

415 Moved Out

One time a dude in New York, you know, this slick dude, he come up to New York, and he started fuckin' *all* the women in New York, started takin' *all* the women. So the *dudes* in New York, they got MAD! So they had to pack up and leave, you know, 'cause all the wives and all the girlfriends was leavin', you know. They got jealous of the dude 'cause they couldn't outfuck the dude. The dude had two warts on the end of his dick and drove the womens *crazy*, you know. All the dudes just move out o' town—went on down South, went on down North Carolina, you know. Then he had all the womens by hisself.

So then 'bout two months later, they seen this dude come on down North Carolina. They tol' the dude, say (everybody gathered around the dude), say, "Man, you come up there where we was at and took all our women. You know the women went for you 'cause you had two warts on the end o' yo' dick, and couldn't nobody else do nothin' once you fucked 'em. So now you comin' down here where we at now and gon' take all o' *dese* women from us. Why you didn't stay up there?"

He say, "I wanted to stay." He say, "But I couldn't."

He say, "Now I know ain't nah nother motherfucker in the world could outfuck you, so why did you *leave*, nigger?"

Dude, he say, "Yeah, man." He say, "I had *all* de women." Say, "I was the fuckingest motherfucker in town, the only one that had two warts on the end o' my dick, until that *dirty* motherfucker come with three warts on the end o' his tongue."

416   That Scared Him

There was this *big* slave and a little one; they had them up for auction. One slave's master says, you know, "My nigger is good and therefore you ought to buy him. He's big and he can do *everything!*"

And here's this little runt standing, you know, the guy's trying to sell him off. So the runt got tired of it, and he jumped up, and he slammed his master in the face. And say that big nigger took off running.

417   John Hatcher

They had a bad character was named Jack Hatcher, a tall, slim, brownskin fellow. He wasn't no *bully*, but he was MEAN! So Jack had got in some trouble and he "went off" [lost his mind] because he had a daughter (a teen-age daughter) and a fellow tried to rape her. So he just "went off" because he couldn't get to this fellow. And while they had 'im down at the streetcar line—they was on their way to Petersburg [mental institution]. This white fellow had 'im handcuffed to him, you know, and he was waiting for the train. And a white girl came on by. So he say, "Hi, honey." She ignored him. He say, "That's my damn gal; she don't pay me no mind." They know he was crazy. So a fellow come on by and laughed at 'im, made fun of 'im. (And the magistrate's name was Mr. Thurston.) He say, "Mr. Thurston, turn me loose; let me get to 'im. I'll eat 'im up and spit 'im out in *two* minutes!"

So he say, "Naw, Jack, I can't let you do that. Stay still."

So he [Jack] decided to carry him [the magistrate] over there wid 'im, you know, 'cause they had 'em handcuffed together. And they down scrambling on the ground, so a policeman ran up, he gon' hit 'im [Jack].

He [the magistrate] say, "Naw, uh, oh, don't hit 'im, don't hit 'im. He ain't fightin' me. He's after that fellow where meddled after him, 'n' he decided he gon' carry me long wid him. That's the only reason I was scrambling."

So Jack went down there and he stayed a while, 'n' he come back. And we used to have what you call festivals up there (just like a party) on week ends. And Aunt Amy Brown, she was always havin' somethin' to sell it. So that night they had everything in full swing. She sold wine and all that stuff. Somebody say, "Lawd, here come Jack Hatcher! Here come Jack Hatcher!"

So they locked the windows and barred the doors and fastened the windows up like that. Jack Hatcher come up with that old—one o' those whatcha call four-barrel pistols. (Muzzle loader had four barrels like that.) So Jack hit the door and say—CLEAN HOUSE! BOOM! Everybody got out. They lit out the door and windows and everywhere like that [dramatizing].

So after they had gone up there for a while, a fellow named Letcher Jenkins (he was a BAD guy, you know), he thought—he got up on this fence like that. He say, "All right, now, I'm a bird. Let somebody shoot *me.*"

Jack say, "BOOM!"

And he lit off [smack of hands to indicate speed], BRRRRRRRRRRRR-RRRRRR!

And the other fellows come on by there. He say, "Tip light, boy, tip light!"

Say they were going through the bushes like a squirrel there.

"Tip light, boy! Tip light!"

418 A Lil' Fight

This fellow put up at a hotel, something like a saloon or a dance hall. And upstairs over top was the quarters. So he went up and went to bed. That night he heard a commotion downstairs, lot of shuffling of feet and every once in a while a voice raised in a yell, you know. He decided that they were having a dance and the loud voices was callin' the figures, you know. So he went off to sleep. And the next morning, he come on downstairs, and the janitor was sweepin' up somethin', you know, down there in the floor. He thought it was magnolia grapes. So he say, "My man, yawl must o' had a swell party down here las' night, throwing 'way magnolia grapes like *that!*"

He say, [laughing] "*Magnolia grapes!* Ha-a-a, *magnolia grapes!* Naw, mister, they had a lil' fight down here las' night. These eyeballs I sweepin' up."

419   Surrogate Cursing

The Orthodox Jewish storekeeper had a problem. He could not curse, and every day a woman would come in with a profane order:

> I want some motherfucking meat for my motherfucking cat;
> Don't want no motherfucking lean touching the motherfucking fat.

The storekeeper decided to find someone to get even for him and curse back at the woman. He walked down the road and came upon some Jewish boys shooting marbles. He kicked the marbles out of the ring. A little boy cried: "Hey, Mister, why the hella you wanna fucka with our marbles?"

The storekeeper continued on. He came upon some white boys shooting marbles and kicked their marbles out of the ring. A little boy shouted: "Hey, Mister, why in the hell did you kick our goddamn marbles out of the ring?"

The storekeeper continued on. He came upon some Black boys shooting marbles and again kicked marbles out of the ring. One of the little Black boys said:

> Put the motherfucking marbles back in the motherfucking ring;
> Then we won't have to start another motherfucking game.

"You are the boy!" the storekeeper said. "I want you to get even with that woman who curses me every day. Come and work in my store."

The next day the woman came in and gave her usual order:

> I want some motherfucking meat for my motherfucking cat;
> Don't want no motherfucking lean touching the motherfucking fat.

The little boy was ready for her. He waited on her, saying:

> Here's your motherfucking meat for your motherfucking cat;
> Ain't no motherfucking lean touching the motherfucking fat.
> Now put the motherfucking money on the motherfucking block,
> And get your motherfucking ass out the motherfucking shop!

The storekeeper was never troubled by the woman again, and he had his revenge.

420   Gay Young Lad

There was a gay young lad and a spry old man
Who sat in a prison cell one day,
Bragging of life and the joys and strife
To pass the time away.
Oh, the kid boasted of the route he had made
While out there playing the game,
And worried not of the sentence he had got,
For the future would bring him fame.
With a voice so grand he spoke of a band
Of real-gone cats he knew.
And when he went free at the gate, they would be
To greet him as he passed through.
The old man listened with eyes that were glistened
Until the kid was through.
He say, "Now, it's your turn, son, to listen what *Dad* have to tell you."
He say, "I played the game, both large and small,
And I always found it rough.
The bluecoated mob stayed on the job,
Trying to call my bluff.
But I too was like you, I was *dap*, for I wasn't afraid.
When I tried the game once more,
When a village cop caught me picking the lock
On the safe of a jewelry store.
I had to draw, but so did the law,
And both of our guns fired lead.
I backed away to see the smoke clear,
And the old village cop lay dead.
I had to run, ditch my gun,
For my life was my treasure then.
I was like a wolf at bay, fighting my way
Through a mob of bloodthirsty men.
I was thrown in jail, without bail
For murder in the first degree.
I tried to be game
When the trial came,
But the chills was running through me.
I tried to grin, but I had to give in,
For my soul was torn in strife.
I held my breath for the verdict of death,
But instead they gave me life.
So here I am, son, all my hopes have fled.
Soon I will join the crowd that lies among the dead.
You are young yet; you have a mother out there,
Perhaps she care.
Take a tip from me: when you go free,
Go kneel beside her chair,
And say a prayer like you once did when you was a lad,

And I'm sure all the things you do, my boy, will make your mother glad.
Forget the game and all the fame,
For throughout all these years it has brought me five numbers, heartaches,
sorrow and tears."

14

Down in the Jungle,
Out on the Farm:
Miscellaneous Animal Tales

From the barnyard, the fields, and the woods
which formed their environment, Southern Negroes
drew a fair portion of their story material.
Richard M. Dorson, *American Negro Folktales*

ANIMAL TALES ARE, and have long been, a popular part of Black folklore. Many originated out on the farms where Southern Blacks lived, but several more recent ones, as, for example, "The Monkey and the Coon" (p. 236), developed in "the jungle" (that is, the city ghetto). The largest group of animal tales, the Brer Rabbit tales, has been discussed at length in the introduction to chapter twelve, since most of the Brer Rabbit tales symbolize the conflict between the white man and the Black man. The Parrot tales that reflect racial strife are also included in chapter twelve; a few others are included here.

A quick glance at the selections in this chapter will indicate that animal tales are not really about animals but about human beings. Most are fables whose main purpose is to point to a moral that we might all do well to heed.

421   Wait on de Lord

A.   This Buzzard went and he lit on a dead pine tree. And he was sittin'
all up there like he ain't got *nobody* in the worl'. So a Hawk come 'long, say,
"Hey, Mr. Buzzard," say, "you look you ain't got *nobody* in de worl'." Old
Buzzard ain't say a *mumblin'* word. After while, a little sparrow pranced
along down below the Buzzard; a little sparrow come along and went un-
derneath the fence to get out. Old Hawk tried to ketch him, you know, and
Hawk like to eat everything fresh. He tried to ketch the little sparrow, and he
run through that wire; he hang up in the wire. So the old Buzzard ain't said
nothin' *yet*. After a while the old Hawk started to smellin' and the old
Buzzard fly down; "It's a good t'ing to wait on de Lord."
   I tell them around home, I say, "Who? I'm a buzzard; I gon' wait on de
Lord."

B.   The Buzzard he was sittin' out there on the post, half-starved, but
hadn't anything died. The ole Hawk, he lit there in a bush beside him,
wanted to try to guy him, you know. "Aw-w-w-w, ain't you sumpin', Old
Buzzard, you got to sit out here and wait till sumpin' die. If sumpin' don't
die pretty soon, then you die. Ain't you sumpin'?"
   He say, "Well, Mr. Hawk, I'll wait on the Lord. Can't all of us be alike."
   "YEAH-H-H-H, you say anything you wanta but ain't nothin' to you. Why
don't you be like *me*. When I get hungry I go out here and *kill* sumpin'."
   "Hummm," he say, "well, Mr. Hawk, Mr. Hawk, I tell you we can't all be
alike. I'll have to just wait on the Lord till sumpin' die."
   "Humph, yeah! I know all that." He say, "Now, wait, I gon' show you how I
get my food."
   A gang of partridge flew over across the field there. He say, "You watch
this." And as the birds came on by, he *dived* at one of the birds 'n' (he had
his eye on the birds; he didn't see the tree before him), and he broke his neck.
   So the old Buzzard say, "Oh, well, it's good to have patience. Something's
dead now. I kin eat!"

422   The Lord Spare Us

   The old Mother Frog and three or four other little Frogs was up on the
hill, and 'twas a ditch down there where the water was. They say, "Well (the
mother and the three smaller ones say), "we going down the ditch and get us
some water, if the Lord spare us."
   The old bad Frog didn't say nothin'. So they went on down there and got
their water and come on back.
   Well, he figured it was safe. He say, "Well, I'm going down there and get

me some water. I don't care whether the Lord spare me or not." So when he got down there and stuck his head in the ditch, a snake grabbed 'im. He say, [choking voice] "I-I-I-If the Lord spare me!"

423   Good to Be on Time

The Snail is s'posed to be one of the slowest things. Say the Snail took seven years to get 'cross a road, and jest as he got 'cross the road, a man drove along with a big, four-horse wagon. Say he said, "It's a good thing to be on time, ain't it?"

424   Don't Trust a Man When He's in His Liquor

Well, in the ole days they had fireplaces, you know, had liquor, what they call pot liquor (where you make soup or salad or somethin'). So this Mouse was around tryin' to get somethin' when he slipped and fell in that pot o' pot liquor. And he couldn't get out. He was 'bout to drown.

So the Cat was laying down there, purring and carrin' on. He [the Mouse] say, "Hey, Cat, take me out, I'll let ya eat me." So the Cat went down, and took his paw like that [demonstrating], lift 'im out, laid 'im down by the fire, let 'im dry off.

So when he dried off, you know, the Cat started to grab 'im. He say, "Naw, Cat, it's impolite to eat before you wash you face." So the Cat she started to doin' one of them numbers [mimicking the Cat washing her face, licking paws, and wiping face as cats do], you know. He got the chance; he slipped in that hole again.

The Cat say, "Mouse, what kinda way is that you doin'? You tol' me if I got you out that liquor I could eat ya!"

He say, "Aw-w-w-w, Cat, don't never trust a man what he say when he's in his liquor; he liable to say anything."

425   Don't Let Anybody Use You for a Cat's Paw

One day the Monkey had done got some chestnuts and put in the open hearth—the fire, you know—to roast 'em. And 'bout time they got roasted, he went to pull 'em out, and he stuck his foot in that fire and it burned his foot. He didn't want to lose his chestnuts, so the Cat was laying down there purring and carrin' on. He say, "Cat, lend me your paw a minute; I'll show ya a trick." So the Cat won't thinking; he reached over there and let 'im take his paw. And he took his paw and reached over there and raked them chestnuts outa the fire and burned the Cat's paw, see.

So the saying is: "Better watch! Don't let anybody use you for a Cat's paw!"

426 Let Us Spray

'Twas four Skunks comin' 'cross the highway, and a car come up the highway, just *speeding!* The Mother Skunk saw they couldn't get out the way. Know what she say: "Let us spray!"

427 You Better Go 'Round

This fellow, he used to travel a whole lot; he used to what you call hobo around, you know—different places. He was a youngster. And he tol' 'em, he say, he got off a freight near some lil' village—it was up on the hill like (the village was sittin'), and down on the level there was a whole lotta trees— look like a swamp like. Say he could see water 'round in there, so he thought one time he'd go on through that swamp and he'd get there without having to go all the way around. And say 'bout that time o' evening, when it's first gettin' sunset, the Frogs begin to sound off. One of 'em say, "KNEEDEEPP, KNEEDEEPPP, KNEEDEEPPP!"

And the other one say, "LILDEEPERRR, LILDEEPERRR, LILDEEPERRR!"

The ole Bullfrog say, [very deep voice in manner of bullfrog] "UP-TOTHECHIN, UPTOTHECHIN!"

So they sounded up again, you know; the lil' Frog say, "KNEEDEEPPP, KNEEDEEPPP!"

Frog say, "LILDEEPERRR, LILDEEPERRR!"

The ole Bullfrog say, "YOUBETTERGOROUND, YOUBETTER-GOROUND, YOUBETTERGOROUND!"

And say he was tellin' the people up there in the village when he got there. They say, "It's a good thing you took that advice, 'cause that was quagmire and quicksand." Say, "You never woulda got outta there."

428 Judgment Up There

He say it was a fire up in these woods, up on the side of what you call the cliff—we call a bluff. And just as he was comin' on by there this ole Terrapin—one of them ole high-land water Terrapin, you know—he was up there and tryin' to get outta the way, he just was clumsy anyway, and he *rolled* all the way down that hill, right down side o' him before he stopped. He say, "AHYAN-N-N-N, JUDGMENTUPTHERE."

429   Buying Wood

A.   This man was goin' 'round sellin' wood and he went to a home he'd been used to goin' to all the time and the man wasn't at home. The wife was at home and she was sweepin' off the front porch. Wood man went along hollerin', "Wood man, wood! Wood man, *wood*."

Ole Polly said, "Put it in the cellar!"

So he gone and put it in the cellar and came 'round to the front to collect. The woman say, "I ain't ordered no wood."

He say, "I beg your pardon." Say, "I hollered wood and you tol' me to put it in the cellar and I *already* put it in there."

So she thought right quick. She looked around at Polly. She say, "Polly, you ordered any wood?

"That damn nigger kep' hollerin' wood and I tol' 'im to put it in the cellar."

So she hauled off with the broom and hit Polly and knocked 'im out his senses. Thought she'd killed 'im. Threw him out in the back in the trash can for the garbage man.

He came to that evenin' late. There was a dead cat out there too. He looked 'round at the cat, say, "Hi, ole cat; you been orderin' wood, too, ain't you?"

B.   This lady had a Parrot, and the Parrot used to repeat everything she said. So when the man would come by, saying, "Wood! Wood!" she'd say, "Throw it over the fence." So the man would throw the wood over the fence. Next time she said the same thing, "Just throw it over the fence and come back next week, I'll pay you."

One day the Parrot was sitting there and the woman wasn't out there. She didn't need any wood. So when the man hollered, "Wood! Wood!" Polly said, "Throw it over the fence, and come back next week."

When the man came back next week to collect for the wood, she said, "I didn't buy *any* wood."

He said, "Oh, yes, you did. I didn't see you, but somebody said, 'Throw the wood over the fence and come back next week.'"

So she went back in the kitchen and she grabbed the Parrot and wrung his neck and threw him out in the back yard. And when she turned around the Cat was on the table. So she grabbed the Cat and threw him out there. And he landed out there by the Parrot. And the Parrot turned around and said, "Well, I be damn! You been buying wood, too?"

430 We Belong Together

The lady had a Polly Parrot, and she would put the Parrot in with the chickens, and they [the chickens] would just be making all kinds of sounds. She went out there, and she said, "You chickenfucker, you got *one* more time to do this, and I'm gon' cut *all* your feathers off. I *told* you to leave those chickens alone."

The next night the same thing happened. She went out there and got Polly and shaved all his feathers off.

Later she carried him to church. So he was sitting up in church beside her. All of a sudden here comes this bald-headed man. He was going on up to the front of the church. He [Polly] say, "Hey! You! with that bald head!" Say, "Come on back here and sit beside me, you bald-headed chickenfucker!"

431 'Tis the Plumber

I have another one about a little old lady. And this is about a Parrot. This old lady lived alone, with the exception of the Parrot, in the home. So one day she discovered she had some plumbing work to be done—and naturally, you know, Parrot sit around and all day long, they're talking or saying something and then he was asking, "Who is it? Who is it? Who is it?"

So after calling the plumber she decided that she would go to the store and get back by the time the plumber came. She went on out to the store and while she was gone the plumber came. He rang the bell and all he could hear was, "Who is it? Who is it? Who is it?"

He [the plumber] thought it was the little old lady. He kept saying, "'Tis the *plumber!*"

Said, "Who is it? Who is it?"

"I said 'twas the *plumber!*"

"Who is it? Who is it?"

Finally, he became disgusted and *whirled* from the door and fell at the foot of the steps.

The little old lady came up. She saw this man; she said, "Oh! My Lord! *Who* is it?"

The Parrot said, "'Tis the plumber."

432 I Would Fall

This man had a real smart Parrot. When he raised his right foot, he could do just about anything, repeat anything he was told to repeat. So the man said, "If you can do all of this—recite so much and repeat so much—when you raise your right foot, I wonder what you would do if you raised your left foot."

The Parrot say, "I would fall and break my ass, you fool, you!"

433   Too Much Tongue

This Squirrel was up this hickory nut tree, you know, jumping and barkin'. And this ole Terrapin, he was around on the ground, eatin' those poisonous mushrooms. And that Squirrel was raising sand, so the Terrapin say, "Mr. Squirrel, I ain't got nothin' to do with your business up there, but you talkin' too much for your own good up there."

[Imitation of Squirrel.] "MINYOBIZNESS, MINYOBIZNESS! MINYOBIZ-NESS! MINYOBIZNESS!"

And so he kep' on jumpin' 'round, 'n' he [Terrapin] said, "Mr. Squirrel, I ain't got nothin' to do with your bizness, but you talk too much."

"MINYOBIZNESS, MINYOBIZNESS!"

'Bout that time the hunter was sittin' up on a log there waitin' for 'im to come 'round. He say, "WHOOMMM!" The Squirrel fall on down [dramatizing tumbling of animal from high tree].

The ole Terrapin drew his head back 'n' say, "I tell ya, too much tongue ain't good for neither soul nor body."

434   Bear 'Round

You know, 'twas a cold, rainy day, and the Rabbit had done made 'im a burrow up the side of the hill there where the sleet was falling over top 'im. And the Fox, he come on up there. He didn't want no rabbit meat that day, so he standin' out there talkin' to the ole Rabbit. So he was talkin' to the Rabbit, showin' 'im 'bout how you duck the hounds: you run in there 'n' bear 'round there and jump over there, and bear 'round there [mimicking ostentatious maneuvers of the Fox].

So he [Fox] say, "I think I want a chicken. I'm going to Farmer Brown's hen yard and get me a chicken." So he went on up there and time he got in the hen yard, the pack o' Hounds jumped 'im. And he come DOWN that hill right straight to that Rabbit. The ole Rabbit say, "Bear 'round, Mr. Fox!" Say, "Bear 'round, bear 'round!"

He say, "Bear 'round hell, I'm comin' straight through here now." [The Fox was coming straight through in the hope that the Hounds would jump the Rabbit.]

435   Root, Root, Root!

Once it was some Pig and the song 'bout them said, "This lil' pig went to the market (that's the first little Pig); and this other (the second) lil' Pig stayed home; the next lil' Pig had roast beef; and the next lil' Pig had none. And the lil' one that didn't have any, he said, "Wee-wee-wee-wee," all the way back home. And they all laughed at each other because one of 'em didn't have any roast beef. They got to squabblin' 'bout this one that had the roast beef. They got to squabblin' 'bout it and then they say, "Let's don't fight about it, don't let's argue about it. Let's divide the roast beef."

But this lil' Pig say it wasn't no more than enough for him. So he just swallowed it all down, lick his tongue out like that [dramatizing pig relishing the food]. And so he licked his tongue out at them 'cause they didn't have any roast beef, so, uh, then the other Pig went rootin' in the ground with his nose, rootin' his nose in the ground—see if he could find some roast beef.

And the Pig that had the roast beef said, "Root, root, root, but you won't get nothin' in your snoot!"

436   Mountain and Squirrel Quarrel

They say it was a mountain and a Squirrel had a quarrel, you know, and the former called the latter a little prig, you know. Say the Squirrel say, "Doubtless you're very big. I can't carry a mountain on my back. I'm not as big as you, and you're not as small as I. I can't carry trees on my back... Neither can you crack a nut!"

437   Well, That's One on Me

A Bird was sittin' on the fence. And this lil' Frog, you know, he was in the pond. He looked at 'im, at the lil' Bird sittin' up there on the fence. He say, "What a puny lookin' lil' fellow. He look like he just ain't nothin'!" Say, "He looks sick. I think I'll sing 'im a song, over there: KCHIRCK-KKCHIRK-KKKCHIRK."

The Bird didn't do anything.

He say, "Now I think I'll show 'im how I can dive." He dived on the water and swung around and come back out. And when he come back on the bank, 'bout that time the Bird took off.

He say, "Well! That's one on me. I can swim and sing, but I can't take off and fly through the air like that."

438   Terrapin and Rabbit Race

The Terrapin and the Rabbit had a race . . . They say, Rabbit was teasing the Terrapin 'bout being so *slow* and ploddy, like this. So he said, "Oh, well, Mr. Rabbit, I'll tell you what: as slow as I am, I kin beat you in a race."

"Aw," he said, "that'll never happen."

They put up a stake and had one of the other animals to goalkeep, to go where they was to meet at. And the ole Rabbit, she set off, like the wind, you know. She ran for a while and then she say, "Oh, I got it—I got that in the bag. I ain't worried 'bout that. I think I'll lay down and take me a nap." So she laid down side o' the trail and went to sleep.

And the Terrapin, he came ploddin' along, ploddin' along. He didn't wake 'im up. He went on down, and when he got up there where the goal was under a big tree, *he* went on to sleep.

So when the Rabbit woke up, it was gettin' kinda late and he say, "Well, I'll gone and finish this race now 'fo' it's night."

And when he went up to the goalpost there, the scorekeeper say, "Where you been all this time, Mr. Rabbit?"

He say, "Well-l-l, I just took a nap, but even now I'm ahead of the Terrapin."

He say, "Naw you ain't." Say, "The Terrapin been in here over a hour ago." Say, "He's over by the tree sleepin.'"

439   Pretty Weather

The Buzzard, you know, he'll sit there on a dead tree and other places like that—'cause tree gon' die anyway. He was sittin' out there one day and 'twas sleetin' 'n' snowin' and carryin' on. He say, "AW-W-W, this won't do for *me*! As soon as this weather let up I'm gon' build *myself* a shelter."

So when the storm passed over and the sun come out, he sittin' up on the bench. He say, "Ah-h-h-h, what kinda shelter anybody want in all outdoors?"

440   Plymouth Rock

This man had some chickens out in the henhouse and ole Polly Parrot, he'd go out there and sleep with the chickens at night. He wanted company, you know. And one night a fellow came there and broke in there and stole all the chickens—stole ole Polly too. He didn't know he had Polly in the bag, you know.

And he was going on down through the alley with this bag of stuff, and the cop stopped 'im. He say, "Hey, what you got in that bag? What you got in that bag?"

"Ain't nothin' but some rocks, Officer, ain't nothin' but some rocks!"

Ole Parrot say, "YEAH! Plymouth Rock! You got me all mixed among these rocks, too!"

441 Scotch!

You know in the country when anything lay out there and die, they'd drag it down the hill for the dogs and everything to eat it, but they claim that the buzzards were spreadin' disease (by eatin' that stuff) wherever he goes.

So this ole horse was laying out in the sun there, you know, ALL-L-L stretched out just like he was dead. And the Buzzard he lit down beside 'im. He walked around 'im and looked at his head, and walked 'round and looked at his tail, you know. (They get one place where they kin go in.)

So the ole Crow, he sittin' up there in the tree. He say, "Try 'im!"

The ole Buzzard, he walk back to the horse's tail.

He say, "Try 'im, try 'im!"

He walked back to the horse's tail again and looked at 'im.

"TRY 'IM! TRY 'IM! TRY 'IM!"

He hauled off and socked his head up in the horse's tail. The horse jumped up [acceleration of voice suggests speed of action here] and took off cross the field like that [gesture indicating speed].

The ole Crow say, "Scotch! Scotch! Scotch!" [put your feet on the ground and steady, or brake, the horse].

He say, "Scotch! How the devil I gon' scotch and I can't get mah foot on the ground."

442 Hard to Kill

You know a Turtle is s'posed to be kinda hard to kill. They claimed that he went down to the river there and caught a Turtle—(you kin ketch 'em on a hook and line sometimes, you know, when you got meat on it). Say he caught the Turtle and brought 'im back up to the house and cut his head off, and threw his head over in the garden. And say the next day, he heard the Chicken holler. Say the Turtle's head was tryin' to swallow the Chicken.

443 He Swallored His Head

This girl and her brother were out there playing in the yard with a

Terrapin, see, and her mother was in the house. And she come in there, she say, "Mama," say, "you know something! Bobby took a stick and hit the Terrapin on the back and he swallored his head!"

444   Didn't You See Me When I Swelled?

You know the Toadfrog, when you tap him like this he'll swell up like that, you know. They say one time Mrs. Toadfrog had cows and she had done churned the butter, and had a way of going down to the spring, puttin' the butter in there, 'cause they didn't have no ice, you know. And she come back crying.

Mr. Toadfrog say, "What's the matter with you?"

She say, "Mr. Terrapin met me and took the butter away from me."

He say, "If I'd been wit' you, he wouldn't o' took it. Next time I'm going wit' ya."

So when she got the butter churned, she say, "All right, Mr. Frog, you say you going 'round there; well, I gon' carry my butter to put in there."

And when they got near the spring, the Terrapin met her and come took it away from her again and went on 'bout his business.

She say, "I thought you was gon' do so much?"

"Woman, didn't you see me when I swelled?"

445   Bravado

The Mouse went into the kitchen and the Cat was layin' down there. And the Cat made a break for 'im. He ran up the steps—steps had a lil' hole like that [indicating something just big enough for a mouse], you know. And he just made it through that hole 'fore that Cat grabbed 'im [dramatizing the Cat grabbing just as the Mouse safely got through the hole].

And the maid had done put a glass of whiskey down on the other side—on the shelf. And that Rat fell in that whiskey, and scrambled out. When he got out, he come back and stuck his head out and say, [in a daring tone] "Where is that DAMN CAT?"

446   Bad Bantam

This man had a Chicken farm. This was his livelihood. But it got to the point that the Chickens weren't producing—weren't giving any eggs at all.

He was losing money *fast*. He couldn't stand anymore. He was about *broke*. His wife told him, she said, "Well, I'll tell you what the problem is. You've got all those Chickens out there and you have just *one* old Rooster out there, and he's just *no* good. He's just worn out!"

He said, "Well, that *could* be the problem." He picked up the paper and looked in there, and in the next town some guy was advertising a Rooster for sale. He flew over there.

He had one of these Bantam Roosters—three hundred dollars!

The guy said, "Are you crazy—a little Bantam Rooster and you want *three hundred dollars* for him!"

The man said, "Well, you say you're going broke over there on your farm—your egg production is down. Now I want three hundred dollars for that Rooster, and if he doesn't increase your egg production *one hundred* percent, I'll give you *all* your money back."

Guy said, "Well, you can't beat that."

He took the Rooster over there on the farm and turned him aloose and [smack of hands] no sooner than he turned him loose, "Bib-bib-bib-bib! Bib-bib-bib-bib! Bib-bib-bib-bib!" He went all *around* that flock of Chickens.

He started around a *second* time, and the man say, "Now *wait* a minute. He ain't gonna last a day out there."

Every day he was out there, "Bib-bib-bib-bib!" And the egg production went up and business was increasing, and that Bantam was still . . .

The man said, "This can't last." He went out there one morning to feed the Chickens, and he couldn't find the Rooster. He said, "I knew it, I knew it. GONE!"

He looked and he looked and he looked. Finally, he went down behind and looked over there, and *there* was that Bantam, all folded up like this [imitating position like a corpse]. He said, "I knew that sonovagun was gone."

The Buzzard was flying around in the air and the man looked over there and saw the Buzzard—the old Rooster waved at him, say, "Shshsh" [indicating that he is waiting for the Buzzard to light].

447   Take Off Dem Fancy Pajamas!

There was a traveling circus; and the circus—as circuses do (they used to start at one point in the country during the winter and criss-cross the country)—anyway, they picked up this African Zebra. She was a female— just newly arrived into the country. So she didn't really know much about it, and anyway, she got sick along the tour. And they decided they were going to leave her at a farm and pick her up on the way back. So they did. They put her out at this farm.

She was walking around sort of getting acquainted with everything; she stopped and she looked down. There was a little Chicken there. And she says, "What are you?"

And the Chicken says, "Cluck, cluck, I'm a Chicken."

The Zebra says, "Well, what do you do around here?"

And she says, "Well, I lay eggs and I eat corn, and I, you know, that kinda thing."

And the Zebra walks over and there's a Donkey, and so she says, "What are you?"

And the Donkey says, "I'm a Donkey."

"Well," the Zebra says, "what do you do around here?"

She [Donkey] says, "Well, I carry things, and I pull things, and I haul things, and I lif' things—and that whole thing."

And so the Zebra says, "M-m-m-m, that's interesting."

And she walks on, and she sees a—up on this hill, there's this *big, black* Bull. Way up on the top of the hill. And so she says, "Ah-h, I'm gonna go up here and see what this thing is." So she goes way up on this hill, and there's this *big, black* Bull just standing there, surveying all the property and just, you know, being a Bull, I guess. And so she looks at him. She says, "What are you?"

So he doesn't even look at her. Just still looking over everything, he says, [proudly] "I'm a *Bull!*"

So she says, "Well, what do you do around here?"

So he looks back *casually*, and he says, "Baby, you take off dem damn *fancy* pajamas, and I'll show you what I kin do!"

448   Mr. Rabbit Is Back

This is the story of a Turtle, a Buzzard, and a Rabbit. They were buddies, and they went on a walking spree one day, and came across a tract of land—about six thousand acres that they could purchase for two hundred dollars—which they did. But the land was very barren and wouldn't grow anything. It had to be fertilized in order to make anything grow on it, so they started talking about where they were going to get this fertilizer and *how* they were going to get it. And the Turtle said, well, he couldn't go get it because he was so slow that it would take him years to go get it and come back. The Buzzard said he couldn't go because the fertilizer would ruin his beautiful feathers, so that didn't leave anybody but the Rabbit. He, being the fastest one in the group, he was chosen to go and get the fertilizer.

He did—and when he returned he didn't recognize the land, because the Turtle and the Buzzard had discovered oil on the place and had become very wealthy, had built a lovely mansion and everything. The Rabbit went to the front door and rang the bell. The butler came and he asked for the Turtle.

The butler said, "Who?"

He said, "The Turtle, where is the *Turtle?*"
He said, "You mean, Mr. Tur-*tell?* Mr. Tur-*tell* is out by the *well.*"
He said, "Well, where is the Buzzard?"
He said, "Mr. Buz-*zard?* Mr. Buz-*zard* is out in the *yard.*"
The Rabbit said, "Well, you tell Mr. Tur-*tell,* who's out at the *well,* and Mr. Buz-*zard,* who's out in the *yard,* that Mr. Rab-*bit* is back with the *shit!*"

449   The Ugliest

The animals of the jungle were having a big feast. Of course, the Lion was the king and he was the head of everything. So when it was all over, the Lion rared back and say, "The ugliest thing in this group gon' wash the damn dishes."
So the Monkey start laughing and looking at the Baboon.
He say, "I don't know what in the hell you pointing at me for. You gon' dry 'em."

450   Monkey Cuts His Throat

This fellow had a Monkey. He'll do anything he see his owner do, you know. And he got tired of 'im. He wanted to kill the Monkey, but he didn't want to kill 'im himself. And wouldn't nobody take 'im. So what he did (he know the Monkey watch 'im and do everything he see him do); so he went into the bathroom and took his razor—straight razor—lathered real good and shaved himself, like that. The Monkey watched 'im. And when he got through he took the back of the razor (you know the back of the razor is thick), turned it over and s-w-i-c-k [pulled razor across throat], and put it back on the shelf.
The Monkey, he watched, and when he put it down, the Monkey he goes in there, gets the razor, lathers, and shaves. Then he took the blade and cut his throat.
That's what he wanted him to do.

451   Crap Game in the Barnyard

The barnyard fellows was up there one evening. It was kinda dull like, so he say, "I tell ya what let's do. Let's get up a crap game."

The old Turkey Gobbler say, "Well, if you do, I'm gon' have the first roll."
He say, "Awright."

So he shook the dice and rolled 'em out there. And the Rooster sittin' up on the fence. He say, [imitating sound of Rooster] "WHATDIDTHEY-THROWWWWW?"

Say ole Duck say, [mimicking Duck] "CRAPCRAPCRAPCRAPCRAP-CRAP!"

Say the ole Gander say, [mimicking Gander] "HE'LLNEVERMAKEIT, HE'LLNEVERMAKEIT, HE'LLNEVERMAKEIT!"

15

Are You Ready for This? Miscellaneous Risqué Tales

> Well, I don't have any more nice tales, but if you
> want to hear some really funny stories, I can tell you
> a few.... But they are pretty dirty.... Are you sure
> you're ready for this?
>
> Comments by Informants

BY FAR THE largest body of materials which I have collected might be classified as risqué and vulgar tales. Until rather recently these tales were either not heard, ignored,[1] or completely expurgated by the "respectable" collectors of Black folktales except when perhaps the collectors were too naive to recognize the obscene allusions in their materials. So notable a collector of Black folklore as Elsie Clews Parsons observed that "the more or less obscene turns occurring now and then in the Bahaman tales are quite lacking in Carolina, whether as a result of natural indifference to the obscene or of greater sophistication, it is somewhat difficult to estimate."[2] One must assume that Parsons failed to recognize the obscene suggestiveness of several of the riddles she included in her volume of folklore from South Carolina, examples of which are the following:

Was an ol' lad an' an ol' man gone to baid. An forgot to slip it in. An'
de ol' man got up an' put it een—*Ans.* Do ba's [bars].

Ol' lady an' ol' man was under de tree. An' de ol' man shook it, an'
de ol' lady take up her dress an' took it.—*Ans.* Apple.[3]

Further, Parsons' observations that several of her informants refused
to tell her toasts and "man's tales" lead one to the obvious conclusion, not that obscene tales were lacking in Carolina, but that her
informants refused to tell her any—at least not any that she recognized as ribald.

Indeed, humor is and always has been largely motivated by the
enjoyment of forbidden themes. Commenting on smutty or obscene
wit, Sigmund Freud noted that "it makes possible the gratification of
a craving (lewd or hostile) despite a hindrance which stands in the
way; it eludes the hindrance and so derives pleasure from a source
that has been inaccessible on account of the hindrance."[4] He continues: "Owing to the repression brought about by civilization many
primary pleasures are now disapproved by the censorship and lost.
But the human psyche finds renunciation very difficult; hence we
discover that tendency—wit furnishes us with a means to make the
renunciation retrogressive and thus to regain what has been lost."[5]
And thus it is that excessive profanity, sex (especially sodomy, oragenital sex, homosexuality, and zoophilia), and scatology are among
the most popular and mirth-provoking subjects in Black folklore as
well as in folklore generally.[6] Albert Rapp's observation about sex
jokes is certainly applicable to all these jokes: "It is *not sex* which
makes these jokes funnier, but it is *the fact of repression.* What
causes the additional laughter is not the obscene; it is man's normal
rebellion against constraint."[7]

Many of the sex jokes derive their humor at the expense of those
who cannot or do not perform "normally." Among these jokes
perhaps the most popular are those about the fool who does not
know how to perform sexual intercourse or who does not recognize a
sexual act when he or she witnesses it. These tales have a long and
wide currency, as Legman points out:

The OLDEST STORES IN THE WORLD, as Dr. Theodor Gaster calls
them, are the Babylonian and Assyrian tales composed nearly four
thousand years ago in Mesopotamia, and written down on clay tablets
in the 7th century B.C. for the library of the great King Ashurbanipal . . .
a library first unearthed only about a hundred years ago. These stories
have been published in English adaptation by Dr. Gaster (1952) and
among them will duly be found, mixed in with the legends of the wars
of the gods, the story of the quintessential fool, *Appu,* who does not

know how to perform sexual intercourse and must ask. Naturally he gets the directions all wrong.[8]

Closely related to the sex fools are other sexual incompetents who, because of age or some other infirmity, are unable to perform sexually. The homosexual who is always out to trap the "normal" man falls into this group, too. He is usually pictured as a highly effeminate, limp-wristed lisper. A final group includes the zoophiliac. Legman informs that "most [animal tales] are not of the cute, anthropomorphic animal type, but concern the sexual intercourse of human beings with other animals...."[9]

A final group of obscene tales deals with "embarrassing" body functions, particularly excretory functions such as menstruation (treated in chapter seven), urination, defecation, and flatus.

NOTES

1. An interesting example may be seen in Elsie Clews Parsons' revelation of the procedure of A. M. H. Christensen, author of *Afro-American Folk Lore: Told Round Cabin Fires on the Sea Islands of South Carolina* (Boston, 1898): "Indeed, Mrs. Christensen has told me that, faithful recorder as she was, on this point she had been selective: the stories she found 'vulgar' she had not taken" (*Folk-Lore of the Sea Islands, South Carolina* [Chicago: Afro-American Press, 1969], p. xx).

2. Parsons, p. xix.

3. Ibid., p. 157.

4. Sigmund Freud, "Wit and Its Relation to the Unconscious," in *The Basic Writings of Sigmund Freud*, ed. A. A. Brill (New York: Modern Library, 1938), p. 696.

5. Ibid., p. 697.

6. D. J. Bennett asserts that even clean jokes, the most innocent kind, are sexually motivated ("The Psychological Meaning of Anti-Negro Jokes," *Fact* [March-April, 1964]: 53).

7. Albert Rapp, *The Origins of Wit and Humor* (New York: E. P. Dutton, 1951), p. 110.

8. G[ershon] Legman, *Rationale of the Dirty Joke: An Analysis of Sexual Humor* (New York: Grove Press, 1971), pp. 125–26.

9. Ibid., p. 206.

452   Come Away, You Dirty Dog

A.   Peter Murphy had a dog,
A dirty dog was he!

He loaned him to a lady friend
To keep her company.
All around the house that night, the dirty dog would run,
He stuck his nose up Mary's clothes and tried to smell her c——
Come away you dirty dog, you make my passion rise,
There is but one man in this town that lies between my th——

Th——ank you ma'am for a glass of milk. I'll drink it for my su——pper,
Damn a man whose got a wife can't raise a hard to f——
F——uss and tumble all night long, sleep so far apart,
Excuse me, mister, I've been eating butter beans, I believe I've got to
     f——
P——ass a girl sitting on a rock;
Got good legs, got good feet, I believe she's got good c——
Cock your pistol before you shoot and let your bullet go free.
If anybody asks you where you got this uh-umn-mm [gibberish],
Tell them you got it from me.

B. Peter Murray had a dog and he didn't know what to name 'im.
Say he loaned him to a lady to keep her company, too.
Say all the little dog would do was run around and hunt.
He stuck his nose up Mary's dress and tried to smell her ———
Say, Get away, you naughty dog, you make my pulse rise.
Only one man in this town can lay between my th——
Thank you, Mr. Father Brown, I'll drink it for my supper,
And when I eat my lima beans you ought to hear me f——
Forty dollars on the table, ten more make a pass,
And if you don't like what I'm sayin', Brother Pole, you kin kiss my
     a——
Ask your father over yonder waitin' on the rock,
Say the littlest girl in this town has the biggest c——
Cock your pistol forty-four, aim before you shoot,
And when I eat my lima beans you ought to hear me poot.

C. Dicky Johnson had a lil' dog and a nice lil' dog was he.
He loaned him to a lady just to keep her compa-nie.
All around the lady's house, this little dog would hunt.
So he ran his nose up the lady's clothes and tried to smell her c——
Come away, you dirty dog, you cause my flesh to rise.
There's only one man in this town can lay between my t——
Thank you for a glass of beer, I'll save it for my supper.
A man is a fool to sleep with a woman, and doesn't have sense enough to
     f——
Forty dollars will I shoot and forty more I'll pass.
Bill Jones took those great big dice and rammed them up his a——
Ask your partner for a match, I'll put it on my list,
Now excuse me people, one and all, while I go down with this.

453   Ole Dan Tucker

They had a song 'bout Ole Dan Tucker. I can't think of all the words.

Ole Dan Tucker, he was a lucky man,
He washed his face in a fryin' pan,
Dipped his foot in a pan of grease;
He say, "HEY, let me pass;
Here I come with a greasy [ass].
He got drunk and fell in the fire
And kicked up a chunk.
Charcoal got down in his shoe,
Bless you, honey, how the ashes flew!
Git out the way, Ole Dan Tucker,
You too lazy to eat your supper.

454   Yankee Doodle

Yankee Doodle went to town
To get a can of peaches,
Let a fart behind the cot
And blew it all to pieces.

455   Over the Hill

It's not the gray hair that makes a man old,
Nor that faraway stare in his eyes, I am told.
But when his mind makes a contract that his body can't fill,
He is—over the hill, over the hill.

Now, life is a conflict, and the battle is keen.
There are just so many shots in the old magazine.
When he has fired the last shot, and he just can't refill,
Then he is—over the hill, over the hill.

He should salvage his energy while he can,
Because Lydia Pinkham can't help a man.
You can't get a new gland from the little pink pill,
So you're over the hill, over the hill.

He can fool the dear wife with the tenderest of lies,
He can shear that poor lamb and pull the wool over her eyes.

But when she calls for an encore, and he pretends that he's ill,
Then he's—over the hill, over the hill.

Now his sporting days are over, and his tail light is out,
And what used to be his sex appeal now is just his water spout.
So that's the story, alas and alack,
When he's squeezed out the toothpaste, he just can't squeeze it back.

So if we want to make whoopie, don't wait until—
We get—over the hill, over the hill.

456 The Man from Ghent

There was a man from Ghent;
He had a rod so long that it was bent;
And to save the girls trouble
He put it in double,
And instead of coming, he *went!*

457 As for You

The father kissed the son good-bye;
And the buttercup kissed the butterfly,
And the morning dew kissed the *grass*
Now, as for you . . .

458 Now That the Party Has Ended

Now that the party has ended,
I hope you have enjoyed it quite a bit.
If anything has caused you to become offended,
Just stick your head in a big bucket of—
Sweet violets.

459 Wrong Bag

This lady was on her way to Washington, this ole colored lady, she's going up there to join the marchers for the civil rights. And she got on the train there in Richmond, and she had her lil' bag there full of chicken. And when the train got up there 'round Alexandria, this old gentleman got on the train there and sat down beside her. So the train was pullin' out of Alexandria, and it went around a lil' curve there, and the ole lady kinda woke up. She stretched and everything, you know, leaned back in the chair, and she said to herself, say, "I feel like a piece o' chicken." So she was lookin' out the window at the scenery there, and she reached over, she went zippp [unzipping something]. And she reached—you know—and she pulled out somethin' there, started out with it. She thought to herself, she say, "Damn, this is mighty long." She felt around again. She say, "Now I know damn well I put more than a neck and two gizzards in this damn bag."

460   Mistaken Identity

Here's a lady was cleaning out her medicine cabinet, and her husband used a straight razor. In turning, the straight razor falls and cuts the nipple off her breast. She in turn goes on, picks up the nipple, and rushes to the doctor, and tells the doctor that she's hoping he can save her—that he can sew it back on, and in time, you know, life will come back into it. Okay. The doctor said, "Well, come on let's X-ray it to see if you're doing any internal bleeding."

So the nipple is in a napkin. He lays it on the counter, the desk, or whatever, and goes in the other room to X-ray her. When they come back, here's a guy cleaning the office, sweeping around. So the guy [doctor] says, "Listen! Did you see something lying around here on this thing?"

He say, "Uhn-un, I just cleaned it."

He say, "You sure you didn't see anything?"

He say, "YEAH! The only thing I saw was a gumdrop, and I ate that!"

461   I Don't Touch That Dirty Dog

It was a Korean War veteran. During this particular time, right after the Korean War, a lot of troops were coming back, you know what I mean. And say this nigger was standin' up at the bus station in the men's room, and he was standin' up there, look like he was shaking and half crying, you know. And this Good Samaritan looked at him and say, "Hey, what's wrong, buddy?"

He says, "Uh, I gotta, gotta, gotta—pee."

So he say, "You got to pee?"

"Yeah."

Say, "Well, what's your problem?"

He say, "Well, do you mind doing me a *favor?*"

The man say, "Doing you a favor? What, whatcha mean?"

He say, "Could you zip my *pants* down?"

So the man looked at 'im: "Zip your *pants* down?" He say, "Well, what the hell! I haven't been overseas . . ." He zipped his damn pants down. The man was still standing there; he was lookin' at 'im. He said, "Uh, uh, what's wrong now, man?"

He say, "C-C-Can you take it out for me?"

So the man say, "What the hell, you know, hell, I mean it ain't no big thing, you know. I'll go 'head and take it out for 'im." So he took it out.

He say, "*Hold* it!"

The man say, "Well, goddamn, this is asking a *whole lot,* but he's a *veteran.* What the hell!" You know what I mean. So he was standin' there holdin' the man's joint 'n' the man was pissing 'n' he was holdin' the joint, you know. And he looked at 'im, you know.

And so he said, "Shake it for me."

He'd gone *this far,* you know, so he shook it, you know what I mean. He shook it and he put it back down in his pants. And he looked at the guy, he say, "I guess you want me to zip your pants back up?"

He say, "I'd appreciate it."

So he zipped his pants on back up and he started to walk off. He thought about it. He say, "Goddamn, I didn't even ask the fellow what was wrong." He said, "Uh, Korea?"

He say, "NAW, gonorrhea!" He say, "I don't *touch* that dirty dog!"

462 Draft

This girl was married to this fellow who apparently didn't know anything about sex. So she tried everything she knew to give him a hint as to what he was supposed to do. And finally she told him, "Honey, I'm so cold."

So he jumped up and got her a blanket. So she was disgusted, but she tried not to let him know.

And she said sweetly, "Sweetheart, I'm still cold."

And he jumped up and got her another blanket.

Then she figured she'd better be more direct, since this fool wasn't taking any hints. So she said, "Dear, you know, I'm made differently from you. I've got a hole down here."

He explained, "Oh, that's where that draft is coming from!"

463   Do Like the Dogs Do

This fellow married this girl. And he was a very timid fellow, but nice. And he went to live with the girl at her parents' home. So they had been living together 'bout two weeks, and one evening, just before time for him to come home from work, she told her mama, she say, "Mama, you know, I'm worried about John."

She say, "Well, what's wrong with John? John seems to be a very nice fellow. He's so nice and mannerable. He comes home. He doesn't do anything wrong. He doesn't go out like most o' these young men—they just running, flying all around. And you got, you ought to be satisfied."

She say, "Well, Mama, John hasn't done or said anything—he hasn't acted any ways like a man."

She say, "What ya mean?"

She say, "You know, he hasn't said anything. He been going to bed every night—he turn over and go to sleep. That's all. He hasn't had anything to do with me the whole time—for two weeks."

She say, "Well, I guess the boy kinda nervous there. When he comes home this evening, I'm gon' talk with him. You go on upstairs and go to bed, and I'm gon' talk with him before he goes to bed."

So John came home and ate and got ready to go upstairs and go to bed. She say, "Wait a minute, John. I wantta talk with ya."

He say, "Yes, Mother."

And she say, "Sit down, I want you to relax, 'cause I know everything is all right." She say, "But my daughter say you not doing your duty, [not] doing right by her."

He say, "Whatcha mean—'not doing right'? Ever since we been married, I come home (I don't go anywhere), and when I get paid, I come home, bring my money here and put it in her lap, and she decides how she's going to spend it. I don't even ask her for any spending money. 'Cause you know, Mama, I don't smoke. I don't drink. I don't need anything but carfare going to and from work. Now what does she mean?"

"But you not doing your *duty* by her."

He say, "Whatcha mean, 'doing my duty,' Mama?"

She say, "Oh, boy! Do like the *dogs* do!"

He say, "Oh-h-h, Mama, now I catch whatcha mean. All right, I-I-I-I realize now that I was wrong. Don't worry. I can take care of business. I'm going upstairs now. Everything'll be all right." So he went on upstairs.

So the next morning, the girl came downstairs *crying!* "Oh, Mama, Mama, I can't stay with John another *day*. I want my divorce."

The first thing the Mama thought was maybe the boy was up there trying to make up for lost time, you know. And she say, "Come here, daughter, don't worry 'bout it. John is all right. You come on tell Mama what happened."

And the girl just *kept* crying. So finally (it took Mama 'bout twenty minutes to get the girl quieted down), she say, "Just tell me, what is wrong with John?"

She say, "Well, I'm gon' tell ya, Mama. I just can't stay with him."

She say, "Why?"

She say, "Because *all* last night—all he's been doing all night long is smelling up my hindparts and pissing up 'gainst the bedpost!"

464 A Devout Reader

This newlywed couple, you know, the daughter after being married for a while, she was real concerned that her husband still never [unclear] her. He just wants to *read*. She told her mother. Her mother said, "I'll tell you what you do. You go home tonight and you undress. Walk around to the bed, and just stand in front of him. I'm gonna watch through the keyhole."

So the daughter went home that next night; husband in bed readin' his book. She showered, perfumed down... So, her mother was watching through the door, and she saw him put his hand in her cock. So she *walked* off.

The next morning she came to her daughter: "Well, I know things worked out for you because I saw it."

Daughter say, "Oh, he just wet his hand to turn the page."

465 Fooled You!

Here's a guy, here; he's going on a honeymoon, you know. He doesn't know anything about sex or anything. He comes outside and sees a guy on the corner. He says, "Listen, how 'bout, uh, uh, uh, how 'bout you doing me a favor?"

The guy say, "What?"

He say, "Look, man, I'm on my honeymoon—from the country—I'm just green about these things, and I really don't know what, what to do." He say, "I want you to come upstairs and show me—come to my room and show me what I'm supposed to do on a honeymoon. My wife laying up in the bed with no clothes on."

He say, "Man, are you crazy or something!"

He say, "I *don't know*."

He say, "Well, okay, come on, come on."

So they got upstairs in the room; there was his wife. But he was suspicious, you know, he was looking around.

"Look, there's nothing wrong. I just *don't know*."

He say, "Okay, you got a piece o' chalk or crayon or anything?"

He says, "Naw."

So he say, "Okay." He took towels and made a circle in the floor. He said, "You see this circle. You get in that circle, and you watch me, but don't you get outta that circle."

He say, "Nawp, I'm not gonna get outta the circle."

The guy gets in the bed with his wife. BAM! BAM! [Gestures to suggest that he is working out.] So when he gets out the bed, here's the guy in the circle. He's like this, "Ha, ha, hee hee." [Jumping around, laughing uncontrollably.]

He say, "What are you laughing at?"

He say, "I-I-I don't know." He say, "Look, I'm very hard at catching on; I just can't catch on. Come on show me again."

He say, "What are you, some quack or something?"

He said, "I *don't know*."

So he said, "Okay. *Don't* get outta that circle."

He said, "Look, I'm not gon' get outta the circle."

So he said, "Okay." He got back in the bed: BAM! BAM! [Gestures again to suggest that he is working out.] Finishes up. He's laying there. [Dramatizing exhausted man lying in bed.]

This guy in the circle: "Ha, hhaaa, haaa, heeheeeeee!" He's laughing again, laughing a lil' harder.

"What in the hell is wrong wit' you?"

He says, "Man, goddog, I ain't got it yet. I ain't got it."

He say, "Okay, look, one more time and no more. One more time and no more!" He got back in the bed with his wife: BAM! BAM! BAM!

He looked: the man was on the floor laughin' and crying, tears coming out—"What in the hell is wrong with you?"

He say, "Ha, haaa, you—haha!"

He say, "You gon' tell me what you laughing at."

He say, "I'll tell ya. Ha, ha." He say, "You know what-t-t, heehee, I got outta that ring *THREE* times and you ain't catch me not once!"

466   Mr. James Know What He's Doing

This is one about Jesse James when he robbed the train. Well, Jesse James and his brother Frank James decided to rob a train. And they rode their horses up beside the train, jumped on like the old days, and say, "This is a stick up! I'm robbing all the women and I'm gon' have intercourse with all the men!"

A lady say, "Mr. James, you must have that *wrong*! You must mean you're robbing all the men and you gon' have an intercourse with all the *women*."

Frank said, "You heard what my brother said. My brother said he's robbing all the *women* and he's going have intercourse—*we* are going to have intercourse with all the men."

Another lady raised her hand, say, "Mr. *Jaaames!* You must have it wrong! It *has* to be wrong. You *must* mean you gonna rob all the men and you gon' have intercourse with all the *ladies.*"

Jesse say, "Goddamn it, you heard what I said—"

And before he could finish, a lil' ole punk in the back say, [shaking his hand and speaking in a very effeminate tone] "Leave Mr. James alone. Mr. James know what he's doing."

467 I'll Take Hymn

A. The minister was encouraging the congregation to just give, give generously, and some sort of compensation would be given them for their generosity. And people were dropping a dollar in the plate, fifty cents, and maybe five dollars, ten dollars. The preacher spied a *one-hundred*-dollar bill in the plate, and he said, "My goodness gracious! Whoever put this hundred-dollar bill in the plate can have a hymn! Oh, you can have three hymns for a hundred dollars."

And this faggot jumps up and said, [very effeminate voice] "I'll take *him* [pointing]—*him*—and *him!*"

B. There was a revival meeting at this little old country church. After shouting and singing and the preaching was over, the ushers passed the plates and took up the usual offering. When they got up to the collection table one usher passed the minister a note, which he read. He then asked the congregation if any one had made a mistake and put a hundred-dollar bill in the plate to please raise their hand. No one responded. He asked the same question again.

A little old lady jumped up and said, "I put the hundred-dollar bill in the plate, but it was no mistake. I intended to give it."

The preacher replied, "Well, in appreciation we shall give you a rising vote of thanks and three hymns of your choice."

The lady jumped up and, pointing her finger, replied, "I'll take *him*, and *him*, and *him.*"

468 This Ain't No Time for Romance

Here's a guy has a wreck. He has about a fifty-one Chevrolet, and he runs into a *seventy-four* Fleetwood Cadillac—Easter pink. And out comes this faggot, raising HELL! Hollering, "Look what you did to my pretty car!"

He says, "Well, take it easy, take it easy, I've got insurance, and I will take—"

He say, "Man, you done messed—"

He say, "Well, I told you I had insurance—"

"I don't care. You done messed my car up!"

The guy say, "Well, kiss my ass then!"

The faggot say, [change from angry to coy tone] "Oh, this ain't no time for romance! I'm really mad."

469   Heltho, Thailor!

Deep in the dense fog of the San Francisco Harbor, you'll hear the cry of the human man-eater [very effeminate voice, very coy, and demure]: "Heltho, thailor."

470   Peaches

These three guys in court. And the Judge looked at one. He said, "Well, what are you here for?"

"For eatin' PEACHES!"

He say, "Well, how 'bout you? What are you here for?"

He say, "For eatin' PEACHES!"

He looked at the other guy. He say, "Well, who are you?"

He say, "*I'm* Peaches."

471   Bubbles

This one is about Bubbles. The policeman was walking up Third Street from Leigh Street towards Clay Street, bypassing the alley which runs parallel to Leigh Street, between Clay and Leigh from Third to Second, and as he approached the alley, right there midway between (on Third Street), between Leigh and Clay, he saw a fellow coming out about two-thirty in the morning. And he said, "Halt in the name of the Law and prepare to be searched."

And the individual raised his hand (he was nervous). He say, "Officer, I haven't done anything, I haven't done anything!"

He frisked the guy; he didn't find anything on him. He say, "What you doing coming out of the alley this time of the morning?"

He say, "Officer, I haven't been doing anything. The only thing I been doing is blowing Bubbles."

He say, "Blowing bubbles this time of morning?" He say, "What you doing blowing bubbles this time of morning?"

He say, "I was just blowing Bubbles."

He say, "Nigger, let me tell you something. Don't ever let me catch you coming out of this alley in this neighborhood any more after twelve o'clock at night." He say, "Now you go ahead."

So the policeman was twirling the stick, walking on 'round the street; got around to the other end of the alley on Second Street, and he saw another individual running through the alley. He say, "Halt in the name of the Law and prepare to be searched!"

Again this particular individual nervously raised his hands and say, "Officer, I haven't done anything."

He say, "What you doing coming out that alley this time of morning?"

He say, "A-a-a-all I been doing is blowing Bubbles, blowing B-B-Bubbles."

He say, "Blowing bubbles! This time of morning!" (That was about fifteen minutes later.) He say, "Listen, nigger, let me tell you something. I just saw one nigger on the other end of the alley. He say he was blowing bubbles. Now you say you were blowing bubbles. Don't ever let me catch you in the vicinity any more!" So he let 'im go.

So he was twirling his stick, and walking his beat, walking all the way around—down Second Street to Leigh Street, up Leigh Street to Third Street and back up Third Street again. He gets to the same part of the alley where he caught the first individual. There's another individual coming out of the alley. He say, "Halt in the name of the Law and prepare to be searched! Now goddamn it, tell me you been blowing bubbles!"

He say, "Naw-w-w, they call me Bubbles! I'm Bubbles!"

472 I'll Show You How Straight *I* Am

Here's a guy who's half-drunk in the bed with a guy. He turned over and patted the other guy on the tail. The cat say, "Hey, what-what-what's wrong wit' you!"

He say, "Man, hell, I don't know what's wrong wit' me. I'm sorry." He say, "Man, look, I don't know what's wrong wit' me. I guess it's the liquor."

He say, "Man, ain't no liquor gon' make you do no stuff like that—feeling on my butt." He say, "I don't go for that!"

He say, "Look, I'm a all-right guy, 'cause, look, I'm married and got three kids. I'll tell you what I'll do. Sunday, you come on by my house, and I'll show you how straight I am." He say, "The liquor or something must o' got me—I don't know what made me do that..."

Okay, he—the guy persuaded him to come to his house. He goes there— nice wife, fine wife, nice kids. So the kids went on out to play and the three o' them sitting down talking.

He say, "Look, I've got to run down the street a minute, and my wife going to entertain you till I come back."

He say, "Well, I'll go now."

He say, "Naw, you stay on here. Don't worry 'bout that. Everything awright! I be gone for 'bout a half-hour."

So he say, "Okay."

So about five minutes after he left, the wife say, "Let 'im go. Come on wit' me."

He say, "Where you going?"

She say, "Come on." She went in the bedroom. She took off all her clothes. She say, "Look, don't worry 'bout 'im. Don't worry 'bout 'im. You come on. We kin get a quick one before he ever get back."

So he say, "Okay, okay." He took off his clothes and got in there [on top of her]. She put her arms around him like that [very tight embrace around his neck]; legs around 'im like that [she locks her legs tightly around his waist, holding him firmly in a position with his posterior up in the air], and then she hollered, "Okay, George—I got 'im! Come on an' get 'im!"

473 Taking the Evidence with Him

This was during the war, you know. And anybody—most of us who've been in the service and you hear all these jokes and things about, like, "Don't bend down in the shower." You know what I mean, this is some shit that—I mean this is something that's really very educational. You can learn a lesson in the shower, you know. Anyway, this fellow bent down to pick his bar of soap up, you know (and he was a private, you know, a lil' ole private), and the Sergeant was in the shower too. The Seargeant hit him in his butt, WHOOMP!

So my man say, [indignant and surprised] "What you do that for?"

He say, "Well, hell, you know..."

He say, "Well, don't do that! You do that again and I'll tell the Captain on you."

He say, "Go ahead and tell him. Don't make me no damn difference."

So the next day he was in the shower again. He bent over and picked his soap up, and ole Sarge hit 'im in his ass again, WHOOP!

He said, "Man, I'm gonna tell the *Captain* on you." He said, "I'm going on and tell the Captain."

He say, "I don't give a damn if you go tell the Captain. I'm a *sergeant!* You a *private.* Captain gon' believe me. Not *you.* And if the Captain believe me and not you, then I'm gon' give you *hell.*"

So the fellow thought about that thing. He say, "Goddog it, he's right. If I go up there and the man got all this rank and all, he gon' believe the Sergeant, you know what I mean. I'm gon' be embarrassed."

So the next day, sure enough, he was in the shower again. He dropped his soap and Sarge hit 'im, BOOMP! [Dramatized.] He *stayed* there. Sarge looked down at him. He say, "You all right, Sarge?"

He say, "Yeah!"

"You got it in, Sarge?"

"Yeah!"

He say, [dramatizing Private locking his hips and walking off with the Sergeant] "Let's go see the Captain!"

My man was takin' his *evidence* with him.

474 That's My Chicken

This guy goes to this house of ill repute, whorehouse or whatever you want to call it. And he say, "Listen, I want some extry good stuff. I don't care who it is, I just want it."

She say, "Well, I tell you what. You want some good stuff. Give me ten dollars and go up there to the first door on your right, and go in."

He say, "Awright." He goes up in there and there's a *big chicken* up there! He say, "This ain't my bag! I don't want to go to bed wit' no chicken."

He come back; he say, "Look, lady, I don't want no chicken. I don't mess around wit' no animals. I don't do that kinda stuff."

She say, "You say you wanted some good stuff, didn't ya?"

He say, "Yeah, but I don't want no chicken."

She say, "You go on up there and try 'im."

He went on up and stayed about a half hour. He come back SMILING-G-G-G. He say, "Look, that's my *chicken!* That's *my* chicken. Don't let nobody ever *touch* that sweet chicken!"

She say, "Naw, next week you come, it's your chicken. Come back. Ten dollars. Up the steps you go! (POP!) [Clapping hands together.] It's *yo'* chicken!"

So the next week he came up here *running.* Ten dollars (BAM!) [slamming money on counter] he give her and run up the steps and turned left instead of right. When he got in the room on the left the people in there looking through glasses—just laughing: "OH! he—glab-de-do-de-doo—oh-h-h-h.

Hey, man, come on in!'' He went on in. There's a guy in there with a donkey, you know.

"Ha-ha-hee-e-e, he-e-ee." He say (boy, he's *laughing*), he say, "Great-t-t-t day—man, I ain't *never* seen nothin' like this!"

He say, "*Shit!* You shoulda been here *las'* week when that guy had that damn chicken . . ."

475   Come on Back!

This guy went huntin' one time, and there he was out there waitin' for something to pass. And up come a *Bear!* "UMPHPH"—hugged 'im. And he was so *scared*. He looked up, and the more he tried to wiggle, the more the Bear held on. He went down there and grabbed the Bear by his privates, started playin' with 'em. The Bear turned him loose, say, "Ughhhh, aahhhh!" and laid out on his back, you know. When the Bear turned loose, he *ran!*

When he got about so many years away, he heard the roar of the Bear, and he looked back; and the Bear told 'im, [mimicking the Bear in a seductive pose, beckoning] "Come on back!"

476   Too Good to Be a Mule

One time this old mule—and he lived in a big barn, and this old drunken man would get drunk every Friday and go down to the barn and fuck this old mule. So one Friday, he got 'im a pint of vodka. He went on down there. Him and the mule start talkin'. But he say, "Fuck the talkin', baby, les fuck a little while." So he went on, start fuckin'. Then he was doing something terrible to that mule's ass. He say, "BABY! If your *head* won't so big, I'd buy you a hat." So he kept on fuckin' that mule. It got good to the mule and the mule start *hollerin'* a little bit. He say, "BABY! IF your *ass* won't so big, I'd buy you a dress." So he kept fuckin' that mule a lil' bit harder—just a lil' bit harder. He say, "BABY! If your *feet* won't so big, I'd buy you a pair o' *shoes*, 'cause you got too good a pussy to be called a mule."

477   Baby, I Wish You Could Spend Money

This farmer was missing his calves and he had 'em all marked down. He couldn't figure where they was going, so one morning he caught 'im; he was sitting down there on the step of the bar. He got the calf—nursing 'im, you know, and the foam just busting out of his mouth. He got a ten-dollar bill in each hand, rubbing his hand. He say, "Baby, I wish you could spend money."

478 Buddy's Travels

I remember one time there was two old Fleas standin' in New York on the corner. So one say, "It's gettin' cold." And then say, "We got to find somewhere to stay warm." Say, "Well, I tell you what to do." Say, "The first day of summer," say, "meet me right here on the corner of a Hundred and Fifty-sebenth Street."

He say, "All right, Buddy, I'll catch you next year."

So this old dog come down the street, so one o' the Fleas say, "Well, I got my ride; see you later, Buddy," and he jumped on the dog's back.

So the other Flea, he walkin' 'round, couldn't find nothing to jump on and hide. So he turned around and went in this whorehouse. He saw the lady laying up on the bed, so he jumped up on the bed and got on her. So he turned right around, and here come next summer; next summer rolled around.

The one that jumped up on the dog, he standin' on the corner, clean, had his tuxedo on, everything, you know. He say—looked at his watch, he say, "I tol' my buddy to meet me up here at twelve o'clock; I wonder what happen to 'im." Buddy ain't showed up yet; it was one o'clock; Buddy still didn't show; at three o'clock, Buddy didn't show. He say, "I ought to tol' my buddy to come on go wid me; maybe he'd been alive today, but my buddy probably dead." 'Bout seben o'clock that night, he seen something staggering down the street—clothes all tore off, one shoe on, one shoe off, needed a shave and everything. He looked at 'im. He say, "Buddy!" He say, "Man," he say, "That dog I jumped on when I seen you last year, man, that was paradise," he say, "but tell me, the way you look—" Say, "What happened to you?"

He say, "Oh, man," say, "I went through some changes. You know that house down there on a Hundred and Fifty-ninth Street?"

He say, "Yeah."

Say, "Man," he say, "I took a walk down there. I couldn't find nothin', so I was gettin' cold, so I jumped on this bed and this woman was on this bed, so I jumped up on the woman; then, man, I went through some changes!"

He say, "Yeah, I kin see that by the way you look, but tell me, what happened to you? Why you so late?"

He say, "Oh!" He say, "Man, I had to hitchhike all the way back."

"Hitchhike all the way back from where?"

He say, "Man, just like I tol' ya, I went to a Hundred and Fifty-ninth Street to that old whorehouse, and I jumped up on this woman and then turned right around, I laying up on this woman, and next thing I know I wind up in a motherfucker's moustache over there in France."

479   Time for Grace

These newlyweds had just gotten married and so they went on to where they were going to stay that night and started to get undressed to go to bed. So after they got undressed, the girl got in the bed first. So the man got down on his knees and said, "Lord, make us thankful for what we're about to receive for the nourishment of our body."

She said, "What are you saying grace for? You say that when you're going to eat."

He said, "What in the hell you think I'm gon' do?"

480   Too Old Fashioned

There was this fellow and he went to see this girl in a kind of old-fashioned car. So he went up to her door and said, "Are you ready to go out?"

The girl looked out to see what kind of car he got; she said, "Hhmph, I ain't going out in that; that's too old fashioned."

So he say, "Mmh!" His feelings were hurt.

So he went on back; he got hisself a sixty-seven Ford. He came back to her house and knocked on the door; she looked out again. She say, "I know I ain't going nowhere, 'cause that's too old fashioned."

So he went back. He wouldn't give up for nothing. He meant that he won't gon' give up.

So he came back with a sixty-nine Oldsmobile. He came up there and he knocked on the door and she looked out. She was really getting pissed off! She was gettin' tired of this mess! She looked out again. She said, "Nope, I'm not going out with you, 'cause that car is too old fashioned." So she shut the door. So he meant that he was really going to get this girl to go out with him. He just meant it! So he went down and got a big Eldorado. He went back there with this big Eldorado and rung her doorbell and said, "Are you going out with me tonight?"

The girl pushed him to the side, looked out and saw that big Eldorado. She said, "Oh, yes! I'm going!"

He said, "Now you sure that's not too old fashioned."

She said, "Oh, no! That's not too old fashioned *at all*." She got her coat and they went on. They was riding. The cat said, "Baby, you *sure* this car ain't *too old* fashioned for you?"

She said, "Oh, no, this is just perfect! And to prove it, I'm going to make love to you." She said, "Park the car; I'm going to take my drawers off."

He said, "Naw! That's too old fashioned; take that bubble gum out!"

481   Shorty Gets a Cadillac

Two buddies, walking down Fifth Avenue in New York, and they passed a palatial residence. A lady hollered out the window, said, "Hey, you!"

So Shorty told Slim, "She must be talking to you."

So the lady say, "Naw, the other one. That one! Come here!"

So Shorty say, "Slim, wait, I'll see what this woman want. She might want me to do some work. Broke as I am, I need to do some work."

So Shorty went into the house and he stayed about an hour. He returned. Slim say, "Shorty, what that woman want?"

He standing there. Shorty say, [incredulous voice, extremely irritated] "You know what the *bitch* wanted me to do?"

"What she want ya to do, man?"

[Long pause.]

"She want me to *eat* her pussy, and if I *did*, she was gon' give me this Cadillac [pointing], this white Cadillac here."

"What you do? Well, well, w-w-what you tell her, man?"

"Oh, man, come on get in this car and roll!"

482   Old Missis and John

This was during the time of slavery days when they used to have the mens doing the housework, too. And the lady told John, "John," say, "I'm going out today." Say, "While I'm gone I want you to clean this house up nice."

Say when she came back from shopping she had a whole armful of packages, and John opened the door for her, grinning. She say, "John, did you do a good job?"

He say, "Yas, M'am."

And she dropped her package. And when she dropped her package and reached down to pick it up, her tiddy fell out; and when she looked, John was looking at her tiddy. She say, "John, do you suck tiddy?"

He say, "Yas, M'am, cock too."

483   French Poussé

This was a nigger who had gone to Paris on some mistaken trip, and he didn't know it, but he had been lucky enough to get past the menu, past the appetizers, without having a lot of trouble, past the entrée, and he had become somewhat emboldened by his success at negotiating these two avenues of the menu, that he asked him, [boldly] "Waiter, what's for dessert?" He hadn't asked before; he been [unclear].

The waiter ran off a whole list of things for him, and he said to him, "Uh, what would you recommend me?"

The waiter said, "What I would recommend is peach poussé."

He didn't know anything about it; he said, "Well, what is that?"

The waiter said, "Well, I could tell you, but I'd rather show you."

He said, "Well, all right, if you want to, show me."

So he called in this lovely French dancing girl, and she pirouetted and danced around the nigger. And he's sitting there. In the meantime the chef had sent him in a half peach, which he cut in quarters and then in eighths, and it was also arranged so that the French dancing girl took each sliver and inserted them in her vagina, and twirled them around. And then she laid them on the sherbert glass.

The nigger say, "What is this?" And by that time there were eight slices out there. He say, "I be goddamn. NO-O-O-O, indeed! What the hell do yawl think? I be damned if I'm gon' eat them goddamn peaches!"

The waiter said, "No, no, no, no-o-o, monsieur! Not the peach! Eat the poussé!"

484   Do You Know How to Party?

Do you know how to party?
Do you know how to play?
Do you know the pleasures of a boss summer day?
You on the fourteenth floor in your duplex pad,
A good stick o' herb [marijuana] was the last thing you had.
You sip a little rum and you sip a little gin
While sassy Sarah Vaughan is singing "Love just walked in."
Here's this nice young lady; she is five-feet-four from her head to the flo'.

She's soft as cotton candy and tastes like Italian brandy.
You groove, move, and try to keep in pace,
And, wow, she slips and sets dead in your face . . .
The yum, yum, yummy of it all.

485   A Beautiful Human Being

Talkin' 'bout sperms down in the scrotum sack, you know. And this one
little sperm—*every* damn day he would take his exercise—do his daily dozens, you know, he "Hup-two, one-two, one-two," *all day long!* Man, this
thing was an obsession with him, you know.

And they say, "What the *hell* is your problem, man?"

He say, "One of these days I'm gon' make a beautiful human being." And
he was "Hup-two, hup-two. . . ."

The rest of the sperm, they sittin' over there to the side, man, smoking
cigarettes, some of 'em smoking pot, you know, bullshittin' around, and
playing cards, you know, hanging out all night long . . . My man, takin' his
exercise. The *only* thing he could think about was "a beautiful human being." So he told the cats, "One of these days, man," he said, "the big tube is
gon' call." He say, "When the big tube calls, I'm gon' be *ready!*"

Them cats said, "MAN, fuck the big tube!"

So anyway, my man was gettin' ready, he was steadily gettin' ready. So
sure enough, about three o'clock one morning, the big tube called, and my
man fell out the sack, Jack, he was steady moving [dramatizing], and my
man was moving, he was steadily rolling, see, and the rest o' them cats
coming out late, you know, they was sluggish [dramatizing], man, tired,
they were coming off the bench, you know, man, "Wait for me, daddy, wait
for me!" And my man was steady out front, he was moving, man. He was
going like he was doing the two-twenty. He was steady [unclear], see. And
this cat made this last turn, he was gettin' ready to go 'round the bend, you
know, and the only thing he could see was this *great big* red object. He could
see this great big red thing, you know, and he thought about this beautiful
human being. Man, he was running! And he looked again . . . he looked
again . . . he start throwing on brakes. He was grabbing hold [dramatizing a
desperate attempt to stop]. He couldn't get no [unclear]. He was holdin' on to
the side of the walls, you know, and he was tryin' . . . He said, [desperate
yell] "Go back! GO BACK!"

And the rest of them, they was runnin', you know what I mean, they were
comin'.

He say, "Go back!" And they were saying, "Wait for me! Wait for me!" He
say, [desperately trying to stop his onward motion] "BLOW JOB! BLOW
JOB!"

486   Every Other Thursday

The man took his wife to the doctor, and after the doctor examined her he called the husband in for a conference. He said to him, "Your wife's problem is that she needs more sex. I'm prescribing sex three times a week."

The man said, "Well, put me down for every other Thursday."

487   Go Git Yo' Mama

Here's a man who educated his kids. He had three sons. And, of course, one was a lawyer, and, of course, one was a doctor. They were doing good. But the third one, he wanted to be a magician. He say, "Now, Pop, you think you waste your money."

He say, "Well, I guess you making a living, but I can't see being a magician, you know. That job won't last."

He say, "Well, like show business. But more than that, Pop. I can do more for you than your other two sons—than your lawyer- and your doctor-son." He say, "Now watch! You a *old* man. Probably ain't been to bed with a woman in *years!*" He say, "Now you watch—YAYYYYYY!" [Thrusting of hands with index finger pointing, in manner of magicians, toward his father.]

And old Pop's penis started to going up, you know.

He say, "Did you see that!"

He say, "YEAH! I see it, son!"

He say, "But wait! Now I kin make it go down just as quick as I kin get it up."

He say, "You bet not *touch* that *damn* thing! You better go git yo' *Mama!*"

488   Just as Dead

One time there was a young man who happened to drop dead. And old Undertaker Jones got his body. Anyway, he was in there dressing 'im. So he got all the way down to his underwear. He was gettin' ready to change his underwear, and he pulled them down. He looked at that thing; he say, "MY GOD! I never seen such a thing on a man!"

All of a sudden he went out the front door there. He ran right out in the middle o' the street. And here come Deacon Jones down the street driving his old A-Model, and he ran out there and he hailed 'im down, and Deacon Jones stopped.

He say, "What in the world is the matter, man?"

He say, "Come here, Deacon Jones. I want to show you something." (So Deacon Jones was hittin' 'round there, 'round sixty-five or seventy years old then.) He say, "Come here. You ain't never seen nothin' like this in your life!"

Deacon Jones say, "What *is* it, man? I done seen dead men before..."

He say, "Yeah, but you ain't never seen nothin' like this in your *life*." So the undertaker took him on in the parlor there, pulled the casket back, and told him, say, "Looka here, man; you ain't never seen nothin' that big in your life!"

Deacon Jones looked at it, say, "Yeah, that might be big, but I got one just as dead as that!"

489 Old Baby

This old couple got married. The woman was eighty-five and the man was ninety. So they KNEW that they wouldn't have any children. So after a while, after about five or six months, she told him, say, "Honey, I think I'm gonna have a baby."

He say, "I don't guess you gon' have no baby."

She say, "Yes, I am." Say, "I can feel him moving."

So finally after nine months she had this baby. And when he was born, he had a bald head and gray hair, moustache, a full set of teeth, HEAVY voice. She picked him up and put him in her lap and started to shake him. She say, "Come on, honey, don't you want tiddy?"

He say, "Naw, I want pussy."

490 Poor Hezekiah

Two old folks (like your mother and me), they were man and wife, and the children were all grown. They were sittin' around reflecting and thinking, you know. And the husband was quite biblical. He liked biblical names. Named all of his children out of the Bible. So he said to his wife, he says, "Look, honey, wouldn't it be nice if we had a child like we did a long time ago." He went on and reminded her about Abraham and Sarah—that was his *selling* point.

So she said, "Oh-h-h" [despairingly], you know, "don't you go by that; we can't do nothin' like that. We can't have no *baby now*."

"You don't *know!*"

She say, "If that's how you feel, well, let's try it."

He say, "I'd like to try it." He say, "I tell you one thing, honey; if we have a baby and it's a boy, I'm gon' name 'im Hezekiah."

So she say, "I don't care what you name 'im."

So she went on in the room to get herself prepared for the—"social event"; and he stayed in . . . She said, "Are you coming on in, honey?"

So he said, "Yeah, I'm comin' on in." Say he put all the lights out; say he started to *runnin'*. He got an erection. In this running, 'twas a chair in the way. Going through the room, when he hit the chair, he said, "O-O-O-OH, LORD!"

She say, "What happened?"

He say, "I just knocked the *hell* out of Hezekiah!"

491   Hey, Hey, Hey!

One Christmas night Santa Claus came down this girl's chimney. He was passing toys out to lil' boys and girls. So Santa was gettin' ready to leave, and the girl say, "Santa, won't you *please* stay with me tonight?"

Santa say, "Ho! Ho! Ho! I *got* to go! I gotta lot o' deliveries, you know!"

So she pulled off her blouse and pulled off her shoes. She say, "Santa, won't you *PLEASE* stay with me tonight!"

Santa say, "Ho! Ho! Ho! I got to go! I gotta *lot* o' deliveries, you know!"

So she jumped on the couch, *pulled all* her clothes off, throwed *both* legs in the air, and say, [seductive voice] "Santa, won't you *please* stay with me tonight?"

Santa say, "Hey! Hey! Hey! I *got* to stay! I can't get up this chimney with my *dick* this way."

492   He's Getting There

This girl was having company downstairs. The mother called down to the daughter, said, "Is that young man there yet?"

The girl said, "Not yet, Mother, but he's *getting* there."

493   If I Had Known

A fellow took his girl to the drive-in theatre, and while the picture was going on, they decided to get on the back seat and have a little pure fun. So when they finished, the fellow told the girl, say, "Honey, if I had known that you were a virgin, I would have taken more time."

And she said, "Honey, if I had known that you had more time, I would have taken off my panty hose."

494 Don't Wait for the Explosion

A. Here's a guy with *muscles*. OOMPH! [Mimicking man proudly flexing muscles.] All [more ostentatious flexing of muscles], you know, that kind of thing. *Muscles!* Do his arms like that [flexing ostentatiously]. So this woman here is fascinated by it, you know. He'd do like this [flexing one arm muscle and then hitting it with the other hand]: Wham! "Two hundred and fifty pounds of TNT!"

She'd go like this [eyes agog in fascination]: "Oooow, OOOOOW, OOOOOOOOOW!"

[Flexing muscle of other arm and slapping it with the opposite hand.] "Two hundred and fifty more pounds of TNT!"

She'd go, "Aaaaaaah, ooooooooow!"

He'd go, "*Five hundred* pounds of TNT! [Flexing leg muscles ostentatiously.] Equal to a *thousand* pounds of TNT."

She'd go, "Wooooowwww, WOOOWWWW!" She was going crazy. So she finally got him to go to the hotel, you know.

He'd done took off everything but his drawers, you know. He laying up there like this: [Starts routine again.] "*Two hundred* and *fifty pounds of* TNT!"

She's going, "WOOOOW! WOOOOOW!" Man, she's going crazy.

"Two hundred and fifty more pounds of TNT!"

"Oh, ooohhhh! Please! Take off your clothes! Take off your clothes!"

He say, [flexing leg muscles] "The rest o' me is *five hundred pounds of* TNT!"

"Ooooooohhhhh, OOOOHHHH!"

"All together—a *thousand pounds* of TNT!" He pull his pants down.

She say, running, running, "HELP-P-P!" She's running, running, RUNNING!

The hotel detective say, "Lady, what's wrong?"

She say, "Mister, if you value your life, you will get out o' here!"

He say, "Well, what's the problem?"

She say, "You know that room—216. There's a thousand pounds of TNT with a blasting cap on it—about *that big!*" [Exhibiting fist to indicate size.]

B. One day this man was walking down the street, and he ran into this lady. So she say, "I'm gon' invite you over my house tonight. I want you to be there at *eight* o'clock."

He say, "Awright. I'll be there."

So eight o'clock rolled around. He went to the lady's apartment. So they was sittin' up drinking beer and talkin' 'bout a whole lot o' different things. And the man say, "I'm gon' tell you somethin'." He say, "In my right arm there are ten *thousand* pounds of *dynamite*." He say, "In my left arm, there is *ten thousand* pounds of *dynamite*." He say, "In both my *legs*, there's *fifteen* thousand pounds of *dynamite*." He say, "In my chest, honey, there's *fifty* thousand pounds of *dynamite*."

And she jumped out the window.

He say, "Lord, hold it, what you do that for, honey?"

She say, "Man, when you pulled down your pants, and I saw that little *fuse*, I thought your ass was gon' blow up!"

495 Katie

A. A fellow went to Washington, D.C., and he wanted some action. And he ran around the city. He was up around Seventh and U Street. And he said, "Look, where can I get some action in this town?"

So this fellow that he talked to stuttered a lil' bit. He say, "Uh, uh, I-I-I-I t-t-t-tell ya, t-t-t-tell ya what to do. Go-go-go-go s-s-s-straight down S-S-S-S-Seventh Street an-an-an-and pass that—brickyard, a-an-an-an-an-and p-p-p-pick up a brick, an-an-an-and s-s-slip it in your right p-p-p-, right rear pocket, an-an-and walk-k-k-k th-th-th-three more blocks to-to-to the s-s-s-second red light, an-an-an-and turn right. Cr-cr-cr-cross the street, and you'll s-s-s-see a brick house facing you. K-k-k-knock on the door an-an-an-and ask for *Katie*. K-K-K-Katie has one *long* leg an-an-and one *short* leg. B-b-b-back Katie up-up-up against a wall a-an-an-an-and slip that br-br-br-brick outa your pocket and p-p-place it under Katie's short leg, and pull Katie's dress up an-an-an-and slip Katie's panties down, an-an-an-and after about f-f-five minutes, *kick* that brick f-f-f-from under Katie's *short* leg. Best damn feeling you ever had in your life—when she start feeling around for that brick [dramatizing]."

B. Back in the days before integration, a white woman was sort of a specialty to a Black man, and if he was in the South, it was sorta like "My goodness, look what *I've* got" kind of thing. So these men were talking one day in a bar, and one said, "You think you've had all the women in the world. I know a *Black* woman that's the best in town, but you have to drive to Paducah, Kentucky, to get it."

He say, "Yeah, well my thing has always been *white* women."

He said, "*Once* you've had *Lucy*, you don't *ever* want *any*body else."

He said, "You said I've got to drive to Paducah?"

He said, "Yes."

He said, "Well, how do I fin' her?"

He say, "Just hit the town! Just hit *Paducah* and tell 'em *who* you lookin'
for—and you got 'er."

He say, "Well, what do I need?"

He say, "Unlike the white women you don't need *nothin'* for Lucy."

He said, "Well, you always tellin' me white women are my thing and you
got this Black woman that kin straighten me out. Good. I *hope* so. I'm not
drivin' all the way to Paducah . . ."

Well he does, and he gets down there and it's night, and he pulls up to a
light, and there standin' on the corner is one *lone* Black man. The town
seemed deserted, and he said, "Say, uh, fellow, I'm new in town. I wonder if
you could help me?"

So the fellow shrugged his shoulders.

He said, "Uh, I'm lookin' for *Lucy.*"

So the fellow said, "Y-y-y-yeah, yeah, yeah, I kin-kin-kin h-h-h-help ya.
Just p-p-p-park yo' car over there by t-t-that p-p-post and c-c-c-come on over
here under the l-l-l-light and I'll sho-sho-show you how to fin-fin to fin-fine
Lucy."

The dude parks his car and he comes over. And he says, "If I could just
find somebody else, 'cause by the time this guy tells me, I'll be out of the
notion."

He said, "Now you see, we-we-we are on Elm St-st-str—Avenue. All you
g-g-g-got to do is just s-s-stay on Elm-Elm Street St-str-str—Avenue, and
you'll come to a *big* w-w-w-white house in the mi-mi-mi-middle o' the
block-bl-bl-block. And it's got green shu-shu-shu-shutters-shu-shu—blinds
on either s-s-s-side of the windows. And ain't no light in the down-down-
downstairs o' the house-house-house at all. 'Tis one light up-up-up-upstairs
i-in the b-b-bedroom, and de house number is f-f-f-four-four, f-f-five, sev-
sev-sev—nine. And-an-an-an you pass on by that house. And you go on
to the n-n-n-next house. It's a bun-bun-bun-bungalo nex' door wit' a f-
f-f-fence 'round the yard and t-two great big black d-d-d-dogs in the yar-
yar-yard, s-s-s-sleep most o' the time, 'cause they l-l-l-lazy as the sh-sh-sh-
shit! And they layin' there sleep and youyouyouyou—ain't no steps to the
front porch. You just pas' on by that house too. But the nex-nex-nex-next
house you come to, mister, is all li-li-lit up like a Ch-Ch-Christmas t-t-t-tree.
An-an-an-an it's got b-b-blue lights in every window, and you push the
g-g-g-gate open, an-an-an-an go up the steps to the house of blue lights and
j-j-j-just k-k-k-knockknockknock-kn-kn—ring the bell, man! Two times, two
times. And a big yellow bi-bi-bitch comes to-to-to the door wit'-wit'-wit'
c-c-c-cockeyes. She so c-c-c-cockeyed when she look at ya and c-c-c-cry, the
t-t-tears r-r-roll d-d-down her b-back. Her teeth look like old folks' toenails,
and her breath smell l-like t-t-ump-ump-t-train smoke. She got one gr-gr-
great big left tiddy, an' on t-t-this side [pointing to the right] she ain't got
n-n-n-n-n-o-o-o-no tiddy atall. Her legs look like b-b-b-bur-bur-burglar
tools." Say, "But now that ain't *Lucy.* You just tell her-tell-tell-tell her you
w-w-want to s-s-s-see Lucy. And she lead you r-r-right s-s-straight out de
b-b-back door o' this ole big house to de w-w-wwo-wo-wo-woodshed. And

in the wo-wo-wo-woodshed ain't no-no-no-no light. You just sort o' f-f-f-*feel* yo' way in. Be-be-before you g-g-go in the woodshed, y-y-you stoop down an' pick-pick-p-p-ick up a brick-br-brick that's inside the woodshed d-d-d-d-door and you carry that brick on in the r-r-room wit' ya 'cause, you see, over in the c-c-corner stands a lil' low ug-ug-ug-ugly, *ugly* lady wit' hair so short you c-c-c-curl it wit h-h-hot t-t-tweezers. She has o-o-o-one eye and n-n-n-no teeth, so don't even t-t-t-try talkin' to 'er. And just put some m-m-mo-mon-money in her hand and the br-br-brick under her l-left leg, which is three inches s-s-shorter than her right leg. And you s-s-see, the brick levelizes the legs. And you have to "git it" s-s-standin' up. And when you git ready to g-g-git yo' c-c-c-cookies, you KICK that brick from under h-h-h-her left foot, and she's gon' start to reachin' for it wid that short leg, and that g-g-grind-GRIND that she puts on you! Man, that ain't n-n-n-nobody in the world b-b-b-but *LUCY!*"

496 Then—Call Me

There's two men that lived next door to each other. Their jobs and their wives—their lives were both similar. The only difference is this: one got *three* children, and the other one don't have none.

So his wife ask him, say, "Why don't you ask him just how—we done done everything we can—ask him what ya do."

"I can't ask that man no mess about how to get no children—what I look like askin' him!"

So one day he was out there talkin' casually. He say, "Man," he say, "I'd like to have me some children; I've done everything I possibly can—"

He say, "Man, you want some children—you want about three or four kids?"

I don't want no *three* or *four* children, but I'd like to have me one or two."

"You want me to tell ya how to get—"

"Yeah!"

"I tell ya what you do. You go and buy your wife a most beautiful neg-ligée, beautiful! Get her hair exotically fixed. Then you go and get a big strong bed for some heavy rocking! Buy her some nice sweet perfume to put on so she'll smell GOOD! And then—"

Guy say, "And then *what?*"

"And *then*, call ME!"

497 I'm Gon' Fin' Her

This young girl [was] from the country—and she was taking her first vacation. So she went to Atlantic City, and she registered in one of the small hotels—way off from the Boardwalk. She goes—puts on her bikini bathing suit, and she didn't know you have to wear a robe or something over it—she went on to the beach and she played 'round on the beach—bathed in the water—and had a good time. So on her way back she walked right on through the street to her hotel. And a policeman saw her, and he immediately arrested her because the law in Atlantic City is that you're not supposed to walk through the streets with a wet bathing suit on.

And they have a court that convenes around the clock during the season, and he took her immediately to the court, but he threw his coat around her while he was taking her through the streets because people were looking at her so because she had on this wet bikini bathing suit.

So when he got to court, the Judge asked him, say, "Officer, what do you bring this woman here for?"

He say, "Indecent exposure, Your Honor."

He say, "Show me the evidence."

So the policeman took his coat from around the woman, and the Judge looked at her. He say, "Young woman, you walk up to the bar."

And she walked up there, and he said, "Now, give me your name."

She gave him her name.

"Give me your address."

She gave him her address.

"Give me your phone number."

She gave him the phone number.

The Judge tells her, "Now, I want you to go *straight* home, take off that wet bathing suit, take yourself a bath and just relax—you stay *right there*, and don't you go out that house the whole day, for the next twenty-four hours. So you hear me?"

She say, "Yes, Your Honor."

The Judge say, "Case dismissed."

So the Clerk *jumped* up and say, "*Judge!* We have a law in this town that says for indecent exposure, it's a automatic fine. You not going to *fine* that woman?"

The Judge say, "You damn right I'm gon' fin' her—unless she gave me the wrong address."

498 Nonsupport

This couple were having a lot of domestic problems. So she had her husband arrested—and she had him arrested for nonsupport. She had three children, and he liked to gamble and drink and run around. So it was a very little money he would bring home. So the children, the woman, and everybody was suffering. So she had him arrested.

So when they went to court, the Judge called her up and said, "Well, what do you charge this man with?"

She said, "Nonsupport, Your Honor."

He say, "Whatta you mean, nonsupport?"

She said, "This man just takes his money and gambles. He likes to drink a lot. He runs around with women. And, to tell you the truth, Judge, that man hasn't give me a piece o' meat in the last six months."

The Judge say, "That's terrible." He say, "Come here, young man. You come before the bar."

He say, "Yes, Your Honor."

He say, "Did you hear the charges that your wife said?"

He said, "Yes, I heard it."

"And you mean to tell me that you haven't given your wife any meat for six months?"

He say, "Just a minute, Judge." So he unzipped his pants, and took out something 'bout nine inches long, and laid it up on the Judge's counter. He say, "Judge, does that look like vegetables to you?"

499   Not for a Coon

This particular master referred to Negroes as coons. One day his slave girl was cleaning his room while he was lying in the bed. Finally his nature rose and his thing stood straight up. She kept watching him and asked if she could help him.

He replied, "No, this was made for a bear's ass and would split a coon wide open."

500   Find Another Scoreboard

This fellow was going with this girl in the country. And he would go down there every night, 'cause he was crazy about this young woman. She was a fine girl. And he wanted to marry her. He said, "Darling, come on let's get married."

And she said, "No, I love you, but I can't marry you because there's nobody but my father and me, and I just can't leave my father. And we don't have but just one room. We cook, eat, sleep—we just have one bed—that old iron bed you see there. I sleep in that—my father sleeps on one side; I sleep on the other. And you know good 'n' well, if I leave him here, he'd die, 'cause he can't do for himself. And I just can't leave him."

He say, "Well, I love you so well that if you'll marry me, I'll come down here and live."

She say, "Well, where you gonna live? We don't have but that one bed. All of us can't sleep in that bed."

He say, "Yes, we can. If you just marry me, I'll sleep in that bed with your daddy. And then if anything happens to him—I'm not gon' hope he die, not gon' push 'im to die—but if he should die, you and I can move to town. But I'll stay here—if it's twenty years—I'll stay here with you."

She say, "Well, if you love me that much, I'll marry you."

So they went on and got married. And the first night they were sitting up there, hugging and kissing and playing. And the old man was sitting up there reading the magazine, Sears Roebuck catalog. He say, "Well, children, yawl stay up long as you wanta. I'm going to bed now." So he took off his clothes, kept on his long drawers, and got in the bed. Got way over in the corner—went on to sleep.

So 'round 'bout twelve o'clock, the old boy got ambitious. He say, "Come on, Baby, les git in the bed here. You know we married now."

She say, "Awright, le's go to bed."

So they got in the bed, and he started playing 'round, say, "Come on."

She say, "Naw, I tol' ya we not gon' do anything like that with my father laying over there. What would he think?"

He say, "Think nothing. After all, you my wife now. I don't care what he think!"

She say, "Naw, I told you this before. I'm not gon' embarrass myself and my father, too." She say, "But I tell ya, if he's sleeping sound, he might not wake. You reach over there on his hindparts, and you break off a hair. And if he doesn't flinch, we can go on and get some."

He say, "All right." So he reach over there and finally found a hair on Pop's hindparts, and he broke it, Blip!

Pop didn't flinch. Pop kept on snoring. So they went on and knocked that piece off. So 'round about two o'clock in the morning, the old boy felt like he wanted another piece, so he said, "Baby, come on, let's, let's—"

She felt all right too. And she was happy. She say, "But I tell ya, you gotta break off another one off Pop." So he reached over there and grabbed a couple of 'em. Pop didn't flinch. So they went on and knocked that piece off.

Around 'bout five o'clock—he wanted to git that wind-up piece now. She say, "Well, now, you know what you got to do."

So he reached over there and grabbed a whole handful of Pop's hair. And just as he got ready to break 'em off, Pop grabbed his wrist, say, "UPPP, hol' it, boy, enough is enough! Now, I tell ya, when you asked me to marry my daughter, I tol' ya yeah, because I know you a nice guy, and she's a nice girl. I think yawl make a nice couple. And personally, I know married people gon' have their little fun—gon' screw and do everything they want to do. And I don't care how much you screw my daughter and how much fun you have. That's yo' business. But be damned if you gon' use my ass for a scoreboard!"

501 Bittersweet Revenge

The ambulance came. They came to get this guy all *cut* up. He's cut up *everywhere!* From his neck, all down, *everything.* He say, "Heyyy, ha, haahahahahaha!" (He's just laughing, laughing.) The man said, "What the hell is *you* laughing about? The man done cut you all up! And you layin' there bleeding to death!"

He say, "Yeah! Hahahaha, but I tell ya something. This is his wedding night, heyheyhey! And I got his dick in my pocket!"

502 Streakers

There were three men and they were streaking. One was a lawyer; and one was a doctor; and the other one was a preacher, or something like that. And they asked them which one was the doctor—could they tell which one was the doctor?

They say the one that had the black bags.

503 Naughty Dollbaby

This little girl, you know, she was, uh, coming through the hall in the house and she seen her old man standin' up in the bathroom taking a shower. She say, "Oooh, *Daddy,* what's that thing between your legs?"

Daddy say, "Oh, girl, that ain't nothin', that's just my dollbaby."

She say, "Oooh, where my dollbaby at?"

He say, "You ain't got nah one. Gone back in there and read a book or somethin'!"

So the lil' girl went on back to her room and start readin' a book. The ole man came out the shower, you know. So they ate and everything, and so then it was time to go to bed; so the ole man went to bed. So this lil' girl went to bed too, but she got up in the middle of the night and went in there where the ole man was, you know, and start' playin' wit' his *dollbaby.*

So the next morning, the ole man got up, you know. He say, "O-O-O-OH! O-O-O-OH, my dollbaby!"

Lil' girl say, "What's wrong?"

He say, "Oh-h-h, my dollbaby hurt!"

She say, "Yeah . . ." She say, "Last night I went in there and start playing wit' your dollbaby and it got all hard and big, and that motherfucker *spit* on me, and I beat the *shit* out of it!"

504   Serving the Cow

This lady had a cow and the cow wanted to serve [to mate] and the lady said, "John, take the cow and go off; the cow want to serve. Take the cow and carry 'im off."

John take the cow and carry 'im off. When he come back: "John, did the cow serve?"

"I don't know whether it served or not, but I seen him lickin' the bull's ass and walk off."

505   Changing His Mind

There was a little white boy and a little colored boy grew up together. And the little white boy's daddy had some cattle, you know. And he was going away. Well, he had some heifers over here in this field, and he had a bull over this side [indicating the opposite side]. But he didn't want the bull to get with 'em, see. And he told his boy when he left home, he say, "Now, be sure to don't let that bull get over there with them heifers."

He said, "All right."

But you know, children playing, by the time he got away, they forgot it, and when they looked, the bull was in there with them heifers, so the colored boy told the white one, say, "You catch 'im—and hold 'im." Say, "I'm gon' *change his mind.*"

So he got 'im a stick and started to beatin' 'im, and then the white man drove up and asked his boy, say, "What is John doin' beatin' that bull like that?"

He say, "Well, he's changing his mind."

So he asked John, he say, "What in the world is you doin'?"

He say, "I'm just changing the bull's mind; I'm tryin' to take it off ass and put it on grass."

506   He Kin Give It, but He Can't Take It

Here's a man with a dog. And he's braggin' about 'im to his friend. He says, "Listen, I got a dog. He's a killer! He's a lover! Every time you see him he's with another girl dog. I mean he's helpin' himself. I mean he's having a good time! But I can train my dog. I can make my dog do *anything I want* him to do."

He say, "Well, there he is. There he is on a girl dog right now. Since you so smart—there he is laying on that dog—try to get 'im off." (That's one thing a person can't do, break up a dog when he's intercoursing.)

He say, "I kin git 'im off 'cause I *know* my dog."

"Man, you can't get them dogs apart."

"I kin get 'im off her!" He took his finger like that [put it in his mouth], went to the dog like that [thrusting finger towards anus], and went BAM! in the dog's tail, you know.

The dog went, "AWNK! AWNK! AWNK!" [Dramatizing dog jumping off other dog.] And he ran off. He said, "I tol' ya I could get 'im off there. I know my dog. He kin give it, but he damn sure can't take it."

507 Put the Snake on Her

Once there was a lady had a little boy. And the boy ask his mother, "Mother, how does you court?"

Mother told the little boy, say, "Next time when the boy come here to see Sister, you go behine the door, and don't let 'im know that you 'hine the door, and you'll see how they court."

So the little boy got behind the door. He was peeping out from 'hine the door. And the boy and girl started doin' the devilment. Little boy say, "Aw, Maw, Maw, I seen that boy put a snake on Sister!"

508 Them Goddamn Potatoes

It was two lil' brothers, and their dad was in service, over in Vietnam. So he finally got his discharge and come on home. So anyway, his wife met him at the airport. And she said, "Hon, I'm very glad to see you. Those two boys that we got at home. I just can't do anything with 'em. Every other word that they use is a curse word."

So he say, "Awright," say, "look, you ain't got no problems now. I'm back. I'm gon' straighten the kids out."

So they goes on home, and they sittin' down eatin' supper. So he looks at Billy. He say, "Bill, what do you want?"

So Billy looks back at him, say, "Daddy, gimme some o' them *goddamn* potatoes."

Old man reached across the table, and, man, he hit 'im, BAM! And knocked him all 'cross the kitchen floor there. Billy got back up and sat in his chair, crying—tears was in his eyes. So the ole man looked over there at Johnny. He say, "Johnny, awright, what do you want?"

Johnny looked at his dad, and he say, "Dad, you kin bet your sweet ass I don't want none o' them goddamn potatoes!"

509 She's Not Going to Believe You Either

A. Say a little girl—she was five, and she was in line. You know, it was the first day of school, and they wanted to know her name. So she told them it was Goddamn. And the lady say, "Oh, honey, I can't help what your mama call you, I wanna know what is your name."

She say, "My name is Goddamn."

The lady looked at her and said, "I cannot write that down. Is there something else they call you?"

"No, M'am."

She said, "Well, you go back home and take this piece of paper and have your mama write your *name* on it."

So the little girl said, "Yes, M'am," and on her way down the line, she pulled a little boy out. She say, "You come on, Motherfucker, they ain't gon' believe you either."

B. This lady had these twins, one named Stinky and the other Shit, see. When they went to school to be enrolled, the teacher asked one what his name was, and he said Stinky. So the teacher wrote a note to his mother, to ask her what was the name of her twins, and the mother wrote a note for each child and sent it back. Well, old Shit, now, he set at the desk, and Stinky goes up with his note to the teacher. The teacher didn't believe him, and she told him to go back home. So when he got to the door, he said, "You might as well come, Shit, 'cause she's not going to believe you either."

C. One time there was two little twins, you know. So they was goin' to school—this was the first day of school. So the teacher there—she wants to know everybody's name in the class. Teacher say, "I want yawl to get up one at a time and tell me yawls' names." She say, "My name is Miz Barnes and I want to know everybody' name."

So the first lil' girl got up; she say, "My name is Sally." She sat down.

The lil' boy behind her got up, say, "My name is William."

Next lil' girl got up, say, "My name is Shirley."

So a lil' boy got up, say, "My name is Charles."

Then the next lil' girl got up. She say, "My name is Motherfucker."

The teacher say, "*What* you say?"

Lil' girl say, "My name is Motherfucker."

So the teacher say, "You come up here." She wrote a lil' note out. She say, "Here you take this note and carry it home to yo' people, and tell your parents that, er, what you said in school. We don't have this type o' language in school."

So the lil' girl grabbed the note and was goin' out the door. When she was goin' out the door she thought about her lil' twin. She called her twin, she say, "Come on, Sonovabitch, she ain't gon' believe you neither."

510   Fire, Fire!

Back when the people had nothing but outdoor toilets, and there were these two young schoolteachers in Pittsburgh (and you know it's a very hilly country there) and they had managed to escape the poverty bond a bit. They were living with their old grandfather. And *they* had a problem. They were destroying all the outdoor privies, tearing them down. And in the process they were making these large excavations in the back yards of these places. Before they had a chance to get out of these holes what was in 'em, they would put signs up saying, "Beware of the holes in the ground." If you fall in them, not only would you hurt yourself, but it was so nasty, so sticky out there, you see.

So they told the grandfather (he was old, and up in his eighties), they said, "Grandfather, stay in and don't go out at night wandering around over the yard because you might fall and hurt yourself, and not only hurt yourself, but you might get *nastied* up." So sure as hell, he promised he wasn't going out.

My man didn't have too much learning, and made it by his own wits. So he came out that night. Sure as hell, he stumbled down and fell into one o' them holes, covered all up to his neck in you-know-what. And he started hollering, say, "FIRE-E-E-E, FI-I-R-E-E-E, FI-I-R-E-E-E!"

So everybody came running to rescue him, picked him up, carried him, hosed him off, brought him on in the house and they called the granddaughters. They got him together and they started talking to him and said, "We *told* you not to go out there. You shouldn't have done it, but we forgive you. We're just happy you're not *hurt*. You really messed *yourself* up, nastied yourself all up with that stuff, but—tell us *something*. Why did you, when you fell into this hole of you-know-what, holler 'FIRE'? How was that gon' save you; it wasn't any *fire*."

He say, "Well, yawl got a lot o' sense. Yawl been out here longer than I have, and I'm eighty-fo' years old. I have *never* heard of *anybody* being rescued hollering 'Shit'!"

511   Sam's Report

for Joy

These children was in class one day, you know, so the teacher assigned homework. She say, "Awright, for tomorrow I want everybody to bring in a report on sex."

So the next day, everybody came to school, you know, got his little paper, report, and everything together, you know. So the first girl she asked, she say, "Sally, what you got to tell me about sex?"

Sally say, "Well, *last* night I peeped up in Mama's room and Daddy was on top o' her and he had his—"

She say, "Hol' it! Hol' it! You got your A, you got your A." She looked around the room and called Jane. Say, "Jane, what you got to say 'bout sex?"

Jane say, "Well, when I looked in the back yard my dog was on top my neighbor's dog and they was—"

Teacher say, "Hol' it! Hol' it! Hol' it! You got your A."

Back in the back o' the room, you know, there was Sam—big, black, *dumb* motherfucker—all the way in the back o' the room. She say, "*Sam*, what you got to say about sex?"

Sam say, [Sam's speech is delivered in the slow, halting manner of a dimwit] "Well, last night, I was lookin' at tele-*vi*-sion, 'n', 'n', 'n' I seen Roy Rogers on tele-*vi*-sion, 'n', 'n', 'n', and this Injun keep jumpin' at Roy Rogers; Roy Rogers shoot 'im, 'BOOM!' so, so—so—"

The teacher say, "Yeah, well, go 'head, go 'head!"

He say, "Well, Roy Rogers jumped on his horse Trigger and they started ridin', ridin', and another Injun jumped at 'im. Roy Rogers shoot him, Boom-BOOM!"

Everybody started lookin' all funny, you know, gigglin' and everything, you know.

Teacher say, "Well, go 'head, go 'head."

Sam say, "Well, Roy Rogers comin' 'round the bend, Chief jumped up there, and Roy Rogers shoot him, Boom, Boom! Boom!"

Teacher say, "But what does all this have to do with sex?"

Sam say, "It teach them goddamn Injuns to stop fuckin' wit' Roy Rogers!"

512 Give Me a Number

A. Billy raised his hand; he say, "Teacher, I got to go to the restroom."
She say, "Okay, Billy."
So he looked at her; he say, "Teacher, I got to piss."
So the teacher say, "Billy, look, when you got to go to the restroom and you got to do something like that, raise *one* finger."
So Billy say, "Okay, teacher." Billy raised one finger.
She say, "Okay, Billy, you're excused."
So Billy's lil' brother, Bobby, he looked at the teacher; he say, "Teacher, excuse me, but I got to *shit!*"
So the teacher looked at Bobby. She say, "Bobby, now look, if you got to go do something like that, you raise two fingers."
So Bobby say, "Okay, teacher."
So Bobby went and come on back, and had his seat.
So the third lil' brother, lil' Johnny (he was the youngest one of the group), was sittin' there. He squirm around in his chair, this thing and another. Teacher look back at him, say, "Johnny, what's wrong?"
He say, "Teacher, I wish you'd give me a number 'cause I got to *fart.*"

B. Well, I'm gon' tell you 'bout this old Wild Man on a airplane with this lady and her three lil' boys. So the big boy come up to the Wild Man. He say, "Wild Man, I got to *piss*."

Wild Man say, "Hey, hey, son, don't you say that 'round them grown people. Say you got to do number one."

He went on to the bathroom, came on back and set down.

So the next boy come up to Wild Man, say, "Wild Man, I got to *shit*."

Wild Man say, "Hey, hey! you little teeny motherfucker. Don't you ever say that around them grown people. Say you gotta do number *two*."

So he went on in the bathroom, came on back 'n' sit down.

So the lil' teeny one, 'bout two years old, come up to the Wild Man. He say, "Hey, WI-I-I-ILD MAN, gimme a number, I wanna fart."

513   Put That Back, Too!

They caught this old lady shoplifting downtown, and they say, "Put those tomatoes back!"

And she put 'em back, and it frightened her so much she passed gas. The guy say, "Put that *horn* back, too!"

514   Two and a Half

One time there was a little boy. He was going to school, you know. He had just started school; and so this little boy had some trouble. It was a funny thing. Every time the boy heard a number, that's how many times that the boy farted! So this day the boy went to his arithmetic class. And so the teacher was puttin' some numbers up on the board, and asked the class, say, "Zero from one leaves how much?"

One little child said, "One," and when he say "One," the lil' boy fart— "Boop!"

Teacher asked, "How much is one and one?"

Somebody in the class say, "I know, teacher, it's two."

The lil' boy say, "Boop-boop."

Somebody say, "How much is two and one?"

Somebody say, "Three!"

The lil' boy say, "Boop-boop-boop!"

The teacher kept the boy after school and asked him why he kept breakin' wind that way. He told her he couldn't help himself; he had always done that when he heard a number. So the teacher called his parents and tol' them to take the lil' boy to see a doctor.

So the next day, they took 'im to see a doctor and the parents explained the trouble to the doctor. The doctor called the lil' boy in there. He say, "One!"

The boy say, "Boop!"

Doctor say, "Two!"

The lil' boy say, "Boop! Boop!"

Doctor say, "I don't know. This a puzzle here!" But then he told the lil' boy's mother and father, he say, "Oh! I know how to catch him," say, "I know how to break him out of this." Doctor say, "One!"

The lil' boy say, "Boop!"

Doctor say, "Two!"

Lil' boy say, "Boop! Boop!"

Doctor say, "That's all right; this'll git him." Doctor say, "Two and a half!"

Lil' boy say, "Boop-boop-shh . . ."

515 Surprise

Here's a guy who loves beans, but they gave 'im so much gas, gave it to 'im, you know, and his wife kinda tol' 'im, you know, "You know when you're around friends and all, you know, we can't have this, you know what I mean, we just don't want it! You burstin' with gas. It's very insulting!"

So he say, [reluctantly] "Well, all right."

So then he got a call one Friday. His wife tol' 'im, "Now listen, I'm goin' outta town. My mother's taken ill and I'm goin' out o' town. Now I've left your food and all that for you on the table and (blab, blab, blab)."

He say, "God! I kin eat all the *beans* that I want and go home and just *root-e-toot-toot* all over the house!" So he ate beans that morning, and he ate beans for lunch, and everything, and came home 'round about ten or 'leben o'clock that night. And when he got home wasn't a *soul* in the house. He said, [exhilarated] "Great day in the morning!" He just laid back and he [comfortably relaxing and raising one leg] BRRRR! BRRRR! I mean he just take care! [Shifting one leg and then the other.] He did that for 'bout three minutes.

Then the light come on. They say, "HAPPY BIRTHDAY!"

A *surprise* birthday party!

516 He Ate the Whole Thing

There was a Ex-Lax salesman, so he was traveling out there in this country. So he had trouble with his car. So he pulled up to this house and asked the lady of the house, say, "Madam," say, uh, "being that it's *late*, could you let me stay here for de night until in the morning 'cause it's a *long* ways back to de city?"

So the lady said, "Well, I can't see why not, but, uh, you have to sleep with my husband tonight."

He say, "All right. I 'preciate that."

So the lady come on down and made supper and then turned around. She went upstairs for to get in the bed.

So the old man asked him, say, "Mr. Salesman," say, "what you selling?"

He say, "Aw, it ain't nothing but some old Ex-Lax."

So the old man, being that he way down in the country, he ain't never heard of no Ex-Lax, you know. So he say, "Mind if I try one?"

Salesman say, "Go ahead, help yourself." So then the old man ate the Ex-Lax. The Ex-Lax taste like Hershey, you know, so it got good to 'im. The old man ate the *whole* box o' Ex-Lax.

So then the next morning the woman called 'im, tol' 'im, say, "Git up and eat breakfast." So he got up and eat breakfast. So then he told the woman how much he 'preciated it. So he gave the woman fifty dollars and tol' her, say, "Look, I shore appreciate it, you lettin' me stay here last night."

He called the wrecker and everything to tow his car in.

So then about two and a half weeks later the old salesman come back down through that way again and turn around, say, uh, told the woman, said, "There go some stockings and what not, you know, for showing me such nice hospitality when I was here befo' and," say, "oh, I got a pipe and a great big can of tobacco for your husband, too." He say, "Where is he at?"

Woman say, "Well, I'm sorry, but," say, "my husband dead."

And the man say, "Well, uh, I'm sorry to hear that." Say, "When did he die?"

She say, "Oh, he died the next day after you left."

He say, "Well, I'm very sorry." He say, "Well, being that it's late like this could I stay, uh, over again tonight?"

Lady say, "Yes."

So he went on upstairs and got in the bed. Next morning lady called 'im, say, "Mr. Salesman, Mr. Salesman, git up so you can eat breakfast."

He say, "All right." So he got up and went on in the bathroom, gittin' ready to wash up. He see her *husband* sittin' in the bathroom on the toilet, you know: "I thought she say he was *dead!*" So he *bust* out the bathroom door, run downstairs, say, "Madam, Madam," say, "I thought you say your husband was dead."

She say, "He is dead, but we gon' bury that bastard soon as he finish shitting."

517 Never Mind!

This guy walks up to a guy and says, "Co-co-co-could you-you-you t-t-t-tell me w-w-w-where a to-to-to-toilet is?"

The guy turned around, an' say, "W-w-w-well, you g-g-g-g-go d-d-d-d-down d-d-d-down and t-t-t-then y-y-y-y-y-you—"

The guy say, "T-t-t-that's a-a-a-a-awright. I-I-I done a-a-a-awready sh-sh-sh-shit!"

518　She Misunderstood

This man had been going to the eye doctor constantly for years with these cataracts, and the doctor was treating him ju-u-ust enough to keep him coming back. And so finally it got so bad, the doctor say, "Well, I've gotten my son through med school, so I'll see what I can do." So he said, "Brother Jones, I've got a new diagnosis and a new medication. Now, this is very touchy, so listen at me carefully. We've discovered that warm fresh urine eyewashes are *magnificent* for cataracts. Now, since this is so personal, it would be easier for your son (if you had a son) to urinate in your eye, because the way he's built it would serve as a funnel, and it would directly wash it out very good." He said, "Now you don't have a son. So we come to the issue of your wife. Do you think in some way she could irrigate your eyes with urine? Now this is strictly personal, but it's good, and you've tried everything else."

He said, "I'm willing. I'm willing to go home and tell her."

Well, she was hard of hearing, but he went home and he told her what the subject was, what had happened, what had transpired, and the doctor said how personal it was.

And she said, "All right, well come on here; we got to figure out some kind o' way. I got to go pee now, anyway."

He say, "I'll tell you what; I'll stretch out here on the bed and hold my head down, and you just irrigate my eye. Now the doctor said you've got to irrigate one at a time."

She say, "Well, it's easier for you to move your eye, your body from one side to the other—"

He say, "Well, all right. Let's try it."

So he stretched out under her, and she urinated in his left eye. He say, "That's fine! Okay, Baby, *shift!*"

And she misunderstood 'im!

519　Musta Been Mustard

This lady had three sons, Jack, Jim, and Mustard. And all three of 'em had terrible colds, so she decided to give 'em some castor oil. So all of a sudden, all of 'em had to go to the bathroom at the same time. Jack went and jumped up on the toilet. Jim ran to the pot. Mustard had nowhere to go. It was a hot day and the windows were up. He was running all around. He had to go so bad. He *ran* and *jumped* up on the window sill.

Here comes this lil' cop down the street. He took off his hat and wiped his head. That time Mustard *broke aloose*. The cop say, "Shit!" BAM! BAM! BAM! [dramatizing cop knocking at the door].

The lady came to the door; she said, "Who is it?"

He said, "Cop! Cop!"

She say, "Well, what's wrong? What's wrong?"

He say, "Somebody don' shit on my head."

She say, "It couldn't o' been Jack; it couldn't o' been Jim. It musta been Mustard."

He say, "I be damned if that's any mustard; that's pure shit! You smell it!"

520   Not for a Quarter

Two city dudes visiting out in the country had to go to the outhouse. It was a two-seater. When one of the guys got up and began pulling up his pants, his pockets with the change flipped over and dumped a quarter down in the hole. After a few seconds' thought, he reached in his other pocket, took out a ten-dollar bill, and dropped it down the hole.

His friend said, "Man, you must be crazy. Why did you drop that ten-dollar bill down in there?"

The guy said, "You don't think I'm going down there for twenty-five cents, do you?"

521   On Guard Duty

This private was standing guard duty at a highly sensitive base, and the general came by in his car, and he saw this private *jumping* up and down and *hollering* and *shouting*—and he got out and started *berating* him for making all that noise and giving away his location. He said, "You'll cause everybody on this base to be killed!"

He said, "I know that, Sir, and I *apologize*, but I have stood at attention while a flock of pigeons flew overhead and dumped on my head, and I didn't *flinch* a muscle. A dog came by and peed on my feet, and I didn't *bat* an eye; but when two squirrels ran up my leg and I heard one of them say, "Let's eat one now and save one for winter..."

522   Come on to Bed

Old man Zeke Johnson had just married Miss Rose, and he was sitting in this old rocker on the porch, but the cane had broke out of it, see. Won't no such thing as pajamas then. He ain't have no pajamas—nothing but them open drawers on, and his nuts ran down through the chair, and the cat setting over there watching him, see.

And she kept on tellin' him, "Come on to bed."

And he tell her, "Awright, I'll be there in a minute."

He was 'shamed to go to bed, setting there with them old black drawers on. The cat kept watching him. Every time he move, the cat *ease* up closer . . . and after a while, the cat grabbed him. He went to bed with *cat* and all.

523   A Golf Lesson

You see, this cat was tryin' to teach this lady how to play golf, you know, and when you teaching somebody how to play golf, you get up, you know, and you bending over, you know, trying to help them, makin' the motions and all [dramatizing man standing behind woman, bending over her, helping her to hold the golf club]. And the fellow looked down and his *pants* was open, and he didn't want to be embarrassed. He reached down and tried to zip 'em up, you know, and caught her damn dress in his zipper. He looked at her, and she said, "What—what happened?"

So he told her, "Well, I got to confess; my pants were zipped down, and I was tryin' to help you, and now you caught in my zipper."

"Well, what you gon' do?"

Say, "I got to get out some way."

So she say, "Well, come on. Let's go in the clubhouse."

She was 'bout like this [bent over in front of man], and he was walkin' [bent over the woman], and they were coming up to the clubhouse, and—a dog—threw some water on both of 'em.

16

A Potpourri:
Miscellaneous Black Folklore

Well, this ain't no slavery-time tale, and this ain't
'bout animals and all of that we been tellin' you
'bout, and I s'pose you ain't really interested in this,
but anyway, let me tell you this one 'bout....

An Informant

IN A SESSION during which material was rather consistently falling
into certain categories, one informant prefaced his contribution with
the comments quoted in the epigraph for this chapter. It is an appropriate introduction to the chapter because the folklore here does not
fit into any of the fifteen other classifications of material collected in
the book. The form and the subject matter of the folklore included in
this chapter vary widely. Here are proverbs, superstitions,
metaphors, home remedies, and exempla. Here are also personal
anecdotes, tales, jokes, folk verses, and songs which treat such varied matters as insanity, cannibalism, stuttering, and the origin of folk
sayings and folk names.

524 Proverbs and Other Bits of Folk Wisdom

A. A whistling woman and a crowing hen
Never come to a good end.

B. Every dog has its day.

C. There's a butcher for every bull.

D. Friends are few and far between.

E. Every good-bye doesn't mean that I've gone,
And every closed eye doesn't mean that I'm asleep.

F. The unseen eye is watching you.

G. If it's for you, you go get it.

H. You can lead a horse to water, but you can't make him drink.

I. No news is good news.

J. We can all sing together, but we can't all talk together.

K. Play big if you want to win big.

525   More Proverbs

A. Leopard don't change his spots.

B. Look before you leap.

C. Money is the root of all evil.

D. You have to take the fat with the lean.

E. Wait? Weight broke the wagon down.

F. You can hide the smoke, but what you go' do with the fire?

G. Live by the sword, you die by the sword.

H. I respect work like I do my Mama. I wouldn't hit her a lick for the world.

526   Superstitions I

A. It's bad luck to sweep trash from the house outside after sundown.

B. Don't hang purse on door knob. It's bad luck.

C. Don't put shoes on the bed. It's bad luck.

D. Don't split a post. It's bad luck.

E. It's bad luck if a woman comes to your house on New Year's Day before a man has been there.

F. It's bad luck to make New Year's resolutions and not keep them.

G. If a black cat crosses the road going to the left in front of you, you should turn around and go back. It's bad luck.

H. If you don't let the telephone ring at least twice, [it's] bad luck.

I. It's bad luck to carry an open umbrella into the house.

J. When a TERRIBLE storm comes, somebody's gon' die that day.

K. When a dog be out there howling and a cat cryin', somebody's gon' die.

527 Superstitions II

A. If your dog who lives outdoors come near the window at night and howls, look out for death in the family.

B. If you dream about a newborn baby, it's a sign of death.

C. If you dream about a fish, it's a sign of death.

D. You should never wash clothes on New Year's Day. You'll wash some members of your family to death.

E. If a picture falls from the wall and sits up straight on the floor against the wall, there will be death in the family.

F. If you touch somebody with a broom, they going to jail. But if he spits on the broom, that cures it.

G. If you sweep on a young girl's feet with a broom, she won't get married.

H. Peanut shells bring police. I don't let my children eat peanuts at my house.

I. When you comb your hair, burn it up so won't nobody get it and work a root on you.

J. Tinting the hair will affect one's brain.

528 Superstitions III

A. Don't let a frog pee on you. You will get warts.

B. If you drop food, someone else must be wishing for it.

C. A ring 'round de moon, gon' be warm weather.

D. My joints feel mighty stiff; I believe we go get some weather [precipitation].

E. When my cut [from surgery] start hurting, I know it's gon' rain.

F. Old folks can tell when it's gon' rain, 'cause their knees start hurtin'.

G. If it rains on a person's funeral, it means the soul has gone to heaven.

H. When it rains and the sun is shining, the Devil is whipping his wife.

I. The first twelve days of the year represent the twelve months as far as weather is concerned.

J. If a pregnant woman doesn't get what she wishes to eat, it may cause the baby to have a birthmark resembling the particular food she wished for.

K. To dream about snakes means you have enemies.

L. If you throw a kiss at a redbird and make a wish, your wish will come true.

529   Superstitions IV

A. It's good luck to eat blackeye peas and hog jowl on New Year's Day.

B. It's good luck to find a four-leaf clover.

C. I found a penny. That means good luck.

D. Right hand itching mean you will get some money.

E. My eye [is] itchin'. Company must be coming.

F. A new nail in an apple tree keeps the tree from being wormy.

G. To make grapes grow on vine, bury old shoes under vine. When shoes rot, grapes grow.

530   Conjuring Your Lover

Wipe your man's discharge in a handkerchief and put it under your mattress, and he won't have no nature for nobody but you.

Cut some hair out of your man's head and put it in a jar in a hole under your step. That'll keep him coming.

Take some of your monthly period and cook it in his food. It'll run him crazy—make him stone crazy 'bout you. When I'm on my period, my boyfriend don't never let me cook nothin' for him.

Take your panties off and don't wash 'em. When he go to sleep, put 'em under the pillow. That'll keep him thinkin' 'bout nobody but you.

Take his bow out of the back of his hat. And don't let him know it. Take it and tie it (pin it) to the back of your panties, and that'll bring him closer to you—keep him comin'. I know my boyfriend don't let me get near his hat.

If you want to get rid of your boyfriend, take a picture and put it up face bottom in your shoe, and he'll fade away from you.

Buy him some new shoes, and he'll walk away from you.

Get rid of a man by taking some pepper when he leave and sprinkle it behind him.

531 Metaphors, Similes, and Other Folk Sayings

A. You're sharp as a 'squito's [mosquito's] peter, and that's sharp at both ends. [You are looking exceptionally good.]

B. You're sharp as a tack.

C. Money is as scarce around here as hen's teeth.

D. They're poor as church mice.

E. He's as ugly as a monkey's uncle.

F. He has more foam [form] than a can of Schlitz. [In reference to a ballplayer's style.]

G. The kettle callin' the pot black, an' the fryin' pan standin' up for witness.

H. He done pissed in the churchyard now. [He has offended someone who has been helpful to him.]

I. He can't smell me when he sniffs.

J. If your shoes start to quake and quiver, Throw them bitches in the nearest river.

532 Yo' Mama

Your mother is like a doorknob. Everybody gets a turn.

Your mother is like a piece of pie. Everybody gets a piece.

Your mother is like a dresser. Everyone gets into her drawers.

Your mother thinks she's sharp 'cause her head comes to a point.

Your mother thinks she's a big wheel because her face looks like a hubcap.

[When one boy told another to go to hell, the latter responded]:

I went to hell,
The door was lock.

I found the key
In your mother's cock.

[Yo' mama's] a sweet old soul.
She got a ten-pound pussy
And a rubber asshole.
She got knobs on her tiddy
That can open a door.
She got hair on her pussy
That can sweep the floor.

Sit on a rock,
  Ooh ah!
Let the boys feel your cock,
  Ooh ah!
Don't be ashame',
  Ooh ah!
'Cause yo' mama do the same.

533   Folk Remedies

A. For dog bites, let dog lick it and it heals.

B. Rub Indian roots soaked in vinegar on joints for rheumatism.

C. Take turpentine and sugar for stomach ache.

D. Take a dirty stocking and put it around your throat for sore throat.

E. Gargle throat with your own urine for sore throat.

F. Gargle with syrup and water for sore throat.

G. Drink vinegar and water for headache.

H. Wet rag in vinegar and lay it across forehead for a headache.

I. Peel a onion and put it at the bottom of baby's feet for fever.

534   All a Matter of Money

They say, when you got money, you have a nervous breakdown and they put you in a mental institution; but when you ain't got no money, they say you crazy, and they put you in a 'sylum.

535   Don't You Forget

This woman went to a mental institution, walking around, visiting, and she ran into this man. Oh! And he was just so intelligent! And she said, "You know, as soon as I get back up to the main desk I'm going to tell them that you have no business locked up in this place."

And so she and the man talked. She said, "I am just convinced beyond a shadow of a doubt that they have put you in here—you really shouldn't be in here."

So he said, "Now, lady, be sure to do that."

So he was working in the brick part of the mental institution. So when the woman got up to the door, he took one of those big bricks, hit her on the back of the head and said, "Now don't you forget!"

536   I Put Sugar on Mine

They tell me this is a true story. This is very true. Somebody was driving by the Williamsburg Asylum. This man had a load of compost on the wagon. So the man yelled out the window to him, and said, "What's that you got in your wagon?"

He said, "Well, it's compost."

He [inmate] laughed, "Oh, how foolish! What you gon' do with it?"

He said, "I'm gon' put it on my strawberries."

He laughed. He said, "Ha, ha, how foolish! How foolish! I put sugar on mine."

537   Just Like One of Us

Matt Carter told this story. He went to, what we call, an insane institution in New Jersey to speak. He said when he got up to speak, he wasn't quite sure just what to say. He didn't want to say, "I'm glad to be here," but he wanted to say something that was pleasant to the people. He didn't want to say, "I'm glad to see so many of you here." So he fumbled around, trying to find the proper words to introduce his speech. I don't remember just what he said, but when he finished one of the inmates came and said, "Man, I'm glad to see you, 'cause you're just like us."

538 Already There

This girl stretched and said, "Oh-h-h, I think I'm *goin'* crazy!" He say, "You already *there*! You already *there*."

539 Oops!

Another man, he had just planted some wheat. And he had a big wheat stack out in the field. And the crows kep' a goin' out there picking up his wheat, you know. So he got his gun out there—he gon' shoot the crows. Before he got out there good, when he leveled down, the crows walked around the stack a lil' bit. So he took his gun and bent the barrel a lil' bit like that [illustrating]. And the crows went a little further. He bent it a little bit more, like that [bending it around as the crows move around]. Crow went way 'round. The next time he bent it, and when he pulled the trigger, he shot his own self in the back!

540 Isn't That Haney?

The other story they used to tell on my great grandfather. He had become very old and he couldn't *see* very well. But the *postman*, who drove a distance of about eighteen miles a day to carry the mail, would bring him his toddy. Many people would call to see him because he was old, he was quite an oddity in the community, a man who was past a hundred years old, a hundred and nine or ten, whatever he was. And of course, if people came to see him and he didn't want to be bothered with them, he "couldn't see good." But he always knew the time of day when the postman was supposed to be coming.

So somebody went to see him—he "didn't know them." He said, "I can't see you." [An obvious effort to put them off because he didn't want to be bothered.] But he looked through the window [dramatizing a man looking through the window, obviously sighting something] and said [smiling broadly], "Isn't that Haney coming?"

541   Mutual Agreement

They say that back in the days of King Hezekiah the Assyrians had surrounded the village in such a way that they couldn't get nothing in there and couldn't get nothin' out, you see. And the people were actually starving. So these two women was livin' together. And they didn't come out until after the war was over. And they came to King Hezekiah, say, "King Hezekiah, I'm gon' tell you somethin'. When the siege was going on, me and this woman lived in the same house. And we both had a lil' son. So we made a agreement to boil and eat my son first; and after he gone, boil and eat her son. Well, I kep' my part of the contract; we boiled and ate my son, but when we come to get hers she put him where I couldn't find 'im. So I want you to do somethin' 'bout it."

542   The Bolsom Dog

Once upon a time there was a big family—seven children, a mother, and a daddy. They were very, *very* poor. They didn't have much to eat, maybe some bread and some milk; that was about all they ever had. And the daddy would go out hunting every day with his little dog, the Bolsom dog. And he'd come back empty-handed—couldn't find anything to eat. And again the children would just eat whatever they had there at home to eat. Well, one morning the father went in there. He said, "Children, I'm going to bring you all some meat this evening if it's the *last* thing I do."

The father went out hunting; he carried the Bolsom dog. The family eagerly waited for him because he promised them some food. And sure enough, Daddy came back with a great big bag over his shoulder. The mama said, "Run, children, RUN! Daddy's got some *food!* Mary, put the kettle on; Johnny, get the water"; and each child had a chore to do. And they got a good-burning fire and Mama put the food in front of them, and they were all sitting around the table, and boy, they were *eating*-g-g to beat the band—everybody except Daddy. Daddy was sitting there under the tree, just swaying back and forth [desolate look on face]. The children called him, say, "Daddy, aren't you hungry?"

"Naw, I'm not hungry."

So everybody ate—all the children just enjoyed the food. So afterwards they cleaned up their plate and they were scraping off the scraps for the dog. And they called, "Here, Bolsom, here Bolsom!" Bolsom dog didn't show. They kept on calling. The daddy was sitting there under the tree:

"Don't know what you callin' 'im for. You just ate 'im."

543   Dolly Bones

There once was a little girl who lived with her mother. They lived alone in this little house out in the meadow. Well, they were very, very poor. And the mother had told Dolly Bones to keep this little lamb there by the house because the lamb was a very nice lamb and a good lamb and he would protect her from all harm and danger, from the wilderness and whatever was out there in the woods. So Dolly Bones said, "Yes, M'am, Mama."

And Mama one day got very sick, and ... then Mama died. And Dolly Bones had this lil' lamb near the house. And one day Dolly Bones moved the lamb down in the meadow a little bit, and she could hear the lamb, "Bah-h-h, baah-h-h." And presently she moved the lamb down a little further. She could hear the lamb, [obviously farther away] "Bah-h-h, baah-h-h." Then she heard, "Boomalanka, boomalanka, dee-e-e-deedum! Boomalanka, boomalanka, dee-e-e-deedum!"

Little Dolly Bones jumped out. She said, "It was nothing but the wind." So that evening, she brought the lamb back to the house. She got up the next morning; she repeated this same thing: each time that the lamb went down, she moved the lamb further in the meadow. And each day the voice would get a little louder: "Boomalanka, boomalanka, dee-e-e-deedum! Boomalanka, boomalanka, dee-e-e-deedum!"

And Dolly Bones couldn't imagine what it was. But the little lamb's voice would get "B-a-a-h-h-h, b-a-a-h-h-h." Finally, she moved the lamb so far away, she couldn't hear the lamb. She heard this loud voice, "BOOMALANKA! BOOMALANKA, DEE-E-E-DEEDUM! BOOMALANKA! BOOMALANKA, DEE-E-E-DEEDUM!" And Dolly Bones was shaking in her boots. And then this creature slammed on the door, and opened the door and found poor Dolly Bones behind the door, and he picked her up and threw her over his shoulder, and took her on down into the woods, and that was the end of poor little Dolly Bones.

544   Headed for the Nine-Mile Lock

The Canal went all the way up into Goochland, past Goochland, all the way up into Lynchburg. And an uncle of his [the speaker's father] drove one of these canal things, you know. When he'd go by, he'd holler, "We're headed for the nine-mile lock" [where the horses would be changed]. And this little saying came to be part of Black folklore. If you were going some place, you know, and you were achieving your goal, then you'd holler, "I'm headed for the nine-mile lock."

545   We Going by Miss Van Lew's House

It was traditional for the Blacks to march to the cemetery on Memorial Day. They would have their shovels and their picks, and everything to clear it out, because this was a once-a-year sort of thing. And when they would be marching, the leader would always holler back, "Hey, you niggers, you straighten up down there now. We going by Miss Van Lew's house!"

And of course, they would all straighten up, you know. They were proud because she had been a Union spy, and was very liberal. And they respected her and her memory.

546   I Gon' Ride the Mule

One time my father had four mules and one mule that couldn't anybody ride, but my uncle said to my father, "Well, I'll ride that mule."

He say, "Well, I'll pay you fifty dollars if you'll ride that mule."

He say, well, all right, he was gon' ride that mule. So my uncle came to the house and they put the saddle and everything on this mule, and my uncle got on. Soon as my uncle got on and stuck his foot in the stirrup and everything, the mule throwed 'im.

He say, "Didn't I tell you you couldn't ride that mule?"

He say, "I gon' ride this mule or kill this mule one."

So he got back on the mule again and by the time he got on it, the mule throwed 'im again.

And he tried to ride that mule five or six times; so then another fellow say, "Well, I'll ride 'im."

And so my father say, "Well, all right. I'll pay anybody to ride that mule."

So he got on 'im and by the time he got on this mule—right over the mule's head he went! He say, "I'm gon' ride this mule 'fo' I go 'way from here."

He consist [insist] that he was gon' ride that mule. So the last one got to ride the mule, he throwed 'im and he broke his arm and his leg—and after that—wasn't any more riding the mule.

547   No Singing Sam

This happened during World War Two when whiskey was rationed. This friend of mine, he was down in North Carolina once, got in a line (the whiskey was rationed) to get some whiskey, you know. And this white fellow came in there—he was one of those what we used to call the hoogies; he couldn't read or write; so he stood in line.

The lady say, "Sir, what are you gon' have?"

"I want a bottle o' whiskey."

She say, "You got any idea what kind of a brand you want?"

"Naw, I don't know nothin' atall about no brand, but I tell ya what I don't want. I don't want none o' dat where that nigger sittin' up there a pickin' on that—uh—banjo."

548 Imagination

This boy had just returned from college, you know, his first trip home. And they were getting ready to eat Thanksgiving dinner. He decided that he would tell his folks about *imagination*. And he told his daddy that, you know, "In college I learned there was a thing called a *keen* sense of imagination, and you really don't have to be there; you can just imagine."

Oh, and that was just so deep, and his daddy was digging this, you know. He had sent this boy to college and he had come back here with this big word, *imagination*.

So finally the Mama brought the turkey and put it on the table. The boy thought he would take the thing a little further. He said, "You know, Daddy, now if you got a real, real keen sense of imagination, instead of looking at *one* turkey on the table, you could see there are really *two*."

His daddy say, "Well, I tell you one thing, me and the children and your Mama gon' eat this other turkey, and *you* eat that imaginary turkey."

549 Literal Translation

An American was asked to lecture in a foreign country. On his arrival he started by saying, "I was dying to get here." The interpreter stated the sentence in this manner: "This poor man in an attempt to get here will die."

550 Retailing without a License

A hobo jumped off a freight train. He had a dog with him, see, and he didn't see the switch engine coming up, so he got across in time. And the dog got across—everything but his tail. It cut his tail off. So he picked up the dog and carried him over there to the lil' village. And he come by a tailor shop, and he said, "I would like to have a needle and thread if you got one to spare."

And the man say, "Yeah, here's one."

So he set out on the curb and sewed the dog's tail back on the dog, you know. And the policeman came along and arrested 'im for retailing dogs without a license.

551 Lost His Head

This dog had run across a railroad track and the train cut his tail off. And he turned around, you know—snapping at the engine—and it cut his head off.

Say that's not the first time a fellow lose his head over a lil' piece o' tail.

552 Who's Mocking Whom?

A guy goes into a restaurant, and the girl comes over to him and says, "C-c-c-c-can I he-he-he-help you?"

So he said, "Yea-yea-yea-yeah, I w-w-w-want a c-c-c-cup of c-c-c-coffee."

So she say, "Uh-uh-uh-uh, you-you-you m-m-mockin' me!"

He said, "No-no-no, I'm not m-m-m-mockin' you. I-I-I-I tal-tal-tal-talk like that all-all-all the time."

So they conversated back and forth, stuttering. In come a guy, sat down, he ordered something, you know. This guy turned around and told the guy who was sitting on the stool, he say, "Nice day."

The guy said, "Sure is—a very nice day. I love it."

So the girl walked over, say, "Oh-oh-oh, so you wa-wa-wa-was mockin' me?"

He say, "No-no-no, I w-w-w-wasn't mockin' you. I was m-m-m-m-mockin' him."

553 False Notes

A minister in this lil' village theater. The village soprano had trilled for 'im, you know, and one of the local natives was enthusiastic about how wonderful it was. So this fellow (he was sittin' there at the time), he saw the pastor; he say, "Oh, it wasn't so hot."

So he say, "Why, man! They tell me she's got a *fortune* in her throat."

He say, "Tell her not to try to raise any money on it, 'cause it's false notes."

554   I Eat Meat Now

This boy went to the zoo and a lion got out, and the boy rushed down to the corridor of the zoo up there, and he was runnin' and runnin'! The keeper said, "Come back here, come on back here. What's the matter?" Say, "That lion," say, "is not going to bother you. That lion was raised up on a bottle."

The boy say, "Yeah, I was too, but I eat meat now."

555   Santa Lied

Once a mother asked her little son (he was about five years old) when Christmas was approaching, what did he want Santa Claus to bring him. And of course, as children are always wantin' the biggest things, he named all of the large things he wanted. And that Christmas his mother wasn't able to pay Santa to bring these things, so therefore he didn't get anything.

So the next year, coming up to Christmas, he never mentioned about Santa Claus. So his mother asked him one day, say, "Alvin, what do you want Santa Claus to bring you this Christmas?"

He say, "I don't want him to bring me *nothin'*, a *scoundrel!* He lied last year."

556   Bob White

Here's a man who had a dog who could spot a bird a hundred yards away, which was exceptionally well for a dog. And he bragged about the dog: "Oh, this dog can *spot* a bird. If a bird's around, he kin spot 'im!"

So then they was walkin' up the street and there was a man over in the corner. The dog went and pointed to the man.

So the man [with him] said, "Look at your dog. Your dog pointing to a man."

The man say, "It's a bird over there somewhere."

After they went over there and looked around, say, "No bird!"

He say, "Man, that dog gone crazy."

He say, "Man, it's a bird over here *somewhere.*"

So he told the guy, "Have you got a bird in your pocket or anything like that?"

The guy say, "No, ain't no birds around here."

He say, "Man, it's a bird somewhere 'round here, 'cause that dog wouldn't point if it wasn't a bird around here."

He say, "That dog done gone mad."

He looked *everywhere* for a bird. No *bird* in the vicinity. So he say, "I just can't understand why he would point to that man."

So they walked off.

He say, "Hey, wait, by the way, buddy, what's your name?"

The guy say, "Bob White."

557 When I Say "Scat"

There was a fellow who had about ten or twelve cats at his house, you know, and he had ten little holes in his door. One day he had a lot of visitors to come to his house, you know—men friends. And so one of 'em said to 'im, say, "John," say, "why is it that you have so many *holes* in that door? You got ten cats, but all of 'em can go out one hole, can't they?"

He say, "Yeah, but when I say 'Scat!' I *mean* scat!"

558 Interesting Names

There is a community or post office in Middlesex Country which is called No Head, and the story is that a man or a horse was seen there with no head. It was a ghost. Of course, these ghost stories were prevalent. Thus for many years, that place was known as No Head.

Now in my own community, there is an area just above me—Horsehead. All my life I knew it as Horsehead. And I wondered why it was called Horsehead, but I was told that there again a man was seen riding down the road (another ghost) on a horse that had no head.

Now you know a place out here in Hanover that they called Niggerfoot. After a long time they changed it and called it Negrofoot. I was anxious to know why they called it Negrofoot. The tradition is that Negrofoot was called Negrofoot because in slave times a Negro lost his foot there, either lost his foot or he was killed and they displayed his foot.

559   Peanut Butter

Two little Peanuts, sittin' on a railroad track, hearts all a-flutter;
Big choo-choo come running down the track, TOOT! TOOT!
Peanut butter!

560   The Vegetable Man

Don't you know I am the vegetable man,
I got sweet po-ta-toes and toma-toes
Beans—peas—cabbage, TURNips, rudibakers, salad, blackeye peas and
    beans.
But when you see me coming, with a basket in my ha-a-a-nd,
Don't—you—know I am the ve-ge-table man!

561   Crokidile Isle

I got something to tel-l-l you—'bout the Crokidile Isle;
I got SOMEthing to tel-l-l you—'bout the Crokidile Isle.
You see ole Crocky, comin' down the aisle,
Comin' down with a walkin' cane,
Comin' down that lane.
I got something to tell you—'bout the Crokidile Isle
When you see old Crocky comin' down the aisle,
Comin' down with a gold-head cane,
He's comin' down that lane.
I got something to tell you 'bout the Crokidile Isle.

562   If You Want to Go to Heaven

If you want to go to heaven when you d-i-e,
Put on your collar with a t-i-e;
If you don't want to die like a d-o-g,
Stop drinking bourbon like a h-o-g.

563 I Must Go

I must go,
Time I was gone;
That old sow is in my low-ground corn.
Track I see, I pursue,
And them lil' pigs was in there too.

564 The Eaf

Have you ever heard this thing called "The Eaf"? Ee-poop-se-de-da-pa-de-da.... Well, Bill Robinson and I used to go around and say that thing:

Went down the river and I couldn't get across;
Paid five dollars for a old gray horse.
The horse wouldn't pull,
I sold him for a bull.
The bull wouldn't holler,
I sold him for a dollar.
The dollar wouldn't pass,
I throwed it in the grass.
The grass wouldn't grow,
I sold it for a hoe.
The hoe wouldn't dig,
I sold it for a pig.
Pig wouldn't run,
I sold him for a gun.
Gun wouldn't shoot,
And I sold it for a boot.
Boot wouldn't wear,
And I sold it for a pear.
Pear wouldn't eat,
And I pitched it down the street.
Kitty had a cow and the cow had a calf;
Sold that calf for seven and a half.
Calf wouldn't pull,
And I sold it for a bull.
The bull wouldn't holler,
I sold him for a dollar.
The dollar wouldn't pass,
I throwed it in the grass.
The grass wouldn't grow,
I sold it for a hoe.
The hoe wouldn't dig,

I sold it for a pig.
Pig wouldn't run,
I sold it for a gun.
Gun wouldn't shoot,
And I sold it for a boot.

And then we start singing, "Ee-dooop, se-da-da-pa-de-da-pa-pop!"

565   February Cold

Oh, when the sun begins to shine,
All the Rounder wants is one thin dime;
For when the grass gets green,
I'm coming clean.
And when the wind begins to blow,
And then it begins to snow,
I tuck my head, and, I softly said,
"So *cold!*—So *cold!*— So *co-o-o-ld!*"
What do you mean when you say it's cold?
Do you mean soft coal? hard coal? nut coal? splint coal? charcoal?
No, I TALKin' 'bout February cold.

   I composed that song comin' down on the elevator, workin' at the Good
Luck Baking Powder [name of company changed] in February—one of the
coldest months I ever witnessed was in February. I composed that song
comin' down on the elevator.

Biographies of
Major Contributors

ASKEW, ELTON. Born in the Bronx, New York, in 1940, Mr. Askew grew up in Norfolk, Virginia, and attended St. Joseph's Catholic High School. He was incarcerated in the Virginia State Penitentiary at the time of our interview.

BOWMAN, CHARLES. Born in Charles City, Virginia, on February 22, 1935, the late Mr. Bowman was educated in the Charles City public schools and attended Virginia State College. Mr. Bowman was very active in political and civic affairs in his home town and was at the time of our interview serving as president of the Charles City NAACP. He worked at the Naval Weapons Station in Yorktown, where he was supervising production controller. A close friend and classmate of mine in public school, Mr. Bowman always had a ready wit and a store of good tales, many of which he learned from his father, the late Spencer Bowman.

BOWMAN, GARY. Born in 1951 in Charles City, Virginia, Mr. Bowman studied at Virginia State College and works as a metallurgical researcher at the Reynolds Metals Company in Richmond, Virginia.

BOWMAN, RICHARD. Older brother of Charles Bowman, Richard Bowman is a striking local oral historian who is full of facts and data about the history of Charles City County, Virginia, as well as numerous anecdotes regarding his family, many of which were told to him by his father. He is very active in the civic and political life of Charles City County and is presently the chairman of the Charles City County Board of Supervisors. He is a general foreman at the Naval Weapons Station in Yorktown, Virginia.

BRADLEY, VIOLA. A resident of Richmond, Virginia, Mrs. Bradley is a member of the West End Senior Citizens' Center.

BROWN, JULIUS. Born in Charles City County, Virginia, on May 8, 1899, Mr. Brown was educated in the public schools there. He worked as a laborer until his retirement. He is presently an active member of the Elam Baptist Church. Mr. Brown enjoys farming (I look forward to fresh vegetables from his garden each year) and is an avid bridge player.

BUCK, BEATRICE. Born and reared in Richmond, Virginia, Mrs. Buck attended the Richmond public schools. She heard most of the superstitions that she related to me from her mother and her mother-in-law.

BUCKRA, CYNTHIA. Born in 1894 in Orangeburg, South Carolina, where she heard many of her tales, Mrs. Buckra was reared by her brother and sister. She has been living in Richmond, Virginia, for at least twenty years.

CALENDER, CHARLES E. Born in Clifton Forge, Virginia, on August 6, 1921, Mr. Calender received his B.S. degree from Hampton Institute. He has also studied at Virginia State College and at Prairie View College. He is now the county farm agent in Charles City County, Virginia. A noted and much-sought-after storyteller in Charles City, Mr. Calender appeared in the 1976 Festival of American Folklife and plans one day to publish his repertoire of tales, many of which he learned in Clifton Forge.

CHEATHAM, CHARLES. Graduated from Armstrong High School in Richmond, Virginia, in 1965, Mr. Cheatham was at the time of our interview incarcerated in the Virginia State Penitentiary, where he is a member of the Creative Writers Workshop. He writes poetry, songs, and plays, two of which have been produced at the penitentiary.

CHEATHAM, MARTHA. Born in Glen Allen, Virginia, Mrs. Cheatham is now a resident of Richmond and a member of the Church Hill Senior Citizens' Center.

CRADDOCK, CLARENCE. Born in Charles City County, Virginia, on March 5, 1901, Mr. Craddock was educated in the Charles City public schools. He is a retired automobile mechanic.

CUMBER, VERONICA B. Born in Waynesboro, Virginia, on December 23, 1911, Mrs. Cumber attended primary school there until after the death of her father, when the family moved to Charles City, Virginia. She attended the Charles City public schools and Virginia Union University. She was graduated from Virginia State College and taught in the Charles City County schools until her retirement in 1974. Mrs. Cumber is active in church and civic affairs in Charles City.

DANCE, ROBERT T., SR. Born in Richmond, Virginia, on October 12, 1907, Mr. Dance attended the Richmond public schools. He began working in the post office when he was eighteen years old and retired as a postal station superintendent in 1969 after forty-two years of service. Active in church and community affairs, Mr. Dance is a deacon and former Sunday school superintendent in the Moore Street Baptist Church. He is a board member of the Richmond NAACP and of the Crusade for Voters. Mr. Dance learned most of his tales many years ago from friends in high school. A raconteur extraordinaire, Mr. Dance, my father-in-law, is a hit at parties, where he often entertains for hours with one tale, joke, or toast after another, always including his popular "Over the Hill" (p. 266).

DAVIS, MARION. Born in Charles City, Virginia, on July 4, 1906, Mr. Davis attended the Charles City County public schools. Now a retired railroad employee, he lives in New Haven, Connecticut.

EGGLESTON, LEMUEL VAUGHAN. Born on January 7, 1882, Mr. Eggleston was ninety-two at the time of our interview. Though he apologized for moving slowly ("Old Arthur has me"), he moves about quite well and has a remarkable memory. He cites the months, days, and years of events throughout his life and reinforces his points with quotations from poems, folk maxims, and the like. He was a close friend of the famed Bill ("Bojangles") Robinson and showed me a "bootblack box" that he and Bojangles used as shoeshine boys in Richmond. Mr. Eggleston eschews racial jokes and refused to allow me to tape-record any of his tales about the church or the minister. He is a highly conscious Black man who praises the beauty of the Blacks and freely cites evidence of the superior history and heritage of the Black race. Always ready with a quip, he greeted me with "I have four sides— inside, outside, religious side, and humorous side; now which side to you want?" He later explained that he didn't know any ghost stories: "If I'd believed in a ghost when I was growing up, we'd ask him to have a drink with us." While Mr. Eggleston portrays himself as something of a swinger in his day, he makes it quite clear that he neither smokes nor drinks now.

ELLIS, EDWARD. Born and reared in Richmond, Virginia, Mr. Ellis attended the Richmond public schools and was graduated from Armstrong High School. Until his retirement he was employed at the Reynolds Metal Company.

ELLISON, JOHN M. Born in 1889 in Reedsville, Virginia, Dr. Ellison has had a long and admirable career as a teacher, principal, college minister, and college president. He is the author of four books, at least ten brochures, and numerous articles. Though retired, Dr. Ellison still spends a few hours each day in his office in Ellison Hall, named in his honor, at Virginia Union University. He is presently the editor of the *Baptist Herald*.

EPPS, ERSELLE. A resident of Richmond, Virginia, Mrs. Epps is a member of the West End Senior Citizens' Center.

HARRIS, ARNOLD. Born in Richmond, Virginia, on September 22, 1903, Mr. Harris was adopted and reared by a Charles City couple. He attended the Charles City County public schools and worked as a laborer until his retirement.

HARRIS, PHILLIP M., JR. Born in Newport News, Virginia, on August 27, 1940, Mr. Harris grew up in Charles City County and attended the public schools there. He is an electronics mechanic.

HARVEY, JACK. Born in Williamsburg, Virginia, on February 20, 1934, Mr. Harvey grew up and attended school in Richmond. He now lives in Henrico County. One of the most prolific storytellers whom I interviewed, Mr. Harvey learned many of his tales during the ten years he spent in the Navy. He also learned some from friends in Richmond. He works as a clerk in the Richmond post office.

HAYES, CHARLES E. Born in Manchester (now South Richmond), Virginia, on May 23, 1879, the late Mr. Hayes was one of my most remarkable informants. A man with a vivid memory, he recalled with relish the days of his youth when he was a musician and a ladies' man ("women was my hobby") and sang some of the songs he made up. Mr. Hayes, who believed that his mother was a slave, furnished me with a great deal of interesting material—and he was well aware of his value to me. He informed me that I wouldn't find many like him. He was, he said, "made out of good leather," and he emphasized his point by comparing shoes made out of paper with shoes made out of leather.

HEDGEPETH, THELMA. Born in Alabama and educated at Fisk University in Nashville, Tennessee, Mrs. Hedgepeth recently moved to Richmond, Virginia. At the time of our interview she was chairperson of the department of mathematics at Virginia Union University. She first heard many of the tales she told me while growing up in Alabama and while attending Fisk University.

HUDSON, CALVIN. Born and reared in Portsmouth, Virginia, Mr. Hudson was at the time of our interview incarcerated in the Virginia State Penitentiary. He heard the toasts that he told me "from winos in Portsmouth around 1966."

HUNTER, MARIE. A talented singer and popular local actress, Mrs. Hunter is a teacher in the Richmond, Virginia, public schools. At the time of our interview she was living in Henrico County.

JOHNSON, PHOEBE. A native of Richmond, Virginia, Mrs. Johnson is a retired LPN. She heard the tales that she told me "from friends long ago."

KERSEY, JOAN. A teacher in Richmond, Virginia, and a resident of Henrico County, Mrs. Kersey told me tales that had been passed down in her family from her great-grandmother, who had been born into slavery in Mecklinburg, Virginia, and who lived until the early 1950s (she died at the age of 105).

LIBRON, ROBERT ("DOG"). Born in 1948 in Richmond, Virginia, Mr. Libron went to school in Philadelphia. Incarcerated in the Virginia State Penitentiary at the time of our interview, he is active in literary and musical projects. Three of his plays have been produced by the Creative Writers Workshop at the penitentiary.

LIPSCOMB, HOPSON. Because of the lack of birth records and the early death of his mother, Mr. Lipscomb can only conjecture that he was born "around about the middle of April" and "probably around about 1904." The most prolific of all of my informants, he was reared by foster parents, who were former slaves in the hills of Virginia. From his parents and their friends, who were also former slaves, Mr. Lipscomb heard many of the tales that he told me. He came to Richmond, Virginia, in the 1930s and worked as a laborer until he was incapacitated by an accident and by arthritis. He is a member of the First Street Senior Citizens' Center.

MICKENS, WALTER, JR. Born in Newport News, Virginia, in 1954, Mr. Mickens attended Carver High School. At the time of our interview, he was incarcerated in the Virginia State Penitentiary. He is a superb teller of toasts.

MOON, QUALLIE, SR. Born and reared in Richmond, Virginia, Mr. Moon was graduated from Virginia Union University and worked as a registered social worker for the state of Virginia until 1965, when he took a position as national alumni secretary and director of development at Virginia Union University, from which he retired in 1972. An avid bridge player who always brings a new tale to each of our bridge club meetings, Mr. Moon's first response when I requested biographical information from him was to ask that I note the grand slam that he and I made on May 7, 1976.

ROBINSON, DELORES. Born and reared in Richmond, Virginia, Mrs. Robinson was educated in the Richmond public schools and at Virginia Union University. Many of the anecdotes and tales in Mrs. Robinson's large repertoire were learned from her father, a native of Charles City County.

ROBINSON, THOMAS ("DYNAMITE"). Born in 1942 in Richmond, Virginia, Mr. Robinson graduated from Armstrong High School. The former boxer was at the time of our interview incarcerated in the Virginia State Penitentiary, where he was active in the Creative Writers Workshop.

ROBINSON, WALTER E. Born and reared in Richmond, Virginia, Mr. Robinson attended the public schools of that city. After serving in the armed forces, he returned to Richmond to found the W. E. Robinson Real Estate Company. A highly successful businessman, Mr. Robinson is active in civic and social affairs in Richmond.

STRAUGHN, WILLIAM JACKSON. Born in Louisa, Virginia, in 1891, Mr. Straughn lived in Englewood, New Jersey, from 1913 until 1952, when he moved back to Louisa. He is a veteran of World War I, a retired gardener, and remarkably youthful man. Mr. Straughn and his wife live in a cozy farmhouse in Louisa, where I visited them and collected several tales and songs that he had heard in Louisa "around the turn of the century."

WILDER, L. D. Born and reared in Richmond, Virginia, Mr. Wilder was graduated from Virginia Union University and received a law degree from Howard University. He has had a successful law practice in Richmond, Virginia, for several years and is the only Black man to serve in the Virginia State Senate since Reconstruction.

WILLIAMS, MOLLIE. Born in Charlotte County, Virginia, in 1888, Mrs. Williams now lives in Richmond. She is a member of the Church Hill Senior Citizens' Center.

WYATT, VIRGINIA. A resident of Richmond, Virginia, Mrs. Wyatt belongs to the West End Senior Citizens' Center.

YANCEY, PRESTON M. Mr. Yancey was born and reared in Georgia, where he learned many of the tales he told me. He was graduated from Morehouse College in Atlanta, Georgia, and is at present working on his Ph.D. degree at Syracuse University. He is acting chairman of the humanities faculty at Virginia Union University.

Annotations

Abbreviations

Afro-American Folk Lore   Christensen, A. M. H. *Afro-American Folk Lore: Told Round Cabin Fires on the Sea Islands of South Carolina.* Boston, 1898.

American Aesop   Pickens, William. *American Aesop: Negro and Other Humor.* Boston: Jordan and More, 1926.

American Negro Folklore   Brewer, J. Mason. *American Negro Folklore.* Chicago: Quadrangle, 1968.

American Negro Folktales   Dorson, Richard M. *American Negro Folktales.* Greenwich, Conn.: Fawcett, 1967.

Baughman   Baughman, Ernest W. *Type and Motif-Index of the Folktales of England and North America.* The Hague: Mouton, 1966.

Black Rage   Grier, William H., and Price M. Cobbs. *Black Rage.* New York: Bantam Books, 1969.

Book of Negro Folklore   Hughes, Langston, and Arna Bontemps, eds. *The Book of Negro Folklore.* New York: Dodd, Mead, 1958.

Book of Negro Humor   Hughes, Langston, ed. *The Book of Negro Humor.* New York: Dodd, Mead, 1966.

Brazos   Brewer, J. Mason. *The Word on the Brazos: Negro Preacher Tales from the Brazos Bottoms of Texas.* Austin: University of Texas Press, 1953.

Buying the Wind   Dorson, Richard M. *Buying the Wind.* Chicago: University of Chicago Press, 1964.

"Cats"   Emmons, Martha. "Cats and the Occult," *Publications of the Texas Folklore Society* 11 (1933): 94–100.

Congaree   Adams, Edward C. L. *Congaree Sketches: Scenes from Negro Life in the Swamps of the Congaree and Tales by Tad and Scip of Heaven and Hell with Other Miscellany.* Chapel Hill: University of North Carolina Press, 1927.

Deep Down   Abrahams, Roger D. *Deep Down in the Jungle: Negro Narrative Folklore from the Streets of Philadelphia.* 1st rev. ed. Chicago: Aldine, 1970.

Dog Ghosts   Brewer, J. Mason. *Dog Ghosts and Other Texas Negro Folk Tales.* Austin: University of Texas Press, 1958.

Dust Tracks on a Road   Hurston, Zora Neale. *Dust Tracks on a Road: An Autobiography.* Philadelphia: J. P. Lippincott, 1971.

Encyclopedia   Spalding, Henry D., ed. *Encyclopedia of Black Folklore and Humor.* Middle Village, N.Y.: Jonathon David, 1972.

Folk Culture on St. Helena Island   Johnson, Guy B. *Folk Culture on St. Helena Island, South Carolina.* Chapel Hill: University of North Carolina Press, 1930.

"Folk Lore from Aiken"   Parsons, Elsie Clews, "Folk Lore from Aiken, S.C.," *Journal of American Folklore* 34 (January-March, 1921): 1–39.

"Folklore from Antigua"   Johnson, John H. "Folklore from Antigua, British West Indies," *Journal of American Folklore* 34 (January-March, 1921): 40–88.

"Folk-lore from Elizabeth City"   Bacon, A. M., and E. C. Parsons. "Folklore from Elizabeth City County, Va.," *Journal of American Folklore* 35 (January-March, 1922): 250–327.

"Folk-Lore from Virginia"   Smiley, Portia. "Folk-Lore from Virginia, South Carolina, Georgia, Alabama, and Florida," *Journal of American Folklore* 32 (July-September, 1919): 357–84.

The Folk Songs   Lomax, Alan. *The Folk Songs of North America.* Garden City, N.Y.: Doubleday, 1960.

"Get Your Ass in the Water"   Jackson, Bruce. "Get Your Ass in the Water and Swim Like Me." Cambridge: Harvard University Press, 1974.

Hoodoo   Hyatt, Harry Middleton. *Hoodoo-Conjuration-Witchcraft-Rootwork: Memoirs of the Alma Egan Hyatt Foundation.* Washington, D.C.: American University Bookstore, 1970.

"I Swear"   Perdue, Chuck. "I Swear to God It's the Truth If I Ever Told It," *Keystone Folklore Quarterly* 14 (Spring, 1969): full issue.

JAFL   *Journal of American Folklore*

Jokes   Haskins, Jim. *Jokes from Black Folks.* Garden City, N.Y.: Doubleday, 1973.

Lay My Burden Down   Botkin, B. A., ed. *Lay My Burden Down: A Folk History of Slavery.* Chicago: University of Chicago Press, 1945.

Laughing   Sterling, Philip. *Laughing on the Outside: The Intelligent White Reader's Guide to Negro Tales and Humor.* New York: Grosset and Dunlap, 1965.

"Miami"   Parsons, Elsie Clews. "Folk-Tales Collected at Miami, Florida," *Journal of American Folklore* 30 (January-March, 1917), 222–27.

Michigan   Dorson, Richard M. *Negro Folktales in Michigan.* Cambridge: Harvard University Press, 1956.

Mother Wit   Dundes, Alan, ed. *Mother Wit from the Laughing Barrel: Readings in the Interpretation of Afro-American Folklore.* Englewood Cliffs, N.J.: Prentice-Hall, 1973.

Motif-Index   Thompson, Stith. *Motif-Index of Folk-Literature.* Rev. ed. 6 vols. Bloomington: Indiana University Press, 1955.

Mules and Men   Hurston, Zora Neale. *Mules and Men.* Philadelphia: J. P. Lippincott, 1935.

"Negro Tales from Bolivar County"   Dorson, Richard M. "Negro Tales from Bolivar County, Mississippi," *Southern Folklore Quarterly* 19 (June, 1955): 104–16.

"New York"   Irvis, K. Leroy. "Negro Tales from Eastern New York," *New York Folklore Quarterly* 11 (1955): 165–76.

Nights with Uncle Remus   Harris, Joel Chandler. *Nights with Uncle Remus: Myths and Legends of the Old Plantation.* New York: Houghton Mifflin, 1883.

"Old-Time"   Brewer, J. Mason. "Old-Time Negro Proverbs," *Publications of the Texas Folklore Society* 11 (1933): 101–5.

Pine Bluff   Dorson, Richard M. *Negro Tales from Pine Bluff, Arkansas, and Calvin, Michigan.* Bloomington: Indiana University Press, 1970.

Positively Black   Abrahams, Roger D. *Positively Black.* Englewood Cliffs, N.J.: Prentice-Hall, 1970.

Rationale   Legman, G[ershon]. *Rationale of the Dirty Joke: An Analysis of Sexual Humor.* New York: Grove Press, 1971.

Sea Islands   Parsons, Elsie Crews. *Folk-Lore of the Sea Islands, South Carolina.* Chicago: Afro-American Press, 1969.

"South"   Fauset, Arthur Huff. "Negro Folk-Tales from the South," *Journal of American Folklore* 40 (July-September, 1927): 213–303.

"Tales and Riddles"   Fauset, Arthur Huff. "Tales and Riddles Collected in Philadelphia," *Journal of American Folklore* 41 (October-December, 1928): 529–57.

"Toasts"   Labov, William, et al. "Toasts," in *Mother Wit from the Laughing Barrel*, pp. 55–76 (reprinted from Labov et al., *A Study of the Non-Standard English of Negro and Puerto Rican Speakers in New York.* Vol. 2. "The Use of Language in the Speech Community." Cooperative Research Project No. 3288 [New York: Columbia University Press, 1968]).

Tone the Bell Easy   Dobie, J. Frank. *Tone the Bell Easy.* Dallas: Southern Methodist University Press, 1932.

Treasury of American Folklore   Botkin, B. A. *A Treasury of American Folklore.* New York: Crown, 1944.

Treasury of Southern Folklore   Botkin, B. A. *A Treasury of Southern Folklore.* New York: Brown, 1949.

Uncle Remus: His Songs and His Sayings   Harris, Joel Chandler. *Uncle Remus: His Songs and His Sayings.* Rev. ed. New York: D. Appleton, 1947.

"West Virginia"   Cox, John H. "Negro Tales from West Virginia," *Journal of American Folklore* 47 (January-March, 1934): 341–57.

Worser   Brewer, J. Mason. *Worser Days and Better Times: The Folklore of the North Carolina Negro.* Chicago: Quadrangle, 1965.

WPA, UVA   Unpublished materials from the Writers' Projects Administration Collection in Virginia, Virginia Folklore Archives at the Alderman Library, the University of Virginia. These materials have been indexed by Charles L. Purdue, Jr., Thomas E. Barden, and Robert K. Phillips (*Afro-American Folklore of the WPA Folklore Files in the Alderman Library*). Interviews from this collection have been published in Charles L. Purdue, Jr., Thomas E. Barden, and Robert K. Phillips, eds., *Weevils in the Wheat: Interviews with Virginia Ex-Slaves* (Charlottesville: University Press of Virginia, 1976).

1 Collected in Charles City, Virginia, on March 19, 1975, from an informant who heard it in Clifton Forge, Virginia, where he grew up.

This account of how the races got their color is a variant of the usual accounts and is one which I have not discovered elsewhere. In the versions closest to this tale all the people except the Blacks respond promptly when God calls the people to get their color. The Blacks come running in late and crowd around the Lord, who yells to them, "Git back!" They misunderstand and think he told them "Git black!" See *Mules and Men*, pp. 48–49; *Dust Tracks on a Road*, pp. 74–77 (reprinted in *Treasury of Southern Folklore*, pp. 482–83); "Figure and Fancy" in *Book of Negro Folklore*, pp. 125–27; and "Why the Negro is Black" in *American Negro Folklore*, pp. 20–21.

Several previously collected tales combine the explanation of the Black's color and hair in the same tale. Joel Chandler Harris' "Why the Negro Is Black" suggests that in the beginning everyone was black and had kinky hair. The news came that people could go to a pond and wash off the black. Those who got there first washed the kinks out of their hair and came out white; the next ones came out mulatto; but the niggers, who were last, only had enough water for the palms of their hands and the soles of their feet. See *Uncle Remus: His Songs and His Sayings*, pp. 166–68 (reprinted in *American Negro Folklore*, pp. 20–21). A similar version is "All Folks Was Born Black" in *American Stuff*, pp. 150–51 (reprinted in *Treasury of American Folklore*, pp. 428–29). In another variant, God made the people and put them out to dry. The nigger went to sleep and didn't go when God called the people to finish them up. When the nigger woke up he was black with kinky hair. See "Sleepy Head, Kinky Head" in *Diddie, Dumps, and Tot; or Plantation Child-Life* (New York: Harper & bros., 1882), pp. 206–7 (reprinted in *A Treasury of American Folklore*, p. 429).

2   Collected in Richmond, Virginia, on January 15, 1975, from an informant to whom the tale had been passed down from her grandmother through her mother.

See Motif A1614.5. "*Negroes made from left-over scraps at creation,*" *Motif-Index*.

3   Version A: Collected in Richmond, Virginia, on January 13, 1975, from an informant who heard it in Alabama, her home state. Version B: Collected in Richmond, Virginia, on October 26, 1970.

I have been unable to discover any previously published versions of these tales. In addition to those previously cited tales in which an explanation for the Blacks' hair and color is combined, some other tales suggest that their "bad" hair is a punishment for tardiness. In "Why the Negro has Curly Hair" in *Michigan*, pp. 78–79 (reprinted in *American Negro Folktales*, p. 136), the other people get all the good hair while the Blacks finish their watermelon. They come in late and all that is left is what the others did not want and had stepped all over. In "How Negroes Got Their Hair" in *Laughing*, p. 170, the Black again gets nappy hair because he is late. (In this same tale he rushes next time to get feet and gets the biggest ones.) Conversely, in "How the Negro Got His Hair" in *Pine Bluff*, p. 184 (reprinted in *American Negro Folktales*, pp. 176–77), the Black gets the kinky hair because he is in such a big hurry.

4   Collected in Richmond, Virginia, on January 30, 1970.

A version is included in "How Negroes Got Their Hair" in *Laughing*, p. 170.

5   Collected in Richmond, Virginia, on November 20, 1974.

I have been unable to discover another previously published version where the Black man selects the small bag. For a discussion of variants see annotation 1.

6   Version A: Collected in Richmond, Virginia, on February 6, 1975, from an informant who heard it in the "hills of Virginia," where he grew up. Version B: Collected in Richmond, Virginia, on March 7, 1975.

In only one collection have I come across a text that closely parallels the versions presented here, and that is in *Positively Black*, p. ix, where the characters are a white man, a Mexican, and a Black man. A very close text is, however, also included by Cecil Brown in his novel, *The Life and Loves of Mr. Jiveass Nigger* (New York: Farrar, Straus, and Giroux, 1970), pp. 59–60. A variant, which explains why the church is split up and in which the principals are Jesus and His disciples, is found in *Mules and Men*, pp. 45–46 (reprinted in *American Negro Folklore*, pp. 25–26), and in *Michigan*, pp. 158–59.

7   Collected in Richmond, Virginia, on January 22, 1975.

My informant, who was ninety-six years old at the time of our interview, accepts this account as historical truth and insists that it is (or at least was) widespread. Exhaustive research on my part has failed to uncover any other close version, but I did discover two other accounts where certain key elements in the tales are similar: the Blacks' attraction to red was used to entrap them, and (in the version above and in one of the variants) their curiosity contributed to their enslavement. In "Red Flannel" one former slave gives an account which she had heard from "Granny Judith," who told her that the white men enticed the Africans onto their ships by dropping pieces of red cloth before them all the way up into the ship. Then when they got as many Blacks as they wanted, they chained the gate up and the Blacks couldn't get off (see *Lay My Burden Down*, pp. 57–58). Another informant, Prince Baskin, related to A. M. H. Christensen his grandfather's account of his captivity: "... an' when dey [white men in Africa] meet up wid my gran'daddy an' a whole parcel more, young boys like, all from de same village, dey hire dem on bo'd de ship dey bring dem ober to dis country an' sell dem for slave" (see *Afro-American Folklore*, p. 4). Richard S. Tallman, co-editor of the *Southern Folklore Quarterly*, informed me that a student of his collected three longer versions of this tale from an elderly Black woman in South Carolina in 1973. Hurston notes in *Dust Tracks on a Road* that she was "brought up" on the folklore "that the white people had gone to Africa, waved a red handkerchief at the Africans, and lured them aboard ship and sailed away" (p. 208).

8   Collected in Richmond, Virginia, on January 31, 1975.

Combination of K371.1. "*Trickster throws fish off the wagon*" and A2216.1. "*Bear fishes through ice with tail*," *Motif-Index*. Variants of this popular tale appear in numerous collections. In most versions Rabbit plays dead and steals Brer Fox's fish, and one of the animals fools Brer Rabbit into fishing with his tail and thereby losing it. For different versions of this tale see "De Reason Br'er Rabbit Wears a Short Tail" in *Afro-American Folklore*, pp. 26–35; "Cartload of Fish" (two versions) and "Who Dives the Longest:

Cartload of Fish" in *Sea Islands*, pp. 39–40; "How Mr. Rabbit Lost His Fine Bushy Tail" in *Uncle Remus: His Songs and His Sayings*, pp. 108–11 (reprinted in *American Negro Folklore*, p. 12); "Playing Dead Twice in the Road" and "Fishing with Tail" in "'Folklore from Aiken," pp. 11–12; "Why Rabbit Has a Short Tail" in "Folklore from Antigua," p. 67; "Playing Dead Twice in the Road" in "Folk-lore from Elizabeth City," pp. 275–76; "Playing Dead in the Road" in *Folk Culture on St. Helena Island*, p. 146; "Why the Rabbit Has a Short Tail" in *Michigan*, pp. 38–39 (reprinted in *American Negro Folktales*, pp. 89–91); "Playing Dead in the Road" in *Pine Bluff*, pp. 28–30 (reprinted in *American Negro Folktales*, pp. 91–92); and "Fox and Rabbit" in "I Swear," pp. 20–21.

9   Collected in Henrico, Virginia, on March 11, 1975.
No previously published versions were discovered.

10   Collected in Richmond, Virginia, on January 31, 1975.
See Motif A2275.5.5. "*Dog loses his patent right; seeks it*," *Motif-Index*. Thompson notes that this slightly similar tale has been collected in the United States by Baughman.

11   Collected in Richmond, Virginia, on February 27, 1975.
The text here is a composite of several different versions that the informant gave me.

12   Collected in Richmond, Virginia, on January 31, 1975.
For a discussion of other versions, see annotation 13.

13   Version A: Collected in Richmond, Virginia, on January 13, 1975. Version B: Collected in Richmond, Virginia, on January 31, 1975.
For other versions of this popular tale see "Zip, Zip" in "Folk-Lore from Virginia," p. 365; "The Hopkins Nigger" in *Congaree*, pp. 2–4; William A. Percy, *Lanterns on the Levee* (New York: Alfred A. Knopf, 1941), pp. 292–93 (reprinted in *Treasury of Southern Folklore*, p. 111); "Colored Man in Heaven" in *Michigan*, pp. 79–81; and *Laughing*, pp. 133–34.

14   Collected in Richmond, Virginia, on January 31, 1975.
For other versions see "Hell in Heaven" in Folk-Lore from Virginia," p. 374; *Brazos*, pp. 81–82; *Positively Black*, p. 133; and "St. Peter Didn't Want Any Trouble" in *Laughing*, pp. 137–38.

15   Collected in Henrico, Virginia, on March 11, 1975.
A version appears in *Worser*, pp. 42–43.

16   Collected in Richmond, Virginia, on March 31, 1975.

17   Collected in Richmond, Virginia, on March 7, 1975.

18   Collected in Charles City, Virginia, on November 12, 1974.

19   Collected in Richmond, Virginia, on December 9, 1974.

20   Given to me in manuscript form by a retired teacher from Charles City, Virginia, on March 15, 1975.

21   Collected in Charles City, Virginia, on November 13, 1974, from a native of Charles City who now lives in Richmond, Virginia.
   A variant appears in *Rationale,* pp. 388–89.

22   Collected in Richmond, Virginia, on January 13, 1975.
   Two versions appear as "The Devil's Choices" in *Deep Down,* pp. 234–35.

23   This variant of the preceding tale, "Don't Make a Wave," was collected in Capahosic, Virginia, on May 12, 1975.

24   Version A: Collected in Richmond, Virginia, on November 20, 1970.
Version B: Collected in Richmond, Virginia, on November 20, 1974.
   Although this is a popular tale in the Richmond area and although I heard several versions, I have discovered no published versions.

25   Collected in Richmond, Virginia, on November 19, 1974.
   See *Motif* V113.1. *"Cripples at shrine frightened and run away without crutches," Motif-Index.*

26   Collected in Richmond, Virginia, on November 19, 1974.
   See Motif X143.1. Lame man is taken on hunt on stretcher . . ., Baughman.
   For other versions see "Miami," p. 184; "South," p. 272; "The Aged Hunter" in *Laughing,* p. 144; and "Master Seth's Cure" in *Tone the Bell Easy,* pp. 38–39.

27   Collected in Richmond, Virginia, on January 31, 1975.

28   Collected in Richmond, Virginia, on January 31, 1975.

29   Collected in Richmond, Virginia, on January 31, 1975.
   This tale is similar to "Belton's Spirit" in *Congaree,* pp. 68–69.

30   Collected in Richmond, Virginia, on February 2, 1975, from an informant who says it is a true incident.
   See Motif E423.1.1. Reverent as dog, Baughman.
   Tales of dog spirits are very popular among Black Americans, as indicated by *Dog Ghosts,* a large collection of these tales. Brewer notes, "As far as I have been able to ascertain, the dog spirit tale is not a part of any oral American tradition except that of the Negro" (*Dog Ghosts,* p. 3). For other tales of dog ghosts, see "Spirit Dog" in *Pine Bluff,* pp. 192–93, and "The Ghost Dog" in "I Swear," pp. 16–17.

31   Collected in Richmond, Virginia, on January 31, 1975.

32 Collected in Richmond, Virginia, on January 31, 1975.

33 Collected in Richmond, Virginia, on January 31, 1975.
See Motif Q223.6.2(e). Men hunting after midnight on Saturday are frightened by ghostly raccoon, Baughman.
A version is found in "Hunting on Sunday," in "Folk-lore from Elizabeth City," pp. 295–96, and in Hoodoo, p. 43, no. 120. Baughman cites a version in Carl Carmer, Stars Fell on Alabama (New York: Farrar and Rinehard, 1940), pp. 163–67.

34 Collected in Richmond, Virginia, on January 31, 1975.

35 Collected in Richmond, Virginia, on January 31, 1975.

36 Collected in Richmond, Virginia, on February 6, 1975.

37 Collected in Richmond, Virginia, on January 31, 1975.
See Motif N384.2. "Death in the graveyard: person's clothing is caught," Motif-Index. This is Type 1676B. Clothing caught in graveyard, Baughman. Thompson points out that versions of this tale have been collected in Ireland, England, and the United States. Baughman cites several versions collected from whites.
For another version from Black Americans see "Tales and Riddles," p. 548.

38 Version A: Collected in Louisa, Virginia, on January 10, 1975, from an informant who heard it from his uncle. Version B: Collected in Richmond, Virginia, on January 31, 1975.
See Motif J1495.1. "Man runs from actual or from supposed ghost," Motif-Index, and Motif J1495.3. Man attempts to stay in haunted house all night..., Baughman.
Variants are "Racing a Ghost" in Sea Islands, pp. 71–73 (four variants); "Racing a Ghost" in "Folklore from Virginia," pp. 367–68; "Nobody but You, Directly" in "Folk Lore from Aiken," p. 21; "Nobody but I and You" in "Tales and Riddles," p. 542; "South," p. 259; "West Virginia," pp. 355–56; "Racing with a Black Cat" in John A. Lomax, Adventures of a Ballad Hunter (New York: Hafner, 1947), pp. 184–85 (reprinted in Treasury of Southern Folklore, pp. 438–39). Other variants are in Hoodoo, p. 62, no. 217; WPA, UVA, Box 2, Folder 1; and WPA, UVA, Box 2, Folder 9.

39 Version A: Collected in Richmond, Virginia, on November 20, 1974. Version B: Collected in Charles City, Virginia, on March 19, 1975.
For versions see "The Three Preachers" in "Negro Tales from Bolivar County," pp. 111–12 (reprinted as "The Baptist, Methodist, and Presbyterian Preachers" in Negro American Folklore, p. 240), and "The Three Preachers" in Book of Negro Folklore, p. 140.

40 Collected in Richmond, Virginia, on December 20, 1974, from an informant who says it is a true incident.
Several cooling board tales are in Pine Bluff, pp. 82–86.

41   Collected in Richmond, Virginia, on January 31, 1975.
See Motifs E451.4.1. *"Ghost asked to identify self in name of God"* and
E451.5. *"Ghost laid when treasure is unearthed,"* *Motif-Index.*
For a version see "Ghost and the Treasure" in "I Swear," pp. 21–22.

42   Collected in Richmond, Virginia, on November 20, 1974. This anecdote
was a response to version B of "Pass the Collection Plate" (p. 29).

43   Version A: Collected in Richmond, Virginia, on November 20, 1974.
This version was given in response to "Pass the Collection Plate" (p. 28)
and "Where Money Is, Evil Is" (p. 30). A part of the tale was missed during
a change of tapes; I have summarized the missing material in brackets.
Version B: Collected at the Virginia State Penitentiary on December 2, 1974.
See Motif H1411.1. *"Fear test: staying in haunted house where corpse
drops piecemeal down chimney,"* *Motif-Index.*
A variant appears in *Deep Down*, pp. 181–82. Two versions appear in
Hoodoo, pp. 62–63.
The term *cush*, which I first heard when I collected this tale, is not gener-
ally found in dictionaries. I discovered, however, that it is a common word
among many Black people. My mother defined it as "a kind of corn bread."
M. M. Matthews says that *cush* is a preservation by the Gullahs of the
African word *kushkush*, which prevails in northern Nigeria and in Angola.
He notes that "in some of the dialects it is used of a thin cake made of
ground-nuts, but in others it means a wheaten food, or parched meal" and
that in the South it is used to mean dressing ("Some Sources of Southern-
isms" in *Treasury of Southern Folklore*, p. 568).

44   Collected in Richmond, Virginia, on January 31, 1975.
Several Charles City correspondents told me similar tales of the appear-
ance of people who had just died.

45   Collected in Richmond, Virginia, on December 20, 1974, from an informant who said that it tells of a true incident.

46   Collected in Richmond, Virginia, on January 22, 1975, from an in-
formant who said that it was told to her by an old neighbor in Spotsylvania,
Virginia.
See Motif E272.1(a). Ghost clings to back of carriage or cart, Baughman.
The belief that spirits make things heavy is discussed in *Hoodoo*, p. 26.

47   Collected in Richmond, Virginia, on January 31, 1975.
See Motif X424. *"The Devil in the Cemetery,"* *Motif-Index*, and Type
1791. The sexton carries the parson, Baughman.
Several versions of this tale, which is also popular in Europe and among
white Americans, have been collected from Black informants in America.
There are two versions in "Dividing the Souls" in *Sea Islands*, p. 68, in
which men divide stolen potatoes. In "Dividing the Souls" in "Folk-lore
from Elizabeth City," pp. 296–97, a slave and an old lame man at the gate are
frightened so much that the lame man runs. In "Voices in the Graveyard" in
Tone the Bell Easy, pp. 39–40 (reprinted in *Book of Negro Folklore*, pp.

79–90), a slave and his master are frightened by two slaves dividing stolen sweet potatoes. In a version in *Mules and Men*, pp. 117–19 (reprinted as "God an' de Devil in de Cemetery" in *Treasury of American Folklore*, pp. 444–45), a slave and his crippled master are frightened, and the master beats the slave back home. In "Negro Tales from Bolivar County," p. 111, white boys and colored boys are in the cemetery with stolen articles, and the colored boys are frightened by the white boys. "Dividing the Souls" in *Pine Bluff*, pp. 48–50 (reprinted in *American Negro Folktales*, pp. 146–47), combines this tale with the tale of the slave who is killed for talking too much; see my "Tongue and Teeth" (p. 84). A slave and his master are frightened in the following versions: "God and the Devil Counting Souls" in *Laughing*, p. 51, and Harry Oster, "Negro Humor: John and Old Marster" in *Mother Wit*, pp. 553–55 (reprinted from *Journal of the Folklore Institute* 5 [1968]). See also WPA, UVA, Box 2, Folder 1. I have additional versions recorded in Charles City and Richmond.

After beginning this tale ("two little boys, they stole some walnuts"), the teller asked me, "You know what walnuts are?" This informant, evidently annoyed by my frequent requests for explanations of unfamiliar, old expressions, had obviously decided by this time that I didn't know anything.

48   Collected in Richmond, Virginia, on January 31, 1975.
   See Motif B343. *"Cat leaves home when report is made of death of one of his companions,"* Motif-Index; Type 113A. "King of the Cats Is Dead," Baughman; and Motif B342(c). A strange cat comes down the chimney . . ., Baughman. See "Cats," p. 99.
   A variant is "The Black Cat's Message" in *Treasury of Southern Folklore*, pp. 540–41 (reprinted from *Spur-of-the-Cock*, ed. J. Frank Dobie [Austin: Texas Folklore Society, 1933], pp. 99–100).

49   Collected in Richmond, Virginia, on February 6, 1975.
   See Motif K1682.1. *"Big 'Fraid and Little 'Fraid,"* Motif-Index, and Type 1676A. "Big 'Fraid and Little 'Fraid," Baughman.
   This widely popular tale, which has been collected in Canada, England, and Wales and among white Americans, appears in the following collections from Negro informants: "Miami," p. 227; "Big-'Fraid and Little-'Fraid" in "Folk-Lore from Virginia," pp. 359–60; "South," p. 269; "Big Fear and Little Fear" in "Tales and Riddles," pp. 549–550; "The Monkey Who Impitated His Master" in *Michigan*, pp. 187–88 (reprinted in *American Negro Folktales*, pp. 349–50); and "Fatal Imitation" in *Lay My Burden Down*, p. 23.

50   Collected in Capahosic, Virginia, on May 12, 1975, from an informant who lives in Richmond, Virginia.
   For variants see "The Settin' Up" in *Congaree*, pp. 29–30.

51   This account of a true experience was related to me in Richmond, Virginia, on February 6, 1975.

52   Collected in Richmond, Virginia, on February 6, 1975.

53   The principal speaker in this interesting conversation delivered the

lines from the song with such feeling that it evoked considerable audience response from the other members of the Church Hill Senior Citizens' Center (Richmond, Virginia) who were present during this session on December 20, 1974.

54 Collected in Richmond, Virginia, on February 6, 1975.

55 Two versions were collected from the same informant in Richmond, Virginia, on January 31, 1975 and February 2, 1975. The text here combines the two.

56 Collected in Richmond, Virginia, on January 31, 1975.
    Several informants relate similar tales detailing the preparations of the black cat bone in *Hoodoo*, pp. 74–75, and a full section (pp. 74–97) deals with superstitions among Blacks and whites regarding the black cat bone. See also a description of this ritual in *Mules and Men*, pp. 272–73.

57 Collected in Charles City, Virginia, on November 12, 1974.

58 Version A: Collected in Louisa, Virginia, on January 10, 1975. Version B: Collected in Richmond, Virginia, on January 13, 1975. Version C: Collected in Henrico, Virginia, on March 11, 1975.
    See Motif X435.1. "What says David?" *Motif-Index*. Type 1833A. "What Says David?" Baughman.
    For other versions see "What John Said" in *Laughing*, p. 116, in which the minister likewise sends his son for meat; "What Did John Say?" in "Negro Tales from Bolivar County," pp. 112–13, in which the preacher sends the slave to John for steak; and "What Did Paul Say?" in *Pine Bluff*, pp. 255–56, in which the minister sends his son to his brother for whiskey (reprinted in *American Negro Folktales*, pp. 366–67).

59 Collected in Richmond, Virginia, on January 13, 1975.
    A variant in which the master reads for the illiterate slave Preacher appears as "Juneteenth" in *Tone the Bell Easy*, pp. 32–33.

60 Collected in Richmond, Virginia, on November 19, 1974.

61 Collected in Richmond, Virginia, on February 24, 1975.

62 Collected in Richmond, Virginia, on January 31, 1975.
    The text here includes additions made by the informant after the story was taped.

63 Collected in Richmond, Virginia, on February 6, 1975. Another version was collected in Charles City, Virginia, in November, 1974.
    See Type 1738. "The Dream: All Parsons in Hell," Baughman, and Motif X459(d). Parson arrives late for meeting of ministers, Baughman.
    For another version see *Brazos*, pp. 91–92.

64 Collected in Richmond, Virginia, on January 31, 1975.

65 Collected in Richmond, Virginia, on March 5, 1975.
See Motif X438. *"The dream: all parsons in hell,"* *Motif-Index.*

66 This popular tale (one that my husband frequently tells) was written out by a student at Virginia State College in Petersburg, Virginia, on November 27, 1970, and given to me by Professor Joseph Jenkins.
Other versions are "Farewell" in *Book of Negro Humor,* p. 35, and in *Encyclopedia,* p. 510.

67 Collected in Richmond, Virginia, on October 23, 1974.

68 Collected in Richmond, Virginia, on March 5, 1975.
A variant is "Why Dooger Woods Changed His Text" in *Worser,* p. 53.

69 Collected in Henrico, Virginia, on March 11, 1975.

70 Collected in Richmond, Virginia, on January 13, 1975.
A version is "Same Tune, Different Words" in *Laughing,* pp. 125–26. See also "The Baptizing Disturbed" in *Michigan,* pp. 172–73, and WPA, UVA, Box 2, Folder 9.

71 Collected in Richmond, Virginia, in June, 1975.
A version is "The Palacios Rancher and the Preacher" in *Dog Ghosts,* pp. 60–61.

72 Collected in Richmond, Virginia, on March 5, 1975.
A variant in which the corpse is a humpback who had been tied down in the coffin appears in *American Negro Folktales,* pp. 330–31.

73 Collected at the Virginia State Penitentiary on December 2, 1974. The text here is slightly condensed to omit a few repetitions from the taped version.
See Type 1833J. "Preacher Says: 'Let Gabriel Blow His Horn!'" Baughman.
For additional versions see "God and Fortune" in *Sea Islands,* p. 58; "Gabriel Blows His Horn" in "Tales and Riddles," p. 552; "Blow, Gabriel, Blow" in *Michigan* (reprinted in *American Negro Folktales,* p. 336); "Guest Artist" in *Laughing,* pp. 118–19; *Deep Down,* pp. 207–8; "Preacher, Ghost, and Trumpet" in "I Swear," p. 33; and "New York," p. 176. In the version collected by Dorson the minister suffers the added humiliation of running into the hogpen in his fear.

74 Collected in Richmond, Virginia, on October 2, 1974.

75 Collected in Charles City, Virginia, on November 12, 1974.

76 Collected in Richmond, Virginia, on December 12, 1974.

77 Collected in Richmond, Virginia, in February, 1975. The facility and delight with which the informant, Hopson Lipscomb, mimicked sounds of

the barnyard animals cannot possibly be described or transcribed, and can only be appreciated when one hears a master storyteller such as Mr. Lipscomb tell the tale.

See Motif X459.2(6). Fowls hide when preacher comes to visit, Baughman.

Several variants of this popular tale have been collected. See "Barnyard Talk" in Treasury of Southern Folklore, p. 511 (reprinted from Stetson Kennedy, Palmetto Country [New York, 1942], pp. 143–44); "What the Fowl Said" in Lay My Burden Down, p. 24; "Preacher and Fowls" in "Negro Tales from Bolivar County," pp. 107–9; "The Preacher and the Guinea" in Michigan, pp. 47–48 (reprinted in American Negro Folktales, pp. 119–20); "Preacher and Fowls" in Pine Bluff, p. 38; and Lydia Parrish, Slave Songs of the Georgia Sea Islands (Hatboro, Pa.: Folklore Associates, 1965), p. 40.

78　Collected in Richmond, Virginia, on October 2, 1974, from an informant who refused to allow me to tape any of his jokes that in any way derogated the church. The text here, therefore, is not verbatim but based on my handwritten notes.

79　Version A: Collected in Richmond, Virginia, on April 4, 1975. Version B: Collected in Richmond, Virginia, on November 19, 1974.

80　Version A: Collected in Richmond, Virginia, on January 13, 1975. Version B: Collected in Charles City, Virginia, on November 12, 1974.

See Motif X4451. "Parson takes a drink of liquor during the sermon," Motif-Index.

This tale, which is very popular in Virginia, is, according to Brewer, also well known in Scandinavia (Worser, p. 50). For other versions collected in this country from American Blacks, see "A Little While I Gone" in Sea Islands, p. 127; "The Preacher, the Deacon and the Fresh Air" in Worser, pp. 49–50; and Positively Black, pp. 104–5.

81　Collected in Richmond, Virginia, on February 24, 1975.

82　This joke was told to me in Petersburg, Virginia, in the fall of 1971. The text here is reproduced from memory.

83　Collected in Richmond, Virginia, on April 4, 1975.

A variant appears in Rationale, p. 538.

84　Collected in Richmond, Virginia, on April 4, 1975.

85　Version A: Collected in Richmond, Virginia, on November 20, 1974. Version B: Collected in Charles City, Virginia, in November, 1974.

Several versions are noted by Legman, who calls this "the best-known of all jokes on English literalism" (Rationale, p. 177).

86　Collected in Charles City, Virginia, in November, 1974.

87　Collected in Richmond, Virginia, on October 2, 1974, from an informant who made me turn off the recorder when he gave me certain jokes which he considered too risqué to be recorded. The text here, therefore, is not verbatim but based on notes taken during the telling of the joke.

88   Collected in Richmond, Virginia, on November 20, 1974.

89   Collected in Richmond, Virginia, on March 11, 1975.

90   Collected in Henrico, Virginia, on March 11, 1975.
   A variant in which the principals are a tired bridegroom and his insatiable new bride appears in *Rationale*, p. 489.

91   Collected in Charles City, Virginia, on April 23, 1975.
   This is a popular tale in the Richmond area, where I have heard it several times though I've recorded it only once. This type of joke is called an action joke because the teller dramatizes throughout, and it relies for much of its humor on the dramatization.
   A version appears in *Rationale*, p. 419.

92   Collected at the Virginia State Penitentiary, on November 27, 1974.
   A greatly condensed version, which was collected by Legman in California in 1952, appears in *Rationale*, p. 552.

93   Collected in Charles City, Virginia, on November 12, 1974.
   See Motif X459.2. Young couple agree to house one of the ministers, Baughman.
   A version is "The Visitors" in *Laughing*, p. 121. Baughman cites a version from a white source.

94   Collected in Henrico, Virginia, on March 11, 1965.

95   Collected in Richmond, Virginia, on November 19, 1974.

96   Collected in Charles City, Virginia, on November 12, 1974.
   Because this anecdote is about an actual member of the community, the name has been changed by me.
   Services at this small rural church were held once a month on the first Sunday.

97   Version A: Collected in Richmond, Virginia, on January 13, 1975. Version B: Collected in Richmond, Virginia, on February 6, 1975.
   See Motif X418, "*Parson is to let a dove fly in the church,*" *Motif-Index.*

98   Version A: Collected in Richmond, Virginia, on April 4, 1975. Version B: Collected in Richmond, Virginia, on January 13, 1975.
   A version appears in *Deep Down*, pp. 199–200. While I was recording tales, I did not hear the version which I had heard innumerable times in the past, in which, after the Deacon indicates he has had the Minister's wife by uttering the agreed upon word, the other repeats that word twice as the Deacon's wife and daughter come in.

99   Collected in Richmond, Virginia, on November 20, 1970.

100   Collected in Henrico, Virginia, on March 11, 1975.

101   Collected in Richmond, Virginia, on October 2, 1974.
See Motif N5. "*Card-playing parson,*" *Motif-Index.*

102   Collected in Richmond, Virginia, on April 4, 1975.
For other versions see "Individualist" in *Laughing*, p. 136, and *Jokes*, p. 22.

103   Collected in Richmond, Virginia, on January 13, 1975.
For another version see *Encyclopedia*, p. 514.

104   Collected in Charles City, Virginia, on November 12, 1974.

105   Collected in Capahosic, Virginia, on May 12, 1975, from an alumnus of Morehouse College in Atlanta, Georgia.

106   Collected in Richmond, Virginia, on October 2, 1974, from an informant who refused to allow me to tape any of his risqué material. The text here, therefore, is not verbatim but based on my notes.
See Motif J1805.1. "*Similar sounding words mistaken for each other,*" *Motif-Index.*

107   Version A: Collected in Henrico, Virginia, on March 7, 1975, from a female informant. Version B: Collected in Richmond, Virginia, on January 13, 1975, from an informant whose hilarious mimicking of the Old Sister's talking with a mouth full of snuff must be heard to be appreciated.
For other versions see *Brazos*, p. 85; *Deep Down*, pp. 205–6; "Out of Jurisdiction" in *Laughing*, pp. 118–19; and "Aunt Dicy and Reverend Jackson's Sermon" in J. Mason Brewer, *Snuff-Dipping Tales of the Texas Negro* (1956) reprinted in *Encyclopedia* p. 121.

108   Collected in Richmond, Virginia, on October 2, 1974.

109   Collected in Richmond, Virginia, on October 4, 1974.
For other versions of this very popular tale see *Brazos*, p. 56; "Baptizing a Hard Candidate" in *Michigan*, p. 173 (reprinted in *Negro American Folktales*, p. 370); *Deep Down*, pp. 209–10; "Down by the Riverside" in *Laughing*, p. 125; and "Sister Sadie Washington's Littlest Boy" in *American Negro Folklore*, pp. 114–16.

110   Collected in Richmond, Virginia, on October 4, 1976.
"The Baptizing Disturbed" in *Michigan*, pp. 172–73, combines this tale with my "I Don't Like That Thing" (p. 48).

111   Collected in Richmond, Virginia, on January 31, 1975.

112   Collected in Richmond, Virginia, on January 31, 1975.

113   Collected in Richmond, Virginia, on January 13, 1975.
A variant is "The Crow" in *Congaree*, pp. 86–87.

114   Collected in Charles City, Virginia, in 1970.

115   Collected in Charles City, Virginia, on November 12, 1974.
I have changed the name of the preacher because this is a true anecdote.

116   Collected in Charles City, Virginia, on November 12, 1974.
I have changed the name of the character because this is a true anecdote.

117   Collected in Richmond, Virginia, in December, 1970.

118   Collected in Louisa, Virginia, on January 10, 1975, from an informant who asserted that it actually happened at a church in Louisa.
The tale appears as "Fair Warning" in *Laughing*, pp. 119–20, where the Minister's name is Cheesehill. Hurston uses the tale as an illustration in her chapter "My People! My People!" in *Dust Tracks on a Road*, p. 234.

119   Collected in Louisa, Virginia, on January 10, 1975, from an informant who asserts that it tells of a true incident.

120   Collected in Louisa, Virginia, on January 10, 1975.

121   Collected in Richmond, Virginia, on January 31, 1975.

122   Collected in Richmond, Virginia, on November 20, 1974.
A variant is "The Cabarrus County Boy Who Told the Church What to Do" in *Worser*, pp. 34–36, in which the butt of the joke is a pompous boy who has been to New York and who considers himself very sophisticated.

123   Collected in Richmond, Virginia, on November 20, 1974.
See Motif J1813.8. Sheep's head has eaten dumplings, Baughman.
For other versions see "Hoghead and Peas" and "Sheephead and Dumplings" in *Pine Bluff*, pp. 56–57 (reprinted in *Negro American Folktales*, pp. 169–70), and "Jack and the Sheep's Head" in *Buying the Wind*, pp. 344–45. Baughman cites several white American sources.

124   This popular tale was collected in Richmond, Virginia, on December 9, 1974.
Variants include "She Knew Whence It Came" in *Laughing*, pp. 54–55, and "The Devil's Hand" in *Book of Negro Humor*, p. 15. I taped another version in Richmond, Virginia, on February 6, 1975.

125   Collected in Richmond, Virginia, on December 9, 1974.
This is Motif J217.0.1.1. "*Trickster overhears man praying for death to take him,*" *Motif Index*.
Variants are "God and Fortune" in *Sea Islands*, pp. 57–58; "The Lord and Toby" in "Folk-Lore from Virginia," pp. 361–62; "Going to Heaven" in "Folk-lore from Elizabeth City," pp. 294–95; "Going to Heaven Without Dying" in "Tales and Riddles," p. 552; "Uncle Pleas's Prayer" and "Uncle Joe's Faith" in *Tone the Bell Easy*, pp. 26–28 and 31–32, respectively; *Mules and Men*, pp. 96–99 (reprinted in *Treasury of American Folklore*, pp. 442–

44); "Efan Prays" in *Michigan*, pp. 61–62 (reprinted in *American Negro Folktales*, p. 168); "How Pompey Changed His Mind" in *Laughing*, pp. 58–59; and "Uncle Jonas and This Sin Cursed World" and "Uncle Israel Changes His Mind" in *Dog Ghosts*, pp. 7–9 and 17–18, respectively. A Wala text of this tale is found in Richard M. Dorson, *African Folklore* (Garden City: Doubleday, 1972), pp. 400–402.

Another version of this tale is my "Ain't No Way in the World for the Lord to Catch Yo' Daddy" (p. 214).

126   Version A: Given to me in manuscript form by Mae Johnson, who had heard it from her father when she was a child; she was unable to recall the third line of the second stanza. Version B: Collected in Richmond, Virginia, on February 6, 1975.

For other versions see "Hoghead and Peas" and "Sheephead and Dumplings" in *Pine Bluff*, pp. 56–57 (reprinted in *Negro American Folktales*, pp. p. 360, is a mixture of prose and verse. "The Preacher and the Bear" in *Laughing*, pp. 122–23, is a prose version.

127   Collected in Richmond, Virginia, on November 22, 1974.

For other versions see E. C. L. Adams, *Nigger to Nigger* (New York: Scribner's, 1928), pp. 223–24 (reprinted in *Treasury of American Folklore*, p. 447); "Bear Meeting and Prayer Meeting," in *Tone the Bell Easy*, pp. 36–37; and "A Change of Tactics" in *Laughing*, p. 123.

128   Collected in Charles City, Virginia, on March 19, 1975.

A variant is "The Preacher and the Runaway Lion" in *Worser*, p. 48.

129   Collected in Richmond, Virginia, on December 9, 1974, from an informant who asserts that it tells of a true incident.

A similar tale appears in Alfred Holmes von Kolnitz, *Cryin' in de Wilderness* (Charleston: Walker, Evans, and Cogswell, n.d.), pp. 30, 44–45 (reprinted in *Treasury of Southern Folklore*, p. 105).

130   Collected in Richmond, Virginia, on January 13, 1975, from an informant who says the incident actually happened in Richmond.

A similar tale was collected by Legman in New York in 1940; see *Rationale*, p. 75.

131   Collected in Richmond, Virginia, on February 6, 1975.

132   Given to me in manuscript form by Joseph Jenkins, who collected it from a student at Virginia State College in 1970.

The same tale appears as "Grace Before Meal" in *Book of Negro Humor*, p. 31, where it is presented as an anecdote involving W. E. B. Du Bois.

133   Collected at Capahosic, Virginia, on May 12, 1975.

The punch lines are a variation on the popular "Good bread; good meat; good food; let's eat!"

134   Collected in Richmond, Virginia, on January 13, 1975.

I have thus far discovered no other versions of this tale, but Brewer records a tale with similar sentiments. In "Elder Lott's Sunday Night Sermon" in *Brazos*, pp. 12–13, white men are shooting at Blacks for holding a church service. As the Steward dodges the bullets, he asks the Elder if he thinks God knows how the white folks treat them; and the Elder, still running and panting, replies, "Sho', he know.... He jes' don' give a damn." My colleague Michael Linn reports that this is a popular joke in Montana, where the butt of the joke is a white man.

135   Given to me in manuscript form in 1970 by Joseph Jenkins, who collected it from a student at Virginia State College who heard it in Texas.
   There are three variants in *Deep Down*: "The Preacher and His Song," pp. 196–97; "The Preacher is Lost," p. 198; and "The Preacher and the Farm Woman," pp. 198–99. Another variant appears in *Positively Black*, p. 101.

136   Collected in Richmond, Virginia, on January 13, 1975.

137   Collected in Louisa, Virginia, on January 10, 1975.
   A WPA worker mentions having recorded this song (WPA, UVA, Box 1, Folder 8), but no text is in the collection at the University of Virginia.

138   Collected in Richmond, Virginia, on January 31, 1975.
   See Motif X1133.3.2. "*If the wolf's tail breaks*," *Motif-Index*. Baughman lists this as Motif X1133.3.2(a). If the bear's tail breaks, and Type 1875A. "If the Wolf's Tail Breaks".
   This tale, which has been collected in all parts of this country, has been found also in Newfoundland, Nova Scotia, Ontario, and Scotland. Versions from Black Americans include "Who Darkens That Hole?" in "Folk-Lore from Virginia," p. 371; "Who Darkens the Hole?" in *Sea Islands*, p. 118; "What Darkens the Hole?" in "Folk-lore from Elizabeth City," p. 292; "South," p. 267; "Who Darkie de Hole?" in *Tone the Bell Easy*, pp. 37–38; and "What Darken de Hole?" in *Book of Negro Folklore*, p. 136 (reprinted from A. W. Eddins, "Brazos Bottoms Philosophy," *TFSP* 2 [1923]:50–51). Several white American sources are also listed by Baughman.

139   Collected at the Virginia State Penitentiary on December 2, 1974.

140   Collected at the Virginia State Peninintiary on December 2, 1974.
   "The North Carolina Negro and the Alabama Deputy Sheriff" in *Worser*, pp. 57–58, is a slightly similar tale in which there is a rhyming dialogue occurring between a Black man and a sheriff, but the ending in Brewer's tale is different, with the Black fellow frightening the sheriff away.

141   Collected in Capahosic, Virginia, on May 12, 1975.

142   Collected in Richmond, Virginia, on January 31, 1975.
   The effectiveness of this tale is greatly enhanced by the mimicking of the squeaky wheelbarrow.

143   Collected in Richmond, Virginia, on January 31, 1975, from an informant who says it is an account of an actual incident.

144 This account of an actual incident was collected in Richmond, Virginia, on February 6, 1975.

145 The text is a combination of two versions given to me by the informant on January 13, 1975, and February 6, 1975.

146 Versions A and B (tall tales commonly called "lies") were collected in Richmond, Virginia, on January 31, 1975.
See Motif X1796.2.2. Lie: man runs as fast or faster than a bullet, Baughman.
A variant is "He Heard the Bullet Twice," in Book of Negro Folklore, p. 135 (reprinted from A. W. Eddins, Negro Tales and Jokes).

147 Collected in Richmond, Virginia, on January 31, 1975.

148 Given to me in manuscript form in 1970 by an informant from Charles City, Virginia.

149 Collected in Richmond, Virginia, on November 20, 1970.
This tale is cited by Legman, Rationale, p. 213, but not as a tale about a Black man.

150 This widely popular tale was recorded in Richmond, Virginia, on March 5, 1975.
See Motif B210.2. "Talking animal or object refuses to talk on demand," Motif-Index.
This tale, which has also been collected in Africa (See Michigan, p. 50), appears in many collections of Black American folklore. See "Talks Too Much" in "Tales and Riddles," pp. 536–37; Tone the Bell Easy, pp. 48–50; Mules and Men, pp. 219–20 (reprinted as "High Walker and Bloody Bones" in Treasury of American Folklore, pp. 717–18); "You Talk Too Much" in Treasury of Southern Folklore, p. 510 (reprinted from William A. Percy, Lanterns on the Levee [New York: Alfred A. Knopf, 1941], pp. 294–96); Pine Bluff, pp. 48–52 (two versions); "Talking Bones," "Talking Turtle," and "The Talking Mule" in American Negro Folktales, pp. 147–51; "How to Stay Out of Trouble" in Laughing, p. 50. "The Talking Mule" in American Negro Folktales is a more direct protest tale than are the other versions; in it the informant emphasizes the fact that the Black man works like a mule without receiving any remuneration for his labors and suggests that the slave John is better off when his master kills him for "lying."

151 Collected in Capahosic, Virginia, on May 12, 1975.

152 Collected at the Virginia State Penitentiary on December 2, 1974.

153 Collected at the Virginia State Penitentiary on December 2, 1974.
I taped another version in Henrico, Virginia, on March 11, 1975.

154 Given to me in manuscript form by Marilyn Gordon, who collected it

from a twenty-year-old female student at Virginia Commonwealth University on April 27, 1976.

This tale, currently popular on the Virginia Commonwealth University campus, appeared in several journals from my folklore class during the spring of 1976.

155　Collected in Richmond, Virginia, on November 19, 1974.

156　This account of the informant's personal experiments with folk beliefs was recorded in Richmond, Virginia, on January 31, 1975.

157　Recorded in Washington, D.C., in November, 1970.

158　Recorded in Charles City, Virginia, on November 12, 1974.
A version of this tale appears in *Encyclopedia*, p. 361.

159　Collected in Henrico, Virginia, on March 7, 1975.

160　Collected in Henrico, Virginia, on March 11, 1975.
A similar tale, in which the Negro responds, "I'd work a lots faster'n that if'n I could read," is "The Smart Mocksville Negro" in *Worser*, pp. 107–8.

161　Given to me in manuscript form in November, 1970, by an informant from Charles City, Virginia.
Though I have uncovered no other version of this particular tale, it is a part of a popular group of stories in which the ignorant Black attempts to pattern his or her behavior after the whites', which he or she assumes is necessarily imitable. The Black person's actions inevitably turn out to be a burlesque of the behavior of his or her paragon, however.

162　This account of a true incident was related to me in Richmond, Virginia, on December 20, 1974.

163　Given to me in Richmond, Virginia, on December 9, 1974, by an informant who says it tells of a true incident.
Though I found no other version of this tale, it is of course a part of that large group of jokes which revolve around a literal interpretation. See my similar tale involving the Irish cook, "Don't Dress It" (p. 161).

164　Collected in Charles City, Virginia, on November 13, 1974.

165　Collected in Richmond, Virginia, on January 13, 1975.
See "Jacob's Cut" in *Pine Bluff*, p. 238, for another version.

166　Collected in Richmond, Virginia, on February 6, 1975.

167　Collected in Richmond, Virginia, on November 19, 1975.
A version in which the man's name is Wash Butts appears in *Encyclopedia*, p. 354.

168　Collected in Richmond, Virginia, on November 19, 1974.

169 Collected in Richmond, Virginia, on February 26, 1975.
A part of the effectiveness of this joke stems from the storyteller's mimicking the expressions of the father which immediately relay the fact that the father doesn't know what the Declaration of Independence is.

170 Collected in Richmond, Virginia, on October 23, 1974, from an informant who lives in Charles City and who says it tells of a true incident.

171 Collected in Richmond, Virginia, on October 23, 1974, from an informant who lives in Charles City and who says it tells of a true incident.

172 Collected in Richmond, Virginia, on November 20, 1974.

173 Collected in Richmond, Virginia, on February 24, 1975.
See Type 1833 E. "God Died for You," Baughman.
A version appears in "Folk-Lore from Virginia," p. 371, and in WPA, UVA, Box 2, Folder 7. A variant is "Sister Patsy's Error" in Brazos, p. 22. Baughman cites several white American references.

174 Version A: Collected in Henrico, Virginia, on March 7, 1975. Version B: Collected in Richmond, Virginia, on January 13, 1975. I taped another version from a Charles City, Virginia, informant on November 23, 1974. Version C: Provided as a sequel to version B by an informant at the same session during which version B was taped.
This group of tales about the stupid husband who is unaware—despite what he sees—of the fact that his wife is committing adultery with the doctor (sometimes it's a priest) is very old. A version which dates back to the Middle Ages has a priest telling the husband that he is eating, and the husband replies: "If I had not heard otherwise, I would have believed you were screwing my wife"; see Russell A. Peck, "Public Dream and Private Myths: Perspective in Middle English Literature," PMLA 90 (May, 1975): 461 (Peck paraphrased the tale from Guerin's "Du Prestre ki Abevete" in The Literary Context of Chaucer's Fablius, ed. Larry Benson and Theodore Anderson [Indianapolis: Bobbs-Merrill, 1971], pp. 268–73). A version collected in New York in 1953 appears in Rationale, p. 131.

175 Collected in Richmond, Virginia, on January 13, 1975.

176 Given to me in manuscript form by Joseph Jenkins, who collected it from a student at Virginia State College in 1970 who noted that she heard it in the dormitory. The same tale was popular during the years when I was living in the dormitories at Virginia State as well, only then the principals were inmates of what we then referred to as "the other hill"—the Petersburg asylum.
A version appears in Alan Dundes, "Texture, Text, and Context," Southern Folklore Quarterly 28 (December, 1964): 259.

177 Collected in Charles City, Virginia, on November 12, 1974.

178 Collected in Richmond, Virginia, on November 19, 1974.

179 Collected in Richmond, Virginia, on February 6, 1975.
   See Motif K401.1. *"Dupe's food eaten and then blame fastened on him,"* *Motif-Index.*
   This tale, which has been collected in India, Japan, Indonesia, Africa, Nassau, and Jamaica, appears in numerous collections of Black American folklore. See "The Man Who Had the Possum" in Joel Chandler Harris, *Uncle Remus and His Friends: Old Plantation Stories, Songs, and Ballads With Sketches of Negro Character* (Boston: Houghton Mifflin, 1892) (reprinted in *Treasury of American Folklore*, pp. 437–38); "Tell Tale Grease" in "Tales and Riddles," p. 536; and "Folklore from St. Helena, South Carolina," *JAFL* 38 (January-March, 1925): 222.

180 Collected in Richmond, Virginia, on February 24, 1975.

181 Collected in Richmond, Virginia, on January 31, 1975.
   This story is related to a group of tales, dating back at least to the Middle Ages, dealing with the actions of a fool who hears the world is coming to an end. A variant is "The Traveling Minister" in *Worser*, p. 49.

182 Collected in Richmond, Virginia, on February 24, 1975.

183 Given to me in manuscript form in 1970 by an informant from Charles City, Virginia.

184 Given to me in manuscript form by Linwood Lewis, who collected it from a Virginia Commonwealth University student in April, 1975.
   A variant appears in *Positively Black*, p. 153.

185 Collected in Richmond, Virginia, on November 20, 1974.

186 Given to me in manuscript form by Leonard Lambert, who collected it in the spring of 1976 from a twenty-three-year-old man from Richmond, Virginia, who first heard it in Lawrenceville, Virginia.
   This tale is included here because it is a variant of the many tales of this type which deal with the malodorousness of Blacks. See, for example, Hurston's tale in which the goat smells so awful that he makes people faint, but, when the Black man is brought in, the goat faints (*Mules and Men*, pp. 110–11).

187 This little episode related from the personal reminiscences of an informant in Richmond, Virginia, on February 27, 1975, suggests that the idea of the tabooed Black male extended even to children.

188 Given to me in manuscript form in 1970 by a female informant from Charles City, Virginia.

189 This popular tale was collected in Richmond, Virginia, on January 15, 1975, from a female informant. Several versions were given to me in Charles City and Richmond, Virginia, by both male and female informants.
   For other versions see *Mules and Men*, pp. 107–9, and "Joke: Putting Hand Under Old Mistress' Dress" in *Lay My Burden Down*, p. 9.

190   Given to me in manuscript form in 1970 by a male informant from Charles City, Virginia.

191   Version A: Collected in Charles City, Virginia, in 1970 from a male informant. Version B: Collected in Capahosic, Virginia, on May 12, 1975. The informant first heard and told this joke in Georgia, where he grew up and to which he refers in the introduction to his joke.

192   Given to me in manuscript form in 1970 by a male informant from Charles City, Virginia.

193   Collected in Henrico, Virginia, on March 11, 1975, from a male informant.
   This tale has had widespread currency in Virginia. In some versions, the first speaker asks the second what he wants all that black stuff for, and he replies, "To go to your funeral." A version, "Over There and Over Here," appears in Laughing, pp. 199–200.

194   Collected in Richmond, Virginia, on November 20, 1970, from a male informant.

195   Given to me in manuscript form by Linwood Lewis, who collected it from a student at Virginia Commonwealth University in April, 1975.
   It may be significant that this joke comes from the youngest informant cited in this chapter. The attraction is suggested in the first line, but the bitterness and violence inherent in the Black male–white woman syndrome seems here to surface more easily and to be expressed more openly, whereas earlier that desire to degrade and to destroy was expressed only in the sexual act, as in my "Pretty Like a Peacock" (p. 106) and in both versions of my "I'd Make Your Ass Sparkle" (p. 106).

196   Collected in Richmond, Virginia, on February 2, 1975, from a male informant.
   See Motif J1549(c). Before I married Louisa, Baughman. Baughman cites one white reference.

197   Collected in Henrico, Virginia, on March 11, 1975, from a male informant.

198   Version A: Collected in Washington, D.C., in November, 1970, from a male informant who originally lived in Richmond, Virginia. Version B: Collected in Richmond, Virginia, on November 20, 1974, from a female informant.

199   Collected in Henrico, Virginia, on March 7, 1975, from a female informant.
   A version appears in Rationale, p. 208 (reprinted from Charley Jones, Laugh Book [Wichita, Kansas, 1951]). I have another version which was collected from a female in Richmond on February 25, 1976, by Marvin L. Robinson.

200   Collected at the Virginia State Penitentiary on February 2, 1974, from a male informant.

A version collected in Texas in which a white girl and a Mexican girl are unable to spell *Peter* while a Black girl spells it, appears in *Positively Black*, p. 116.

201   Collected in Washington, D.C., in November, 1970, from a male informant who is originally from Richmond, Virginia.

202   Collected in Charles City, Virginia, in November, 1974, from a male informant.

203   Collected in Charles City, Virginia, on March 29, 1975, from a male informant. I also heard a female recite "Shoot the Habit" in Richmond, Virginia, in January, 1976.

204   Given to me in manuscript form by Joseph Jenkins, who received it from a Virginia State College student in 1970.

205   Given to me in manuscript form by Leonard S. Lambert, who collected it in Richmond, Virginia, on February 21, 1976, from a twenty-three-year-old male.

206   Told to me in Gaithersburg, Maryland, in 1974, and in Richmond, Virginia, in July, 1975, by a female informant. The text here is reproduced from memory.

A variant, collected in Washington, D.C., in 1947, in which the girl uses an apple, an orange, and a banana appears in *Rationale*, p. 496.

207   Collected in Richmond, Virginia, on December 2, 1974, from a male informant.

208   Collected in Richmond, Virginia, on October 23, 1974, from a male informant from New Kent, Virginia.

209   Told to me in Arlington, Virginia, in March, 1974, by a female informant and in Richmond, Virginia, on May 8, 1975, by a female informant and on July 17, 1975, by a male informant. The text here is reproduced from memory.

210   Collected in Henrico, Virginia, on March 11, 1975, from a male informant.

A variant appears in *Rationale*, p. 434.

211   Collected in Richmond, Virginia, on October 23, 1974, from a male informant who is originally from Charles City.

A variant in which a man thinks he has given birth to a monkey appears in *Rationale*, p. 601.

212   Collected on October 2, 1974, in Richmond, Virginia, from a male

informant. Two lines omitted from the taped version were added during a later session.

The following variant of this verse was given to me in manuscript form by Ms. Marilyn Gordon, who collected it from a white student at Virginia Commonwealth University:

Mary had a little lamb,
A lobster and some stew,
A piece of meat, a piece of pie,
And some macaroons.
It made the haughty waiter laugh,
To see her order so,
And when they carried Mary out,
Her face was white as snow.

213   Collected in Henrico, Virginia, on March 11, 1975, from a male informant.
A variant appears in *Rationale*, p. 64.

214   Collected in Washington, D.C., in November, 1970, from a male informant who is originally from Richmond, Virginia.

215   Collected in Richmond, Virginia, on October 23, 1974, from a male informant from New Kent, Virginia.

216   Collected in Richmond, Virginia, on December 2, 1974, from a male informant.

217   Collected at the Virginia State Penitentiary on December 2, 1974, from a male informant.

218   Collected in Richmond, Virginia, on February 6, 1975, from a female informant.
Legman traces a variant of this tale back two hundred years to Thomas Hamilton, Earl of Haddington's poetized version, "The Sutler" in *Select Poems* (1735); see *Rationale*, p. 378.

219   This tale was collected in Richmond, Virginia, on November 20, 1970, from a male informant.

220   Collected in Richmond, Virginia, on January 13, 1975, from a female informant.

221   Collected in Henrico, Virginia, on March 11, 1975, from a male informant.

222   Collected in Richmond, Virginia, on November 20, 1970, from a male informant.

223   The text here, based on a tale told to me in Richmond, Virginia, in

June, 1975, and on other versions that I have heard for many years, was reproduced from memory.

A version appears in *Rationale*, p. 70.

224   Collected at the Virginia State Penitentiary on December 2, 1974, from a male informant.

A version appears in *Rationale*, p. 204. Legman cites two other versions appearing in Conrad Aiken, *Blue Voyage* (1927) and Neil Rosenberg, "An Annotated Collection of Parrot Jokes" (M.A. thesis, Indiana University, 1964). A variant is "If You Get Well with Your Cut" in "I Swear," p. 26.

225   Collected at the Virginia State Penitentiary on December 2, 1974, from a male informant whose mimicking of the parrot was hilarious.

226   Told to me in Richmond, Virginia, on May 17, 1975, by a male informant. The text here is reproduced from memory.

227   Collected in Richmond, Virginia, on November 19, 1974, from a female informant.

228   Collected in Richmond, Virginia, on November 20, 1970, from a male informant.

A very close version of this tale, which Legman collected in New York in 1943 and which he describes as "my favorite joke," appears in *Rationale*, p. 582.

229   Written out for me in 1970 by a female informant from Charles City, Virginia.

230   Told to me in Richmond, Virginia, on October 2, 1974, by a male informant. The text here is based on my notes.

231   Collected in the Virginia State Penitentiary on December 2, 1974, from a male informant. The text here is slightly condensed.

232   Version A: Collected in Richmond, Virginia, on January 13, 1975, from a female informant. Version B: Collected in Henrico, Virginia, on March 11, 1975, from a male informant.

233   Collected in Richmond, Virginia, on February 2, 1975, from a male informant.

234   Collected in Henrico, Virginia, on March 7, 1975, from a female informant.

235   Collected in Richmond, Virginia, on February 27, 1975, from a male informant.

Because this is a true anecdote involving a prominent Richmonder, I have changed the name of the character.

236   Version A: Collected in Charles City, Virginia, in November, 1974, from a male informant. Version B: Collected in Richmond, Virginia, on October 23, 1974, from a male informant, a resident of New Kent, Virginia.

237   Collected in Richmond, Virginia, on October 23, 1974, from a female informant from Charles City, Virginia.

238   Collected in Richmond, Virginia, on November 19, 1974, from a female informant.

239   Collected in Richmond, Virginia, on November 19, 1974, from a female informant.

240   Version A: Collected in Richmond, Virginia, on November 19, 1974, from a female informant. Version B: Given to me on the same occasion as Version A by another female informant.
A version of this tale appears in *Rationale*, p. 644, with the comment, "[This story has been] collected in America only once, in 1945, from a soldier of Greek origin." The tale is, however, well known among some of Richmond's Black community.

241   Collected in Richmond, Virginia, on January 31, 1975, from a male informant.

242   Collected in Richmond, Virginia, on October 4, 1974, from a male informant.

243   Collected in Richmond, Virginia, on October 23, 1974, from a female informant.

244   Collected in Richmond, Virginia, in February, 1975, from a male informant.

245   Collected in Richmond, Virginia, on November 19, 1974, from a female informant.

246   Collected in Richmond, Virginia, on January 31, 1975, from a female informant.

247   Collected in Richmond, Virginia, on January 13, 1975, from a female informant.

248   Collected in Richmond, Virginia, on October 23, 1974, from a female informant from Charles City, Virginia.

249   Collected in Richmond, Virginia, on October 2, 1974, from a male informant.
See Motif J2212. *"Effects of age and size absurdly applied," Motif-Index.*

250   Collected in Richmond, Virginia, on January 31, 1975, from a female informant.

251   Collected in Richmond, Virginia, in February, 1975, from a male informant who asserts that it tells of a true incident.

252   Collected in Richmond, Virginia, in February, 1975, from a male informant.

253   Collected in Charles City, Virginia, in July, 1975, from a female informant.

254   Collected in Richmond, Virginia, on October 4, 1975, from a male informant.

255   Collected in Richmond, Virginia, on October 2, 1974, from a male informant.

256   Collected in Richmond, Virginia, on October 4, 1974, from a male informant.

257   This drinking toast was collected in Charles City, Virginia, on April 23, 1975, from a male informant.
Get Your Ass in the Water includes a group of drinking toasts, one of which begins with the line, "And here's to the duck that swim the pond," but the remainder of that toast is completely different from this one; see p. 229.

258   Collected in Richmond, Virginia, on January 13, 1975, from a male informant.
A version appears in *Rationale*, p. 96, where Legman notes, "This exact story will be found in the *Cent Nouvelles Nouvelles*, written in Burgundy, between 1456 and 1461, to entertain the Dauphin of France." Another version appears in *Positively Black*, p. 98, where Abrahams interprets it as an airing of the "incest motive" and as an "aggressive act against his father."

259   Version A: Collected in Henrico, Virginia, on March 11, 1975, from a male informant. Version B: Collected in Richmond, Virginia, on December 2, 1974, from a male informant.

260   Song collected in Louisa, Virginia, on January 10, 1975, from a male informant who recalls hearing it sung by "a old fellow in Louisa" around the turn of the century. The informant furnished music for this lively and delightfully rendered tune with an inverted wash basin. The text here is based on a tape recording and on a written version.
Though I discovered no other versions, one verse from "I Would Not Marry a Black Girl" in Thomas W. Talley, *Negro Folk Rhymes: Wise and Otherwise* (Port Washington, N.Y.: Kennikat, 1968), p. 63, is very close to the fourth verse of the text here. Talley's verse is "I wouldn' marry dat yaller

Nigger gal,/ An' I'll tell you de reason why;/ Her neck's drawed out so stringy an' long,/ I'se afeared she 'ould never die."

261 Song collected in Richmond, Virginia, from a male informant. The inconsistencies in rhyme and rhythm so apparent in my efforts to transcribe the song are not apparent in my informant's performance of it (during which he accompanied himself on the guitar). The text here is based on a tape of the song made on January 22, 1975, and on corrections which the informant gave to me on April 30, 1975.

262 Collected in Richmond, Virginia, on April 4, 1975, from a male informant.
    Another version is my "Revolving Jones" (p. 144).

263 Collected in Richmond, Virginia, on January 13, 1975, from a male informant.
    Another version is my "Pinwheel Charlie" (p. 144).

264 Collected in Charles City, Virginia, on March 19, 1975, from a female informant.
    I was told several versions, including one which I recorded in Richmond, Virginia, on November 3, 1975. For other versions see "Father and Mother Both 'Fast'" in Buying the Wind, pp. 78–79, and Rationale, pp. 444–45.

265 Given to me in manuscript form by Joseph Jenkins, who collected it from a male student at Virginia State College in November, 1970.

266 Collected in Richmond, Virginia, on January 13, 1975, from a male informant.
    A version is "Holding Mama Down" in "I Swear," p. 35.

267 Collected in Richmond, Virginia, on January 13, 1975, from a female informant.
    A version is "The Iceman Cometh" in Deep Down, p. 251.

268 Collected in Richmond, Virginia, on January 13, 1975, from a female informant.

269 Recorded by hand in Richmond, Virginia, on November 20, 1974, from a female informant.
    Though my informant never alludes to the fact that the men were lovers of the wife, except in sexually allusive lines such as "I want to butcher a hog, but I ain't got no barrel to butcher it in," the actions and comments of the men obviously suggest that the tale deals with marital infidelity. See Type 1419. "The Returning Husband Hoodwinked," Baughman. It is a version of an old and popular tale about the lover who hides in a barrel. The Second Story of the Seventh Day of Boccaccio's Decameron deals with this theme. Another version, collected by Barbara K. and Warren S. Walker, is "The Lovers" in Nigerian Folk Tales (New Brunswick, N.J.: Rutgers University

Press, 1961). Richard Chase also has a version, which he collected in Beech Creek, North Carolina (*American Folk Tales and Songs* [New York: New American LIbrary, 1956], pp. 43, 46–47). Baughman cites two white references.

270 Collected in Richmond, Virginia, on January 13, 1975, from a male informant. See Type 1360c. "Old Holdebrand," Baughman.

271 Version A: Collected in Richmond, Virginia, on April 4, 1975, from a male informant. Version B: Collected in Richmond, Virginia, on January 13, 1975, from a female informant. Note in these versions that the sex of the avenger in the joke differs according to whether the informant is male or female.

272 Collected in Henrico, Virginia, on March 11, 1975, from a male informant.

A version of this tale, which Legman collected in New York in 1953, appears in *Rationale*, p. 773.

273 Collected in Washington, D.C., in November, 1970, from a male informant from Richmond, Virginia.

274 Collected in Richmond, Virginia, on October 4, 1974.

275 Version A: Collected in Capahosic, Virginia, on May 12, 1975. Versions B and C: Collected in Henrico, Virginia, on March 11, 1975, from the same informant. Version D: Collected in Washington, D.C., in November, 1970, from a former resident of Richmond, Virginia.

For other versions see *Brazos*, pp. 88–89; "Doing Business with the Devil" in *Laughing*, p. 132; and "White Man, Jew, Colored Man" in *Pine Bluff*, pp. 89–90 (reprinted in *American Negro Folktales*, pp. 174–75).

276 Related to me by several men at the Old Timers' Club in Richmond, Virginia, on March 6, 1975. The text here is a composite of the different versions.

For other versions see *Brazos*, pp. 86–87, and "Colored Man, Jew, and White Man" in *Michigan*, pp. 76–77 (reprinted in *American Negro Folktales*, p. 173).

277 Collected in Richmond, Virginia, on January 31, 1975.

A version with Pat and Mike as the central characters is "Jumping into Heaven" in "Tales and Riddles," p. 550. A variant is "The Preaching of the Sinful Brother's Funeral" in *Worser*, pp. 47–48.

278 Collected in Richmond, Virginia, on February 6, 1975.

See Motif K231.13. "*Agreement to leave sum of money on coffin of friend,*" *Motif-Index*.

For other versions see "South," p. 271, and "Colored Man, Jew, and White Man" in *Michigan*, pp. 77–78 (reprinted in *American Negro Folktales*, p. 175).

279 Collected in Richmond, Virginia, on February 6, 1975, from an informant who says this is a true incident.
See Motif J1141. Confession obtained by ruse, Baughman.

280 Collected in Richmond, Virginia, on February 6, 1975.

281 Version A: Collected in Richmond, Virginia, on December 2, 1974.
Version B: Collected in Richmond, Virginia, on January 13, 1975.
A version appears in *Rationale*, p. 421.

282 Collected in Richmond, Virginia, on December 2, 1974.

283 Collected in Richmond, Virginia, on December 2, 1974.

284 Version A: Collected in Richmond, Virginia, on February 6, 1975.
Version B: Collected in Richmond, Virginia, on January 13, 1975.

285 Collected in Richmond, Virginia, on November 20, 1974.

286 Collected in Richmond, Virginia, on January 13, 1975.
A version of this tale is "Jim Johnson and His New Suit of Clothes" in *Worser*, p. 80.
This same tale was told to me on June 31, 1975, by a white secretary at Virginia Commonwealth University, who noted that her father related it to her as an actual occurrence in Alabama.

287 Collected in Richmond, Virginia, on January 13, 1975.
See Motif J1499.13(g). Man is amazed at high prices in hotel, Baughman. Baughman lists one white American source.
A variant in which Abe Lincoln touches a girl's breasts and says, "everything is so high around here, I though they might be your buttocks," appears in *Rationale*, p. 245 (reprinted from *The New Anecdota Americana*, no. 491 [1944]).

288 Collected in Richmond, Virginia, on December 2, 1974.

289 Collected in Richmond, Virginia, on March 5, 1975.
A lengthy version appears as "John and the Twelve Jews" in *Pine Bluff*, pp. 125–26 (reprinted in *American Negro Folktales*, pp. 311–13).

290 Collected at the Virginia State Penitentiary on December 2, 1974.

291 Collected in Richmond, Virginia, in February, 1975.

292 Collected in Richmond, Virginia, on January 31, 1975.

293 Collected in Richmond, Virginia, on January 31, 1975.
See Type 1319A. The Watch Mistaken for the Devil's Eye, Baughman; Motif J1769.4. Terrapin thought to be watch, carried, Baughman, and Motif J1772.21. Watch is taken for sea tick, Baughman.

"Watch or Rattlesnake: 'Knee-Deep' and 'Better Go Round'" in *Sea Islands*, pp. 65–66, combines this tale and my "You Better Go 'Round" (p. 250). Other versions with the Irishman as the principal include "Mother of All the Ticks" in "Folk-lore from Elizabeth City," p. 303; "Irishman and the Watch" in *Michigan*, p. 4; and one in *Pine Bluff*, pp. 251–52. The tale is told about a colored man in *Mules and Men*, pp. 115–16. Dorson collected a version in Ireland. Baughman cites several white American references.

294 Collected in Richmond, Virginia, on January 31, 1975.

295 Collected in Richmond, Virginia, on November 20, 1974.
    Two versions of this tale appear in *Sea Islands*; see "Landing Is Hell," pp. 92–93.

296 Collected in Charles City, Virginia, in November, 1974.
    Michael Linn informed me that this was a popular joke in Montana, where it was told about lumberjacks or sheepherders.

297 Related to me as a true incident on February 6, 1975, in Richmond, Virginia.
    Though I heard only this one joke about the Chinese restaurateur since I have been collecting jokes for this volume, I heard several during my high school and college days (in the fifties). Apparently these tales have lost their popularity since many of the conditions that motivated them have changed.

298 Collected in Henrico, Virginia, on March 11, 1975.

299 Collected in Richmond, Virginia, in February, 1975.
    A variant appears under "Adults' Rhymes and Songs" in *Worser*, p. 172, and in *Rationale*, p. 664.

300 Collected in Charles City, Virginia, on October 12, 1974.

301 Collected in Charles City, Virginia, on November 12, 1974.

302 Collected in Richmond, Virginia, on January 31, 1975.

303 This comment was made by an informant from Richmond, Virginia, on February 27, 1975, about a judge in Richmond notorious for his treatment of Blacks. I have changed the name here and in other anecdotes about him.
    Tales about this same judge collected by the WPA workers are WPA, UVA, Box 1, Folder 2.

304 Collected in Richmond, Virginia, on March 5, 1975.

305 Collected in Richmond, Virginia, in February, 1975.

306 Collected in Richmond, Virginia, in February, 1975.
    "Short'nin' Bread," like many other blues and secular songs, has sexual connotations that would make it objectionable to many. For a discussion of

the double meanings in this and in other songs, see Guy B. Johnson, "Double Meaning in the Popular Negro Blues," *Journal of Abnormal and Social Psychology* 12 (1927–28): 12–20. A verse of this song appears in WPA, UVA, Box 1, Folder 1.

307   Collected in Richmond, Virginia, in February, 1975.

308   Collected in Richmond, Virginia, on November 19, 1974.
   See Motif B2751. *"Animal executed for crime," Motif-Index.*
   A version of this tale is "Ole Missy, the Mule and the Buggy" in *Pine Bluff,* pp. 229–30 (reprinted in *American Negro Folktales,* pp. 306–7).

309   This true anecdote was recorded in Richmond, Virginia, on February 24, 1975.

310   This true anecdote was related to me in Richmond, Virginia, on February 24, 1975.

311   Collected in Henrico, Virginia, on March 11, 1975.
   A version in which a Dutchman tells an Irishman, "All Irish is used to dis," appears as "Used to It" in *Sea Islands,* p. 92.

312   Collected in Richmond, Virginia, on January 13, 1975.

313   This true anecdote was recorded in Richmond, Virginia, on February 24, 1975.

314   Given to me in manuscript form in July, 1971, in Charlottesville, Virginia.

315   Given to me in manuscript form by an informant from Charles City, Virginia, in December, 1970.
   For other versions see "Bill Adams and Georgia the Peach State" in *Pine Bluff,* pp. 123–24 (reprinted in *American Negro Folktales,* pp. 318–19), and "Revised Version" in *Laughing,* p. 180.

316   Given to me in manuscript form in December, 1970, by an informant from Charles City, Virginia.
   A version appears in *Book of Negro Humor,* p. 254. A similar tale in which the question is posed by a Black man and in which the response comes from a white man is found in *Jokes,* p. 81.

317   Given to me in manuscript form in December, 1970, by an informant from Charles City, Virginia.
   For variants see "Whatever Became of the Seminoles?" in *Laughing,* p. 180, and *Jokes,* p. 87.

318   Collected in Charles City, Virginia, on November 12, 1974.
   For other versions of this tale see "Divine Discretion" in *Laughing,* p. 206; *Encyclopedia,* p. 506; and *Jokes,* p. 82.

319 This true anecdote was recorded in Richmond, Virginia, on February 24, 1975.

"Cleansing the Temple" in *Laughing*, p. 182, in which a white deacon warns the Black janitor that he'd better not pray in the white church, bears some interesting similarities to my informant's experience.

320 Collected in Charles City, Virginia, on November 12, 1974.

For other versions see *American Aesop* (reprinted as "An Exclusive Church" in *Book of Negro Folklore*, p. 158); *Laughing*, pp. 155–56; "Joining the Church" in *A Treasury of Southern Folklore*, p. 100 (reprinted from *Life in Old Virginia*, ed. James J. McDonald [Norfolk: Old Virginia, 1907], pp. 281–82); "White Minister and Sam" in *Michigan*, p. 78 (reprinted in *American Negro Folktales*, pp. 175–76; "The Church That Jesus Couldn't Get In" in *Worser*, pp. 38–39; and *Book of Negro Humor*, p. 262.

321 Collected in Charles City, Virginia, on November 12, 1974.

For other versions see *Book of Negro Humor*, p. 263; "Total Immersion" in *Laughing*, p. 129; "Immersion, Integrated Style" in *Encyclopedia*, pp. 514–15; and *Jokes*, p. 85.

322 Collected in Richmond, Virginia, in February, 1975.

See Motif W154. "*Ingratitude,*" *Motif-Index.*

This tale is included here since the Parrot is usually pictured as an accomplice to white bosses who oversees and informs on the Black. Variants which deal with the Black's securing revenge on the Parrot or attempting to outsmart the white boss appear in chapter twelve. It should be noted that Parrot stories have a long currency. An early example is cited by Legman: *Tuti-Namah*, or "Seventy Tales of a Parrot," written about 1306; see *Rationale*, p. 200.

323 Given to me in manuscript form by Linwood Lewis, who collected it from a student at Virginia Commonwealth University in April, 1975.

324 Collected in Richmond, Virginia, on January 31, 1975.

For other versions see "On a Streetcar" in *Book of Negro Folklore*, pp. 507–8; "Help from a Stranger" in *Laughing*, p. 189; and *Jokes*, pp. 98–99.

325 Collected in Charles City, Virginia, on November 12, 1974.

326 Collected in Charles City, Virginia, on March 29, 1975.

For other versions see "Desegregation" in *Book of Negro Folklore*, p. 508; "Who's Ready for Who?" in *Worser*, pp. 105–6; "Unfair Bill of Fair" in *Laughing*, pp. 207–8; *Book of Negro Humor*, p. 265; "Who's Ready for Who?" in *American Negro Folklore*, pp. 88–89; and *Jokes*, p. 63.

327 Given to me in manuscript form by Linwood Lewis, who collected it from a Virginia Commonwealth University student in April, 1975.

328 Given to me in manuscript form by Linwood Lewis, who collected it from a Virginia Commonwealth University student in April, 1975.

329 Collected in Richmond, Virginia, on October 27, 1970.

"Sam is Definitely Left Out" is one of a large group of tales dealing with the Black person's revenge (usually obscene) when he or she is left out of a party (and this may be extended to include all of the brighter aspects of American life from which Blacks are excluded), beginning with "Brother Rabbit Breaks up a Party" in Joel Chandler Harris, *Nights with Uncle Remus* (New York: Houghton Mifflin, 1883), pp. 61–68, in which Rabbit frightens the other animals away from the party, goes to the house, kicks the door open, puts his feet on the sofa, and spits on the floor. A more modern version of Harris' tale was collected by Abrahams; in it Brother Rabbit kicks the door open, eats and drinks all he wants, does whatever he wants with the wives of the other animals, and then defecates in the middle of the floor; see *Positively Black*, p. 53.

330 Collected in Richmond, Virginia, in February, 1975. It is a true account, passed down in the informant's family, of an experience of either his great-grandmother or his great-great aunt.

331 This true anecdote was collected in Richmond, Virginia, on February 27, 1975.

332 Collected in Richmond, Virginia, on January 22, 1975.

The accounts of the slaves' efforts to muffle the sounds of their secret meetings are very popular. Similar accounts are found in "Unwritten History [of Slavery]" and "Memories of Slavery" in *Book of Negro Folklore*, pp. 45–61 and 89–91, respectively.

333 Collected in Richmond, Virginia, on December 20, 1974.

334 Collected in Richmond, Virginia, on December 20, 1974.

335 Collected in Richmond, Virginia, on January 16, 1975.

A variant with a similar line is "Uncle Bob's Voyage to New England" in *Tone the Bell Easy*, pp. 42–43.

336 Collected in Richmond, Virginia, on February 6, 1975.

337 Collected in Richmond, Virginia, on January 16, 1975.

A variant appears in "South," pp. 262–67. A version appears in *Mules and Men*, pp. 112–14, in which John is victorious in the end by frightening the master who attempts to punish him; this version is reprinted as "Massa's Gone to Philly-Me-York" in *Treasury of Southern Folklore*, pp. 74–75, and in *Laughing*, p. 45. For other versions see "Master Disguised" in *Sea Islands*, pp. 76–77; "Fooling Master and Catching John" in *Lay My Burden Down*, pp. 3–9; "Old Marster Takes a Trip" in *Michigan*, p. 59 (reprinted in *American Negro Folktales*, pp. 136–37); "Master's Gone to Philly-Me-York" in *Pine Bluff*, pp. 44–45 (reprinted in *American Negro Folktales*, pp. 151–52); and "Old John Blow-out" in *Dog Ghosts*, pp. 9–14.

338 Version A: Collected in Richmond, Virginia, on December 20, 1974.

Version B: Given to me in manuscript form in 1970 by an informant from Charles City, Virginia.

This tale is combined with my "I Run My Hand Up Missis' Dress" (p. 105) in *Mules and Men*, pp. 107–9. For other versions see "Cussing Master" in *Lay My Burden Down*, pp. 8–9 (reprinted in *Treasury of Southern Folklore*, p. 72); and "He Didn't Have the Knack" in *Laughing*, p. 45.

339   This true account of his father's experience was related to me by an informant from Charles City, Virginia, on November 13, 1974.

340   Given to me in manuscript form by Linwood Lewis, who collected it from a Virginia Commonwealth University student in April, 1975.

341   Collected in Richmond, Virginia, on October 27, 1970.

This is one of a popular group of tales in which a man takes a magical potion that causes his penis to grow to enormous proportions. A variant may be found in *Rationale*, p. 307.

342   Collected in Richmond, Virginia, on November 20, 1975.

This and the immediately following selections belong to a popular group of tales involving fornication contests between the Black man and other men.

A variant appears in *Positively Black*, p. 70.

343   Collected in Capahosic, Virginia, on May 12, 1975.

344   Given to me in manuscript form in 1970 by an informant from Charles City, Virginia.

345   Collected at the Virginia State Penitentiary on December 2, 1974.

346   Collected in Richmond, Virginia, on January 13, 1975.

My informant said that this tale is told as were those frequently told in college, in which the Black stereotype was shifted to other men. The tale was immediately corrected by another member of the audience; the corrections are included in brackets. The tale generally pictures the Black man as the one having the largest penis (and this is how my informant originally heard it).

Other versions may be found in *Positively Black*, pp. 69–70, and in Roger D. Abrahams, "The Negro Stereotype," *JAFL* 83 (April-June, 1970): 236.

347   Versions A and B, which my informant says are true accounts, were recorded in Charles City, Virginia, on October 23, 1974.

I have changed the name of the individual, whom I happen to have known and about whom I have heard these and similar tales many times.

A version is "Uncle Aaron and the Baby Chickens" in *Dog Ghosts*, p. 29, but the butt of the tale is evidently a Black man.

348   Collected in Charles City, Virginia, on March 19, 1975.

349   Collected in Richmond, Virginia, on December 9, 1974.

See Motif K741, "*Capture by Tarbaby,*" *Motif-Index.*
This is certainly the most popular of all Black American folktales. Versions have been collected also in Africa, India, Spain, South America, Alaska, Indonesia, Barbados, and Jamaica. Newbell Niles Puckett says that the tale was imported into America from Africa; see *Folk Beliefs of the Southern Negro* (New York: Dover, 1969), p. 39. In his study of 152 versions of the tale collected from all over the world, Aurelio M. Espinosa concludes that it originated in India, passed into Europe, and then to Africa. He contends that the American versions are of European and African origins; see "Notes on the Origin and History of the Tar-Baby Story," *JAFL* 43 (April-June, 1930): 130–209.
For other versions see "De Rabbit, de Wolf an' de Tar Baby," *Afro-American Folklore;* "The Wonderful Tar-Baby Story" in *Uncle Remus: His Songs and His Sayings,* pp. 7–11 (reprinted in *Treasury of American Folklore,* pp. 653–54, and in *American Negro Folklore,* pp. 4–5); "How Mr. Rabbit Was Too Sharp for Mr. Fox" (this is the briar patch part of the tale) in *Uncle Remus: His Songs and His Sayings,* pp. 16–19 (reprinted in *Treasury of American Folklore,* pp. 654–55, and in *American Negro Folklore,* pp. 5–6); and "Tell-Tale Grease: Mock Plea" and "Fire Test: Mock Plea" in *Sea Islands,* pp. 12–14. Several other versions also appear in *Sea Islands,* pp. 25–26; in "Folklore from Antigua," pp. 53–56; and in "Folk-lore from Elizabeth City," pp. 256–60. Three versions appear in "Playing Godfather: Tar Baby: Mock Plea" in "Folk Lore from Aiken," pp. 4–6. Three versions appear in "Tales and Riddles," pp. 532–33. See also *Book of Negro Folklore,* pp. 1–2; *Pine Bluff,* p. 17; "De Wolf, de Rabbit, and de Tar Baby" in *American Negro Folklore,* pp. 7–9 (reprinted from *The Hillsborough Recorder* [Hillsborough, N.C., August 5, 1874], where it appeared as "A Familiar Legend"); "The Tar Baby" in *American Negro Folktales,* pp. 75–76; "Bowki and the Rabbit and the Well" in *Buying the Wind,* pp. 248–49; "Tar Baby" in "I Swear," pp. 24–25; and "Mr. Rabbit Steals Mr. Fox's Butter" and "The Tar Pole" in S. G. Armistead, "Two Brer Rabbit Stories from the Eastern Shore of Maryland," *JAFL* 84 (October-December, 1971): 442–44.
I also collected versions of this tale from informants in Charles City, Virginia, on October 4, 1970, and in Richmond, Virginia, on December 20, 1974, and February 6, 1975.
In an interesting study of this tale, Philip Sullivan points out that the story suggests that the best way to defeat the enemy is to "know him thoroughly. Buh Fox is basically cruel and knows next to nothing about Buh Rabbit's real life. And on that cruelty and ignorance Buh Rabbit can surely rely," Sullivan concludes; see "Buh Rabbit: Going Through the Changes," *Studies in Black Literature* 9 (Summer, 1973): 29.

350   Collected in Richmond, Virginia, on January 22, 1975.

351   Collected in Richmond, Virginia, on February 6, 1975.
See Motif K171.1. "*Deceptive crop division,*" *Motif-Index,* and Type 1030. "The Crop Division," Baughman.
This popular tale has been collected in countries all over the world. In most of the versions collected among Black Americans, the Rabbit fools other animals, including the Fox, the Wolf, and the Bear. See "Under the Ground and Over the Ground" in *Sea Islands,* pp. 109–11; "Above Ground

and Below Ground" in "Folk-lore from Elizabeth City," pp. 277–78; "South," pp. 218–19; "Underground and Overground" in "Tales and Riddles," p. 535; "Sheer Crops" in *Treasury of American Folklore*, pp. 659–61 (reprinted from A. W. Eddins, "Brazos Bottoms Philosophy," *Southwestern Lore: Publications of the Texas Folk-Lore Society* 9 [1931]:153–56, ed. J. Frank Dobie); "Sheer Crops" in *Book of Negro Folklore*, pp. 13–16; and "*Sheer Crops*" in *American Negro Folklore*, pp. 14–16 (also reprinted from Eddins). Baughman cites several white European and American references.

352   Collected in Charles City, Virginia, on March 19, 1975.

353   Version A: Collected in Washington, D.C., in November, 1970, from an informant who moved there from Richmond, Virginia. Version B: Collected in Charles City, Virginia, on April 23, 1975.

For other versions of this popular toast, see "The Elephant, the Lion, and the Monkey" in *American Negro Folktales*, pp. 98–99 (reprinted from Richard M. Dorson, "Negro Tales," *Western Folklore* 13 [April, 1954]:77 [this is a prose version]); *Book of Negro Folklore*, pp. 363–66 (a completely expurgated version); *Worser*, pp. 164–75 (also expurgated); Roger D. Abrahams, "The Negro Stereotype," *JAFL* 83 (April–June, 1970): 244–46; *Deep Down*, pp. 113–19, 142–56 (which includes a history and several versions of the toast. Abrahams considers "The Pool-Shooting Monkey" as a version as well, but there seems to be no similarity between the Signifying Monkey and the Poolshooting Monkey beyond the fact that they are both monkeys); *Positively Black*, pp. 88–90; *Get Your Ass in the Water*, pp. 161–72 (which includes six versions); and Neil Eddington, *The Urban Plantation: The Ethnography of an Oral Tradition in a Negro Community* (Ann Arbor: University Microfilms, 1973), pp. 178–79.

354   Version A: Collected in Richmond, Virginia, on November 19, 1975. Version B: Collected in Richmond, Virginia, on October 23, 1974, from an informant who is originally from Charles City, Virginia.

See Motif K406. "*Stolen animal disguised as person so that thief may escape detection*," *Motif-Index*.

A version is "Eyes Had He But Saw Not" in *Laughing*, pp. 180–81. A variant with a similar punch line is "Hog in the Cadillac" in *Michigan*, p. 82 (reprinted as "The Hog and the Colored Man" in *American Negro Folktales*, p. 184).

355   Collected in Charles City, Virginia, on November 12, 1974, from an informant who heard it in Mississippi.

For other versions see "The Whole Wide World" in *Book of Negro Folklore*, pp. 510–511; "The Governors' Convention" in *Pine Bluff*, pp. 122–23 (reprinted in *American Negro Folktales*, pp. 319–20); *Positively Black*, p. 34; and *Encyclopedia*, pp. 471–72.

356   Version A: This true account of an incident was recorded in Henrico, Virginia, on March 7, 1975. Version B: Given to me in manuscript form by Joseph Jenkins, who collected it from a student at Virginia State College in 1970.

Other versions may be found as "Menu Trouble" in *Laughing*, p. 207, and in *Jokes*, p. 73.

357 Collected in Richmond, Virginia, on January 13, 1975.

358 Given to me in manuscript form by Professor Joseph Jenkins, who collected it from a Virginia State College student in 1970.

See Motif K444. "*Dream bread*," *Motif-Index*, and Type 1626. "Dream Bread," Baughman.

For other versions see "The Three Dreams" in *Sea Islands*, pp. 68–69; "The Three Dreams" in *Treasury of American Folklore*, pp. 452–53 (reprinted from Archer Taylor, "The 'Dream-Bread' Story Once More," *JAFL* 34 [July-September, 1972]: 327–28); and Paulette Cross, "Jokes and Black Consciousness: A Collection with Interviews," in *Mother Wit*, p. 660 (reprinted from *The Folklore Forum* 2 (November, 1969): 140–61.

359 Collected in Richmond, Virginia, in February, 1975.

360 Given to me in manuscript form in Richmond, Virginia, on November 25, 1974.

361 Collected in Charles City, Virginia, in September, 1974.

See Motif H1595.1. "*Test of Memory*," *Motif-Index*.

A version is "Uncle Samuel's Marvelous Memory" in *Laughing*, p. 143.

362 Version A: Collected in Richmond, Virginia, on November 20, 1974. Version B: Given to me in manuscript form in 1970 by a resident of Charles City, Virginia.

See Motif N688. "*What is in the dish: 'Poor Crab,'*" *Motif-Index*, and Type 1641. "Doctor Know-All," Baughman.

This popular tale has been widely collected. Dorson notes that Helen L. Flowers ("A Classification of the Folktales of the West Indies by Types and Motifs" [Ph.D. diss., Indiana University, 1952]) lists examples from Antigua, Dominica, Grenada, Guadaloupe, Haiti, Jamaica (2), Martinique, Puerto Rico (8), St. Kitts, St. Lucia, St. Martin, and Trinidad; see *Michigan*, p. 209, note. For other versions see "The Diviner" in "Folk-Lore from Virginia," p. 370; "South," pp. 264–66; "The Diviner" in "Tales and Riddles," p. 542; "The Prophet Vindicated" in *Tone the Bell Easy*, pp. 24–25 (reprinted in *Book of Negro Folklore*, pp. 73–74); *Mules and Men*, pp. 111–12 (reprinted as "The Fortune Teller" in *Treasury of American Folklore*, pp. 445–46); "Coon in the Box" in *Michigan*, pp. 51–53 (reprinted in *American Negro Folktales*, pp. 126–29); "The Old Coon" in *Pine Bluff*, pp. 172–73; John Q. Anderson, "Old John and the Master," *Southern Folklore Quarterly* 25 (September, 1961): 195–97; *Deep Down*, pp. 187–88 (reprinted as "The Coon in the Box" in *Positively Black*, pp. 64–65, and in *American Negro Folktales*, pp. 80–81; and WPA, UVA, Box 1, Folder 1.

363 Related to me by an informant from Charles City, Virginia, who says that it is true.

364   Collected at the Virginia State Penitentiary on December 2, 1974.

A version appears in *Deep Down*, p. 82, where Abrahams notes that a version in which the Jew has the punch line appears in the original *Anecdota America* 1 (1927): 314.

365   Collected in Richmond, Virginia, on December 2, 1974. Version B: Collected at the Virginia State Penitentiary on December 2, 1974.

A version appears in Neil A. Eddington, "Genital Superiority in Oakland Negro Folklore: A Theme," in *Mother Wit*, pp. 645–46 (reprinted from the *Papers of the Kroeber Anthropological Society*, no. 33 [Fall, 1965]), and in *Rationale*, p. 159. Legman indicates that the tale appears in *Kryptadia* 2 (1884): 344 (note) (*Rationale*, p. 160).

366   Given to me in manuscript form in 1970 by an informant from Charles City, Virginia, and taped in Richmond, Virginia, on October 23, 1974, from the same informant. The text here is a composite of the two versions.

A variant without racial designations is found in *Rationale*, p. 160.

367   Version A: Collected in Richmond, Virginia, in February, 1975. Version B: Collected in Richmond, Virginia, on January 31, 1975.

For other versions see "John Doe in Self-Defense" in "Negro Tales from Bolivar," p. 110, and *Book of Negro Humor*, p. 257.

Although both versions here were collected from elderly persons, the tale still circulates among young Blacks and was collected on February 21, 1976, from a twenty-three-year-old Richmond male by one of my students.

368   Version A: Collected in Richmond, Virginia, on December 2, 1974. Version B: Collected in Henrico, Virginia, on March 11, 1975.

Other versions appear in *American Aesop*, p. 82; in Arthur J. Prange, Jr. and M. M. Vitols, "Jokes Among Southern Negroes: The Revelation of Conflict," in *Mother Wit*, p. 631 (reprinted from *Journal of Nervous and Mental Disease* 136 [1963]: 162–67); as "The Defense Rests" in *Laughing*, p. 81; and in *Rationale*, p. 159.

369   Collected in Richmond, Virginia, on November 20, 1970.

370   Collected in Richmond, Virginia, on October 2, 1974.

371   Collected in Charles City, Virginia, on November 12, 1974.

Variants appear as "Saturday Night" in *Book of Negro Folklore*, p. 509; as "Saturday Night" in *Pine Bluff*, pp. 61–62 (reprinted as "Saturday Night and the Colored Man" in *American Negro Folktales*, p. 135); and in Arthur J. Prange, Jr., and M. M. Vitols, "Jokes Among Southern Negroes," in *Mother Wit*, p. 632.

372   Collected in Richmond, Virginia, on January 13, 1975.

373   Collected in Capahosic, Virginia, on May 12, 1975.

374   Collected in Louisa, Virginia, on January 10, 1975.

For other versions see "The Poll Parrot, the Hawk, and Jim" in *Michigan*,

p. 48 (reprinted in *American Negro Folktales*, pp. 12–21), and "Poll Parrot" in *Pine Bluff*, pp. 38–39.

375   Collected in Richmond, Virginia, on February 18, 1975.

376   Version A: Collected in Richmond, Virginia, on January 22, 1975. Version B: Collected in Richmond, Virginia, in December, 1974, from an informant who changed the ending line to "Hot biscuits burn you," but a member of the audience immediately corrected her. My informant agreed that the closing was "Hot biscuit burn yo' ass," but said she didn't want to say that on tape. I have taken the liberty to reproduce the line as they all agreed it should be and as I have heard it numerous times in Richmond, where the tale is quite popular.

For other versions see "Polly Parrot" in *Lay My Burden Down*, p. 7; "Poll Parrot and Biscuits" in *Michigan*, p. 48 (reprinted in *American Negro Folktales*, pp. 122–23); "Poll Parrot" in *Pine Bluff*, pp. 40–41 (two versions); and "Burn Your Ass, Mister" in "*I Swear,*" p. 27.

377   Collected in Richmond, Virginia, on January 22, 1975.

Much of the humor of this tale comes from the informant's remarkable imitation of the Parrot, which must be heard to be appreciated.

378   Collected in Richmond, Virginia, in February, 1975.

379   The informant from whom this tale was recorded in Richmond, Virginia, in February, 1975, says that it tells of a true incident.

380   Collected in Richmond, Virginia, in September, 1974.

Versions appear in *Mules and Men*, pp. 125–26; as "Master Paying Off John" in *Michigan* (reprinted in *American Negro Folktales*, pp. 142–43); and as "Lazy John" in *Pine Bluff*.

381   Collected in Richmond, Virginia, on January 31, 1975.

382   This popular tale was given to me in manuscript form by an informant from Charles City, Virginia, in 1970.

See Motif K1761. "*Bluff provisions for the swimming match,*" *Motif-Index*.

For other versions see "The Fake Swimmer" in "Folklore from Antigua," pp. 72–73; Elsie Clews Parsons, "Folklore of the Antilles, French and English," *Memoirs of the American Folklore Society* 26, Part III (1943): 284–85; J. Mason Brewer, *Humorous Folk Tales of the South Carolina Negro* (Orangeburg: 1945), pp. 3–4; "The Champion Swimmer" in *Michigan*, p. 55 (reprinted as "The Swimming Contest" in *American Negro Folktales*, pp. 131–32); and Harry Oster, "Negro Humor: John and Old Master" in *Mother Wit*, pp. 550–51 (reprinted from *Journal of the Folklore Institute* 5 [1968]: 41–57. In her article cited above, Parsons cites West African versions.

383   Collected in Richmond, Virginia, on January 13, 1975.

For annotations and another version see my "I Ain't Ready to Go Yet" (p. 71).

384 Collected in Richmond, Virginia, on February 6, 1975. On January 31, 1975, the same informant gave me a version in which the Rabbit and the Cat both escape while the cocky Fox dies.

This is Motif J1662. *"The cat's only trick," Motif-Index.* Thompson indicates that the tale has been found in Rumania, Spain, India, and Africa.

385 Recorded in Washington, D.C., in November, 1970, from an informant who moved there from Richmond, Virginia. Version B: Recorded in the Virginia State Penitentiary on December 2, 1974.

I collected another version of this toast in Capahosic, Virginia, on May 12, 1975, which ended, "When all them white folks went to heaven/ Shine was at Sugar Ray's Bar drinking Seagram's Seven./ He wasn't a minute too soon; he wasn't a minute too late,/ He was the swimmingest motherfucker in the forty-eight states."

"Sinking of the Titanic" in *Book of Negro Folklore,* pp. 366–67, is a completely expurgated text of this toast. Sections of the toast are given with prose summary in "Toasts," pp. 334–36. A discussion of the toast and several versions appear in *Deep Down,* pp. 7–8, 101–4, 120–29. Two versions are included in Eddington, "Genital Superiority" in *Mother Wit,* pp. 646–47. A completely expurgated version appears in *Book of Negro Humor,* pp. 91–92. A version appears in *Positively Black,* pp. 44–45. Jackson includes ten versions in *"Get Your Ass in the Water,"* pp. 180–96.

A story was circulated that Jack Johnson was denied passage on board the *Titanic.* Allegedly he was told, "We don't haul no coal." Huddie Ledbetter sang, "Jack Johnson wanted to get on board,/ Captain he said I ain't haulin' no coal,/ Fare thee, *Titanic,* fare thee well"; see Harold Courlander, *Negro Folk Music, U.S.A.* (New York: Columbia University Press, 1963), p. 78. Thus, according to the legend, the only Black person on board was a worker in the boiler room. (Actually there were no Black passengers, nor were there Black crew members.) The toast lends itself to a symbolic interpretation, with the *Titanic* representing the United States, where the Black is denied first-class passage and relegated to menial positions. Now that the ship is sinking (i.e., the country is foundering, languishing), he is implored to help. But Shine rejects the pleas, rejecting at the same time its status symbols—so long withheld from him—white women and money. This symbolic rejection brings Shine close to the principles of the contemporary militant writers such as Calvin C. Hernton, who eulogizes Shine in "Elements of Grammar" in *The New Black Poetry,* ed. Clarence Major (New York: Major-International, 1969), pp. 66–67. See also Larry Neal's interpretation of "Shine" in "And Shine Swam On," in *Black Fire: An Anthology of Afro-American Writing,* ed. Leroi Jones and Larry Neal (New York: William Morrow, 1968), pp. 638–59.

386 Collected in Charles City, Virginia, on November 12, 1974.

This tale usually ends with the white man humbly serving the Black man. See "He Gets the Tank Filled" in *Deep Down,* pp. 237–38; "Lesson in Etiquette" in *Laughing,* pp. 213–14; Pauline Cross, "Jokes and Black Consciousness" in *Mother Wit,* pp. 650–51; and *Positively Black,* p. 72.

387 Collected in Richmond, Virginia, on November 20, 1970.

388   Version A: Collected in Charles City, Virginia, on November 12, 1974. Version B: Collected in Henrico, Virginia, on March 11, 1975.

This group of tales about Blacks frightened into submission who later turn the tables on their white persecutors is very popular. Several variants have been collected. In "Old Marster Eats Crow" (*Michigan*, p. 74), Old Marster holds a gun on John and makes him pick the feathers and eat the crow halfway down. John then gets the gun and orders Old Marster, "Start at his ass and eat all the way up." In "John Whips Old Master" in "Negro Tales from Bolivar County," pp. 108–9, when John finds out Old Master doesn't have his pistol, he prepares to whip him. Similar to my version B is "The New Dance Step" in *Pine Bluff*, pp. 234–35, in which Blacks make whites dance.

389   Collected in Richmond, Virginia, on February 6, 1975.

See Motif N332.1. "*Man accidentally fed bread which his father has poisoned,*" *Motif-Index.*

390   Given to me in manuscript form by Linwood Lewis, who collected it from a Virginia Commonwealth University student in April, 1975.

391   Collected at the Virginia State Penitentiary on December 2, 1974.

392   Given to me in manuscript form by Linwood Lewis, who collected it from a Virginia Commonwealth University student in April, 1975.

393   Given to me in manuscript form by Linwood Lewis, who collected it from a Virginia Commonwealth University student in April, 1975.

394   Given to me in manuscript form by Linwood Lewis, who collected it in April, 1971, from a Virginia Commonwealth University student.

395   Given to me in manuscript form by Linwood Lewis, who collected it from a Virginia Commonwealth University student in April, 1975.

396   Version A: Collected in Charles City, Virginia, on March 29, 1975. Version B: Collected in Richmond, Virginia, on January 31, 1975.

See Motif K651. "*Wolf descends into well in one bucket and rescues fox in the other,*" *Motif-Index*; Motif J179.3. Diving for cheese, Baughman, and Type 34. "The Wolf Dives into the Water for Reflected Cheese," Baughman.

For other versions see "Old Mr. Rabbit, He's a Good Fisherman," *Uncle Remus: His Songs and His Sayings*, pp. 76–81 (reprinted in *A Treasury of American Folklore*, pp. 661–63); "In the Well" in "Folk Lore from Aiken," pp. 16–17; *Pine Bluff*, pp. 167–68 (reprinted in *American Negro Folktales*, pp. 97–98); "Brother Rabbit and Brother Terr'pin" in *Positively Black*, pp. 51–52; and "Buh Rabbit and Buh Wolf in deh Well" in Lydia Parrish, *Slave Songs of the Georgia Sea Islands* (Hatboro, Pa.: Folklore Associates, 1965), p. 40.

In his review of *Uncle Remus: His Songs and His Sayings*, T. F. Crane ("Plantation Folk-Lore" in *The Negro and His Folklore in Nineteenth-Century Periodicals*, ed. Bruce Jackson [Austin: University of Texas Press,

1967], p. 160) points out that this tale has a version in La Fontaine's *Le Loup et le Renard*, which was taken from the *Roman de Renart*. He points out also that there is an earlier version in *Disciplina Clericalis*, a collection of Oriental stories made in the first years of the twelfth century.

397   This true anecdote was related to me in Richmond, Virginia, on February 24, 1975.

398   Given to me in manuscript form by Linwood Lewis, who collected it from a student at Virginia Commonwealth University in April, 1975.

399   Given to me in manuscript form by Linwood Lewis, who collected it from a student at Virginia Commonwealth University in April, 1975.

400   Given to me in manuscript form by Linwood Lewis, who collected it from a Virginia Commonwealth University student in April, 1975.

401   Collected in Richmond, Virginia, on December 2, 1974.
    A variant is "That's Illegal Too" in *Laughing*, p. 212, in which a beautician, after being paid $125.00 by a Negro, puts out a sign, "No White Trash Served Here."

402   Given to me in manuscript form by Linwood Lewis, who collected it from a student at Virginia Commonwealth University in April, 1975.

403   Version A: Collected in Richmond, Virginia, in February, 1975. The informant who gave me these lines was the only one of my informants who talked about "John Henry." He enthusiastically recalled the recitations of the ballad that he heard from "the guys who used to be on the railroad," adding that, in the country where he grew up (western Virginia), if a man couldn't play "John Henry," "he couldn't play no guitar." He spoke authoritatively of the real John Henry and noted that a statue had been planned "right there at that place where he used to drill steel [Big Bend]." The informant said he never learned "John Henry," but, during the course of his account, he related these verses, some of which are prose summary (see the third verse). Version B: This parody of "John Henry" was given to me in manuscript form by Marilyn Gordon, who collected it from a twenty-one-year-old male in Richmond, Virginia. The informant noted that, when he was in elementary school in Newport News, Virginia, the children used to sing it. Miss Gordon also gave me a parody which she collected from a young white man at Virginia Commonwealth University on March 25, 1976:

When John Henry was a little boy,
Sitting on his pappy's knee,
His pappy picked him up
And threw him on the floor,
And said, "This boy don' pissed on me."

See Motif X991. Lie: remarkable rock driller, Baughman.
Tales of John Henry have been collected since 1909, when Louise Rand

Bascom published two lines of the ballad; see "Ballads and Songs of Western North Carolina," *JAFL* 22 (April-June, 1909): 249. Since that time versions have appeared in sources too numerous to list here. Anyone interested in this ballad should seé the chronological survey of John Henry scholarship in Richard M. Dorson, "The Career of 'John Henry,'" *Western Folklore* 24 (July, 1965): 155–63. See also Guy Johnson, *John Henry: Tracking Down a Legend* (Chapel Hill: University of North Carolina Press, 1933), and Louis W. Chappel, *John Henry: A Folklore Study* (Port Washington, N.Y.: Kennikat, 1968).

Though most versions do not present the direct sexual assertiveness that is characteristic of the Bad Nigger tales, a few deal specifically with the hero's sexual prowess. See, for example, a version collected by Abrahams in Philadelphia in *Deep Down*, p. 75. Further, the standard verses present very definite sexual allusion in the images of the virulent John Henry driving his steel and dying with his hammer in his hand, as Lomax has suggested: "John Henry, then, with its list of his numerous female admirers, its account of steel-driving so violent it shook the mountain (a phallic image), probably began as a testament to the erotic prowess of John Henry..."; see *The Folk Songs*, p. 553.

404   This tale was collected at the Virginia State Penitentiary on November 27, 1974.

Numerous and varied versions of "Stagolee" have appeared in print. A detailed discussion of the history of this toast, including several versions, may be found in *Deep Down*, pp. 129–42. Howard W. Odum and Guy B. Johnson include two texts in *The Negro and His Songs* (Chapel Hill: University of North Carolina Press, 1925), pp. 196–98. Several versions appear in Mary Wheeler, *Steamboatin' Days* (Baton Rouge: Louisiana State University Press, 1928), pp. 100–2. John and Alan Lomax include two versions in *American Ballads and Folk Songs* (New York, 1934), pp. 93–99. A version is found in Sterling Brown et al., *The Negro Caravan* (New York: Dryden, 1941), pp. 462–65. Prose and poetic versions are found in Onah Spencer, "Stackolee," *Direction* 4 (Summer, 1941): 14–17 (reprinted in *Treasury of American Folklore*, pp. 122–30). Dorson includes a version in *Michigan*, pp. 16–62. Hughes and Bontemps reprint the versions from *The Negro Caravan* and from Spencer's "Stackolee" in *Book of Negro Folklore*, pp. 359–63. Lomax discusses the legend of Stagolee and includes a text of the tale in *The Folk Songs*, pp. 559–72. Expurgated verses of "Stagolee" appear in Harold Courtlander, *Negro Folk Music, U.S.A.* (New York: Columbia University Press, 1963), pp. 178–79. Bruce Jackson presents a rhyming verse and several prose narratives about Stagolee from John Hurt, in many of which Stagolee is presented as a positive hero, helping little old ladies save their homes, for example; see "Stagolee Stories: A Badman Goes Gentle," *Southern Folklore Quarterly* 29 (June, 1965): 188–94. A brief text, "Stackolee," appears in *Book of Negro Humor*, pp. 93–94. Labov et al. include verses from "Stagolee" and comment on the toast at varied points in their study; see "Toasts," pp. 336, 343, 345. Another interesting study is Richard E. Buehler, "Stacker Lee: A Partial Investigation into the Historicity of a Negro Murder Ballad," *Keystone Folklore Quarterly* 12 (Fall, 1967): 187–91. A long prose version appears in Julius Lester, *Black Folktales* (New York: Grove Press,

1969), pp. 113–35. Another version appears in *Positively Black*, pp. 45–46. Seven versions, two of which were collected from white informants, are included in *"Get Your Ass in the Water,"* pp. 43–55. The earlier versions of "Stagolee" cited above, as well as a few of the more recent ones, are expurgated.

Numerous recordings of "Stagolee" have appeared. For a listing of these see *Deep Down*, p. 133 (note).

For a literary version see Margaret Walker, "Bad-Man Stagolee" in *For My People* (New York: Arno Press, 1968), p. 35.

405   Toast collected at the Virginia State Penitentiary on December 2, 1974.

Two versions, one manuscript version from a Harlem correspondent collected in 1967 and the other, a version recorded from a performance of Rudy Ray Moore in New York in June, 1970, appear in *"Get Your Ass in the Water,"* pp. 57–62. The text here corresponds very closely to the version by Rudy Ray Moore.

Mabel's allusion to cunnilingus here is the gravest insult to the Bad Nigger in toasts. For a discussion of views of cunnilingus and fellatio in the toasts, see *"Get Your Ass in the Water,"* pp. 19–20. For a discussion of the views of cunnilingus and fellatio in the Black ghetto areas of San Francisco and Washington, D.C., see Christina and Richard Milner, *Black Players: The Secret World of Black Pimps* (Boston: Little, Brown, 1972), pp. 143–44 (note). Of course, it should be noted that the taboo of oragenital sex is not limited to Blacks but is widely accepted in American society in general.

406   Collected at the Virginia State Penitentiary on November 27, 1974. A few lines were added during an interview in December, 1974.

A version, "The Fall," appears in "Toasts," pp. 331–33. A few lines appear in Wepman et al., "Toasts: The Black Urban Poetry," *JAFL* 87 (July-September, 1974): 216.

Regarding *to boost* as slang for *to shoplift*, see Neil Eddington, *The Urban Plantation: The Ethnography of an Oral Tradition in a Negro Community* (Ann Arbor: University Microfilms, 1973), p. 197.

407   Collected in Washington, D.C., in November, 1970, from an informant who moved there from Richmond, Virginia. I have changed the name to "Murphy" because the informant used his own name.

Though I have discovered no other versions of this toast, it makes use of several formulaic lines. The closing lines are standard in many of these narratives. See, for example, the closing of "The Signifying Monkey" in *Positively Black*, p. 90, and " 'Flicted Arm Pete" and "Junkies' Heaven" in *"Get Your Ass in the Water,"* pp. 150–51 and 206–7, respectively. Lines 12 and 13 in the text here are the opening lines of a short toast, "I Woke Up This Morning with a Hard On" in *"Get Your Ass in the Water,"* pp. 218–19. It is not unusual for an expert reciter of toasts such as my informant to take certain of these standard lines and develop his own variations.

408   Collected at the Virginia State Penitentiary on November 27, 1974.

409   Collected at the Virginia State Penitentiary on December 2, 1974.

Four versions appear in *"Get Your Ass in the Water,"* pp. 103–12: "Pimping Sam," "Wicked Nell" (two versions under this title), and "The Pimp." One text under the title of "Wicked Nell" was recorded from a performance of Rudy Ray Moore and obviously is the model for my informant's version.

410   Collected at the Virginia State Penitentiary on November 27, 1974.
A carefully expurgated version which appears as "The Pool-Shooting Monkey" in *Worser*, p. 173, recounts the pool game but does not include the card game. A few verses are found in *Deep Down*, p. 74. This toast is treated by Abrahams in his discussion of the Signifying Monkey in *Deep Down*, pp. 142–57, and other versions are included there. Four versions appear in *"Get Your Ass in the Water,"* pp. 173–78.
Charlie Russell has the character Sweetmeat recite a version of this toast in his play, *Five on the Black Hand Side* (New York: Third World Press, 1973), p. 37.

411   Collected at the Virginia State Penitentiary on November 27, 1974.
Portions appear in "Toasts," pp. 333–34. A much longer version appears in Michael H. Agar, "Folklore of the Heroin Addict: Two Examples," *JAFL* 84 (April–June, 1971): 177–81, with a more detailed account of the buying and shooting of the heroin and including also an account of the trial. Agar's version is a sharp protest against the stiff punishments meted out to drug abusers.

412   Collected at the Virginia State Penitentiary on November 27, 1974.
Variants appear as "A Hard Luck Story" in *Deep Down*, pp. 158–60, and in *Positively Black*, p. 125. *"Get Your Ass in the Water,"* pp. 115–23, includes four variants: "Sweet Lovin' Rose," "No Good Whore and Crime Don't Pay," "Whores Are No Good and Crime Don't Pay," and "No Good Whore." The second of Jackson's texts was collected from a white informant. Some of the lines appear in "Once I Lived the Life of a Millionaire" and "Down and Out" in *"Get Your Ass in the Water,"* pp. 200–1. "The Letter" in "Toasts," pp. 336–37, is also a version.
Labov et al. explain the pimp's virulent reaction to the whore's request for money: "We see once again a statement of the crucial question as to who takes money from whom. A 'ho' takes money from her 'tricks.' Thus she is superior to men who pay her. Her asking him for money is understood as an attempt on her part to convert him from 'superior' pimp to 'inferior' trick. This is why, according to the rules of the 'game,' the pimp adamantly refuses to pay her what she asks" ("Toasts," p. 337).

413   This burlesque of Henry Wadsworth Longfellow's "Paul Revere's Ride" was collected in Henrico, Virginia, on March 11, 1975, from an informant who first heard it in Richmond, Virginia, in 1950.
This toast bears similarities to the account of the fornication contest in "Schoolteacher Lulu and Crabeye Pete" in *Deep Down*, pp. 164–65.

414   Collected in Richmond, Virginia, on November 20, 1970.
Though I discovered no versions of this tale in any folklore collections, there is a version related by Ludlow, the protagonist of William Melvin

Kelley's novel *A Drop of Patience* (Chatham, N.J.: Chatham Bookseller, 1965), pp. 202–3.

415   Collected at the Virginia State Penitentiary on December 2, 1974.
Legman collected this tale in New York from a foreign source in 1940 (*Rationale*, p. 563).

416   Collected in Charles City, Virginia, on November 12, 1974.
In most versions the slave kisses or slaps the white mistress, the ultimate act of audacity. See "The Fight" in *Michigan*, pp. 55–56; "Big John and Little John" in *Worser*, pp. 108–10; and "What Made Micajah Run" in *Laughing*, pp. 52–53.

417   Collected in Richmond, Virginia, in February, 1975, from an informant who says it is a true account.

418   Collected in Richmond, Virginia, in February, 1975.

419   Originally related to me in Capahosic, Virginia, on May 12, 1975. This was, however, the one session where I was so enthralled by the tales that I failed to notice that my tape had run out. The informant was kind enough to furnish me a handwritten copy of the tale in July, 1975, from which the text here is taken.

420   Collected at the Virginia State Penitentiary on November 27, 1974, from an informant who learned it in Norfolk, Virginia, in 1958.
Admittedly this is an exhortation against the life of the Bad Nigger rather than the usual acclamation of it. The principals are, however, a contrite Bad Nigger and a budding Bad Nigger, and thus it seemed appropriate as a closing selection for this chapter.
Jackson has two texts of "Feeble Old Man and a Kid Named Dan," which are versions of "Gay Young Lad," in "*Get Your Ass in the Water*," pp. 72–77. He also gives three versions of a similar toast, "My Reflections," in "*Get Your Ass in the Water*," pp. 68–72. All of these narratives, as Jackson points out, are homilectics in which an experienced, convicted criminal catalogues his experiences to substantiate his authority ("*Get Your Ass in the Water*," p. 69).

421   Version A: Collected in Richmond, Virginia, on November 19, 1974. Version B: Collected in Richmond, Virginia, on February 6, 1975.
For other versions see "Mr. Hawk and Brother Buzzard" in *Nights with Uncle Remus*, pp. 372–76; "Fasting-Trial" and "Wait upon the Lord" (two versions) in *Sea Islands*, pp. 118–19; and *Mules and Men*, pp. 153–54 (reprinted as "The Hawk and the Buzzard" in *Treasury of American Folklore*, pp. 672–73).

422   Collected in Richmond, Virginia, on February 6, 1975.
See Motif J151.4. "*Wisdom from old man: always say, 'if it pleases God,'*" *Motif-Index*.

423   Collected in Richmond, Virginia, on February 6, 1975.
A version in which the Snail says, "It pays to be fast," appears in *Mules and Men*, p. 165.

424   Collected in Richmond, Virginia, in February, 1975.
See Motif K611. *"Escape by putting captor off guard," Motif-Index.*
For other versions see *Sea Islands*, p. 75; "In Liquor" in "Folk-lore from Elizabeth City," p. 279 (this tale does not include the episode in which the Mouse escapes by fooling the Cat into washing his face); *Michigan*, p. 206 (reprinted as "The Rat in the Whiskey" in *American Negro Folktales*, p. 105); and "The Mountain Rat Who Outwitted the Cat" in *Worser*, pp. 100–1. Hurston has a tale about a Rat who gets away by reminding the Cat to wash her face before eating, but the whiskey episode is omitted; see *Mules and Men*, pp. 303–4.

425   Collected in Richmond, Virginia, in February, 1975.

426   Collected in Richmond, Virginia, on January 31, 1975.

427   Collected in Richmond, Virginia, in February, 1975.
See Motif J1811.5(c). Simpletons interpret frogs' cries as "knee deep!" Baughman. This tale is combined with my "It's 'Leven O'Clock" (p. 162) in "Watch or Rattlesnake," "Knee-Deep," and "Better Go Round" in *Sea Islands*, pp. 65–66. See also "South," p. 268.

428   Collected in Richmond, Virginia, in February, 1975.
As in many of his other tales, this informant's impressions of the sound of the animal adds to the effectiveness of the tale.

429   Version A: Collected in Charles City, Virginia, in November, 1974.
Version B: Collected in Richmond, Virginia, on February 24, 1975.
For other versions see Veronica Huss and Evelyn Werner, "The Conchs of Riviera, Florida," *Southern Folklore Quarterly* 4 (September, 1940): 143–44; "Poll Parrot" in *Pine Bluff*, p. 42 (reprinted as "The Parrot and the Wood-man" in *American Negro Folktales*, p. 123); and "The Mountain Man and the Parrot" in *Worser*, pp. 101–2. See also my "Talk So Much" (p. 212).

430   Collected in Richmond, Virginia, on January 13, 1975.
Variants appear as "Poll Parrots and Hens" in *American Negro Folktales*, p. 123, and in *Rationale*, p. 201.

431   Collected in Richmond, Virginia, on December 9, 1974.

432   Related to me in Henrico, Virginia, in June, 1975. The text here is reproduced from memory.
A version appears in *Rationale*, p. 202.

433   Collected in Richmond, Virginia, in February, 1975.
See Motif J2351. *"Animal betrays himself to his enemies by talking," Motif-Index.*

434   Collected in Richmond, Virginia, on January 31, 1975.
This is a version of my "Turn Out the Sack" (p. 214).

435   Collected in Richmond, Virginia, on December 9, 1974.

436   Collected in Richmond, Virginia, in February, 1975.

437   Collected in Richmond, Virginia, in February, 1975.

438   Collected in Richmond, Virginia, on February 6, 1975.
See Motif K11.3. "*Hare and tortoise race: sleeping hare,*" *Motif-Index.*
Thompson notes that this tale has been found among Japanese, North
American Indians, Africans, West Indians, and Bahamans as well as among
Black Americans.
For another version from Black Americans, see "The Hare and the Tor-
toise" in Ambrose Gonzales, *With Aesop along the Black Border* (Columbia,
S.C.: State, 1924), pp. 75–81.

439   Collected in Richmond, Virginia, on February 6, 1975.
See Type 81. "Too Cold for Hare to Build House in Winter," Baughman.
For other versions see "Mr. Hawk and Brother Buzzard" in *Nights with
Uncle Remus,* pp. 372–76, where this tale is combined with my "Wait on de
Lord" (p. 248); "Dilatory Buzzard" in "Folk-Lore from Virginia," p. 374; and
"Lazy Buzzard" in *Michigan,* pp. 44–45 (reprinted in *American Negro
Folktales,* p. 115). Baughman lists several white American sources.

440   Collected in Richmond, Virginia, in February, 1975.
See Motif K427. "*Clever animal betrays thief,*" *Motif-Index.*
A variant is "The Polly Parrot and the Chickens" in *Worser,* p. 98.

441   Collected in Richmond, Virginia, on February 6, 1975.
See Motif K1047. "*The bear bites the seemingly dead horse's tail. Is
dragged off by the horse,*" *Motif-Index.*
A variant appears as "Brother Fox Catches Mr. Horse" in *Nights with
Uncle Remus,* pp. 6–11, in which Rabbit fools Fox into letting him tie him
[Fox] to the horse's tail. In the variant "Crow, Buzzard and Mule" in *Michigan,* pp. 43–44, the Mule runs himself to death, and Buzzard dies, too; then
the Crow eats both of them (reprinted in *American Negro Folktales,* pp.
114–15). Other versions appear as "Take My Place" in *Pine Bluff,* pp. 20–22,
and *American Negro Folktales,* pp. 83–86.

442   Collected in Richmond, Virginia, in February, 1975.

443   Collected in Richmond, Virginia, on January 31, 1975.

444   Collected in Richmond, Virginia, on February 6, 1975.

445   Collected in Richmond, Virginia, in February, 1975.

446   Collected in Richmond, Virginia, on December 2, 1974.

The effectiveness of this joke is enhanced by the dramatizations which accompany it.

447 Collected in Capahosic, Virginia, on May 12, 1975.

448 Collected in Richmond, Virginia, on December 2, 1974.
A variant of this popular tale is "Mr. Buzzard and Mr. Rabbit" in *Deep Down*, pp. 247–48.

449 Collected in Henrico, Virginia, on March 11, 1975.
This is one of a large group of tales about the hypersensitivity of the Monkey (as well as of other primates other than man) regarding his looks. In *Where Animals Talk: West African Folk Lore Tales* (Boston: Gotham, 1912), R. H. Nassau mentions an African tale in which the Gorilla is sensitive about his looks. Other variants are "The Ugliest Animal" in "Tales and Riddles," pp. 533–34, and "He Made His Position Clear" in *Laughing*, p. 184.

450 Collected in Richmond, Virginia, on February 6, 1975.
See Motif J2413.4.3. "*Monkey cuts his throat, thinking that he is imitating cobbler*," *Motif-Index*.
"The Monkey Who Impitated His Master" in *Michigan*, pp. 187–88, combines this tale with my "Big Fraid and Lil' Fraid" (p. 34). Dorson reprints this tale in *American Negro Folktales*, pp. 349–50. "Fatal Imitation" in *Lay My Burden Down*, p. 23, is another version. A variant in which the Monkey thumbs his nose at the men when he pretends to cut his throat appears in *Rationale*, p. 195.

451 Collected in Richmond, Virginia, in February, 1975, from an informant whose rendering of the cries of the barnyard animals was masterfully done.
In another version given to me by the same informant the Gander says at the end, "DATSHISASS, DATSHISASS, DATSHISASS!" [that's his ass]. I also collected a version from a Richmond woman on January 13, 1975.
"Fowls at the Crap Game" in *Pine Bluff*, pp. 170–71, combines this tale with my "Preacher Comin' Today" (p. 51).

452 Version A: Tease song collected in Richmond, Virginia, in November, 1970. Version B: Collected in Washington, D.C., in November, 1971, from an informant who moved there from Richmond, Virginia. Version C: Collected in Richmond, Virginia, on April 4, 1975.
This verse, which is highly popular in Richmond (I have three excellent versions), teases the reader by creating the expectation of an obscene word to complete the rhyme pattern and then substitutes a word with the same initial consonant sound. It is very entertaining when properly performed. (The timing must be perfect.) The only variant that I have seen in a collection is "Ringo" in "*Get Your Ass in the Water*," p. 220, which Jackson's informant said he learned from someone in Tennessee. Jackson notes that he recorded several versions in Texas.
Interestingly enough, Stephen Henderson (*Understanding the New Black Poetry* [New York: William Morrow, 1973], p. 34), quotes a "poem" by Reginald Butler (Henderson does not indicate a source; perhaps the "poem"

has not been published) which bears a striking similarity to the versions that I have collected in Richmond, Virginia. It turns out that the poet is a native of Richmond, Virginia, who now lives in California.

Legman alludes to two alliterative and bawdy tease songs, "Two Irishmen" and "Peter Murphy's Dog," but he does not reproduce any lines from either (*Rationale*, p. 443).

Several of my white students at Virginia Commonwealth University sing a similar but less obscene song, "Lulu":

> Lulu had a steamboat,
> The steamboat had a bell;
> Lulu went to heaven,
> The steamboat went to _____
> *Hell*-o, Operator,
> Give me number nine;
> If you disconnect me,
> I'll kick you in the _____
> *Behind* the 'frigerator,
> Lulu found a glass,
> Slipped and fell upon it,
> And cut her little _____
> *Ask* me no more questions,
> I'll tell you no more lies.
> This is the true story
> How Lulu lived and died.

453   Collected in Richmond, Virginia, in February, 1975.

For a discussion of the history of this song, see Curtis Owens, "Whose 'Dan Tucker'?" *JAFL* 84 (October–December, 1971): 446–48. Curtis credits Dan Emmett with composing the original "Ole Dan Tucker," but adds that the song "at least in many of its variants belong[s] to the people—to the Negroes especially, but also to some of the whites" (p. 248).

I added *ass* (see line 5 of the song); my informant merely said, "You know what."

454   This parody of "Yankee Doodle" was collected in Richmond, Virginia, in February, 1975.

455   Collected in Richmond, Virginia, on April 4, 1975, from an informant who says it was a very popular verse in Richmond, where he has heard it and recited it many times. After the first verse, the performer simply throws his hand over his shoulder and the audience invariably fills in "Over the hill, over the hill."

Lydia Pinkham (see stanza 3) was an old medication for female trouble, the informant told me.

456   Limerick collected in Richmond, Virginia, on April 4, 1975.

457   Collected in Richmond, Virginia, on April 4, 1975.

458 Collected in Richmond, Virginia, on April 4, 1975.

459 Collected in Charles City, Virginia, in November, 1970.

460 Collected in Henrico, Virginia, on March 11, 1975.

461 Collected in Washington, D.C., in November, 1970, from an informant who moved there from Richmond, Virginia.

462 Told to me in Richmond, Virginia, on July 17, 1975. The text here is reproduced from memory.
See Motifs J1744.1. "*Bridegroom does not know what to do on his wedding night*" and J1745. "*Absurd ignorance of sex,*" *Motif-Index.* A version appears in *Rationale*, p. 119.

463 Collected in Richmond, Virginia, on April 4, 1975.
See Motif J2462. "*Foolish bridegroom follows instructions literally,*" *Motif-Index.* Versions appear in *Rationale*, p. 126, and as "Family Duty" in "I Swear," p. 30.

464 Collected in November, 1970, in Washington, D.C., from an informant who moved there from Richmond, Virginia.
A variant appears in *Rationale*, p. 668.

465 Collected in Henrico, Virginia, on March 11, 1975.

466 Collected in Richmond, Virginia, on January 13, 1975.
A version, which Legman collected in Bloomington, Indiana, in 1963, appears in *Rationale*, p. 264.

467 Version A: Collected in Richmond, Virginia, on March 7, 1975. Version B: Given to me in manuscript form by an informant from Charles City, Virginia, on March 15, 1975.
Though this tale is very popular in the Richmond area, I have found no printed versions. I have another excellent version collected in Henrico, Virginia, on March 11, 1975.

468 Collected in Henrico, Virginia, on March 11, 1975.

469 Collected in Henrico, Virginia, on March 11, 1975.

470 Collected in Henrico, Virginia, on March 11, 1975.

471 Collected in Richmond, Virginia, on January 13, 1975.

472 Collected in Henrico, Virginia, on March 11, 1975.

473 Collected in Washington, D.C., in November, 1970, from an informant who moved there from Richmond, Virginia.

474   Collected in Henrico, Virginia, on March 11, 1975.

475   Collected in Henrico, Virginia, on March 11, 1975.
A version is "Masturbating the Bear" in "I Swear," p. 31.

476   Collected at the Virginia State Penitentiary on December 2, 1974.

477   Collected in Richmond, Virginia, on October 23, 1974, from an informant who was born and reared in Charles City, Virginia.

478   Collected at the Virginia State Penitentiary on November 27, 1974.

479   Collected in Richmond, Virginia, on October 23, 1974, from an informant from Charles City, Virginia.

480   Collected in Richmond, Virginia, on October 27, 1970. The text here is slightly condensed.
A variant appears in *Rationale*, p. 555.

481   Collected in Richmond, Virginia, on November 20, 1970.

482   Collected in Richmond, Virginia, on November 19, 1975.

483   Collected in Richmond, Virginia, on November 20, 1970.

484   Collected at the Virginia State Penitentiary on November 27, 1974.

485   Collected in Washington, D.C., in November, 1970, from an informant who moved there from Richmond, Virginia.
A variant appears in *Rationale*, pp. 586–87.

486   Related to me in the fall of 1974 in Richmond, Virginia. The text here is reproduced from memory.

487   Collected in Henrico, Virginia, on March 11, 1975.

488   Collected in Charles City, Virginia, in November, 1970.
A version which Legman collected on a transcontinental train in 1943 appears in *Rationale*, p. 303.

489   Collected in Richmond, Virginia, on October 23, 1974, from a resident of Charles City, Virginia.

490   Collected in Charles City, Virginia, on November 13, 1974.

491   Collected at the Virginia State Penitentiary on December 2, 1974.
Though I have heard this joke many times in Virginia (at least since my college days [1954–1957]), I found no version of it in the collections studied.

492   Collected in Richmond, Virginia, on December 2, 1974.

493   Collected in Richmond, Virginia, on April 4, 1975.

494   Version A: Collected in Henrico, Virginia, on March 11, 1975. Version B: Collected at the Virginia State Penitentiary on December 2, 1974.
A variant in which the bride brings the groom down by saying, "with a three-inch fuse," appears in *Rationale*, p. 536. Legman collected his joke in Washington, D.C., in 1943.

495   Version A: Collected in Richmond, Virginia, on January 13, 1975. Version B: Collected in Henrico, Virginia, on March 7, 1975.

496   Collected in Henrico, Virginia, on March 11, 1975.
A version appears in *Rationale*, p. 789.

497   Collected in Richmond, Virginia, on April 4, 1975.

498   Collected in Richmond, Virginia, on April 4, 1975.

499   Given to me in manuscript form in the fall of 1970 by an informant from Charles City, Virginia.

500   Collected in Richmond, Virginia, on April 4, 1975.
For other versions see "The Hairy Scoreboard" in *Deep Down*, pp. 220–21, and *Rationale*, p. 773.

501   Collected in Henrico, Virginia, on March 11, 1975.

502   Collected in Richmond, Virginia, on October 23, 1975, from a resident of New Kent, Virginia.

503   Collected at the Virginia State Penitentiary on December 2, 1974.
A variant appears in *Rationale*, p. 100.

504   Collected in Richmond, Virginia, on November 20, 1974.

505   Collected in Richmond, Virginia, on October 23, 1974, from a resident of New Kent, Virginia.

506   Collected in Henrico, Virginia, on March 11, 1975.

507   Collected in Richmond, Virginia, on November 20, 1974.

508   Collected in Charles City, Virginia, in November, 1970.

509   Version A: Collected in Richmond, Virginia, on January 13, 1975. Version B: Collected in Richmond, Virginia, on October 23, 1974, from an informant who was born and reared in Charles City, Virginia. Version C: Collected at the Virginia State Penitentiary on December 2, 1974.
Variants appear in *Worser*, p. 65, and in *Rationale*, p. 66.

510   Collected in Richmond, Virginia, on November 20, 1970.

511   Collected at the Virginia State Penitentiary on December 2, 1974.
512   Version A: Collected in Charles City, Virginia, in November, 1970.
Version B: Collected at the Virginia State Penitentiary on December 2, 1974.
    A version appears in *Rationale*, p. 63.

513   Collected in Capahosic, Virginia, on May 12, 1975, from a resident of
Richmond, Virginia.

514   Collected at the Virginia State Penitentiary on December 2, 1974. The
text here is slightly condensed from the taped version.

515   Collected in Henrico, Virginia, on March 11, 1975.

516   Collected at the Virginia State Penitentiary on December 2, 1974.

517   Collected in Henrico, Virginia, on March 11, 1975.

518   Collected in Henrico, Virginia, on March 7, 1975.
    See Motif X111.7. *"Misunderstood words lead to comic results,"* Motif-
Index.

519   Collected in Richmond, Virginia, on January 13, 1975.

520   Given to me in manuscript form by an informant from Richmond,
Virginia. This was one of the items missed when my tape ran out during a
session in Capahosic, Virginia, in May, 1975.

521   Collected in Richmond, Virginia, on December 2, 1974.

522   This "true" anecdote was related to me in Richmond, Virginia, on
October 23, 1974, by a former resident of Charles City, Virginia, the setting
for the tale.
    Names of the principals have been changed by me.

523   Collected in Washington, D.C., in November, 1970, from a former resident of Richmond, Virginia.

524   A: Given to me in manuscript form in March, 1976, by an informant
from Charles City, Virginia. B: Given to me in manuscript form by Thomas
Beatty, who collected it on March 26, 1976, from a twenty-year-old female
student at Virginia Commonwealth University. C: Ibid. D: Ibid. E: Given to
me in manuscript form by Leonard S. Lambert, who heard a Black youth
(whom he estimated to be between twelve and fifteen years old) say this to
some of his peers with whom he was joking on a Richmond street corner on
March 14, 1976. F: Given to me in manuscript form by Mr. Dennis Folly,
who heard it from a street worker in Richmond, Virginia, on March 17, 1976.
G: Given to me in manuscript form by Dennis Folly, who collected it in
Hanover County, Virginia, in the spring of 1976. H: Ibid. I: Ibid. J: Ibid. K:

Given to me in manuscript form by Dennis Folly, who collected it from a student at Virginia Commonwealth University on April 1, 1976.

525 A: Given to me in manuscript form by Dennis Folly, who collected it from a female student at Virginia Commonwealth University on March 12, 1976. B: Ibid. C: Ibid. D: Ibid. E: Given to me in manuscript form by Dennis Folly, who collected it in Hanover County, Virginia, on April 5, 1976. F: Given to me in manuscript form by Dennis Folly, who collected it from an eighty-six-year-old woman in Hanover County, Virginia, on March 27, 1976. G: Ibid. H: A version of this familiar wisecrack, one of my aunt's favorites, appears as "Respect for Work" in *Book of Negro Folklore*, p. 497.

526 A: Collected from a Charles City, Virginia, woman in March, 1976. B: Given to me in manuscript form by Dennis Folly, who collected it from a female student at Virginia Commonwealth University, on April 5, 1976. C: Ibid. D: Given to me in manuscript form by Dennis Folly, who collected it from a sixteen-year-old Hanover County, Virginia, girl in April, 1976. E: Collected from a Charles City, Virginia, woman in March, 1976. E: Ibid. F.: Ibid. H: Given to me in manuscript form by Dennis Folly in May, 1976. I: Collected from a Charles City, Virginia, woman in March, 1976. J: Collected from a Richmond, Virginia, woman on May 20, 1976. K: Ibid.

527 A: Collected from a Charles City, Virginia, woman in March, 1976. B: Ibid. C: Collected from a Richmond, Virginia, woman on May 20, 1976. D: Collected from a Charles City, Virginia, woman in March, 1976. E: Ibid. F: Collected from a Richmond, Virginia, woman on May 20, 1976. G: Collected from a Charles City, Virginia, woman in March, 1976. H: Collected from a Richmond, Virginia, woman on May 20, 1976. I: Ibid. J: Collected from a Charles City, Virginia, woman in March, 1976.

528 A: Given to me in manuscript form by Dennis Folly, who collected it from a sixteen-year-old Hanover County, Virginia, girl in April, 1976. B: Given to me in manuscript form by Dennis Folly in May, 1976. C: Ibid. D: Ibid. E: Collected from a Richmond, Virginia, woman on May 20, 1976. F: Ibid. G: Collected from a Charles City, Virginia, woman in March, 1976. H: Ibid. I: Ibid. J: Ibid. K: Ibid. L: Ibid.

529 A: Collected from a Charles City, Virginia, woman in March, 1976. B: Ibid. C: Given to me in manuscript form by Dennis Folly, who collected it in Hanover County, Virginia, on April 5, 1976. D: Given to me in manuscript form by Dennis Folly, who collected it in Hanover County, Virginia, in April, 1976. E: Ibid. F: Given to me in manuscript form by Thomas Beatty, who collected it from a twenty-year-old female student at Virginia Commonwealth University on March 26, 1976. G: Ibid.

530 All of these directions for conjuring a lover were given to me on May 20, 1976, by a Richmond, Virginia, woman.

531 A: Collected from a Charles City, Virginia, woman in March, 1976. B: Ibid. C: Ibid. D: Ibid. E: Ibid. F: Given to me in manuscript form by Gregory

Pleasants, who collected it in Richmond, Virginia, on February 14, 1976. G: Given to me in manuscript form by Dennis Folly, who collected it in Hanover, Virginia, on March 27, 1976, from an eighty-six-year-old woman. H: Given to me in manuscript form by Gregory Pleasants, who collected it in Richmond, Virginia, in January, 1976. I: Given to me in manuscript form by Gregory Pleasants, who collected it in the spring of 1976 from a young woman from Richmond, Virginia, who had heard it from her grandmother in Charles City. J: Given to me in manuscript form by Gregory Pleasants, who collected it from an eighteen-year-old senior at John F. Kennedy High School in Richmond, Virginia, during the spring of 1976.

532   Given to me in manuscript form by Gregory Pleasants, who recorded all except the last of these lines of "the dozens" from a "cracking session" between two high school boys in Richmond, Virginia, during the spring of 1976. The last verse is directed to females rather than to other males; it was recorded from a sixteen-year-old Richmond boy in the spring of 1976.

533   A: Given to me in manuscript form by Thomas Beatty, who collected it from a forty-year-old Richmond, Virginia, woman on March 29, 1976. B: Given to me in manuscript form by Thomas Beatty, who collected it from a Charles City, Virginia, man during the spring of 1976. C: Ibid. D: Collected in Richmond, Virginia, on May 20, 1976. E: Ibid. F: Ibid. G: Ibid. H: Ibid. I: Ibid.

534   This interesting bit of folk wisdom was recorded in Richmond, Virginia, in February, 1975.

535   Collected in Richmond, Virginia, on January 13, 1975.

536   Collected in Richmond, Virginia, on February 24, 1975.

537   This true anecdote was collected in Richmond, Virginia, on February 24, 1975.
   My informant refers to one of his former students, the former mayor of Montclair, New Jersey. The dubious compliment at the end probably refers to the fact that Carter is a Black man.

538   Collected in Richmond, Virginia, in February, 1975.

539   Collected in Richmond, Virginia, on February 6, 1975.
   The informant's dramatization of the movement of the crow and the bending of the gun add to the effectiveness of this tale.

540   Collected in Richmond, Virginia, on February 24, 1975.

541   Collected in Richmond, Virginia, on February 6, 1975.
   See Motif K231.1.1. "*Mutual agreement to sacrifice family member in famine,*" *Motif-Index.* Thompson indicates that the tale has been collected in India, Africa, Jamaica, the West Indies, and America, among other places.

542 Collected in Henrico, Virginia, on February 2, 1975.
"Feasting on Dog" in *Sea Islands,* pp. 115–16, is a variant. See also "Feasting on Dog" in "Folk Lore from Aiken," pp. 19–20.

543 Collected in Henrico, Virginia, on February 2, 1975.
I have come across no other versions of this interesting tale, which has been passed down for generations in my informant's family.

544 Collected in Richmond, Virginia, on February 27, 1975.
The informant's husband explained that the horses would pull the boat for nine miles; then at the next lock they were changed.

545 Collected in Richmond, Virginia, on February 27, 1975.
Elizabeth Van Lew ("Miss Lizzie"), who lived at 2311 East Grace Street in Richmond, Virginia, had been a Union sympathizer and reputedly a spy, concealing escaped Union prisoners and serving the Union in other ways during the Civil War. General Grant sent his aide to protect her during the Evacuation of Richmond. After the war she became a legendary figure, hated and taunted by whites for her aid to the Union and for her sympathy for Negroes but idealized and adored by Blacks for the same reasons. For further information see Mary Wingfield Scott, *Houses of Old Richmond* (Richmond: Valentine Museum, 1941), pp. 68–74.

546 Collected in Richmond, Virginia, on December 9, 1974.

547 Collected in Richmond, Virginia, on January 31, 1975, from an informant who says it is a true anecdote.
"Hoogies," the informant explained, was a slang expression for "poor white people, crackers." The informant also explained that the man was referring to a brand called Singing Sam Whiskey, the label of which had a picture of a Negro playing a banjo on it.

548 Collected in Richmond, Virginia, on January 13, 1975.

549 Given to me in manuscript form by Joseph Jenkins, who collected it in 1970 from a student at Virginia State College.

550 Collected in Richmond, Virginia, on April 16, 1975.

551 Collected in Richmond, Virginia, on April 16, 1975.

552 Collected in Henrico, Virginia, on March 11, 1975.

553 Collected in Richmond, Virginia, in February, 1975.

554 Collected in Richmond, Virginia, on October 4, 1974.

555 Collected in Richmond, Virginia, on December 20, 1974, from an informant who says it tells of a true incident.

556   Collected in Henrico, Virginia, on March 11, 1975.

557   Collected in Richmond, Virginia, on March 5, 1975.
    See Motif J1649(i). Man has a hole in door for each of his cats, Baughman. Baughman lists three white American sources.

558   John M. Ellison has long had an interest in the origins of unusual names. During an interview in his office at Virginia Union University in Richmond, Virginia, in February, 1975, he shared with me some of his findings regarding places that derived their names from folk beliefs.

559   Collected in Richmond, Virginia, in February, 1975.

560   Street cry recorded in Richmond, Virginia, on January 22, 1975.
    For a discussion of street cries with examples, see "Street Cries of Charleston" in *Treasury of Southern Folklore*, pp. 667–71 (reprinted from Harriette Kershaw Leiding, *Street Cries of an Old Southern City* [Charleston: Daggett, 1910], pp. 1–12), and "Street Cries of New Orleans" in *Treasury of Southern Folklore*, pp. 671–74 (reprinted from R. Emmet Kennedy, *Mellows: A Chronicle of Unknown Singers* [New York: Albert and Charles Boni, 1925], pp. 19–23). Other examples of street cries may be found in "Street Cries" in *American Negro Folklore*, pp. 339–41 (reprinted from Lyle Saxon, *Gumbo Ya-Ya* [New York: Houghton Mifflin]).

561   Song recorded in Richmond, Virginia, on January 22, 1975.

562   Collected in Richmond, Virginia, on November 20, 1974.

563   Song recorded in Louisa, Virginia, on January 10, 1975.

564   The text here is based on a version taped on October 4, 1975, and on additional lines and corrections provided during an interview on April 30, 1975, in Richmond, Virginia.
    Bill ("Bojangles") Robinson is of course the famed entertainer, whose home was Richmond. The informant noted that he and Bill Robinson made up the song and that "a fellow recorded it in New York."

565   Song taped in Richmond, Virginia, on January 22, 1975. Additional lines and corrections were provided during an interview on April 30, 1975.
    The informant's definition of *rounder* may be of interest: "Fellow who's dressed nice and looking for a girl friend and good times. *Rounder* means good times."